# SEVEN TRIBES
## OF
# CENTRAL AFRICA

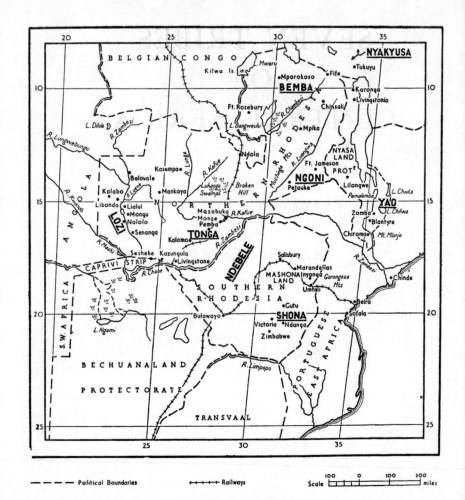

CENTRAL AFRICA

- - - - Political Boundaries     +++++ Railways

Scale |100 0 100 200| miles

# SEVEN TRIBES
# OF
# CENTRAL AFRICA

*Edited by*
ELIZABETH COLSON
*and*
MAX GLUCKMAN

*Published on behalf of*
THE INSTITUTE FOR SOCIAL RESEARCH
UNIVERSITY OF ZAMBIA *by*
MANCHESTER UNIVERSITY PRESS

First published 1951 by
OXFORD UNIVERSITY PRESS
AMEN HOUSE, LONDON E.C.4.
Reprinted with minor corrections 1959
by MANCHESTER UNIVERSITY PRESS
316-324 OXFORD ROAD, MANCHESTER 13
and distributed in the U.S.A. by
HUMANITIES PRESS, INC.
303 PARK AVENUE SOUTH, NEW YORK, N.Y. 10010

Reprinted 1961
Reprinted with amended title, 1968

GB SBN 7190 1014 4

*To*

EDWIN W. SMITH

# PREFACE

*Seven Tribes of British Central Africa* represents an early result of the enlarged research scheme of the Rhodes–Livingstone Institute. The Institute was founded in 1937 to investigate the social systems and changing social conditions of Central Africa. After the war, grants from the Colonial Development and Welfare Fund and from the Beit Railway Trust allowed it to expand its staff and to undertake new research. Three officers were appointed from Colonial Development Fund grants. Barnes was appointed to study the Ngoni of the Fort Jameson area of Northern Rhodesia; Colson to study the Plateau Tonga of the Mazabuka District, Northern Rhodesia; and Mitchell to study the Yao of Nyasaland. Holleman, the officer appointed under the Beit Trust grant, went to the Shona tribes of Southern Rhodesia. Gluckman, then Director of the Institute, continued his work among the Lozi of Northern Rhodesia.

In 1947, when Gluckman left to accept a lectureship at Oxford, the Trustees of the Institute decided to send its officers to Oxford to begin the preliminary analysis of field data under his direction. The Institute of Social Anthropology kindly invited them to give a series of lectures on the social organization of the tribes with which they had worked. Gluckman suggested that the lectures should be published as preliminary reports. Gradually we conceived a more ambitious plan which resulted in this book. Holleman, who had been unable to accompany the other officers to Oxford, was persuaded to write a general description of the Shona, and Gluckman agreed to produce one for the Lozi.

Our plan was to produce a general description for each tribe which might be useful to government officers working in the region and which could be used by students of anthropology who wished for some knowledge of the types of social organization to be found in the area. Two general accounts of tribes in the region, which were in a sense similar to the ones which we were writing, had already appeared in *Bantu Studies*, but unfortunately they had long been out of print. We therefore invited Dr. Audrey Richards to add to our collection her preliminary description of the Bemba of Northern Rhodesia and Professor Monica Wilson to contribute the preliminary description of the Nyakyusa of South-western Tanganyika, written by her late husband,

Mr. Godfrey Wilson, with whom she had worked in the field. Both agreed, and made a few corrections in the light of further field research. Neither, however, could undertake the task of rewriting the accounts to include more research material or to equal the length of the four main studies. They therefore stand, with a few amendments, as they were originally written. We are extremely grateful to them and to the Editor of *African Studies* (formerly *Bantu Studies*) for giving permission to include the two accounts and thus to widen the scope of the collection.

We also feel that these two accounts, in a sense, represent the Institute, for Mr. Wilson was the first Director, and Dr. Richards has helped actively in the development of the Institute and at one time was Director-select. The research work which they did before the Institute was founded led directly to its creation.

It has been impossible to produce the seven papers in the collection to a single scheme or to insist on a standard terminology. They have had too diverse an origin. The papers by Dr. Richards and Mr. Wilson were written in the middle 1930's. Holleman was not at Oxford with the rest of the Institute team when the book was planned and much of the writing for it was done. Nor do the articles represent the same length of experience. Gluckman began work among the Lozi in 1939. His paper is the fruit of three tours spaced over a number of years. He has previously published on the Lozi and can summarize many aspects of Lozi life which he has described fully elsewhere. Holleman began his work among the Shona in 1945 and had finished two tours when he began to write his article. He also has written other papers on the Shona, one of which appeared in 1949 as a Paper of the Institute. Barnes, Mitchell, and Colson had finished only one tour, a matter of approximately twelve months of field-work, when they produced their accounts.

The studies are therefore not in all ways comparable. In addition, as each writer attempted to give an account of the tribe he or she had studied, the lines of each analysis were partly dictated by the culture. For this reason, and those outlined above, it has not been possible to have a comparative introduction.

We hope that this is only the first of a number of similar studies which will ultimately cover the whole region. In addition the Institute plans to produce from time to time symposiums on special topics, such as modern political organization, kinship, and local organization. As in this present work, we hope to enlist the co-operation of others who are at work within the area though they are not officers of the Institute.

As a group the officers of the Institute wish to express their gratitude to Professor E. E. Evans-Pritchard and Dr. Meyer Fortes of the
Institute of Social Anthropology, Oxford, for their aid, criticism, and
friendly encouragement. We also thank Professor I. Schapera of the
University of Cape Town for many favours to us collectively and as
individuals.

The bibliographies include items published or in the press up to the
setting of page proofs, and the data in some of them, partly obtained
in research after some of the articles were written, have not been
included here. Miss M. M. Tew supplied some references. In the text
quotations are referred to by author's name, with title of work where
there are several works by the same author. Details of publication are
given in the bibliographies. Most of the material was prepared for
press during 1948.

We have dedicated our essays with respect and admiration to Dr.
Edwin W. Smith, in tribute to the book which he and the late
Captain Andrew Dale wrote over thirty years ago: *The Ila-speaking
Peoples of Northern Rhodesia.* It founded modern anthropological
research in British Central Africa.

ELIZABETH COLSON
MAX GLUCKMAN

*December* 1949

## NOTE TO THE THIRD IMPRESSION 1968

THIS is a new impression of a book which has won some reputation as *Seven Tribes of British Central Africa*. It was originally published in 1951, at a time when most of Africa was under colonial rule. At that time, simple expediency led us to use 'British Central Africa' in the title as a means of alerting readers to the fact that we had included studies of societies drawn from a limited area which did not include those parts of Central Africa then under Belgian or Portuguese rule. In this new edition, the title becomes *Seven Tribes of Central Africa*, reflecting the fact that the region is no longer under British domination and that the old title is now inappropriate even though the former presence of the British has continuing effects. English is commonly spoken. English literature is widely read. Most of the region is still influenced by British political, legal, and other institutions though the present Rhodesian regime, which rules the area known by many as Zimbabwe, is now modelling itself upon the South African example.

We trust that potential readers of this new edition will not be misled by the change in title into thinking that the book represents a wider coverage than it once did. The title has changed, but the contents stand as originally written. We are well aware that much has changed since the 1940s, both in Africa and in the discipline of social anthropology, but it would be foolhardy to seek to update the individual articles without further intensive field work; and this would mean quite another book. *Seven Tribes of Central Africa* therefore stands substantially as it was written in the 1940s, as a record of an era important for the development both of Central African and of social research.

ELIZABETH COLSON
MAX GLUCKMAN
*Editors*

*April* 1968

# CONTENTS

## THE LOZI OF BAROTSELAND IN NORTH-WESTERN RHODESIA

Max Gluckman, B.A. Hons. (Rand), M.A., D.Phil. (Oxon.). Professor of Social Anthropology in the Victoria University of Manchester; sometime University Lecturer in Social Anthropology, Oxford; formerly Director of the Rhodes–Livingstone Institute

## THE PLATEAU TONGA OF NORTHERN RHODESIA

E. Colson, M.A. (Minnesota), Ph.D. (Radcliffe). Director, Rhodes–Livingstone Institute

## THE BEMBA OF NORTH-EASTERN RHODESIA

AUDREY I. RICHARDS, M.A. (Cantab.), Ph.D. (London). Director of the East African Institute of Social Research, Makerere; sometime Reader in Social Anthropology in the University of London; sometime Senior Lecturer in Social Anthropology in the University of the Witwatersrand

## THE FORT JAMESON NGONI

J. A. BARNES, *D.S.C.*, M.A. (Cantab.). Lecturer in Social Anthropology at University College, London; Fellow of St. John's College, Cambridge; formerly Research Officer, Rhodes–Livingstone Institute

## THE NYAKYUSA OF SOUTH-WESTERN TANGANYIKA

GODFREY WILSON, M.A. (Oxon.). Rockefeller Fellow, 1935–8; first Director of the Rhodes–Livingstone Institute

## THE YAO OF SOUTHERN NYASALAND

J. C. MITCHELL, B.A. (Natal), D.Phil. (Oxon.). Research Officer, Rhodes–Livingstone Institute

# CONTENTS

## SOME 'SHONA' TRIBES OF SOUTHERN RHODESIA

J. F. HOLLEMAN, M.A. (Stellenbosch), Ph.D. (Cape Town). Beit Research Fellow of the Rhodes–Livingstone Institute; sometime Lecturer in Native Law and Administration at the University of Stellenbosch

# LIST OF MAPS, TABLES, AND DIAGRAMS

## 'SHONA'

# LIST OF PLATES

B

## 'SHONA'

# NOTE

KINSHIP symbols have not been standardized save for the articles by Barnes, Colson, Gluckman, and Mitchell. In the main we have followed accepted usage, but have introduced new symbols in one or two places to exclude the necessity for using symbols composed of two letters, as in the common symbol for sister, Si.

| | | |
|---|---|---|
| M—Mother | B—Brother | P—Parent |
| F—Father | Z—Sister | H—Husband |
| S—Son | G—Sibling | W—Wife |
| D—Daughter | C—Child | E—Spouse |

Other symbols are built up on these, as Father's Sister, FZ; Mother's Mother, MM; Mother's Mother's Sister's Daughter's Husband, MMZDH. Seniority is indicated by a plus or minus, thus: older Brother is B+, younger Brother is shown as B—.

# THE LOZI OF BAROTSELAND[1] IN NORTH-WESTERN RHODESIA

*By* MAX GLUCKMAN

## I. BAROTSELAND AND THE BAROTSE PEOPLE

*Lozi Origins and History*

THE Lozi people, who are the dominant tribe in the region of north-western Rhodesia usually called Barotseland, live in a great flood-plain which stretches along the Upper Zambezi for about 120 miles, between 14½ and 16 degrees south latitude. At its widest the Plain is some 25 miles wide. It is enclosed by bushed scarps of various heights up to 200 ft. From this Plain the Lozi conquered outwards until they ruled as far as Wankie, south of the Victoria Falls, to the Zambezi valley below the Victoria Falls where it is inhabited by the We, to Lake Lukanga and Kasempa, as far north as Balovale, and south by the Kwito river across to the Kwando-Mashi-Linyanti-Chobe river. Within their kingdom were the members of some twenty-five tribes, many of diverse origin. In this essay I deal mostly with the Lozi themselves.

The name *Lozi* is of comparatively recent origin. Formerly the people were known as Aluyi or Aluyana. In the middle of the nineteenth century they were temporarily conquered by the Kololo, a horde with a Basuto nucleus, under whom their name seems to have been changed to Barotse. Since the Luyi liberated their country from the Kololo, but retained the Kololo language, *Rotse* has become *Lozi*, in accordance with regular phonetic changes of *r* to *l* and *ts* to *z*. The surface similarity of Rotse with Hurutshe, the parent stock of the Tswana (Bechuana), and with Rozwi, the dominant 'Shona' group, has led some ethnologists to relate the Luyi to these peoples in the south. But the Lozi's own legends, and the ecological, linguistic, and ethnological evidence undoubtedly give them a northern origin,

[1] I collected the data for this study while working for the Rhodes-Livingstone Institute. My visits to central Barotseland were: ten months in 1940, ten months in 1942, three months in 1947; and I spent five weeks at Sesheke in 1944. At the Rhodes-Livingstone Institute in Livingstone I mixed constantly with Lozi and was visited by many from Loziland, including King Imwiko, the Princess Chief Mulima, Ishee Kwandu Mtwaleti, Ngambela Wina, and other senior councillors.

# SKELETON GENEALOGY OF THE LOZI ROYAL FAMILY

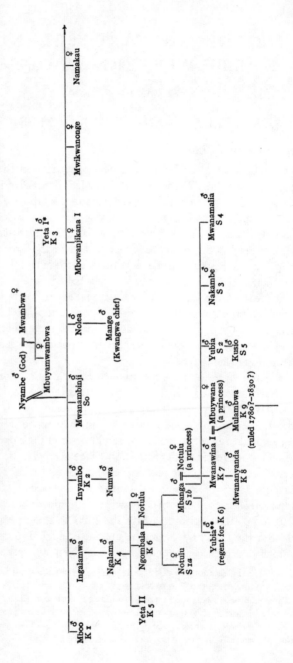

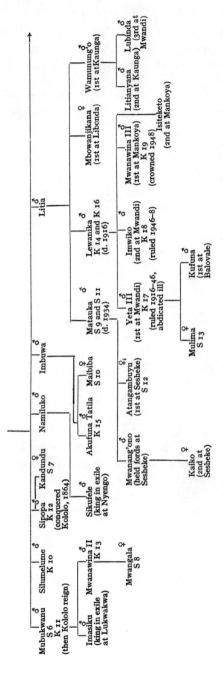

K = king of northern capital, followed by numeral in order of ruling.
S = king of southern capital, followed by numeral in order of ruling.
Order of ruling at outer-district capitals, or those of exile during Kololo
incursion, shown in brackets.

* Jalla gives Yeta I (K 3) as younger brother of Mwanambinji (♂), but informants
now say he was brother of Mbuyamwambwa.
** Jalla gives Yubia as 7th king, as do many Lozi. I present version of other Lozi
who say Yubia ruled as regent for Ngombala, died before him, and was not crowned.

probably in a region of great watershed plains cut by rivers, somewhere about Lake Dilolo. The Lozi themselves say they are kin to the Lunda. They do not claim descent from the great Lunda king Mwatiamvo, but say they and the Lunda are descended from Mbuyamwambwa, the daughter and wife of God Nyambe. No published record that I know from the Lunda peoples mentions this relationship, nor is the Luyana language grouped with Lunda.[1] To support the Lozi legend, we know that many other tribes in both north-western and north-eastern Rhodesia are derived from the Lunda. Even if this particular connexion be incorrect, it is probable that the Lozi are of common stock with the peoples of the southern Congo basin. Their state organization, royal bands, and other customs connected with the kingship show certain basic affinities with the southern Congo cultures, though they lack circumcision ceremonies, masked dancers, and secret societies. Finally, in Mr. Trapnell's judgement, their system of grasslands gardens, unique in the region, could only have developed in the plains to the north-west.[2]

One section of the Kaonde claims to have been driven from the Barotse Plain by the Luyi[3] (hereafter Lozi), but the Lozi do not have this story. They tell of related people who were 'produced' about the same time as themselves in the Plain, where God made wives and begat the tribes. Some of them, like the Lozi, were born to Him by Mbuyamwambwa, daughter of one of these wives by Him. These were the Kwangwa, Kwandi, and Mbowe. Other peoples, such as the Imilangu and Ndundulu, were living to the west. These peoples peacefully accepted Lozi domination. Indeed, the tale is that it was they who showed the Lozi what a good thing chieftainship was by presenting part of the catch at a fishing battue to the sons of Mbuyamwambwa. The Lozi then subdued the Kwangwa, who were living on the east margin of the Plain, and later moved them to work iron at the circular plains which are interspersed in the encircling bushed plateau. The young brother of the first king made big conquests to the south, and these were consolidated and extended southwards along the river, and inland from both banks, by later kings. The Lozi subdued many

---

[1] Doke (p. 142) and Guthrie (p. 52) group Lozi with different languages. Doke seems the sounder classification (see review of Guthrie's book by C. M. N. White in *African Studies*, vii. 4, December 1948).

[2] C. G. Trapnell, Government Ecologist, Northern Rhodesia: personal communication. See Trapnell and Clothier, *The Soils, Vegetations and Native Agricultural Systems of North-western Rhodesia*, pp. 48 ff.

[3] Melland, *In Witchbound Africa*, pp. 31-2.

peoples, who are shown in an appendix (see pp. 87–9). They did not wage war to the north until the reign of their ninth king, when they report the failure of their armies to conquer the Luena, whom they defeated three generations later.

Around 1800 there came to seek refuge among them from the west two groups of people: Mbalangwe under Mwenekandala and Mbunda under Mweneciengele. Both were welcomed and they were settled on the east margin of the Plain in the region of the present Mongu. This area had previously been inhabited by Nkoya, brought from their homeland to the east, who were now moved to colonize the west of the Plain and stand as a buffer between the immigrants and their own tribes. These immigrants have now largely been assimilated to the Lozi; I call them Old Mbunda.

In 1838, shortly after a civil war, the Lozi were defeated by the Kololo, who had been set in flight by the Zulu Shaka's wars. A group of Lozi princes fled north and established three small kingdoms, each with all the royal symbols. Their followers were largely Old Mbunda and the few Lozi became Mbunda-ized. A number of princes remained under the Kololo, who had their capital on the Linyanti, with a deputy in the Plain itself. One of these Lozi princes, Sipopa, fled north and killed one of his cousins ruling in exile. He formed an army and in 1864 annihilated the Kololo to re-establish the Lozi domination. Under his successor Lewanika the Lozi conquered part of the Luena (Lubale) and gave protection to Shinde's Lunda. They also raided the Kaonde, the Ila, and the southern Tonga and We, and thereafter drew tribute from them.

Some Portuguese visited Loziland early in the nineteenth century and when the Kololo invaded Loziland it was being regularly visited by Mambari (Ovimbundu) and half-caste traders and slavers from the west coast and Arabs and half-castes from the east. Griqua traders were the first to reach the Kololo from the south, but historical records date from Livingstone's visit to them in 1853–4.

In 1883–7 the Paris Evangelical Mission from Basutoland began work in the Plain, and largely on its advice in 1890 and 1900 the king Lewanika accepted the protection of Britain through the British South Africa Company under treaties which reserved to the Lozi kings and people considerable rights which they still enjoy. Under these treaties Britain retained for the Lozi from the Portuguese the land lying west of the Zambezi which the Portuguese had claimed, but in fact the Lozi had ruled farther to the west than the international boundary laid down by the King of Italy. The Lozi also withdrew from the present Caprivi Strip to the north bank of the middle Zambezi in the face of German colonization and they had already abandoned their holdings towards Wankie before Ndebele threats.

The Barotse Province of today is considerably smaller than the area of the old kingdom. The Ila, Tonga, Toka, and Leya countries were taken over by Government, as well as the Kaonde District of Kasempa. In 1941 a Commission decision excised from Barotse Province the northernmost district of Balovale, after the local peoples had protested their independence. The grounds of the decision were not made public.

During this century there has been an important accretion to the Barotse population in thousands of immigrants from Angola to the west and Balovale district to the north. These immigrants are mostly Luena (Lubale), Mbunda, Cokwe, and Lucazi. They give as the reason for their move the oppression they suffered under the Portuguese. Undoubtedly it is also part of the general drift of peoples towards the central railway line which forms the backbone of modern Central Africa, from where people move southwards to the richer territories of southern Rhodesia and the Union of South Africa and northwards to the Katanga Province of Congo Belge. Northern Rhodesia peoples, including the Lozi, are involved in these movements. The Lozi call these immigrants *Mawiko*, the peoples of the west.

Thus what I call the Barotse nation, as against the ruling Lozi tribe, has always consisted of many different tribes. These tribes have intermarried considerably and nowhere has this been more marked than among the Lozi themselves. Though the Lozi look down on *mang'ete*, the foreigners, despite their chiefs' disapproval, the Wiko are the only people whom they are reluctant to marry. Members of all the other tribes, but chiefly children, were in the old days brought to Loziland by the chiefs. They were called *maketo* (honoured by choice of the king). Razzias in the outer provinces also brought in children, called *mahapiwa* (the seized). They were placed in various villages in the Plain, where they grew up as Lozi and are today indistinguishable from them. Another category was people captured in war, *batanga* (serfs),[1] with whom also the Lozi intermarried. Today the Lozi

---

[1] I translate *batanga* as 'serfs' because they were bound to a master in a village but could not be sold to another as 'slaves'. *Mahapiwa* and *maketo* were all in royal villages.

# MAP I.

## TOPOGRAPHY OF LOZI LAND

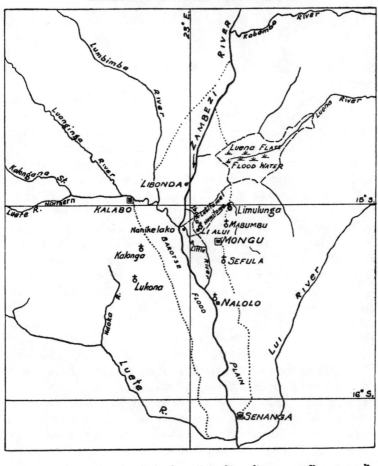

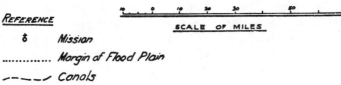

SCALE OF MILES

themselves say that there is practically no Lozi who is a pure Luyi. Almost all of them point without shame to Nkoya, Kwangwa, Subiya, Totela, Mbunda, Kololo, and other blood in their ancestry.

## Production in the Flood-plain

The Plain provides the Lozi with a habitat[1] that is unique in the whole region, and it so constrains their settlements and their technology that their social organization presents certain exceptional forms within a general pattern characteristic of this part of Central Africa.

The Plain floods every year about December with the rains which fall on the divides between the Zambezi and the Congo, Kafue and Kwando rivers. In an average year, by February–March the whole Plain becomes a vast lake from where it opens at Lukulu in the north to beyond Senanga in the south where the bounding scarps meet. The Lozi have therefore to build their villages on mounds in the Plain, which to some extent stand above the flood-waters. Even on the mounds huts are destroyed by the waters if these reach a fair depth. Thus the sites in the Plain which can be inhabited are limited in number, and each site is limited in area. The number of people who can reside on a single site is limited in addition by the amount of garden-land and the fishing-sites which are attached to each mound. Lozi plains gardens consist of pockets of fertile soils in the lower parts of the Plain which are enriched by the alluvium of each flood, and of certain fertile mounds whose soils they refresh by kraaling cattle on them. These gardens are usually very small ($\frac{1}{4}$ to $\frac{1}{2}$ an acre or less) and are dotted about the Plain. Every garden is attached to a village built on a mound. The waters of the main river and its tributaries, and of large pans in the Plain which probably are cut-off meanders of the rivers, can be fished by any member of the Barotse nation. But on the banks and shallow gulfs off the rivers and pans and in the shallow depressions which score the Plain and up which the flood finds its earliest course are valuable fishing-sites where fish can be isolated and trapped in reed-fences and earth-dams. Other dams are built between the higher parts of the Plain. All these sites are attached to particular villages. Thus the Lozi's villages, since they are placed on the only possible building-sites, have histories running back to their first colonization of the Plain. Their gardens and fishing-sites too have long histories and

[1] For a full description of the Plain and economic activities see my *Economy of the Central Barotse Plain*.

often have specific names and praise-songs. The villages therefore are enduring groups of fundamental importance in Lozi social structure.

In addition to these gardens and fishing-sites, the Plain provides rich grazing for large herds of cattle at two seasons of the year: in winter after the flood has fallen (May–July) until the hot dry months (August–October) have shrivelled the grasses, and in spring when the rains bring on new grass (November–January). During the flood months (January–May) the cattle move out of the Plain to graze in the bush or at the small plains and river valleys which are interspersed in the woodland stretching east and west of the flood-plain itself.

Since about 1880 the Lozi have also cultivated gardens on the margin of the Plain. They say that before the Kololo invasion they themselves lived more or less permanently in the Plain, and only moved out of it to herd their cattle or to live in temporary camps at the margin for a couple of months because of the discomforts of living in the flood. Early records confirm this tradition. Some Lozi still do this, and a few stay out in the Plain, often in camps, even when the flood is very deep. But many of them now cultivate margin gardens, a technique which was probably developed by the Mbalangwe and Mbunda immigrants of the early nineteenth century, though the original cultivators of this form of garden were Kwangwa and Nkoya. These gardens are made where there is underground seepage under the steeper slopes in marshy land which is drained by canals. In this land and other places root crops are planted in heaps of soil raised to be above the waters. Farther towards the margin there sometimes occurs a belt of humic soil which is watered by underground seepage, but is naturally drained, and which can be cultivated in perpetuity. Beyond this, up the slope, is a belt which has some underground seepage but which has to be artificially fertilized, and beyond that a further belt of dry soil, but not bushed, which is cultivable with manuring. Beyond that belt lies the bush, which is worked on a cycle of cropping and regeneration, with clearing and burning to provide a first enrichment with ash. These different belts do not occur continuously round the margins of the Plain; where all exist, they attract dense populations.

The Lozi as a whole thus have some eight different kinds of gardens, spread from the Zambezi into the sand scarps. Not every Lozi owns every kind of garden, but many do; and most have several. The work in these gardens is spread over all the months of the year. Low-lying gardens in the Plain, drained gardens, and seepage gardens are

planted in the winter (July), though the rains do not begin until
November, since the crops are fed by underground waters. They are
reaped in December to February. The bush gardens, dry-margin
gardens, and gardens made on the higher patches in the Plain are
planted in the rains in November and reaped in April to May. Bush
gardens have to be cut in April to June to dry for burning in September. Thus a Lozi who has several of these kinds of gardens has
work in almost every month of the year, and often in a single month he
has to work in gardens which are widely separated.

Fishing and herding of cattle increase labour difficulties. The Lozi
have some two dozen ways of catching fish. The main methods are: a
brief season when the flood is rising and fish can be trapped in non-
return traps set in reed-fences (December–February); similar trapping in fish-dams and -fences when the flood falls (April–July); netting
with trawl- and gill-nets when the waters are low and confined in
July to November; communal battues with fish-spears when the waters
are low in pans (September–November). The fishing-sites to be worked
thus at one time may be widely separated. Meanwhile the cattle have
to be taken out to bush-grazing in the flood season and return emaci-
ated to the rich grasses of the Plain before the people move back to
their Plain villages.

The Lozi have a number of subsidiary productive activities which
also largely depend on the flood, such as the trapping and hunting of
birds and game in the Plain.

The Lozi thus have a mixed economy in which they make efficient
use of a variety of resources. Their gardening system has been lauded
by agriculturists and they are undoubtedly proficient fishermen. But
what is most relevant for a study of their social organization is
that their resources consist of small areas of land or water which are
dotted about the Plain and which have to be worked from the villages
built on mounds similarly scattered. These resources are worked in
perpetuity and thus differ markedly from those of most other tribes
of the region who are shifting cultivators working their way through
an area of woodland, and constantly moving their villages. Since the
Lozi use their sites in perpetuity, rights of ownership in them are
precisely defined in a complicated pattern.

There is one further important environmental condition of Lozi
social organization. The Plain is unique for the region and its products
differ from those of all the surrounding areas. The river-routes all
centre in the Zambezi. Therefore generally trade lies between the

Plain and the surrounding region as a whole, and not between adjacent areas of basically similar woodland. The Plain produces cattle, fish, sorghum, maize, and root-crops. From the woodland areas come tobacco, cassava, millet, ground-nuts, honey, dugouts, mats, baskets, fishing-nets made of tree-roots, bark-rope, wooden dishes and other utensils, drums, skins, iron implements, baskets, beeswax.

## The Flood in Lozi Life

The flood dominates Lozi life. It covers and uncovers gardens, fertilizing and watering them; it fixes the pasturing of the cattle; it conditions the methods of fishing. All life in the Plain moves with the flood: people, fish, cattle, game, wildfowl, snakes, rodents, and insects. The Lozi calendar is largely defined by the state of the flood. The two great national events of the year are the moves of the king between his Plain and his margin capitals. In theory no one should move out before he does. When the flood is rising his people may be living in discomfort as the water creeps up to their huts, and rodents, snakes, and warrior ants invade their homes. The royal drummers sing songs beseeching him to save the people and move. At last, after new moon, sacrifices are made at all royal graves. The national drums are beaten at night. The king begins the drumming, followed by his chief councillor (the NGAMBELA[1]) and then by other councillors in order of rank. After that, young men struggle for the honour of sounding the drums. These thunder over the Plain, and men from the *sifukambanda* (the area round the capital) come hurrying to escort the king on his voyage. He travels in a barge with forty paddlers, all princes and councillors, dressed in bright cloths and caps, and wearing head-dresses with long black plumes. Behind his white shelter his personal bands play. The national drums travel in a separate barge, for they represent the people. The councillors and princes who paddle it wear reed-buck skins and lion-mane head-dresses. During the voyage the national drums or the king's bands must play; one set of players takes up from the other. The two main barges 'play' (*fumba*) about in the flood, dashing hither and thither in quick zigzags. A whole fleet of other barges (the queens', the chief councillor's, the king's baggage barge, the councillors' baggage barge) and of dugouts escort the king. His

---

[1] Lozi councillors, as will be described below, are appointed to specific offices carrying titles which pass to new incumbents. The institution of these titles is so important that I shall print them in small capitals, to distinguish them from personal names.

barge must always be in front, following the *Natamikwa* royal dugout which bears the national war- and hunting-spears. When the voyage ends these are first carried to be placed on their altar in the palace courtyard.

When the flood falls, the drummers again enjoin the king to move. They complain of the hardship of life in the woodland. The Lozi are happy only in the Plain, that is their real home, where a man can look about him. The people want to return to their homes and to begin planting their plains gardens, and fishing. This time the king voyages down a canal dug by one of his predecessors. The ceremony is less attended, for people can move back to the Plain in advance of the king. Only the chieftainesses who have capitals to the north and south of his must wait for him.

*Lozi Transhumance*

When they move from Plain to margin homes the Lozi do not all move simply from one village to another. Some do, and many Plain villages have margin counterparts. Some Lozi remain permanently in the Plain in their own villages or they may move to temporary camps on larger mounds which are not inhabited. A village in mid-plain may move to a village in the outer plain, whose members move a short distance to the margin. The inhabitants of other villages disperse in the flood season, going to different villages along the margin where they seek homes with various relatives or friends. Some members of a village may go to the west margin, others to the east. Young men may escort the cattle to graze at small plains in the woodlands, either camping or staying with relatives or with blood-brothers or friends. As the inhabitants of one village may scatter temporarily, the members of neighbouring villages may go to widely separated places on the margins. Through a year, the same people are not associated in territorial units.

Since the establishment of British rule in this century there has also been an increasing tendency for Lozi to establish themselves permanently in villages on the margin. Administrators have encouraged this and some of them pressed the Lozi to abandon their Plain homes. This building of permanent homes on the margin has been most marked round the administrative centre of Mongu and various missions, which offer markets for vegetables and milk and nearby employment. Many villages have abandoned their huts on mounds near the margin of the Plain to live permanently on the margin. Time and labour are more valuable now, for there is money to be earned, and they shirk the task of keeping two sets of huts. In the old days serfs helped with this; nowadays a man must employ someone to help him, probably a Wiko. These Lozi are settled among the Old Mbunda and Mbalangwe in a line of villages which north and south of Mongu tends to form a continuous street. Pressure of population on Plain resources has also contributed to this movement.

Nevertheless, we may say that most Lozi move seasonally between two sets of homes; that the same people do not always reside together throughout the year; and that people may go to different flood-season homes from one year to another. Until the 1930's there was not always a fixed flood-season capital; the king might make a temporary 'camp' anywhere he chose.

*Limiting Economic Conditions*

Before I analyse Lozi social structure in its specific environmental and technological background, I refer briefly to a limiting economic condition which is general for the simpler peoples. Despite their developed technology and the varied products they acquired by it, the Lozi's goods were primary consumable goods. A man could only consume a limited quantity of these goods. They were not storable in the tropical climate of a land of pests and had to be used at once, except for a few ornaments, dugouts, tools, and cattle. As grazing was limited, men with large herds distributed their cattle. Moreover, with their tools and implements a worker could not produce very much beyond what he could himself consume, so despite the organization of certain co-operative working groups about dugouts and fishing-nets and fish-dams, it was impossible for a wealthy man to employ labour to raise his own standard of living markedly above his fellows. The Lozi had many serfs, but serf and master lived at approximately the same standard. Serfs were described as 'my children', and though they were bound to particular people as freemen were not, relationships with them were otherwise assimilated to those of kinship. Since the serfs have been freed under a treaty with the British, many have chosen not to return to their ancestral homes in other provinces but have remained on their masters' lands. It is impossible for an outsider observing a neighbourhood to detect those of servile origin: only inquiries into genealogies elucidate this. The Lozi, moreover, did not have debt-slavery, though this was present among Ila and Lamba and Bemba to the east.

c

Not even the king could use the wealth that came from his own land and waters, from tribute, and later from trading-caravans, to improve his own standard markedly above that of his subjects. The people emphasize most in chiefs the quality of generosity, and their tales and anecdotes of the past, and even of today, constantly recount the distribution of goods and food by the king among his people. The subject peoples were drawn into this distribution. After European trade-goods entered the country this continued; and missionaries have described how King Lewanika, after the arrival of a trading-caravan, shared out the cloth among all the people present until every man flaunted a half-yard of cloth. Cattle raided in war were similarly distributed—and even returned. After Lewanika raided 50,000 small Ila cattle, and made the Ila his subjects, he sent thousands of large Barotse cattle to be herded by the Ila for him. These herds of the king are still known in Ilaland today.

## Class and Tribal Divisions, Past and Present

Despite this overall equality of living standards, there were certain broad class-divisions of the Lozi. The royal family, the descendants of all kings through males and females, were identified as *linabi* (Luyiroyals) or *bana bamulena* (Kololo-children of the king) for some four-five generations. Husbands of princesses (*boishee*) and commoner relatives of the royal family (*likwanabi*) were also accorded reflected respect. The consorts of princesses sat on the royal mat in council on behalf of their wives and administered affairs for them. Next came the Lozi freemen themselves, with certain tribes regarded as true Lozi: Kwandi, Mbowe, and Kwangwa. Grouped with them are the Nkoya, Muenyi, Simaa, Ndundulu, Old Mbunda and Mbalangwe, Makoma, Totela, Subiya, who were long-time subjects of the Lozi. They were not subjected to razzias: their children were brought to Loziland by order from the king, as he might honour any Lozi by choosing his child. Kaonde, Ila, Toka, Humbe, Yeyi, Mbukushu occasionally were swept for children. The Mashi are now honorifically Lozi, since in the 1880's they provided a refuge for King Lewanika in temporary exile from his throne. Today only the Wiko immigrants are markedly despised by the Lozi, though they live together amicably in neighbourhoods and even single villages, and though the Lozi authorities constantly stress that 'we are one people; there is no one who is a Lozi or a Wiko, we are all people of the king'. This is in accord with their whole tradition of absorbing foreigners. Thus the differences of tribal and cultural origin have not been institutionalized, though there are feelings of tribal pride and tribal contempt. Today Lozi men are averse to marrying Wiko women and even Old Mbunda women, though they allow their daughters to marry men of these groups. They say that differences in customary behaviour make it difficult for them to live together successfully. Nevertheless, despite this feeling of national identity in subjection to the king and despite considerable intermarrying through many generations and the wholesale adoption of each other's customs, each tribal group is conscious of its identity and identified by the others. Each is noted for particular skills of which it boasts and particular evils which it denies. The Lozi ascribe, notably to the Old Mbunda and Mbalangwe and to the Wiko, great powers of magic and sorcery.

*Lozi* means not only a member of the dominant tribe, but any man who is subject to the king; just as Loziland (*bulozi*) means both all the country he rules as well as the Plain itself. The kings themselves have consistently emphasized this common nationality. Lewanika made it a punishable offence to refer to anyone as *Mung'ete* (a foreigner) and his sons who have succeeded him have supported this with laws of their own. However, the enacting of these laws itself indicates that the process has not been altogether successful. The tribes are considerably mixed through most of the region about the Plain, and, as stated, they live together amicably. But the tribes have differences in culture, and in disputes and quarrels insults to a man's tribal origin are liable to arise. Tribal distinctions are slightly reflected in the build up of the Lozi king's bands of drums and xylophones: he has Lozi, Simaa, and Nkoya sections.

In general, the Lozi have not attempted to impose their laws on any other tribe. They now state their policy has always been that in national matters (i.e. in public law: theft, murder, beer-drinking, &c.) all tribes have to follow national laws, but that in matters of inheritance and other aspects of family law (private law) each tribe can follow its own customs. 'We hope they will see that our laws are better and follow them', the PRINCESS CHIEF Mulima told me. The Lozi themselves point to a recent dispute with Luena and Lunda who were excised from the modern Barotse kingdom by the award of a Government Commission, and say how foolish the prince sent to rule there was in trying to enforce Lozi laws. But the other tribes today increasingly resent Lozi dominance.

The characteristic feature of Lozi polity was that it was not divided

# MAP II

## TRIBAL DISTRIBUTION IN BAROTSELAND

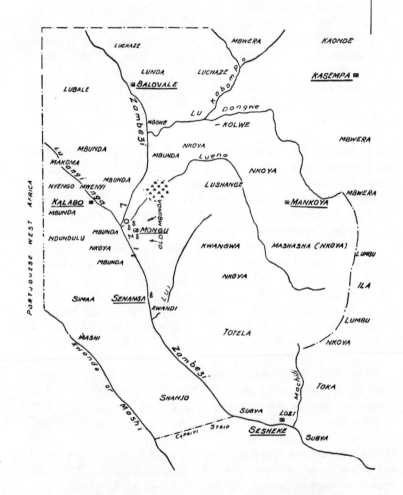

### RECENT WIKO IMMIGRANTS SCATTERED
### IN NEIGHBOURHOOD OF LOZILAND

— SCALE OF MILES —

20   10   0      20      40      60      80      100 Miles

into territorial provinces, but into a series of non-territorial political sectors (as I translate their *makolo*), each centred in an important title at one of the capitals. Since these administrative groups were not local groups and only united temporarily for war or labour for the king, they do not seem to have developed a sense of corporate loyalty setting them not only against each other but also against the central power of the State. Some of this tension developed between the adherents of the king's own capital and those attached to a subordinate capital established not far to the south in the Plain. The few rebellions there have been showed largely accidental cleavages. Men supported one or other claimant to the throne according to which was nearest to them at the time or what line was taken by prominent men among them. Adjacent villages frequently took opposite sides. But in the outer provinces tribes tended to take sides as wholes. These outer provinces were not administered by princes sent out to establish capitals among them as is usual in Bantu kingdoms. They were left under their own chiefs, where they had them, and the chiefs were allowed to retain their drum and xylophone bands, the main symbols of chieftainship. The Lozi kings sent 'representatives' (*lindumeleti*) to watch over the districts for them and to forward tribute. Only in the 1880's, under the threat of Ndebele invasion from the south-east and the coming of Whites from the same direction, were two capitals established in the Sesheke region near the Victoria Falls—they were built almost alongside each other. In the 1930's two more capitals were built in the Balovale and Mankoya Districts to meet the needs of modern administration. Both these establishments provoked mutiny: the Lubale claimed and got independence and the Nkoya chiefs have constantly quarrelled with the Lozi councillors at their capital until in 1947–8 one chief had to be temporarily deposed. In Sesheke District, and even in the homeland districts of Mongu, Senanga, and Kalabo, the subject tribes have begun to protest, I think encouraged by the attitude of District Officers, that the national councils are filled with Lozi and that they should get more seats on the councils. In 1947, under Government persuasion, representatives of most tribes were given seats in the National Council. I have found no evidence in the writings of early visitors to Barotseland, or in what I heard of the past from Lozi and subject peoples, that there was such a movement until recently. I consider the present tendency stems from the following situation. In the past the council was rarely concerned with matters which affected the day-to-day life of the peoples concerned: they discussed the waging of wars, how to cope with famines, the organization of royal hunts and royal moves from capital to capital, the appointment of officers within the Plain. I have recorded only one debate on a problem involving all the people of the kingdom. When Lewanika became king in 1880 he argued that the Lozi should themselves plant food and not live on the tribute of the subject tribes; some of his councillors wanted to continue the Kololo practice of living on tribute. This is said to have provoked these councillors to rebel; they drove out Lewanika, but with the support of subject tribes he regained his throne. The other obligation of citizenship was to bring in tribute; but since the tribute-bringers were usually rewarded with other goods, it was not merely a burden. Today the council is constantly concerned with matters of urgent importance to the people in their relations with Government and the Whites generally: missions and schools, wages, cattle-sales, control of prices, the price of trade-goods, treatment of Africans by Whites, &c. Posts of councillors are considered to be well paid, often sinecures. The tribes which in the past got a return in gifts from the king for the tribute they brought, now do not see that they get a return in social services for their taxes, and indeed social services are better developed in Loziland proper than in the rest of Barotse Province. Finally, some tribesmen, especially the more literate, are in contact with other tribes and British ideas of political organization. However, on the whole, even in Mankoya, these peoples are attempting to strengthen their position *vis-à-vis* the Lozi in the national organization; they are not attempting to break out of it as the Lubale did. It may be—I have no evidence on this point—that they see that the Lubale have lost, with the gain of their independence, certain rights preserved for Barotse under their treaty with the British. Certainly all Barotse politicians of all tribes stress the importance of the treaty, the symbol of their independence within the protection of the British Crown to which they manifest great loyalty. Associated with the treaty is the kingship itself. Recently, reforms of the Barotse councils were carried through by the Administration after negotiations with the councils themselves. 'Foreigners' publicly upbraided senior councillors for consenting to these changes without consulting them: 'The kingship is our house. One day we will find that the Government has taken our house. When we complain, Government will truthfully answer, "You gave it to us".'

The coming of the Europeans has of course introduced a consciousness of African identity against the superior colour-group of

whom Lewanika ruled: 'all white men are chiefs, even traders'. In
towns, in more onerous conditions, Barotse of all tribes who go out
to work live segregated with members of other African nations and
tribes. Thus they are being welded with others into a common African
group, and this is reflected in a tendency of tribes now independent of
the Lozi king to turn to his strength and power under the treaty. This
counters the other tendency for the different tribes to play off the
Administration in their interest against the king.

## II. KINGSHIP, NATION, AND LAND

*Identification of the Three*

Lozi nationhood is generally referred to in three terms: the nation
(*sicaba saMalozi*), the land (*bulozi*), and the kingship (*bulena bwama-
lozi*). Nation, land, and kingship participate in one another and the
systems of relations centring in all the concepts interpenetrate inex-
tricably in reality, though they can be isolated in analysis. For the
Lozi themselves they are absolutely identified: each is always referred
to in terms of the others. The land is *mubu wamulena* (soil of the king),
and the king's most specific title, used otherwise only for the Princess
Chief, LITUNGA, means 'earth'. The king is MBUMU-WA-LITUNGA,
'great-one-of-the-earth'; the Princess Chief is LITUNGA-LA-MBOELA,
'earth-of-the-south'. LITUNGA is an ancient Lozi (Luyi) word and is
never used to refer to other superiors, as *mulena*, the modern Lozi
(Kololo from Sotho *morena*) word for chief, may be used. Lozi emphasize all the time: 'the king is the land and the land is the king'.
Similarly the nation *sicaba*, the Lozi people *Malozi*, are the king. The
king is saluted and referred to as *Malozi*, as are his councillors in
council and his people *en masse*. The nation and the land, the Plain,
are also for the Lozi the same thing: no one can call himself a true
Lozi unless he can point to ancestral land in the Plain. In the following
sections I describe part of the network of relations involved in this
triple identification.

The Lozi feel themselves to be a distinctive people from all others,
the *mang'ete* (foreigners). *Malozi*, however, also describes all subjects
of the king. But only the Aluyi of the Plain are *Malozi tota* (true Lozi),
though other related tribes (Kwandi, Mbowe, and sometimes Kwangwa) are considered 'true Lozi' in contrast with the other conquered
peoples. True Lozi, the people who form the proud conquerors, are

distinguished by certain criteria: in one or other line of descent they bear a Lozi descent-name (*mushiku*—see below); they can point to ancestral mounds in the Plain; they file a reversed V between their upper incisors; they tattoo a certain pattern on their cheeks; and they have a series of burns on the forearm and holes in the ear-lobes, which after death are passports for men to God *Nyambe* and for women to His wife, *Nasilele*. These are the outward marks which symbolize the deep sense of unity which the Lozi have and which they express in the phrase *sicaba saMalozi* (the Lozi nation).

The kingship now pertains to, and represents, not only the unity of the Lozi but also of the conquered tribes with the true Lozi; neverthe-less the Lozi consider it to be particularly theirs. The ruling king must be descended agnatically from the line of Lozi kings: he has the Lozi descent-name *ndandula*. But even the Lozi admit that all the con-quered peoples are *batu bamulena*, 'people of the king'.

Every Barotse, of the Lozi or any subject tribe, has a direct allegiance to the king. He is *mutu wamulena*, 'a person of the king'. This allegiance —which is Barotse citizenship—obliges him to pay the king the respect of the king's office; to fight for the king; to work for the king; and to render the king tribute. These duties are owed directly and personally to the king, though in practice they are usually rendered through officials. In return every subject is entitled to claim the king's help and protection; to take his troubles to the king; to ask the king directly for land; to use the products of the king's land, fish and game and wild fruits and crops in the king's own gardens; and to beg goods of the king. In practice, Lozi hold land from the king in an elaborate hier-archy of estates, and work and fight for him, or approach him, through an elaborate hierarchy of officers; but Lozi love to cite stories of how kings overrode their officials to set right the complaints of their people or some person. Ideally, for the Lozi, the relationship of each subject and the king is individual and personal. Even serfs, prisoners of war in the power of a master, claimed the direct protection of the king.

As the Lozi see this direct allegiance of all to the king, the kingship exists in its subjects and the subjects are nothing without the king. In all groups leader and followers are in the Lozi mind identified; chief-tainship is the relation of chief and people. At the installation of an heir to any position of authority the officiators always stress: 'You, heir, remember that you do not rule alone, but by the power of those behind you [the followers sit behind the heir as he is exhorted]. Wis-dom does not come from one man, but from many men.' And they tell his supporters: 'You will be weak and lost without a leader. Strengthen him and you strengthen yourselves.'

Thus for the Lozi, kingship is now their nation itself. Nevertheless, it is not, like kinship, something that came with them into the world. They have a myth which tells how kingship originated when Mboo, son of Mbuyamwambwa, the daughter and wife of God, was given a share of a communal fish-catch by the Ndundulu.[1] Before that, there was chieftainship and a royal family; but men instituted the kingship. Since then, however, kingship has been something absolute without which the Lozi cannot be a people, and there can hardly be life. The king is *mushemi* (parent) to everyone; he is praised as 'my father' (*bondate*) and 'my mother' (*bome*). Kingship is as ultimate as birth: subjection to the king and kinship by blood are the basic elements of all Lozi social relationships.

The king is thus the nation. 'When the king dies, the nation falls into a coma', Lozi say.[2] In theory, fires throughout the kingdom should be extinguished until his successor, with the help of the priest of Mbuyamwambwa, lights with friction-sticks new fire which should be carried to the confines of the kingdom to kindle afresh every village's fire. Then food is cooked and people warm themselves by the fires of King so-and-so. The national drums are played at the orders of the king and belong to him; some are sunk in a pan near his burial-village. But they also belong to the nation, and the final act of the king's installation is to enthrone him on one: 'he is placed on the nation'. Nation and king are brought together.

I have tried briefly to describe how the Lozi feel the identification of their land, their king, and themselves as a nation. It emerges constantly in all discussions about the king, the land, or the people. It is manifest in the royal salute with which the Lozi acknowledge gifts of land from the king. Most notably, this general diffuse feeling is observable in how people flock to see the king when he travels, delight in visiting his capital, and approach him with an elaborate etiquette of words and actions as semi-divine.

## Kingship and the Royal Family

The kingship itself, though it is one fountain-head of authority, *bulena*, is distributed in several institutions and among many social personalities. Kingship at any moment is owned particularly by the

[1] See my *Economy of the Central Barotse Plain*, p. 89.
[2] *Ku shwa* is to die, to faint, to suffer, to be unconscious: *mulena ha'ashwa, sicaba sashwa.*

reigning king, but he holds it as a temporary representative of the royal family. It belongs to that family and it is therefore represented in the person of every prince and princess. The king and the princess chief are entitled to certain emblems, modes of salute and address, &c., some of which can be used for no one else. Others have been granted also to the chiefs and chieftainesses who, in the last two generations, have been established in outer provinces. But every prince or princess[1] is approached and treated with great respect. Wherever a royal is, he represents there the kingship; for kingship is diffused with the blood of kings. When a prince is elected king (or a princess to be princess chief) he moves into a status which differs absolutely from mere princeship (*bunabi*), but he remains in another aspect a prince. Some of his land and people are his 'things of princeship' (e.g. *munzi wamulena wabunabi*, the village of the king as a prince).

Kingship belongs to the royal family. The king is chosen from the male descendants through males of ruling kings. Ideally he should be a son of a king, born after his father was enthroned, by a woman on whom one of a number of queenly titles has been conferred and after that conferment. But any male in the agnatic line can be chosen. A man who lacks a prince in any generation of his ancestry is excluded. A princess chief should also come of an agnatic line. When the daughter of a princess chief was installed as her mother's successor at her mother's wish, she could not be enthroned on the national drum or have royal bands and other insignia: after three years she was deposed and replaced by a daughter of the reigning king. Nevertheless, all descendants of any king, up to some four or five generations, are 'children of the king' (BANA BA MULENA, Lozi), LINABI (royals, Luyi). This prestige of the royal blood even reaches back into a royal's commoner line to ennoble it. Commoner relatives of important princes or princesses are LIKWANABI, and entitled to respect. The prestige extends also to all those whom royals marry. There are general titles for all categories of these spouses and each has a specific title. The queens are BO MOYOO; husbands of princesses are BO ISHEE; wives of ruling chiefs (not the king) are BO MEYANA; wives of princes are BO NATANDI. When commoners thus marry into the royal family they are to some extent cut off from their kin by the elaborate etiquette which rules between royals and commoners. This is particularly true of queens and of the husband of the princess chief.

[1] To cover both princes and princesses I use the word 'royal' as a noun, which is unusual, but justified by the dictionary definition.

The right of the royal family to the kingship is unquestioned; no Lozi commoner can think of himself taking the throne. At the selection of a new king, or during a rebellion, the actual contenders for power may be councillors or groups of councillors. Always they have served their interests by supporting a particular prince. When a group of councillors mutinied against a king, because of his own policy or because he favoured another group of councillors, they attacked neither the kingship itself nor the rights of the royal family to it. Each party put forward its royal candidate for the throne and fought in his name. Thus when the councillors Mataa and Numwa drove out King Lewanika in 1884, they installed Prince Akufuna Tatila as king. Lewanika returned with an army and drove them out in turn. Mataa fled to the north, to the kingdom in the Lukwakwa where some Lozi had taken refuge from the Kololo. He persuaded the ruler there, Sikufele, to return as his leader to fight for the Lozi throne. It is clear that commoner councillors could only seek for power by serving their own royal candidate for the kingship.

### The Northern and Southern Capitals

Kingship resides especially with the reigning king in his capital (*muleneng'i*, 'place of the king', 'place of ruling'; in Luyi, *mbanda*). In Loziland there are two real (*tota*) capitals. Outstandingly the greater is that of the king. Nowadays wherever a particular king may reside, his capital is *Namuso*, 'the-mother-of-Government', after the capital of King Mulambwa (1780?–1830?). Since about 1866 this capital, the northern one, has been at Lialui, which was founded by King Sipopa who defeated the Kololo. Seven kings have ruled there, though three for but a few years. Before the Kololo invasion it is said that every king established his own capital. Twenty-five miles south of Lialui is Nalolo, the seat of the southern capital, referred to as *Lwambi*, which was the first capital built in the south in the reign of the sixth Lozi king. Here, too, every chief or chieftainess used to establish his or her own capital, but Nalolo has been the seat of rule since the defeat of the Kololo.

The Lozi homeland runs from north to south along the Zambezi and is divided thus into two major parts, the north and the south, under the main capitals. The southern capital is a duplicate of the northern one. Both have a LITUNGA (king) living in a royal palace (*Kwandu*, 'at the house') which has a special reed-fence with pointed stakes and a particular binding. Each palace contains the same structures, the same shrine for royal spears, and the same type of royal band. Within the capital there are on the whole the same buildings (*Kuta*, 'council house'; *makolo*, 'royal storehouses') in the same positions relative to the palace. It is said that when the chief-of-the-south was a man, the two capitals were duplicates of one another; but with the ruler a woman there are necessarily differences. The king's capital has a number of queen's courtyards—at Nalolo there is now one only for the princess chief's husband, ISHEE KWANDU ('consort of the palace'). However, till recently the northern king kept two to four wives at Nalolo. Each capital has also the same national drums and royal barges, paddles, and spears. The two councils are similarly organized.

The seeming equivalence of the northern and southern capitals, between which the Lozi kingship is primarily divided, is obscured in the modern Lozi (Kololo) terms for their rulers, MULENA YOMUHULU (the king, lit. 'the great chief') and MULENA MUKWAE (princess chief, lit. 'Chief Princess'), since *mulena* is often used for princes established in capitals as well as generally for Whites and all Lozi superiors, and *mukwae* is any princess. The equivalence of the real capitals and their distinction from the recently established outer district headquarters are manifest in the restriction of the Luyi term *Litunga* to these two principal rulers. *Mulena Mukwae* implies that the sex of the southern ruler is of absolute importance, as it is not. She is indeed, except when the context might cause her to be confused with the king, usually referred to as *Mulena* (king, chief) and more rarely as *Mukwae* (princess). But as we have seen, technically she is 'earth-of-the-south' against the king's 'great-one-of-the-earth'. That she is a woman is partly irrelevant. Though legend says that the first 'earth-of-the-south' was a princess, her successors until the Kololo invasion were men. The Lozi hold that it was a civil war between the southern prince and the northern heir to their dead father which enabled the Kololo to defeat them, and since then they have a custom, which is not a law, that the 'earth-of-the-south' should be a woman. For only a man can be 'great-one-of-the-earth'. Indeed, they regard the princess chief in some ways as if she were a man; a princess ruling at Sesheke told me, 'When I go into council, I change—I am a man.'

The rulers of the capitals established in the 1890's at Sesheke and Mwandi on the south-eastern borders of Barotseland, those which grew great at Libonda and Kaunga at the same time, and those established at Balovale and Mankoya in the 1930's, are often referred to as *mulena*, but never *litunga*. However, the Lozi regard the extension of the term *mulena* to them as courtesy; strictly, they say, the princes should be addressed and referred to as *mwana' mulena*, 'son of the king', and the princesses as *mukwae*, 'princess'. These rulers are entitled to the royal salute and to use white cloths on their barge shelters, but they have not royal drums, pointed stakes to their fences, or the right to the eland-tail fly-switch. The capitals became important in the administration of outer districts to meet threats of Ndebele invasions and to cope with the entry of Whites into Loziland, and later with the needs of the White administration. Four of these capitals have only marginal significance for the present analysis. However, they are capitals (*milineng'i*), though Lozi say, 'when you are at Namuso and Lwambi they are *matakanyani*' (out-of-the-way-places).

Loziland as a kingdom is thus mainly divided into north and south, with Namuso and Lwambi as the two chief centres of kingship. Of the other capitals, the short-lived one in Balovale District and the one at Mankoya were created to rule districts demarcated by the British Administration; those established by the Lozi were geared into the north–south division. Libonda, under a princess, now ruling Kalabo District, is a dependency of Namuso, part of it. It is a day's journey to the north-west of Lialui. Outside the Plain, in the bush a few days' journey south-west from Nalolo, is a small capital Kaunga (abolished in 1947) under a prince, which is a dependency of Nalolo. It was ostensibly created to watch the Mashi frontier, but it appears to me that it may be a balance against Libonda. On the south-eastern marches, where the Lozi faced the Ndebele, they first established a number of fighting councillors, with a prince as *primus inter pares*, to 'watch the fords'. Later, King Lewanika sent his son to establish a capital, Mwandi, there, and the daughter of the princess chief, his sister, a couple of years later built a capital, Sesheke, some 50 miles away. The prince's Mwandi was steadily moved nearer to Sesheke till they stood half a mile apart. Mwandi was considered an outpost of Namuso, Sesheke of Lwambi. They ruled the same region, though villages were allotted to each. In time, they became the Native Authorities of Sesheke District.

This primary division of the Lozi kingdom into north and south appears to me to reflect the tendency to dichotomy which is inherent in many African states, as related to the simple means of communication and the absence of an overall economic system. Until recently it appeared in all political establishments. Kaunga as a dependency of the south balanced Libonda in the north, and Mwandi and Sesheke represented north and south at a point of danger. The division did not meet administrative necessity. The known northern and southern capitals are all near the centre of the north–south axis of the Plain, very much nearer to each other than either is to the extremity of the axis. Lwambi rules villages to the north of Namuso and Namuso rules villages to the south of the Lwambi. At the centre their villages are intermingled, and when these villages move to margin sites for the flood-season they cross each other's tracks. Administrative control appears to be complicated, not made easy, by the dual organization.

Though the southern capital was established fairly late in Lozi history, as they tell it, the dichotomy is reflected in the legends of their first king, Mboo. He did not get on well with his younger brother, Mwanambinji, and they had a series of contests which Mwanambinji won with the help of magic. Mwanambinji moved south with great herds of cattle. These went down the centre of the Plain while he marched along the margins. There he raised headlands so that he could watch his cattle. In the south Mwanambinji built a kingdom: he subdued many people, including the Subiya and the Mbukushu, from whom he took their *maoma* (now the national drums). Ngalama, the fourth king of the north, sent many armies against Mwanambinji, but they were always defeated by magic. At last, worn out with fighting, his son decided to migrate, but Mwanambinji said he was tired and he and his councillors and cattle entered the ground at Imatongo, leaving only his cattle-pegs and ropes and porridge spoons. The pegs became trees. Imatongo is at the extreme south of the plain and is one of the most hallowed of Lozi cenotaphs. When Lozi pass here it is not sufficient for them to crouch and clap as at other royal graves, but they must give the royal salute and should leave some gift at the grave or on the river-bank. From there Ngalama brought the royal drums to the capital.

The hallowed northern cenotaph, Imwambo, the grave of Mboo, is not correspondingly as far north as Imatongo is south, but it balances it ritually. Between them is Makono, the cenotaph of their mother, where the king gets his kingship. The princess chief gets her kingship at the royal grave of Ngombala, the sixth king, who first sent his daughter and then a son to establish Lwambi. His daughter, Notulu, visited the south to get fibre for ropes and the people were so good to her she sought her father's leave to rule there. Later she asked that her brother Mbanga be sent to help her, for ruling was beyond her power as a woman.

Ikatulamwa, the capital of Mboo, and Makono, are taboo to the princess chief; indeed she must never even pass Ikatulamwa because of the feud between Mboo and Mwanambinji. NOYOO, of Mboo, should not pass Nalolo. Wherever the king and the princess chief move, they must occupy the same positions relative to one another. When they came to Livingstone to meet King George VI, the princess chief's tent was placed due south of the king's hut; and the homes of all other chiefs or their representatives were sited geographically in relation to this axis. If king and princess chief travel together going south, the princess chief embarks and lands first; going north the king embarks and lands first.

These then are the beliefs and myths and legends about the northern–southern division. They indicate what is confirmed by history and observation, the competitive relationship of north and south. There are authentic accounts of several occasions in Lozi history when the south has mobilized against the north, though only once did a real battle occur; but in legendary times the chief of the south attacked the king several times seeking kingship. However, the southern chief is generally regarded as being not a rival to, but only a sanctuary from, the northern chief. Since the chief is a woman, she cannot become king. Ritually, the opposition is symbolized in the taboo on her passing Ikatulamwa and in the reverence paid to the grave of Mwanambinji. His spirit is more powerful than the spirit of any departed king, and nearly all Lozi stories to prove the power of royal spirits are about him. Namuso has in its control more royal graves, but the greatest single ritual centre lies in the south. That is, where the secular power is weaker, the supernatural power is greater.

For though north and south are regarded as equivalent in their constitution, the main power of the kingship resides with the king in the north. The princess chief has all ritual appurtenances and royal rights, she has a full council and she should be consulted on all important national affairs, but she is under the king. Her councillors in court always refer to 'the laws which come from there', indicating the north. When the two councils combine, the order of seating is: (1) The NGAMBELA (chief councillor of the north); (2) ISHEE KWANDU (husband of the princess chief, who represents her); (3) NATAMOYO-WA-NAMUSO (the sanctuary of the north); (4) SAMBI (chief councillor of the south); (5) SOLAMI (or other title—the king's own councillor); (6) NATAMOYO-WA-LWAMBI (the sanctuary of the south); and so on. Thus the councillors of the south sit below those of the north. At flood and fall of flood the princess chief cannot move until the king has moved. When they are together, the national drums of the king must play first and last. The south as a whole has its specific place within the administrative and military organization of the north and not vice versa. The princess chief, as we have seen, cannot compete for the king's throne. In discussion and in reply to direct questions the princess chief herself, like the people, stresses that ultimate power resides in the king.

In this situation I expected to find that the princess chief would have some ritual control over the north in some such form as the Swazi Queen-mother has over her son, the king,[1] in that she might refuse to co-operate in playing her part in an integrated national ritual. In over two years of residence in Loziland and in associating for five other years with Lozi in Livingstone, I have never heard the slightest suggestion of this and it was denied at both capitals. The princess chief told me that she could reprove a king who was ruling unwisely and she might for good reasons object to some proposal, such as waging war, but that ultimately she would give way. She would not refuse to make offerings at her royal graves, 'for are we not one people and one land?' Again, how could she refuse to send her army to fight a war of which she did not approve, for 'they would be fighting for us'. Only in the cult of Mwanambinji, the magician hero-chief of the Lozi who got the national drums, does ritual superiority appear in the south.

For despite the division into north and south, the Lozi kingship is strongly integrated under the king. The two councils interlock into a single council, in which every member knows his place: and this was, till 1947, the real ruling body of Loziland. In this, as we have seen, southerners rank below northerners. When they visit each other's capitals the councillors know where they fit in and a councillor from either has the right to speak in his appropriate place at the other.

In recent years when the Government has steadily been 'reforming' Lozi political organization, the south has always lost in importance. Though the kings have consulted the south, the princess chief does not participate in the continuous discussions with the Provincial Commissioner which produce matters ready to be laid before the full council. Her capital has tended more and more, in the seven years I knew Loziland, to become the headquarters of a district, while the northern capital remains a national and district headquarters. The multiple sub-councils of her council are overridden: they are still important in the north. The retiring of 'redundant' councillors has

[1] See H. Kuper, *An African Aristocracy: Rank among the Swazi of the Protectorate.*

reduced their ranks more than the ranks of the northerners. Her dependent capitals at Seseke and Kaunga have been abolished, the former without her prior knowledge. Appeals in law could not go from Lwambi to Namuso—'from one king to another'. Now they do.

This is the inevitable result of the centralization and speeding up of Lozi rule necessitated by civilized British rule. Nevertheless for the Lozi the princess chief remains far more powerful than any other district ruler—she is still, like the king, *Litunga*, the earth. The Lozi are still divided into *Ba-Namuso*, 'the people of Namuso', the northerners, and *Ba-Lwambi*, 'the people of Lwambi', the southerners.

## Secular and Ritual Royal Villages

Namuso and Lwambi are the two real places of kingship in Loziland, but all villages which have been capitals of kings or princess chiefs, or at which kings and princess chiefs, certain princes and princesses, and two queens, are buried (*litino*, sing. *sitino*), and any village where a prince or princess, or a queen, or an important councillor title-holder, resides, is a *muleneng'i* (capital) for its neighbourhood. These villages are all *minzi ya mulena*, 'villages of the king', *minzi ya luu*, 'villages of the title'. I call them royal villages. They are distributed throughout the Plain which is thus divided into a large number of small areas each centred on a royal village, and into neighbourhoods with royal graves as centres of mystical power. The distribution of these capitals is not by any means even. In some parts of the Plain several may be built close together; in other parts one capital may serve in isolation a large area. The neighbourhoods acknowledging these capitals therefore vary greatly in size and population and frequently overlap one another. For they are not territorially demarcated as compact blocks with defined boundaries and they do not form the basis of the military, administrative, and jurisdictional organization of the state. A royal village may have attached to it a number of other villages whose headmen in ranked order form a council 'to look after', 'to care for', the royal incumbent or title-holder: his village, gardens, fishing, personal affairs, &c. But often the royal village has among its adherents other villages many miles away and in flood-season its villagers near by may move away, while other people, living at a distance, settle for a time near to it. In addition, in the administrative organization the villagers have allegiance to other princes and title-holders. Villages in one small local area may be attached to different royal villages in that neighbourhood. But affairs

D

affecting land in the neighbourhood of a royal village should properly come to it, and there is a feeling that other disputes among people in the neighbourhood should come to it, though they are not properly in its jurisdiction. Therefore there are frequent disputes between princes and councillor title-holders over their commoner followers and between them and commoners about the allegiance of the latter. Commoners also dispute about the relative status of the royal villages to which they are attached, since by different criteria a royal grave, the village of a powerful prince, the village of an important council-title, and the capital of an old king can each be considered superior to the others. At this level then Lozi political structure shows a large number of competitively orientated small groups which are in some ways localized and in others consist of attached but scattered villages, all of which have other attachments; and the composition of the groups varies between flood and dry seasons.

This competitive orientation of neighbourhoods is not present in the relations of royal graves (*litino*), considered as homes of dead royals, and not of their living heirs and councillors. Each king (or princess chief) selects or builds a village where he or she will be buried and places in it a number of councillors and priests with titles, and people. When he dies a huge grave is dug and there the king is laid to rest. A fence, with the pointed stakes and the lashings of royalty, is erected round the site of the grave. When the village is selected, trees from the bush are planted there, so that most royal graves with their clumps of trees stand out sharply on the Plain, which is largely treeless. A number of princes and princesses who ruled small areas, for various reasons have been buried in their own *litino* and not in one of the cemetery villages for royals; and two queens, one in the north and one in the south, have *litino* in reward for service to their husbands. The Lozi speak of these dead royals as 'the lord there', 'the lord who is sleeping', 'the lord of the earth', to distinguish them from the living prince or princess who has inherited the name and is regarded as the owner of the village. The Lozi believe that the sleeping chief still rules the neighbourhood and its people. He or she can strike with misfortune the whole neighbourhood or any of its inhabitants or anyone passing by, or grant good crops, big catches of fish, many calves, many children, unexpected luck like finding dead game, and so on. Thus the royal grave exerts particular power over its neighbourhood and the people who reside there, 'who are known to it'. It represents, for that locality, the mystical power of the kingship, of its past-holders, and of the stock which owns the kingship. However, though the grave's power is at its strongest for the neighbourhood, it is not limited by distance. Any royal grave also contains the full power of the kingship, though in practice the Lozi think the exercise of that power depends on the position of the sleeping chief when alive. Any royal grave can afflict any member of the royal line anywhere. It can cause misfortune to the whole of Loziland. It has power to trouble any Lozi, anywhere, even in White country, if it knows of him and his forebears, and particularly any member of the political sector attached to it (see below). Though the kingship is distributed over the land, every village which enjoys it represents its full power.

Individuals make offerings through the resident priests. In national enterprises and disasters there were sacrifices or offerings at all the graves. The spirits are approached by the resident priests, appointed by the king in council, at the king's orders, and he controls the cult. In extremity the king might himself go to make offerings to a recalcitrant spirit.

The cult of the royal graves thus reflects the ultimate unity of the kingship, though it is apportioned between different people and places, and presented to small communities in many localities. Its virtue (*mata*, strength; *moya*, breath) is present in full wherever it touches or in whomever it resides. At this ritual level those who hold kingship or may have struggled for it do not compete for people. Therefore many powerful royal spirits can sleep in amity in one small area, as near Lialui King Lewanika does at Nanikelako, King Mulambwa at Lilundu, King Mwanawina I at Lieneno, King Inyambo at Liondo, and now King Imwiko (died 1948) near his forebears at Naloyela.

*Administrative and Military Organization*

I have described how Loziland is divided and the Lozi people are grouped into neighbourhoods centred in royal villages, and pointed out that this was not the administrative and military organization of the nation. This organization consisted[1] of a number of sections called *makolo* (sing. *likolo*) or *likuta* (sing. *kuta*). The members of any *likolo*, which I translate as (political) sector, did not live in a compact block, within a defined area, but were scattered over the whole of Barotseland. People in adjacent villages, and sometimes even people in the same village, belonged to different sectors. This was particularly

[1] I move here to the past tense. What I have recorded so far is still observable; the organization described in this section still functions but within and sometimes in conflict with the organization overlaid upon it in recent times under the British Government.

so in Loziland itself, the Plain, though there were several pockets of members of a single sector at the margin of the Plain where people resided throughout the year, especially when they were foreigners. Moreover, as we have seen, people of Namuso, the northern capital, lay south of Lwambi, the southern capital; and Lwambi people dwelt north of Namuso. Lwambi itself had a separate sector organization. However, outside of the Plain, in the conquered areas, blocks of people or tribes might be attached as groups to particular sectors, though there were usually among them members of other sectors. Thus the Ila and Kaonde were mostly Njeminwa sector; the Kwangwa were mostly Kabeti; the Totela settled by King Sipopa north-west of the Lui river formed a sub-sector Macelafasi under stewards SIKOTA-MUTUMWA and AWAMI and entered Njeminwa. These Totela lived among Kwangwa largely of Kabeti.

Each sector had as its head (*toho*, head; *mung'a*, owner; *muzamaisi*, director) the holder of a senior office with title at the capital. The council (*kuta*) at the capital is divided in several ways. The chief division is into what are usually called 'mats' (*miseme*), after the mats on which the councillors sit. In the middle of the rear of a courthouse at the capital is a dais on which only the king or princess chief, or honoured White visitors, may sit. On the right are mats where sit the councillors-of-the-right (*manduna*), whose senior members are generically *makwambuyu* and whose junior members are *malume*. For them I shall use the term *indunas*, which from Zulu has crept into English and is a suitable word to describe African officials with mixed functions. 'Councillors' covers all members of the council. On the left of the dais is the mat of the *likombwa*, which is usually translated as 'stewards', whose junior members are also called *malume*. On their left is the mat for princes and husbands of princesses (*boishee*, prince consorts) who represent their wives. At the front sit the council's police and attendants and the king's bandsmen and attendants. Every title of each councillor, steward, prince, or prince consort has a fixed position on his mat. Successors to all titles are appointed by the king in council, though a few titles pass in kin-groups. On the right, at Namuso, next to the king, sits the NGAMBELA,[1] the chief councillor. Beyond him is the NATAMOYO, the giver-of-life, a title held by a prince. NATAMOYO is a sanctuary—a condemned man who can reach him or his courtyard is

---

[1] I believe an anthropologist should as far as possible avoid using African terms once he has defined an English equivalent, but I feel I must from now on use NGAMBELA and not chief councillor, for reasons which will become apparent.

PLATE I

1. The Plain in the dry season, showing the line of villages on the margin and villages in the Plain

2. Liyala, a large village near the northern capital

LOZI

PLATE II

3. The king's nets, attached to floating trays, are drawn up a branch of the Zambezi

4. A Kwangwa smith, one of many Barotse
specialists

LOZI

temporarily reprieved. Each king has the power to appoint a new senior induna of the right with a new title, described as 'his own NGAMBELA', whose seat is below the NATAMOYO's. When a king does so, all other titles move one seat farther away from the king. Not all kings have made the appointments, and the regular order of indunas' titles has been upset by the creation of other titles, by shifting of titles, and by death of titles, but I have shown elsewhere[1] that the history of the kingship is deposited in the indunas' titles which may be likened to a series of geological strata. The personal 'NGAMBELAS' of kings sit in order in distance from the present king, from him of the latest king to him of the first king. When a king created the title of his own 'NGAMBELA', he attached to it a large number of people, scattered over Barotseland, to form a new political sector. I say 'attached', because though titles are still created thus, people are no longer carefully attached to them. The modern administrative division is territorially organized.

The senior induna, the owner or warden of each sector, had under him a number of other indunas, both on the senior and the junior mats of the right. Every induna belonged to one or other sector, but the members of each sector were not always specifically allotted to its junior councillors. Where an induna also had a position in a royal village the people in the neighbourhood might take affairs first to him and consider him their immediate head, but they had the right to go to any councillor of the sector to which they belonged. Members of other sectors in the neighbourhood also attended on him. At two places on the Plain's eastern margin were the Old Mbunda foreign immigrant chiefs who sat in council and whose people were attached as blocks, through them, to specific sectors. Thus of the Old Mbunda chiefs, MWENEKANDALA, who sits with the royals, was attached to Kawayo sector, and MWENECIENGELE who sits with the senior indunas, to Imutakela-Nandinde sector.

The councillors of a sector formed a court, *kuta*, and council for that sector, which met at the house in the capital of the owner of the sector if two sector-members were involved in a dispute. A dissatisfied litigant appealed from this court to the full council of all sector indunas, stewards, and royals. When two members of different sectors disputed, the courts of the two sectors united to form a single court sitting in the capital house of the owner of the senior sector. From this court, too, appeal lay to the full council. These were the formally

[1] *Administrative Organization of the Barotse Native Authorities.*

## ROYALS

F 1. DANIEL KUFUNA
F 2. ISHEE MUKOLA (= L 8)
F 3. MBOO SIPOSA (= R 18)
F 4. MULMUI NAMABANDA
F 7. ISITEKETO LEWANIKA (1948, Chief Mankoya)
F 12. MWENE-KANDALA

## JUNIOR STEWARDS

*Katengo Council*

L 12. INGUU
. . . . . . .
(also F 3)
L 8. ALULEYA-IFUNGA
L 7. AWAMI
. . . . . . .

*Saa and Sikalo Councils*

## STEWARDS

L 5. SIKOTA-MUTUMWA
. . . . . . .
L 1. INGANGWANA

**KING'S DAIS**

Bandsmen and King's attendants
Police

*Lialui Council Seating, 1942 (showing titles referred to in text)*

## INDUNAS

*Katengo Council*

R 33. NAMUYAMBAUTALE
. . . . . . .
R 42. NAWALA
. . . . . . .
R 46. MBASIWANA
. . . . . . .
R 49. ANANDALA
. . . . . . .

*Saa and Sikalo Councils*

R 1. NGAMBELA
R 2. NATAMOYO
R 3. SOLAMI
R 4. MUKULWAKASHIKO
R 5. NALUBUTU
R 6. IMANDI
R 7. INYAMWINA
R 8. NAMUUYAMBA-ISINEKE
R 9. MUYUMBANA
R 10. KATEMA
R 11. NAMUNDA-KATANEKWA
R 12. MAAMBA
R 13. NOYOO
R 14. SIMUNDA
R 15. KALONGA
R 16. NAMBAYO
R 17. SUU
R 18. MBOO SIPOPA (also F 3)
. . . . . .
R 23. MUNONO
. . . . . .
R 32. MWENE-CIENGELE

CLERKS

instituted courts of the nation, but as we have seen, courts sat in many royal villages, and any prince or councillor might hold a court on his travels. Also, at the plains and stream valleys at which people were settled in the bush, there were prominent men who held courts. Nevertheless, on the whole the administration of justice was strongly centralized in the capital, and all important affairs were settled, or at least reported, there. However, where disputes occur inside a village or among kindred including affines, the Lozi feel strongly that they should be settled inside these small groups, and the authorities may refuse to hear them until it is clear that the village headman or senior kinsman cannot settle them.

The sectors were the divisions of the nation for state labour works, and the army assembled in sectors. We shall later examine how this was organized.

The sectors now vary greatly in numbers, and I think they must always have done so. In recent times the largest were *Njeminwa* and *Mooka* (the latest formed), which in some contexts are regarded as one sector, and which belonged specifically to the recent ruling kings under their own 'NGAMBELAS'; *Kabeti*, the sector of the NGAMBELA of the nation; and *Imutakela-Nandinde* under title MUKULUWAKASHIKO. The other sectors, going into the past, were *Imutakela-Indila* under title NAMUYAMBA-ISINEKE, *Kawayo* under title NAMUNDA-KATANEKWA, *Ng'ulubela* under title KATEMA, *Mbanda* under title MUYUMBANA, and *Ng'undwe* under title NOYOO, making nine in all in this century. (Lwambi in the south had three or four sectors: Njeminwa of the princess chief, under her own 'NGAMBELA', the title BIUNDANG'ONO; *Kabeti* of Lwambi's 'NGAMBELA' the SAMBI; and *Mbanda* under title MUKWAKWA, and an *Imutakela* which had 'entered' Njeminiwa.) All the stewards belonged to the king's Njeminwa and Mooka except two of the NGAMBELA's Kabeti; and at Lwambi all stewards were Njeminwa. Almost all royals at both capitals belonged to Njeminwa (though there are a few in other sectors) through the royal sub-sector, *Nakapu*, which contains them and their personal adherents (*Banakapu*); and so did the *Bamitana* (the personal adherents of queens) and the adherents of powerful consorts like ISHEE KWANDU (husband of the princess chief). Note, however, that the princes holding the sanctuary-title NATAMOYO, which exists in north and south, belong to the Kabeti sector of the chief induna of the council (i.e. of the 'NGAMBELA' of that capital). The sector system was not working properly when I was in Loziland. It seems, however, that the king put nearly all princes and stewards into the sector he formed, where they took their adherents. As we shall see, the stewards were his immediate supporters and the royals were part of the kingship in so far as it exists apart from the nation.

When the army assembled in sectors, smaller sectors entered into the larger ones, until all had ultimately entered into either the king's Njeminwa or the NGAMBELA's Kabeti. The same thing happened in the south, and in addition the south as a whole had a position in the king's Njeminwa. The king's and the NGAMBELA's sectors always remained distinct.

The sector system did not coincide with another administrative division of the people, in which they were allocated, also not on a territorial basis, to royal 'storehouses' (also *makolo*, or *malapa*). The king had a private storehouse, *Nayuma*, where he kept his personal property, and four public storehouses, *Mushukula, Newa*, and *Newanyana*, specifically his, and *Nateyo*, which was the storehouse of the council rather than the king. Certain wives of the king were given the general title MOYOO (queen) followed by a specific title (e.g. IMWAMBO, MUKENA, MALUNDWELO, KEYI). In these titles they represented the chief queens of early kings, as MALUNDWELO is the wife of Mboo, MAONDO of Inyambo, NAMABANDA of Yeta I. Each of these queens had her own house with its attendants and also its supporters. Each storehouse and each queen's house (also called a storehouse) has a specific position in the capital in relation to the palace. Both indunas-of-the-right and stewards are responsible for the storehouses, but here lies more specifically the work of the stewards. To the storehouses came all the royal store of tribute and all gifts and goods of the king, and the stewards looked after these and the queens and royals in the storehouses.

Finally, the NGAMBELA has his own people, the *Bamukowa*, but he has no steward, though a junior induna, ANANDALA, looks after them for him. The NGAMBELA must receive a piece of everything coming to the capital: part of his title's praises say, 'even if it is only a tortoise which comes to the capital, to him comes one leg'. I mention the Bamukowa here because they had no royal attachment, though they belonged to storehouses. Otherwise all the people, Lozi and subject tribes, are divided in attachment to storehouses and queens, and in this attachment they come under stewards. The people attached to a storehouse belonged to several sectors and members of a sector were placed in different storehouses. For example, Mutondo, holding the title

NAWALA, in that title is of Ng'ulubela sector under Induna KATEMA, he is chief councillor of Princess MBUYWANA, he is attached to Queen KEYI under steward KAMAKUNYI, and an adherent of Newa storehouse under steward KOLOLO. Muyongo is of Imutakela-Nandinde sector under Induna MUKULWAKASHIKO, his nearest important royal is Princess MWIKWANONGE, he is attached to Queen MUKENA under steward LIOMA, and an adherent of Newa storehouse under steward KOLOLO. Other members of Imutakela-Nandinde sector may work for other royals and other queens and be attached to other storehouses. These names for queens, royals, indunas, and stewards are not personal, but are all titles, and may be cited followed by a personal name, as NAWALA Mutondo.

In all these different attachments a man looks on every superior as his *mulena* (lord or chief). Thus NAWALA Mutondo, cited above, regards as his lords the king, the NGAMBELA, KATEMA, Princess MBUYWANA and her husband ISHEE KAMBAYI, Queen KEYI, stewards KAMAKUNYI and KOLOLO. NAWALA itself is a title in the Ng'ulubela sector of KATEMA. The present incumbent, Mutondo, by that name belonged to Njeminwa sector, and he still regards himself by sentiment in his private capacity as a member of it, and its leader, KALONGA, as his lord. He takes gifts to all these people. When he was only Mutondo (for from there he had the title MBASIWANA under NAWALA before becoming NAWALA) and resided near Princess MBUYWANA's, he still served her but not KATEMA; though he was even then under Queen KEYI and steward KOLOLO. He has also a series of other attachments, including a special one directly to the king, for whom he worked as an attendant and later became a vegetable grower. The previous NAWALA was of Kabeti sector before he got that title: his other lords were then councillors of that sector. Under British rule a local court was established some 3 miles from NAWALA's title-village under Induna MUNONO of Imutakela-Nandinde sector, and Induna MUKULWAKASHIKO, owner of that sector, was made responsible for it at the capital. The District of Mongu-Lialui was also put under a section of the Namuso council with Induna SOLAMI, owner of Mooka sector, as its head. Since then NAWALA Mutondo has regarded these three councillors as specifically his lords singled out from the mass of councillors, stewards, and royals who are all his lords in the widest sense. I have taken here the set of specific political attachments of one man and even then I have left out some.

Of all NAWALA Mutondo's lords only the Princess MBUYWANA has a residence near his home (both in a village of her own and in a village which is a royal grave), in addition to her house in the capital. The others all have their own villages, both familial and of-the-title, but his adherence is to their positions in the capital. Every Lozi thus is linked in several ways, for different purposes, with the capital. On the whole his lords and their assistant indunas and stewards are all con-centrated in the capital, so that formally the system is strongly centralized.

Many of a man's neighbours are not members of all the same chains of links as he is, while his fellows of each chain are scattered widely through Barotseland. Since these administrative divisions of the nation were thus not localized units, they assembled as groups only on rare occasions, for hunting or war, or for the major works of the king, such as digging a canal or building up a mound, when the king's interest specifically united them. Their leaders were resident in the capital, and the incumbents of titles were selected and did not directly and inevitably inherit them. Men attached high value to their member-ship of administrative units, esteemed their leaders and squabbled over their adherence, but the sectors and other units did not develop an internal sense of loyalty and autonomy which set them against the State as such. They resemble in this, for example, Zulu 'sectors' into which the age-regiments were divided and not the Zulu territorial provinces under their own princes or chiefs into which the nation was segmented. These princes and chiefs represented their provinces in the councils of the Zulu king.[1] The Lozi show strong feelings of loyalty in the small neighbourhoods attached to royals, but these were not clearly demarcated or organized for State administrative purposes. The people of these localities altered with the seasons and they were themselves divided by the administrative and other divisions. I sug-gest that this explains why the administrative divisions of the nations and the neighbourhoods attached to royals have never as corporate units dominated Lozi politics.

We have been looking at these attachments to titled offices as an absolutely existing system of political relationships, and the Lozi see and describe them in this way. But the relationships are highly fluid, for some of them alter as people make seasonal moves or change their residence, which Lozi frequently do, and others alter when the king moves people by royal command, or incumbents of titles change or new royal villages are established. Therefore to some extent for the

[1] See Gluckman, 'The Kingdom of the Zulu of South Africa'.

Lozi only certain parts of the system, to which his loyalties never waver, persist. The king in his capital with his council under the NGAMBELA, where all attachments lead, is the most enduring of all objects of loyalty. As one lives with the Lozi one sees that every Lozi, even a young man or a woman, is the centre of a nexus of ties to a particular number of lords, in a whole body of titled councillors, royals, queens. Every Lozi has specific and direct allegiance to the king and the NGAMBELA: his other lords may change. A Lozi in his political, and in his everyday, activities has to balance his obligations to all these lords and try to obtain his due rights from them. At this Lozi show consummate skill and they can fit in new lords with ease. I have described how NAWALA Mutondo had added to his old ties new ties to SOLAMI, MUKULWAKASHIKO, and MUNONO, to whom we may add the District Officer and other Government officials. When I arrived in Loziland he was placed to care for me, and I can vouch that his devoted service of my interests did not affect his service of his Lozi lords—or of his Lozi underlings. I found it extremely difficult to work out the framework of this very complicated administrative system, but I was always struck by the certainty with which each Lozi knew his own complex of attachments, and by the deft sureness with which he served his lords and used them to his own satisfaction.

The Lozi esteem their attachments to sectors, to storehouses, to queens, to royals, and to the titles and histories of all these and of those connected with them, very highly. Each one has its own praise songs, many of which contain both historical lore and proverbial wisdom. These praises are recited on big occasions and may be sung by the king's bandsmen; they are also quoted in many everyday situations. The Lozi's attachments in this network of chains of administration and service enter into every aspect of their lives. Though every man is a person of the king, with direct rights of appeal to him, normally he goes to the king along one of these chains. The network is part of the organization of the kingship: for the Lozi it is the kingship itself. They are not merely administrative devices as the British officers regard them. Therefore British insistence on reforming their administration in the interests of efficiency and economy has appeared to the people as an attack on 'the house of kingship' itself. The councillors who gave way to this attack have been discharged by the whole nation, after the death of the Paramount Chief who agreed to the reforms. *Bulena*, kingship, is represented to the Lozi in many ways, and among them are the sector and storehouse systems. Every person holding

rank in them partakes of the kingship which he represents to the
people. He is, in relation to the people, the king himself. As the most
important titles of the council were established by different kings, so
the present incumbents, who are commoners, represent those kings.
For the Lozi they are, without any idea of spirit-incarnation or
possession, those kings themselves. Induna NOYOO in virtue of holding
that title is King Mboo, the founder of the kingship. Mboo is also in
his royal grave, Imwambo, and in his capital, Ikatulamwa, and in the
reigning king. This is obvious to the Lozi, for the kingship contains the
virtue of all past kings, of God, of the land, and of the nation. Thus
the holder of the title NAMUNDA-KATANEKWA is the Kings Ngalama
and Ngombala who made the greatest Lozi conquests. These councillors are in charge of those kings' old capitals and their royal graves
where the kings sleep. There the kings are also represented by the
priests, who have their own titles.

### Ranking of Princes, Princesses, and Councillor-titles

When tribute was brought to the capital, a first portion was taken at
night for the reigning king. In the morning, before all the people, he
took a second share. Loads were then given to ILINANGANA, the priest
at Nakaywe which was the capital of King Ngombala. These are
tribute to God, Nyambe, for there He once saved the Lozi and there
ILINANGANA in national extremity offers prayers to Him. Loads of
tribute are next given to Induna NOYOO, for he is Mboo the first king,
since Noyoo was Mboo's 'NGAMBELA', and then to the priests of Kings
Ngalama and Ngombala, who are 'owners of the tribute', since it was
they who conquered the tribute-giving tribes. The people of the
NGAMBELA, the chief induna, next get loads, and then the councillors
and stewards in order of rank.[1]

This order of distribution of tribute reflects a manifold assessment
of rank. The reigning king is the powerful king and the titles of his
appointed councillors and those of his immediate predecessors occupy
the seats of greatest power. They are nearest to the king and they
speak last in court and council. When a decision is being taken[2] after

---

[1] See my *Essays on Lozi Land and Royal Property*, p. 93.

[2] Com. T. S. L. Fox-Pitt, O.B.E., R.N., sometime Acting Provincial Commissioner
of Barotse Province, informs me that since I last visited Barotseland there have been
votes by shows of hands on some matters. I previously noted majority votes only in
secret ballots on succession to vacant titles.

full and free discussion, the lowest councillor gives his opinion first. In it he defers constantly to those above him by phrases such as: 'to my mind it seems that . . ., but you will hear from your lords there', 'I consider that . . ., but I do not know what my lords will say', and so on. Senior councillors similarly defer to those below: 'my lords here have said and I join their words', or 'I cannot enter into the words which my lords have spoken', and so on. But in practice the newer titles have most power, for they give the final decisions and they are regarded as superior to the old titles. Yet on another scale the older titles, the ancestral ones, are more esteemed: they are the history of the nation and even more. They are the kings of the past themselves. It is similar with the ranking of royals. The sons and daughters of the reigning king are most important in some respects: their father is likely to give them posts, people, and goods. The three last kings, including the present ruler, King Mwanawina III, have all been sons of the great King Lewanika (ruled 1878–84, 1885–1916): they and their brothers are Lewanika and great in his name and the positions he gave them. It is probable that all future kings will be descendants of Lewanika. But because these descendants of Lewanika are specifically Lewanika they are not often referred to his grandfather King Mulambwa (1780?–1830?), as are the descendants of other of Mulambwa's lines. Some of the princes by other lines, though they have begun to lose the chance of being chosen for the throne, are thus reckoned greater: for they are Mulambwa, the parent. One of them, Muimui NAMABANDA, is considered the senior of the princes who should settle disputes in the royal family. So too for princesses. Daughters of the recent kings have power and people and their husbands sit high on the royal mat. A daughter of King Yeta III, son and successor of Lewanika, is princess chief. Her half-sister was destined to succeed a sister of Lewanika, Mbowanjikana, who rules at Libonda and who is over 100 years old. Since King Yeta's abdication,[1] a daughter of Lewanika is considered to be the likely successor. But the Princess MBUYWANA, who represents a princess taken to wife by her half-brother King Mwanawina I and who bore King Mulambwa, is in other ways the greatest of all princesses: 'she is the parent'. And with her are associated other princesses of ancestral status, inheriting names from the past: Mbowanjikana was a sister of King Mboo, the first king, as were Mwikwanonge and Namakau who is owner of Mbanda sector under Induna MUYUMBANA;

---

[1] He was crippled by a stroke and abdicated in favour of his half-brother, Imwiko, after several years.

Notulu,[1] whose father King Ngombala founded a sector for her the people of which became absorbed in the capital (Ng'ulubela of Induna KATEMA), and others. Some of them have national royal graves. Further complications are introduced by the princesses who have been placed in the names of the kings' mothers, where these were commoners, as Inonge who represented the mother of King Lewanika, and who was married to Induna SOLAMI (No. 3 on the right). ISHEE MUKOLA, married to the princess who inherited the place of King Yeta III's mother, by that title sat second on the royal mat at Namuso to Daniel Kufuna, eldest son of King Yeta III, then reigning, while by the title ALULEYA-IFUNGA he sat eighth among the stewards. Third on the royal mat was Mboo Sipopa, surviving son of King Sipopa who drove out the Kololo; Mboo had the eighteenth seat on the mat-of-the-right. Fourth on the royal mat was Muimui NAMABANDA who, we have seen, is warden of the princes; he is said to be a son of King Lewanika's physical father, Mando, who gave his pregnant wife to Litia, another son of Mulambwa. But ISHEE KWANDU, husband of the princess chief, sits on the right in full national council, second only to the NGAMBELA himself; he is a commoner exercising power in place of a 'king' (*litunga*).

## Rank—Lords and Underlings

Arguments and even disputes over the relative ranking of royals are frequent. These are a fraction of this type of argument, for Lozi are always disputing their own and others' relative ranking. Lozi society and thought are permeated with the ideas of *bulena* (kingship, chieftainship, rank, overlordship) and of the proper and appropriate behaviour between persons of different rank (*likute*, politeness, respect, appropriateness, good taste). In Lozi conversation, public addresses, and writings, *likute* is constantly emphasized. High praise of a man is to say *unani likute* (he has *likute*); a boor is damned, *utokwa likute*, he lacks *likute*. This is said of an impertinent underling and of an important person who reviles, or is impolite to, or is familiar with, his subordinates. The Lozi consider that *likute* is one of the two qualities which distinguish them from other tribes. Lozi have an elaborate code of etiquette between people of different ranks or sex, &c., and they know how to observe it; foreigners do not. Their other quality they consider to be the art of government: as they sometimes put it, 'we know how to rule', or 'other people have magic; we need none, we have the medicines of government'.

[1] Not the Notulu of the same father who founded the southern capital.

Rank—the relationship of lord (*mulena*) and underling (*mutanga*); of parent (*mushemi*) and child (*mwana*); of warden or owner (*mung'a*) and a person (*mutu*) or thing (*nto*)—is implicit in every Lozi relationship. Each of these three types of relationship, these three kinds of ranking, is contained in the others. The parent is lord over his child and owns him; the husband is lord over his wife and owns her; the king is parent of his followers and owns them. But the Lozi also think of these relationships as reversible. The child is lord over his parent and the wife is 'another kind of lord' to her husband. The king is not only the child of the nation but he is also its *mutanga*, its serf, its servitor. 'Chieftainship is slavery', say the Lozi, like the Ila. When Lozi reported to me King Imwiko's accession speech, they all recalled several times his saying: 'You have chosen me, you have killed me.'

*Bulena*, overlordship, kingship, and *likute*, respect for others, are dominant values for the Lozi, explicitly expressed. All relationships, even those of siblings and blood-brothers, are conceived in its pattern. Every part of their social system has these elements. The epitome for the system as a whole is the relation of king to subject, and all other relationships take significance from it. The kingship is thus again more than an administrative institution: it is the concept which integrates every relationship in Lozi life. But though other relationships are patterned on the relation of king and subject, the kingship is distinctive from them all. Kingship itself is unique.

## The NGAMBELA *and the King* —NGAMBELA*ship*

The use of kingship, *bulena*, in defining status relationships throughout Lozi society appears also in the use of the titles of his councillors and particularly that of the NGAMBELA, the chief induna. There is only one real NGAMBELA, and in the nation as a whole he is next in secular power to the king. He is not a king, *litunga* the earth, as the princess chief is, and he defers to her, saluting her with royal titles, eating on the ground before her, &c. But in the full national council he sits above the ISHEE KWANDU who represents her.

Though there is only one true NGAMBELA, whom every king has as his chief adviser, executive and judge, the title NGAMBELA is also used generally in the sense of 'chief councillor' of anyone in a position of authority. The true NGAMBELA, the NGAMBELA of the State, is an office which endures through the generations of kings as an essential part of kingship, but, as we have seen, every king also has his own 'NGAMBELA', the head of his own sector. Thus Noyoo, head of the first King Mboo's sector, is still referred to as the 'NGAMBELA' of Mboo, and Solami, head of Lewanika's sector, Mooka, is the 'NGAMBELA' of Lewanika. The State NGAMBELA is the man who rules for the king; the reigning king's own 'NGAMBELA' is some favourite whom he raises with a new title to sit above all titles save the true NGAMBELA and the NATAMOYO. The king's 'NGAMBELA' is the head of the Saa, the senior council described below; the State NGAMBELA does not sit on it. SAMBI, chief induna at the southern capital, is the 'NGAMBELA' of the princess chief. The senior councillor of every royal is his 'NGAMBELA', e.g. NAWALA is the 'NGAMBELA' of Princess MBUYWANA. The NGAMBELA also has his own 'NGAMBELA', Induna IMANDI, now seventh on the right above many sector heads. IMANDI is second to the NGAMBELA in his sector Kabeti, and holds Kabeti for him; he is also 'NGAMBELA' to the NGAMBELA in the capital, for which he is the warden on behalf of the NGAMBELA. In another set of relationships people speak of ANANDALA, a junior induna, as 'NGAMBELA' of the NGAMBELA, since he is responsible for the Bamu-kowa, the people attached to the title NGAMBELA. Similarly, in every sector the councillor next to the head is spoken of as his 'NGAMBELA'. The term is also used in defining respective positions among com-moners; thus every headman in every village throughout the land has his 'NGAMBELA'. NGAMBELA is almost equivalent to 'deputy'. As *bulena*, generically *overlordship*, is distinct from *mulena*, the king, so there is a concept of NGAMBELAship distinct from the specific title NGAMBELA. Similarly, the other titles of councillors at the capital apply precisely to particular positions and incumbents, but are also used in extension to define relationships in the hierarchical organization of all Lozi groups. Besides NGAMBELA, the one I have heard most generally used is INGANGWANA, that of the senior steward of the king, which is applied to the senior steward of all royals and also to the closest personal body-servant of any prominent person. Lozi define the relative positions of the members of any group by the council's titles. This is most commonly done in the councils of men which meet at royal villages, but I have heard both villagers and siblings placed on this scale. The council epitomizes all Lozi relationships.

To be an 'NGAMBELA' is not only to be a deputy who can act for his overlord. The NGAMBELA has his own authority, his own chieftainship —it is derived from the king, yet it is independent of the king. The Lozi express this by describing the NGAMBELA in relation to the king as *mulena usili*, 'another chief'. One praise of the NGAMBELA states: 'the king is owner of Loziland (Luyiland) and its trees and his servants·

and its cattle [game, fish, birds], the NGAMBELA is owner of the Lozi (Luyi) people'. We shall later examine further this contrasting definition.

In tales of the past Lozi always identify NGAMBELAS with particular kings. King and NGAMBELA are intimately associated, so closely that some Lozi consider that a holder of the NGAMBELAship should give up office when the king dies or abdicates and not continue to rule for his successor. The rule has not been followed in this century, though it contributed to the grounds for an attack in 1948 on NGAMBELA Wina which led to his dismissal. Nevertheless, as king and NGAMBELA are distinct and separate rulers, they are even opposed in certain senses: one is owner of the land, the other of the nation. Because of this opposition they must not sleep in the same building or travel together in one dugout. Some Lozi say the taboo is lest both rulers be killed together, but in a storm the NGAMBELA and all councillors must rush to sit with the king. Another way in which this opposition is expressed is in Lozi defences of kings who have failed to reward or have even cast aside those who brought them to power or helped them in adversity. They knew their king when he was insignificant, they would not be able to render him the proper respect due to a king.

To appreciate the position of the NGAMBELA it is necessary to grasp that all Lozi councillors are 'chiefs', in the current use of the word in anthropology, and that the NGAMBELA is the greatest of them. The mightiest of princes, even those who now rule districts, approach the NGAMBELA with respect and even fear, and the princess chief and king treat him with deference. King and princess chief refer to him as owner of the country, of the nation, of the capital. Princes and senior councillors salute him or his messages, clapping his words, delighted with his notice. He is expected to constrain and upbraid the king in private.

Underlying the relation of king and NGAMBELA is the fact that in Lozi society, as soon as a man is appointed to an office, he is lifted out of the ranks of his fellows and placed in some ways in opposition to them. I cannot elaborate or give detailed evidence to support this here, but I have observed the repercussions of the situation on many occasions and have frequently heard it described by Lozi. They put it in some such way as, 'a prince is loved till he is made king; everyone hates the king'; or 'if you become heir [to a village], you must expect to be hated'. The heir represents the power of state and law which constrain individuals. As one aspect of this, all positions of authority

E

tend to be divided in power between the incumbent and someone who wields part of his power—who is his 'NGAMBELA'. The 'NGAMBELA' then exercises authority on behalf of his lord who sanctions his appointment, but also has power from their underlings whom he represents against their common lord. In an organization as elaborate as that of the Lozi state there is therefore a continuous series of these bifurcations and delegations of power. The series obviously decreases in range as the group involved gets smaller, but it is present in every village and in every family.

In the most notable of these divisions of authority, that in the state, one principle of distinction which recurs frequently is into royals and commoners. The NGAMBELA has enormous power, but he must not be of the blood royal. He is not approached with the royal salute, or the elaborate etiquette that attends the king; he dare not use the eland-tail fly-switch or aspire to any other emblems of kingship. His power is so great that it is inconceivable for a possible claimant to the throne to be NGAMBELA. When King Yeta III in 1921 made a prince whose mother was a princess NGAMBELA, the people felt it was wrong, though he could not become king. Their prognostications of evil were confirmed when he was deposed after being charged with murder. In addition, the NGAMBELA must represent the commonalty, the Lozi people, and individual NGAMBELAS are judged by the politeness with which they treat commoners.

The king is the land, the NGAMBELA the commonalty; together they exercise kingship. It is the duty of the NGAMBELA to protect the nation against the king. The king has to protect people against the NGAMBELA and the commoner councillors. Therefore the sanctuaries in council are all closely related to the king; if a condemned man can reach the royal bandsmen and their instruments, or the Prince NATAMOYO who sits among the senior commoner councillors, he is respited. Farther down the council sits the NATAMOYO's assistant, also a sanctuary, INYAMAWINA, a title which should be held by a *sikwanabi*, i.e. a commoner relative of a prominent royal or a royal so distant from the ruling line that he is beginning to merge into the commonalty. As a *sikwanabi* he links royals and commoners. Since the council, and not the king, executes most business, it is liable to trespass on people's rights and there are many other royal sanctuaries: the king's palace, his mother's or queens' courtyards, his storehouses, all royal graves. The NGAMBELA's courtyard, and the council's storehouse Nateyo, are the main sanctuaries from the king.

The balance in the positions of the king and the NGAMBELA, as head
of the council, appears clearly in the disposition of buildings at the
capital. The king stands for *bulena*, kingship, the NGAMBELA represents *mulonga*, government (possibly the same word as *mulonga*, load).
The capital as a whole belongs to the king and to the NGAMBELA for the
nation: both are spoken of as its owners. The king, the NGAMBELA,
and every title have more specific rights to particular sites in the
capital, which are placed in relation to the palace (*Kwandu* in *Lian-
gamba*), before which is a large open space, *Namoo*. Across Namoo from
the palace is the *kuta*, the council-house. The place Namoo has to be
respected: no man with a load and no woman may cross it between
palace and council-house and no one may play or dispute on it. In the
palace courtyard is the *Limbetelo*, the hut where the king's own
drums and xylophones (Lozi, Simaa, and Nkoya) are kept, and there
the drummers on duty through the night beat the *mwenduko* Lozi
drum. As long as it plays, the king is well: the drums are his life. A man
meeting another who comes from the capital is asked: 'are they still
drumming?' and if the answer is 'yes', then all is well with the king
and his capital.

In or near the council-house are kept the great national drums, the
*maoma*, which are beaten only for war, or a great hunt, or to summon
the nation in emergency, or regularly when the king travels as between
his capitals. They are in charge of the council, under the Prince NATA-
MOYO, who is the sanctuary.

The two types of drums symbolize the dual elements of the state.
After the death of a king the council selects a prince as heir. He is then
escorted by the NGAMBELA and other councillors and princes at night
'to fetch kingship' from Makono, the home and royal grave of Mbuyamwambwa, daughter and wife of God and original ancestress of the
royal family. The king spends the night in vigil by a small lake out of
which comes a monster to hold commune with him. In brief, here the
king-elect gets kingship from God, from his ancestors, and from the
land (nature). Here too the priest helps him kindle the new fire of his
reign. He returns to the capital with the national drums thundering
and the NGAMBELA seats him on one of the drums, as on the nation, to
bring the kingship to the people.

As the king and NGAMBELA stand apart in their representative positions in the capital, so, as we have seen, they may not sleep in the same
house or travel together. The king with his own bands travels in his
royal barge, the *Notila* or *Indila*. The national drums travel in the

*Nalikwanda,* which the NGAMBELA commands and may ride in, but not the king. Royal and national drums play one after the other; both may not be silent, but both may not play together. The Notila of a king is sunk after his burial, as he is buried with his drums; the Nalikwanda and most *maoma* national drums go on from reign to reign. Nalikwanda may temporarily take the lead, but Notila usually leads behind the dugout Natamikwa which carries the national spears in charge of a senior steward. The NGAMBELA's official barge is *Nalikena.* Nalikena travels close behind Notila and constantly draws alongside so that the NGAMBELA may enter and consult with the king; the NGAMBELA should not be long in Notila. Other councillors and princes paddle Notila and Nalikwanda.

Yet ultimately though the national drums, the *maoma,* are thought of as the nation's in contrast with the king's own bands, the king is spoken of as owner of the national drums. So too the NGAMBELA's barge, Nalikena, belongs to the king. For as all rule ultimately is kingship, so all symbols of that rule rest in the kingship, even where they represent separate elements making up the kingship. All ritual objects of rule are the king's: the spears which rest on the altar, *Kaole,* in his palace, against a pole from a many-fruited tree signifying fertility; the *likululume,* magic horn, which leads the army into action, &c. The NGAMBELA has only emblems of office (a rhinoceros horn walking-stick peculiar to his office, and skins and a lion-mane head-dress and bells which may also be emblems of other important offices). The king is ritually installed, the NGAMBELA ceremonially. The king's spirit has power over the nation and the land, not the NGAMBELA's. The king's ancestors are national gods, not the NGAMBELA's.

The king makes formal appearances in the council, he does not participate in the trying of cases or the public discussion of national affairs, except nowadays when pronouncements are made in the presence of British officials. When the senior induna (for decisions always end on the right) gives his judgement, he defers to the king's name: 'I do not know what the king will say . . .' He then instructs a councillor, usually a steward, to report the matter to the king in his palace, with the grounds of his own decision and what other councillors have said. On this report the king gives his verdict and the reporter informs the senior councillor who informs the council. I have never seen the king sit in court, though I have been with him in full formal council.[1]

---

[1] During most of my visits to Loziland King Yeta was ruling but not appearing in public because he had had a stroke which left him speechless.

PLATE III

5. The king's royal barge on the return from his visit to Livingstone to pay homage to King George VI in 1947

6. Senior-councillor SOLAMI beating the national drums as the barge *Nalikwanda* travels to the margin-capital out of the flood. In the centre is the NGAMBELA Wina

LOZI

PLATE IV

7. The court-house in the northern capital from the mat of the stewards. On the right is the king's dais with councillors-of-the-right beyond it; litigants sit at the support on the left

8. Ceremonial installation of a Kwanga heir, succeeding his father, in his home village. Beyond is his mother

LOZI

I have frequently been in court with the princess chief and at Mwandi with the late Chief Imwiko (afterwards king). Discussion of affairs went on as if the ruler were not there. Though the princess chief heard everything, a councillor was instructed to report to her and the reporter returned her verdict to the head councillor who announced it. The council must inform the king of everything that comes to its knowledge and the king must inform the council of all his affairs or what he is told. All day long streams of messengers go backwards and forwards between king and council. As I sat in the council, or with the king, I felt vividly that rule is exercised by the two, as matters came from one to the other. Patently kingship is divided between the king and the government balanced against one another. Every man who is successful in a suit at the capital—a law case, a request for land, begging for goods, a pass to visit somewhere else—gives the royal salute first to the palace, then to the council: he rises before the palace, he only kneels at the council. But here again, though administrative and judicial work is performed by king and council in separation, all verdicts are ultimately in the king's name.

## The Sub-Councils of the Council

Rule is also distributed between the three mats, of indunas-of-the-right, stewards, and royals. When a decision is taken, members of each mat in ascending seniority speak after one another. The distinction of the mats is spatially clear and constantly emphasized by speakers, though both for themselves and for the people in unity they form *kuta* (the council), they are all *Malozi* (The *Malozi*). The councillors and people consider that representatives of all three mats should be present when an affair is decided. Nowadays if a delegation of the council goes anywhere or discusses any matter, it should contain ideally representatives of each mat; and if it is a matter of national importance, representatives of each mat of northern and southern capitals. The three mats represent three important components of the State. The most powerful, the mat-of-the-right, is the mat of the nation, the commoners, and it contained in 1940–2 only two princes nearly related to the king: the sanctuary NATAMOYO and by special gift Mboo Sipopa. A few distant princes who are not of the pure agnatic line get appointed to positions on the right, but this is comparatively rare and disliked by the people. The royal mat represents the royal family and its rights over and obligations to the nation, as well as its rights to the kingship. The stewards, on the third mat, are described as 'the wives of the king', 'the women', 'the boys of the king', and are thought to stand for the ruling king against the mat of the nation and the mat of the royal family. Therefore the king is described or greeted politely as BO INGANGWANA (the polite plural of the title of the senior steward) or *Bo Mtwaleti* (for King Lewanika, the polite plural of the name of his personal steward, later the husband of the Princess Chief Mulima). Similarly, the princess chief, her husband, the recently created provincial chiefs, a queen, and any royal, are politely referred to or addressed by the plural of the title of his or her senior or personal steward. Throughout, these stewards, who always sit on the left, are closely identified with the rulers. At capitals they should stand for the interests of their present ruler. Therefore the stewards are 'the king's wives'. But though the stewards are thus called 'women' and 'boys', they are also powerful councillors, who decide, judge, and execute. Though their status is much lower than that of indunas-of-the-right, as was shown for example in 1943 when Steward No. 2 was promoted to Induna No. 7 at Namuso, 'they too are chiefs'.

Though the king is especially represented in the council by the stewards, he stands above this particular representation. The whole council is the king's: he is its owner, and the owner of the NGAMBELA, who is more specifically its owner. The three mats are held together in their common subordination to the NGAMBELA and through him to the king.

The council is divided also into three sub-councils on each of which sit members of each mat: the Sikalo, the Saa, and the Katengo. The Katengo consists[1] of the *malume*, the junior indunas-of-the-right and stewards who sit on mats behind the mats of their seniors, and of all unimportant princes and consorts. The Saa consists of all other members of the council, except the NGAMBELA and NATAMOYO, so it is under the reigning king's own 'NGAMBELA'. The Sikalo consists of the NGAMBELA and NATAMOYO and an undetermined number of varying senior members of the Saa. The Saa and Katengo met in the day in the council-house or at the courtyards of their leaders; the Sikalo met at night in the *Limbetelo*, the king's drummers' shed in the palace. These divisions were found only in the two main capitals, not in the councils of the new provincial capitals. These councils were not a division into junior, senior, and highest courts for judicial purposes; as described

---

[1] The council is still divided thus, but formally the titles have in addition been applied to new bodies. Nevertheless it is still possible to write of this old division in the present tense, though I use the past where procedure has changed.

above, cases went first to the courts of political sectors, then to the full council. The division into the three councils was into equivalent units to discuss matters of national importance. That is, the Katengo as a separate body in these discussions was more powerful than Katengo members' standing in the full council of all title-holders (*the* Kuta). Matters might originate in any of the sub-councils. They were then discussed in all separately. The head of Katengo sat also in the Saa, and reported the arguments and decisions of each to the other. Most of the Sikalo consisted of members of Saa. Discussion went backwards and forwards between the councils in an attempt to get agreement before the king was called on to give the final decision. The king was also advised by two women (ANATAMBUMU), one a princess, the other a commoner, who listened outside the drummers' shed to the Sikalo's deliberations. In addition, any very important matter was also referred to the southern capital with its own three sub-councils.

Besides the formal sub-councils, the king meets informally with his advisers or anyone he pleases by day and night in the *Kashandi*, a structure in his courtyard where he may converse with and feed people.

In the past there were very few matters on which these sub-councils were likely to split markedly in their wishes. There was no economic basis for a cleavage of the nation into classes with divergent interests. The problems generally were: against whom and when should war be waged; where should raids for children be made; did the nation have enough food to undertake the digging of a canal or building up of a mound; where should they hunt; who should succeed to a vacant title, and other administrative matters. New laws, such as rules of marriage or land-holding, were discussed, but these were rare occasions. With the coming of Europeans, cleavages of opinion developed, as over the treaty with the British South Africa Company, beer-drinking, &c.

Nevertheless the three sub-councils were considered to stand for different interests. The Sikalo members were the most important councillors, who met the king quietly at night in the palace, and, with other senior councillors, met as the Saa in the day. The Saa represented the capital, with its councillors, the Sikalo the king and NGAMBELA and their advisers. The Katengo was the council of the mass of the nation, called 'the council of the many'. It consisted of a large number of petty princes, councillors, and headmen widely dispersed through the nation and therefore in fact as in theory knowing better the people's wishes and feelings. Though its members were subordinate to the senior councillors in the council sitting as a whole, when they separated to meet apart it was as an independent body with its own specific powers. Katengo councillors have told me, 'we too are chiefs', and I have heard senior councillors refer to the Katengo as 'another kind of chiefs'. The Katengo councillors are *malume*, which means 'men', 'warriors', 'veterans'. They were expected to be bold in opposing senior councillors, and I was told that the senior councils would hesitate to force their will on the Katengo. The king has on occasion taken the Katengo's advice against the seniors.

Obtaining a seat in the Katengo was one path by which an able and courageous man could get promotion to senior posts, though in practice, at least in recent times, most senior councillors have not come from the Katengo.

The Katengo represented the mass of people, as a council in which princes and men from many small local areas could be assembled. The Lozi do not seem to have had regular meetings of all men of the nation like the Zulu *ibandla* or Sotho *pitso*. Meetings of this kind were held on affairs of very grave importance, as for example, apparently to discuss the treaty with the British South Africa Company.[1]

Here again, though each of the three sub-councils was considered to represent a specific part of the state, together they formed the council as a whole. The Sikalo was more particularly the king's inner sub-council, but all three councils are spoken of as the king's. He stood above uniting them all, for the whole council was his.

Since there were no cleavages of class, based on economic interests, in Barotse society to be represented by mats or sub-councils, we may say that these various internal intersecting divisions of the national council exist autonomously in the political structure. Moreover, in Loziland the powerful councillors do not represent territorial segments which have a corporate identity within the kingdom. The councillors are powerful only in virtue of their offices, the positions of their titles on the council, and in virtue of their recognition by the council and king, and not because they lead bands of followers, even though having followers is a path to promotion. Thus, though the Lozi council was, and is, intricately organized into 'mats', sub-councils, and sets of titles heading sectors, which are held to represent various components of the state, they do not in fact represent organized groups. Nevertheless we may say in summary that the royal mat represents the rights of

[1] Coillard, *The Threshold of Central Africa*, pp. 356–7.

the royal family in the kingship and the obligations of royals to defend commoners against council and king; the indunas' mat represents the rights of the mass of commoners in the state, and within this mat the Saa seniors represent the state's power and the Katengo juniors represent the commoners against their own powerful representatives who come to stand for the state against them; the stewards' mat represents the ruling king's rights in the state, and the Katengo junior stewards represent the commoners' rights in the king's estate against him and the powerful stewards who are identified with him. The administrative organization is an elaborate arrangement of checks and balances between units which are referable to components of the state, but the machine works largely within the capital itself. Therefore the nation and its organization in the kingship are very strongly integrated. The capital is full of intrigues which are worked out in debate and discussion within the council. Tribal legends are unreliable, but it is perhaps significant that early Lozi history is marked by an absence of rebellions against kings. Since the expulsion of the Kololo, and the coming of Whites which followed shortly afterwards, there have been frequent rebellions leading to the expulsion of kings or the dismissals of particular councillors.

In this situation, the average Lozi manages to get his quarrels with his neighbours settled at the capital; he goes there to beg for land and have his inheritances confirmed; his wars and hunts were planned there; the king distributed goods to all his subjects there. These were and are the satisfactions that he sought and seeks in the capital, and the very satisfaction of being there: of being noticed by the king and the senior councillors, of talking with them, of serving them. Here too the individual Lozi strives for his own advantage by proceeding from one lord to another, playing one against the other. In doing so he likes to feel that he has a personal direct allegiance to some councillors, who speak for him in court.

The king had in the capital for his service an organized group of warriors who could exercise force: his privileged *mabuto*. But it was a small force, available also to the council by the king's permission. For, as we have seen, though in this system of checking and counter-balancing administrative units the king was specifically represented by certain units, yet he stood above them all. It is held that the king can do no injustice, and should a commoner feel that he is unjustly affected by an action of the king's he can sue the councillor or attendant who carried it out. The king never acts: 'he is not a policeman'.

For a ruler or councillor or headman to take violent action is a heinous offence, for which he may be discharged. Even a king has been threatened with deposition[1] for doing this. The ruler is ideally wise, gentle, and soft-tempered; for 'the anger of a chief kills'.

The man who carries out the king's orders cannot quote them in defence: 'he cannot work (spoil) the king's name'. The kingship is thus outside of their internal disputes. Since the Lozi still, on the whole, hold common values, the kingship stands, both secularly and ritually, for the unity of the Lozi themselves and their union with their land. The three mats, the three sub-councils, the sectors and store-houses, all belong to the kingship through its officiating councillors or stewards and are integrated in it. No Lozi has ever attacked the kingship, though Lozi have fought in attachment to different claimants for it.

The king and his council rule through the complex administrative system which embraces the whole nation. But the system is clearly far more than a machine for settling disputes, organizing armies, and meeting contingencies. The council with its sectors and its store-houses, to which all Barotse are attached, has been an enduring if changing framework of the Lozi state. Within this framework the state has accommodated its increasing numbers, both those born to its subjects and those added by conquest. All villages are set in it. It enables the Lozi, and beyond them the Barotse nation, to be marshalled as a strong, powerful group which can settle internal disputes and combat external foes. Therefore it is the source of their power and their enduring existence, valuable in its own right. The titles in this framework stand for the mighty kings of the past who still affect the welfare of the land: these titles are therefore Lozi history and great-ness. The system is an essential part of kingship, for the organization is locked in the kingship and the person of the ruling king.

## The Kingship

The kingship at the capital is more elaborate than my description, but I have not space to describe all the relationships of councillors and stewards or the many other attendants on and workers for the king—the *Baliyenga*, people of the king's kitchen, fishermen, hunters, carvers, bandsmen, jesters, &c.—who visibly for the Lozi 'make kingship'.

Kingship thus consists in having many subjects, distributing land,

---

[1] In the past usually possible only by a rebellion.

possessing ritual power, holding emblems, receiving ceremonial attention, and in exercising organized power through an elaborate structure
of officials. For the Lozi, as a nation, there are these three autonomous
but interpenetrating elements in their political structure: the kingship
as such, which is the epitome of the concepts of rank which enter into
all their relationships; the administrative organization which embraces everyone and which works through its junction in the king; and
the land which belongs to the king. These elements are all reflected
in the cult of the royal graves. The royal spirits had in them the
virtue and power of kingship to affect the whole nation, the royal
family, the land, and the fortunes of any subject. These graves are not
only of kings and princess chiefs, but also of princes and princesses who
had been given people. The virtue of kingship is in the royal family as
a whole. Two queens have royal graves because they helped their
husbands. They link royal family and commoners who constantly intermarry: the royal family is not completely isolated from commoners.
The graves are worked in the sector system, for almost all royal graves
are of kings with sectors or princes and princesses who were given
sub-sectors. The spirit can affect anyone, but particularly a member
of its sector, for it 'knows' him. Finally, each grave has immediate
power over its immediate neighbourhood, in relation to local dispositions of the people; and yet it also has undivided power over all
Loziland.

The state thus has a mystical value for the Lozi, and its ritual
centres have power to affect any Lozi's fortune or life. Primarily,
however, the Lozi are concerned with the secular work of the state.
In fact, the chiefs and councillors organize them to deal with outside powers or recalcitrant sections, arrange for public works (and
tribute), distribute goods and services, allocate land and protect
holdings in it, deliberate and decide on matters affecting the interests
of nation or individuals, and adjudicate in disputes. The last two functions are those the Lozi emphasize most: 'government', they say, 'is
ruling people', and ruling people involves above all settling quarrels
impartially according to well-known rules, and taking action to meet
problems arising in the life of the people. In ruling thus the king and
his council enable the Lozi to live an ordered life in which they can
plan their work, their marriages, and all other activities. The state
represents the common and general interests in the rule of law,
prosperity, and continuity, and it may be this which is reflected in
the ultimate indivisibility of kingship.

*Modern Political Developments*

When a British protectorate was established over Barotseland under the treaties with the British South Africa Company, the king retained the right to rule his people according to Lozi custom, subject to the demands of good government and of natural justice. He gave up his rights to try theft, murder, witchcraft, and other offences, and later serfdom (1906) and then tribute (1925) were abolished in return for money payments from the British authorities.

Overall power now rests in the British Government, though certain exercises of that power are limited by the treaty. The Lozi and their subject peoples realize this very well. As in the rest of South and Central Africa, the people are suspicious of the Whites and hostile to them. But though the Lozi have lost some of their outer provinces which they held in tribute but did not administer, Loziland itself and land for many miles around it has been preserved to them. Officials, missionaries, and traders in the Province itself treat Barotse, and especially the rulers, with a respect which contrasts markedly with the way Africans are treated elsewhere. Therefore, though the British Government is conceived as an alien protecting and ruling power, Lozi frequently say, 'we are one Government with the British'. This feeling of unity appears most strongly in loyalty to the British King. The feelings of doubt are realistically divided between Parliament in the United Kingdom and Legislative Council in Northern Rhodesia. With the former the Lozi consider they may be secure in their treaty: they are petitioning for the same status as the High Commission Territories of South Africa. Of the intentions and promises of the local government they are highly suspicious; they even hesitated before agreeing to send representatives to the African Representative Council of the Territory. Nevertheless, in most situations in which they deal with the Administration, these suspicions do not arise.

Yet, in the internal structure of the Province, Lozi and British have been involved in a long struggle, despite easy co-operation in many affairs. District Officers have frequently regarded themselves as protectors of the people against their native rulers, while the latter think they must protect the people against their British overlords. Thus Barotseland shows the same balance of black and white authorities found elsewhere in Africa, though the tension is not as acute as in most areas. The balance of authorities nevertheless appears, for example, when litigants appeal to the High Court of Northern Rhodesia in civil matters or the Provincial Commissioner in criminal matters from the Barotse authorities: frequently they allege corruption, favouritism, &c., among the Lozi councillors. The position is similar in administrative matters.

The British Government has developed a considerable number of activities—public works, schools, hospitals and dispensaries, transport services, veterinary treatment, &c.—in which it strives to co-operate with the Lozi Government, but of which its officials are the main focus. Similarly, in its local offices is centred much of the administrative work resulting from the presence of Whites in Barotseland, the movement of Lozi to labour centres, the presence of police and their control of public order, and so on. The two sets of centres of government, British and Barotse, function partly independently but with frequent interlocking.

This trend of development has been described elsewhere,[1] so that I shall here indicate only its influence on the internal structure of the Lozi state. Lozi society, like all African societies, is becoming more and more diversified. A number of distinct interest groups have emerged: traders, clerks, teachers, labourers, Christians, &c. Generally the introduction of Christianity has not created a specific group alinement, for the Lozi have absorbed Christianity. Many chiefs and councillors who are polygynists and not members of the Church attend services and consider themselves Christians, and so do many ordinary folk. The Paris Evangelical Mission's schools have educated very many Lozi, and most councillors can read and write. The nation wholeheartedly supports schooling. Though between 1942 and 1947 I noted a growing hostility to the missions, Christianity does not seem to form a focus of political struggle. There are a number of 'intelligentsia', as they call themselves (clerks, traders, store foremen, &c.), who form a political grouping, but they include pagans. Generally they do not attack the kingship but aim at acquiring increasing power in the king's councils. The grouping is split by internal jealousies between Lozi, and between Lozi and Nyasaland Africans who hold important positions in White service. These clerks and other skilled workers both in the Barotse and the British services are very resentful of their comparative unimportance in Barotse national affairs. Here Barotseland differs from other parts of Central Africa where the educated clerks have acquired considerable power because, unlike illiterate chiefs and

[1] See H. Kuper, *The Uniform of Colour: A Study of Black–White Relationships in Swaziland*, and my essay on 'The Kingdom of the Zulu of South Africa'.

councillors, they can to some extent cope with Government needs.[1] In Barotseland rulers and/or important councillors usually can read and write and many speak English so that they can handle business with the Government directly, though it is customary for them to work through interpreters. The Lozi government has maintained its power and councillors are too powerful to be awed by education. A few 'secretaries' to rulers and councils have, however, become important in the nation and are resented by senior illiterate councillors. In the councils of small sub-districts clerks are relatively more powerful.

Secondly, as described above, the subject tribes constituting the Barotse nation have tended to assert themselves against the Lozi. The Lunda and Luena have been granted independence, and a movement among the Nkoya demands independence. But the Nkoya movement, and movements in some other tribes, are mainly for increasing their representation in central councils and their control of local affairs, and are not simply attempts to break from the Lozi kingship.

There is just detectable an emerging cleavage between the rulers and the mass of commoners, but it has not yet attained political significance as a mass movement. For to commoners, as to subject tribes and intelligentsia, the king and his treaty rights are a protecting shield against the Whites.

Up to the present, therefore, the pressures created by the diversification of Lozi society have been expressed in demands for changes in the personnel of offices. This has accorded with the pressures applied by Government to Lozi authorities. Government recognizes its obligations to the Lozi under the treaties and has no wish to upset the powerful kingship which controls a vast area and many people. In any case, it has no substitute to offer. Therefore officials for various reasons at various times have pressed for changes in the personnel and constitution of administration.

I have elsewhere described in detail administrative changes up to 1942[2] and here summarize these and note more recent changes. From the inception of their rule the British, who thought the sectors were military units, required a territorial basis for their administration.

---

[1] See articles on modern political problems among the Mazabuka Tonga and the Fort Jameson Ngoni of Northern Rhodesia by E. Colson and J. A. Barnes respectively, and among the Nyasaland Yao by J. C. Mitchell.

[2] See my *Administrative Organization of the Barotse Native Authorities.*

Magisterial posts (*bomas*) were established as the centres of Districts with defined boundaries. Obvious sites were near Lialui and Nalolo, the main capitals, and near the capitals, Mwandi and Sesheke, on the south-eastern border at Sesheke. The small capital Libonda later grew as the centre of the District of Kalabo Boma. In 1934 a Lozi capital was founded near Balovale Boma, but it did not begin work before it provoked the Balovale peoples to get independence. The Lozi capital established at Mankoya Boma in 1936 has also created difficulties with local chiefs. In Lialui in 1937, when Native Authorities and Treasuries were started by agreement between the two Governments, a so-called Sikalo council (which the Lozi referred to as *ofis*, 'office') was placed in charge of Provincial estimates and to oversee affairs in the several Districts and hear appeals from them, while a council called Saa-Katengo was placed in charge of Lialui District affairs. The Sikalo and Saa-Katengo divisions were also made at Nalolo where the Sikalo had power only in Nalolo (Senanga) District. A National Council met annually at Lialui: it consisted of Lialui Sikalo and Saa (not Katengo) with representatives from the outer districts, especially Nalolo.

The system, regarded as an administrative organization, was still untidy, and the Administration exerted pressure to have it made neater. The allocation of intermingled villages in Sesheke District to two capitals built almost alongside each other was inconvenient, and as the reigning chiefs quarrelled continually, in 1942 the district was divided territorially between them; in 1947 one capital was abolished. In 1946 the small capital Kaunga in Nalolo District was also abolished. At Lialui the Sikalo and Saa-Katengo did not keep Provincial and District affairs distinct, and Sikalo and Saa consulted each other and met together continually. In 1946 this organization was altered: two councils were established at Lialui, a Provincial Council and a Mongu-Lialui District Council. The Sikalo and Saa-Katengo Councils at Nalolo were combined into a single District Council. Barotse Province in theory is now tidily organized: it has a Provincial Council and five subordinate councils each in charge of one of the Districts. As we have seen, the Nalolo Council has steadily been forced into a position in practical affairs akin to that of other District headquarters. All the councils still sit as three 'mats'.

The division into Districts cuts across indigenous political groups, and this was even more marked in the partition of each District into sub-districts each with its own court of prominent local personages.

These sub-districts have ousted the sectors in judicial and administrative affairs.

District Officers, who tended to look on the Barotse Government as an administrative machine, have pressed for other changes. Most of them thought the councils were riddled with corruption, nepotism, and favouritism, and by their standards the councils were inefficient; they seemed to be cliques battening on a mass of poor commoners. Councils had already begun to give members technical duties connected with hygiene, canals, agriculture, &c. The District Officers wanted the abolition of what it considered redundant posts, and aimed at smaller councils consisting of a few trained judges and executives, with a number of men trained as medical, veterinary, forestry, agricultural, &c., assistants. They argued that salaries of useless councillors consumed so much of the Barotse Treasury's funds that little was left for social services or to raise salaries to attract better-trained men. Finally, they felt that the 'exploited' commoners and subject tribes should be given seats on the council.

Their proposals encountered considerable opposition, but by various means the king and his advisers were persuaded to agree to certain changes in 1946. Changes in the councils have been described. The Barotse Government also abolished a large number of titles, compensating the then holders with gratuities. Seats on the Provincial Council were given to nominated representatives of most of the subject tribes, and to councillors of District Councils who serve six months at a time 'to learn to govern'. Finally, a new Katengo was established consisting of five nominees from each District who were not members of its council and all old Katengo title-holders: gradually these nominated members are to be replaced by men elected by sub-districts. National debates, I gather, will be in two houses: the Katengo, and the National Council consisting of the Provincial Council and representatives from District Councils.

These changes have to some extent been made to cope with problems which face all African governments today. One group of problems is the institution of an efficient bureaucracy, the use of technically trained men, &c. Secondly, since the councils are now dealing with debatable problems affecting all subjects, in a way they did not in the past, and as there is increasing differentiation in the nation, subject tribes and interest-groups demand representation. Later events have shown that the changes, apparently largely administrative, have brought new forces and personalities into Lozi politics.

However, the most striking feature of the first 'New Katengo' meeting was the way in which members defended the kingship and the old Lozi councils, though they asked for more representation on them, and the vigour with which they attacked their rulers for agreeing, without consulting them, to the radical changes which had diminished the glory of their kingship. The rulers had been persuaded that the people were dissatisfied, when they were not.

This Katengo debate indicated that both for the Lozi and the other Barotse tribes the kingship still has dominant worth. It is the centre of their unity, and that unity now includes a struggle against the Whites. With the kingship are still bound up the capitals, the councillors' titles, the storehouses, the royal graves, the king's attendants and regalia, and all other personalities and institutions involved in it. What District Officers regarded as a series of administrative changes in the interests of economy and efficiency was to the Lozi, even to most Barotse, an attack on something far greater than personnel to execute and judge affairs. For them the kingship, in its relation to nation and land, is still satisfying. There are few Christians or educated men who do not participate in this loyalty and in the cult of the royal graves which is its supreme expression. Therefore the Lozi still think and act in terms of old councils and sectors, which remain at work within the new forms of organization.


## III. LAND, STATE, VILLAGE, AND KINSHIP

*Land-holding from King to Villages*

We have seen that the Lozi identify their kingship with their land and that each king at his installation is brought into contact with the supernatural powers of the land and after death enters into these. In addition the ways in which people settle and work the land are part of a system of social relations which again is dominated by the king. It is through this system of land-holding that the two basic sets of Lozi relationships—political and kinship—are mainly integrated, in the village and the position of the village headman.

All Loziland and all its products belong to the nation through the king. Though one right of Lozi citizenship is a right to building and arable land and the use of public lands, it is by the king's bounty that his subjects live on and by the land. Commoners think of themselves as permanently indebted to the king for the land on which they live

F

and its wild and domesticated products which sustain them. The Lozi say this is why they gave tribute and service to the king and still give gifts. Since tribute was abolished the king has had to purchase many of his necessities from his people, and this is a standard by which Lozi assess their present poverty: 'even the king bought fish today'. Sometimes people refuse payment for goods bought by the king: 'how can we take money from our father who gives us our food, for goods which are his?'

The king thus is the owner (*mung'a*, Kololo; *minyo*, Lozi) of 'Lozi-land and its cattle [the wild game and fish and birds] and its trees', in the sense that ultimately he has a right in every piece of Lozi land. Though he owns the land, the king is obliged to give every subject land to live on and land to cultivate, and to protect him against tres-passers; and he must allow every subject to fish in public waters, to hunt game and birds, to gather wild fruits, and to use the clay, iron ore, grasses, reeds, and trees with which the Lozi make their pots, utensils, mats, baskets, weapons, implements, nets and traps, furni-ture, huts, medicines, &c., and protect him against anyone interfering with the exercise of these rights. The king's rights are to claim the allegiance of everyone living on his land, to demand (in the past) tribute from their produce, to control the building of villages, and to pass laws about the holding and use of land. He may make treaties affecting the land. He also holds directly in his power land which has not been allocated to any subject, he takes over land to which an heir cannot be found, and he has a 'potential right' to unused land, i.e. he can beg it from the holder in order to give it to a landless person or use it himself or for public works, and it is morally difficult for the holder to refuse the land. In exercising his rights to land the king must bear in mind the interests of his subjects: for example, if he moves a man he must give him land elsewhere. The king thus owns the land as trustee for his people.

The king's holdings of land as part of the kingship are very large, particularly in the Plain, but also in the provinces. Many villages, gardens, fishing-sites, pans, reed-beds, are specifically his. As I travelled through the Plain over several years, this became more and more impressed on me. Village after village was pointed out to me as belonging to the king, though it might be held by a queen, a prince or princess, or by a councillor's title, or by an ordinary commoner. Everywhere are *namukao*, the king's gardens, which may not be pro-tected by magic against thieves, for every hungry person has a right to help himself from them, and the king's fenced-off shallow fishing-sites (*litindi*) where in the dry season communal battues are held at which he gets a share of the catch. Most reed-beds are his and he is entitled to one-eleventh of all reeds cut, and when the nestlings are caught in these and in clumps of trees he gets a share. All over the Plain are the king's fishing-sites for non-return traps, though they are worked for him by commoners who take the catch on alternate days. He has pans where turtles are bred and villages where royal cattle are grazed. The Lozi who work these gardens and other resources do not feel themselves in the least exploited by the king's rights; they look on the king as a father who generously gives them the means of sustenance. Nor indeed does the king exercise his rights rigorously, for he forgoes them when the catch or crop is small. Also, he distributes to others the fish, &c., which come to him, though nowadays less than in the past. For the rest, the Lozi are happy to contribute to the upkeep of the capital from which they get so many good things, though the cost to them is heavy.

Thus besides the king's ritual guardianship of the whole land his secular ownership is always manifest to the Lozi in his own villages and sites. One important sign of this ownership is the canals which score the Plain and which have been dug at the order of successive kings. Each king should dig such a canal, to make easy the travels of his people, as his distinguishing mark (*sisupo*) on the land itself.

The king's ownership also appears constantly in the Lozi's own holding of land. Whenever they discuss land, they continually have to introduce the king. He enters into the history of every garden: he asked for it, he borrowed it for someone else, he exchanged it for another garden, and ultimately he or a predecessor gave it. Title to land is defined: 'My ancestor gave the royal salute for it to King so-and-so', perhaps centuries ago. Whenever the holder dies, the heir is installed both at home and in the capital and his title is referred to the royal salute he gave when he was presented to the king and his council.

Once the king has given land to a Lozi, the latter has in it rights which are protected against all comers including the king himself. Should the king desire the land he must ask for it, he cannot take it: 'the king is also a beggar'. Lozi have security in their holdings within a well-established and defined system of law, administered by an organized judiciary and executive, who are alert to protect this security and its premises.

The king may give a piece of land to an individual, but in practice all land is held by villages in the names of their village headmen. Even when an individual is given land by the king, his title to it accrues to his position in a village. The pattern of Lozi land-holding is the attachment of numerous small, distributed, and intermingled gardens and fishing-sites to specific villages, either of titles or of families. The Lozi emphasize strongly laws which prevent a man from 'taking land from one village to another'. If a man leaves a village he loses his rights in all land which he worked as a member of that village; and though a man may work land at his mother's home while living in his father's, or vice versa, he cannot move the title to the land to his village of residence. He works the land by grace of the headman to whom it is attached.

The primary allotment of land from the king to his people is therefore to villages, and this allocation is in a political relationship. This is so even where the headman is a prince or princess, who occupies that position because of kinship with the king. In land-holding the village is the largest and the ultimate political unit.

The land of a village is distributed by a headman among his villagers, or had been distributed thus in the past; for each heir to a headmanship inherits the obligations of his predecessor. Once a member of a family homestead by right of blood or adoption, that is excluding wives or strangers, has been granted land, he retains the right to use that land, and to transmit it to his own heirs, and the courts will protect his rights against the headman. The holder cannot give the land to anyone, and if he leaves the homestead the land reverts to the headman. Every member by blood or adoption of a village by virtue of residence in it has a right to some land from the headman.

Lozi family villages are inhabited by groups of cognates related to the headmen and to each other in a variable pattern. Almost all inhabitants of such a village are kindred, with their wives, and in the past serfs, who were adopted as kinsmen, though with lesser rights. The Lozi have a bias to father-right, but in practice a man can claim the right to settle in the village of any of his ancestors. The courts protect the rights of people in the villages and land of their maternal kindred, though Lozi say: 'Why do you claim land at your mother's? Claim at your father's.' The heir to a headman is selected from any of a man's kindred for his ability to hold the village together. Preference is given to his brothers and sons, but a son of a junior wife or the younger son of a particular wife may be chosen and often a uterine nephew or grandson is selected.

Lozi villages are strong corporate groups which, since they can only be built on mounds in the Plain, have long histories. Through a village there has flowed a stream of kinsmen, related at any moment in a variable pattern, but always bound by ties of blood. Relationships with fellow villagers do not constitute the total field of a man's kinship ties, nor even a large part of that field. A man's relatives by blood and marriage are spread very widely over the land, scattered perhaps through the whole nation; and every man is the centre of a very complex network of ties. In local areas I found that, owing to intermarriage, almost everyone was related in some way to almost everyone else. These kinship ties are particular to each individual, or at most are shared by his or her siblings. The high rate of divorce and remarriage of both men and women decreases the number of people who share largely the same sets of ties. A man's kindred in this sense never come together as a group. The villages are the only corporate groups of kindred, pulled together as it were in common habitation out of the vast complex of kinship which links Lozi and subject tribes together. Around the village is a peripheral grouping of other kinsfolk who assemble for illnesses, funerals, &c., within it.

The Lozi family village is thus a political unit, and membership of the village is a political affiliation; but in addition the village is a kinship group whose members are interlinked by ties of blood and marriage. Thus the village is the group in which political and kinship ties, which are the two ultimately important ties for the Lozi, are intertwined: it knits together the political and kinship systems. In land-holding, a villager here has rights because he is attached in a political sense to the headman, and because he is kin to the headman.

In villages-of-a-title the position is somewhat different. Some villages-of-titles are inhabited by family groupings (expanded families) attached to titles; a member of the grouping is headman on behalf of the title-holder. The inhabitants of many other of these villages have been brought together by the king or by joining the village with his permission. Many of them are Lozi or foreign *maketo* (chosen by the king), *mahapiwa* (seized in the razzias in the outer provinces), and *batanga* (prisoners-of-war from foreign tribes). In a village of this kind there are many families or expanded families of different stocks and tribal origins which have often intermarried and become interrelated. They are bound together primarily by allegiance to the queen or royal or title-holder who holds the village. The Lozi consider the holder of the title to be parent to all the villagers; and the patterns of behaviour in such a village tend to be assimilated to those in family villages. When the royal village is old, many inhabitants tend to be kinsmen to each other; in new royal villages they are 'strangers'. The inhabitants of such a village have the same rights in their land as those of a family village have in its land. Nevertheless the royal village is dominantly a group which is held together by political ties though these are stated in kinship terms, and in which actual kinship ties are initially of secondary importance.

Thus if we examine the chains of relations in which Lozi hold land from the king, the links between king and village headman, and those between headman and his followers, differ greatly. A further change occurs within the partition of land inside the village. The headman distributes land to the heads of the households which constitute the village, in a relation which is partly political and in a family village also one of kinship. Allocations of land within each household's share is purely in kinship relationships. Nevertheless as the Lozi see the allocation of land, it is in a chain of distribution from the king to the village headman, to household head, to subordinates in the household; and therefore land-holding is formulated in legal terms in a straightforward series of allocations.

Lozi rights to land in this series of holdings do not correspond with the rights defined by jurisprudence as usufruct or use or feudal tenure, though they have elements in common. I have therefore suggested[1] a neutral term, 'estates of holding', to describe them. The headman is 'the primary holder' of the 'primary estate of holding'. His position *vis-à-vis* his dependants is similar to that of the king *vis-à-vis* his subjects. The king must give his subjects land and they retain these rights while they remain members of the nation; the headman must give his villagers land and they retain these rights while they remain in the village. Thus the headman, the primary holder, distributes secondary estates to secondary holders and they distribute tertiary estates to tertiary holders, and so on. I grade these estates in order of priority, for each estate consists of similar legal rights against and obligations to the person from whom it is derived, and similar legal obligations to and rights against the people given land within it. If a tertiary holder abandons his estate by leaving the homestead or dies without heirs within the stock of the village, the estate reverts to the secondary holder, not to the primary holder; if the secondary holder abandons his estate it reverts to the primary holder, not to the owner, the king;

[1] *Essays in Lozi Land and Royal Property*, pp. 28 ff.

and only if the primary holder abandons his estate does it revert to the king. Here I am confining the term 'estate of holding' to a certain pattern of rights and obligations between superiors and inferiors. There is a hierarchy of these estates, between king and primary holder and through him to subsidiary holders by right of political affiliation, which reflects the hierarchical organization of the society. Between estate-holders, ownership is a right by virtue of membership of a group, of nation in relation to the king, of a village in relation to the primary holder.

The preceding analysis oversimplifies the hierarchy of estates in bringing out the relations between the adjacent holders of estates in the descending series. But holding of a subsidiary estate also involves acceptance of a share in the obligations of the superior estate to all holders of higher status in the series, and holding of a superior estate involves acceptance of obligations to all holders of junior status. All villagers accept obligations to obey and respect the headman and help him in his work, from whomsoever they get their holdings immediately; and everyone, however small his holding, is considered to get his land from the king to whom he has a direct allegiance. 'Soil has no owner; it is soil of the king', the judges say. Conversely, the king recognizes direct obligations to all his subjects, however inferior their estates may be, and the headman recognizes these to his most junior holders. The series of estates parallels directly the organization of the society in nation-group, village-group, household-groups in the village, each group being under a leader who is a superior estate-holder dividing his estate into subsidiary estates; but in addition each group has an autonomy of its own, with all the members owning rights directly from and owing obligations directly to the head of the group. Therefore any subsidiary holder can claim from the king directly a holding in the national land which the king owns, and similarly any member of a village can claim land anywhere in the primary estate, however subsidiary may be his previous estate. Conversely, any subject who fails to render due obligations to the king can be expelled from the estate he holds directly from intermediate holders, and the holder of a tertiary or other inferior estate can be expelled from it for failing in his dues to any of his superiors.

Therefore, though in fact, as we have seen, the social relations in which Lozi hold land vary at different stages in the series, we are justified in describing their land-tenure system as a series of estates embracing similar patterns of rights and obligations. In this series of estates the dominant position, which gives significance to the whole, is vested in the king's ownership. Below that the crucial position is occupied by the headmen of the villages.

## Central Significance of the Village

The village occupies a position of central significance in Lozi social structure. Lozi life is marked by constant movements of people over the land in response to ecological demands and in consequence of kinship pressures and pulls and of political action. As described, the members of a village, and even more of a locality, may disperse widely during the flood-season and go to different places from one year to another. In these moves the Plain village remains 'home', the base from which people move to their temporary flood-season destinations. Over a period of years the inhabitants of a village also change frequently. Since the resources centred in a village are limited in area, the population which can be supported on that village's estate is limited; and after some time there is an eruption of people out of the village. If they leave vacant resources other kinsmen move in to replace them. As the Lozi see it, agnates, those who have rights in the village through their father, move out, and the village accepts uterine kinsmen to replace them. These movements of kinsmen out of the village are often accompanied by violent quarrels and charges of sorcery. Quarrels between kinsmen in the village, and frequently quarrels with the headmen, of themselves cause people to leave the village and go to villages of other kindred. 'If you live badly at your father's you have a right to seek a home at your mother's.' Other moves are produced by the frequency of divorce. A divorcee may return to one of her parents' homes taking her children with her, and some of these children may later elect to return to her husband; or if they remained with her husband they may decide to join their mother. Or if the divorcee remarries, her children by her first husband may grow up with her at her new husband's home, holding land by grace of their half-siblings till some quarrel induces them to go to an ancestral village. Widows' children move about similarly. Some men for various reasons build in their wives' homes, though this is despised. They are treated respectfully as affines, speaking in the names of their wives at family councils; but they have no legal rights in the village. Their children have rights through the mothers. The extent of these movements is marked in all genealogies and life-histories.

The king, or other important personage, may also order people to move to other villages. The kings were constantly forming new royal villages, moving people to join old ones, promoting people from their homes to positions of responsibility in other royal villages. Movements of people at royal command occur constantly in every genealogy and life-history.

All these movements are between villages, many of which have traditions of centuries, and the Lozi always refer to them by the names of the villages. The villages thus have been corporate groups which, like the state and the land, have provided enduring bases in the shifting links of Lozi interrelationships. Hence the Lozi attach great emotional value to each village and celebrate its name with praises. Hence, too, they select the village headman with care, calling all kindred to long deliberations. The heir is elected by the kindred and confirmed in his position by ceremonial at the capital.

In the past the headman used to make important offerings on behalf of the village to God. In September before the rains broke he would ask God's blessings on all the villagers' seeds and implements, and thank Him for a good harvest in May. He might also make offerings for luck in hunting, and appeal for rain. It is the headman who officiates at these ceremonies. I do not know a headman who still performs these ceremonies, but I am told many do. We may note too that lightning magic placed on the headman's hut is considered to protect his whole village and people.

The village thus occupies a critical position in two sets of relations. It is the basic unit, below the state, of the political structure as it exists territorially: in land-holding and in the headman's responsibility for his followers the state consists of villages. Secondly, it is the one set of kindred which acts as a group, and as such, with other villages in a system of villages, is one of the knots which shape the network of kinship ties. Membership of a village involves political allegiance to the headman; it is also a kinship and domestic organization in which the people make their living and spend most of their time, and where it is proper for a man to die.

Rivalry between villages is not acute, but in many situations they act as units distinguished from each other. In land disputes or other quarrels villages appear as units. At a sacrifice at a local royal grave the meat is distributed among the people by villages, and they appear for local public works by villages.

The headman symbolizes the corporate identity of the village and he should attend its members in disputes at the capital. The Lozi attach great value to a village being 'big' and 'remaining strong' and to the headman's maintaining peace in the village by wise, impartial, and generous rule. But the headman is involved in at least two sets of struggles. One is with his followers who wish themselves to become headman. The other set of struggles emerges from his kinship links with his followers. As he interlocks two distinct systems of social relations, the attitudes of his followers to him are fundamentally ambivalent. As we have seen, his very election to authority makes him an 'enemy' of the people who chose him. He is a kinsman, but he is also the law of the state. He symbolizes their common corporate values and yet he is caught personally in their internal struggles, for he is closely involved in every matter over which he should preside impartially. Thus he is the centre for fears and charges of sorcery.[1]

## Inter-village Linkages

For any Lozi the village where he is resident at any time is the centre of other sets of important relationships. As we have seen, in Loziland the same people are not associated in constant common residence within a defined area, formally demarcated, through the year or over a number of years. Royal villages, and especially royal graves, form local centres whose supporters are not absolutely defined, though their core is clear. But a Lozi's everyday economic and other activities are not constantly influenced by these capitals. It is chiefly with his fellow villagers that he works the land, co-operates in that work, and shares the products of that work. The nature of the building land prevents the village growing in size beyond a certain limit or the development of a group of neighbouring villages related by kinship in an association of corporate unity. In the Plain there are occasionally found two villages on nearby mounds which are spoken of as *mundi ummweya*, 'one village', since they belong to the same stock; but the villages are independent. Where the Lozi have settled at the margins a number of related independent villages may be found building together, working land in largish blocks and referring to themselves as, for example, *ndandanda ya ndandula*, 'the line of villages of Ndandula', which may also be called *mundi ummweya*. 'They recognize a single head.' In some situations this line of related villages is considered and acts as a corporate group. However, *ndandanda* also

[1] See M. Gluckman, J. C. Mitchell, and J. A. Barnes, 'The Village Headman in British Central Africa'.

refers to any line of villages, even if not related.[1] *Ndandanda* is an Mbunda, not a Lozi, word.

The village is also the centre from which a Lozi is associated with his neighbours in other villages, and he is often related to many of them by some tie of blood or marriage. He co-operates with them in fishing, herding, gardening, hunting, and he plays and drinks beer with them, relies on them to help him bury his kin and treat his sick. These people he describes as *basilalanda saka*, 'they of my *silalanda*'. *Silalanda* does not describe a definite group or locality, but is roughly equivalent to 'neighbourhood', and I have translated it as 'a vicinage' —the 'relation of neighbours'. In a group of villages ABCDEFGH, ABCDE are in one vicinage in relation to C, BCDEF in another in relation to D, and so, too, CDEFG for E, and DEFGH for F. This illustration is not intended to indicate that a vicinage covers five villages, but merely the shifting connotation of the term; for one village is in several overlapping vicinages in some of which are included some of the same villages but not all. A man's vicinage embraces normally the villages close enough to his for him constantly to meet and see the villagers and associate with them in common social life. Its membership varies according to season, with the movement of people. Vicinages differ too in size, for many factors operate. There are varying ties of diverse cognatic and affinal relationship, and of friendship, between vicinage co-members, and tribal distinctions are also important: Wiko among Lozi villages cannot have as many ties with their vicinage fellows as other Lozi, since the Lozi do not as readily intermarry with them and have a different culture. Old Mbunda are of yet another culture. But they are all in Lozi's vicinages.

The impress of a cultural stamp in the form of this special territorial name with shifting connotation reflects the constant movements of people from place to place. It refers to a changing group of people and shifts in relation to every individual, while people enter into the overlapping vicinages wherever they go for any length of time. Vicinage defines neither a definite locality nor a demarcated group. For the Lozi, however, it has a fixity which arises from its being centred in a village.

### The Web of Kinship

The village is the only corporate group of kinsmen among the Lozi, but kinship links with people outside the village, stretching often to

[1] I omitted to point this out in my *Economy of the Central Barotse Plain*, p. 88, where I noted only its more specific use.

the borders of Barotseland and beyond, are important to all Lozi. Kinsmen from other villages, near and distant, constantly visit a Lozi at his home; he calls on them for help in his work and illnesses, his marriages and funerals; he visits them, and may spend the flood-season with them; he has a potential right to claim a permanent home with them if they are kin of the blood. The Lozi and their subject tribes are knit together in a web of ties of kinship which, whatever their character, of marriage or blood, of paternity or maternity, in-clude rights and obligations of mutual help. Furthermore, to these kinship ties are added others which are assimilated to kinship. The Lozi hold that 'the kinsmen of a man's kinsmen are his kinsmen' (*mwaboyu ta mwaboyu*). A man's *mayenda*, supporters attached to help him by the king, and his *batanga*, serfs, are quasi-kinsmen, though he may marry them. Lozi also make many pacts of friendship (*bulikani*), especially with members of other tribes, and treat their friends as kins-men, though they may marry with them unless they enter into blood-brotherhood (*manyinga*).

In this web of kinship ties no corporate unilinear group of kinsfolk is distinguished. The difference among the Lozi in a child's relations with its father's and mother's kin is one of emphasis only.[1] A child's proper home is with its father, and it should go to his village to live and inherit, but this may be the village of his father's father or his father's mother. If a child does not get on well with his father, if his father fails to provide properly for him, or if he quarrels with his paternal relatives, he will go to his mother's home, which again may be that of any of her progenitors. Lozi say 'the child belongs to both sides', and the courts will not constrain a young boy (or girl) to leave his mother's home to go to his father. In any of these homes he has the right to inherit any position if his kin esteem his character. When he becomes heir, he assumes the titular name of his predecessor and takes over land and cattle, including those allocated to wives of the dead man, and divides them among all the kin, retaining the largest portion for himself.

The large choice of homes which is open to a Lozi is reflected in the mode of tracing descent. Instead of having a single important kin-group, reckoned from father through all his male ancestors or from mother through all her female ancestors, or both groups, the Lozi reckon descent theoretically in all, including mixed, lines, and in

---

[1] For a fuller analysis of the relations dealt with in this section, see my 'Kinship and Marriage among the Lozi of Northern Rhodesia and the Zulu of Natal'.

practice in every line with whose members they maintain connexions. They have no clans, but they have *mishiku* (sing. *mushiku*), which I translate as *descent-names*. This defines their attributes clearly, for the people sharing a single descent-name are not considered to be a group, nor do they have any specific obligations to each other, nor are there any ritual beliefs or practices attached to any descent-name. Nevertheless people who share a descent-name feel that they are kinsfolk. The descent-name indicates that somewhere in his ancestry a man has a male or female ancestor or ancestors who, again in any one or more of his or her or their lines, had that descent-name. A Lozi remembers the descent-names of those kinsmen with whom he lives and co-operates. Lozi say that everyone has eight descent-names, one from each grandparent, though these may have had descent-names in common. In practice, Lozi usually give four to five descent-names, but very many know only two and others only one.

People who share descent-names do not expect to trace genealogical relationship. The Lozi, except for the royal family, trace their descent genealogically for only three or four generations from adults. There are no broadly based unilineal groups associating in common rights of residence, ownership, inheritance, production, &c., and consequently the structural depth of the kinship system is shallow, while it ramifies widely in all lines. The Lozi is interested in tracing his genealogical relationship with particular kin through any of the many lines of his descent rather than to claim or trace a distant relationship with someone in one special line.

A Lozi may marry a woman with the same descent-name as himself. He should not marry a woman with whom he can trace genealogical relationship in any way, and we have seen that Lozi fail to do so beyond four generations. Intermarriages do occur earlier, while relationship can still be traced. Young people claim that their kindred has become so big that the relationship is broken, and insist on marrying despite their elders' protests. Such a marriage is cursed: only death may break it, the parties may not divorce. It establishes new ties of affinity which in the next generation renew cognatic ties.

As part of this widely ramifying system, in which every line counts equally, all siblings, half-siblings, and cousins, however related, are called 'brother' and 'sister'. In lower generations the children of all these people and of relatives-in-law of the same generation are 'children'; their children are 'grandchildren'; and thereafter alternate generations are 'children' and 'grandchildren' again. In the first ascendant generation paternal and maternal relatives are distinguished. All men and women on the father's side are 'father' (the paternal aunt is descriptively 'female father'); all men and women on the mother's side are 'mother' (the maternal uncle is descriptively 'male mother'). Nevertheless, the pattern of behaviour on both sides tends to be the same, though paternal aunt jokingly calls her fraternal nephew 'my husband' and her niece 'my co-wife', and maternal uncle calls his uterine niece 'my wife' and his nephew 'my fellow-husband'. The nephew may indeed marry his maternal uncle's widow, as he cannot his father's widow. In the second ascendant generation the difference between the nomenclature for the two sets of kin is obliterated: all men and women are 'grandparent'. In the third, men and women are distinguished as 'father' and 'mother' respectively, whatever side they be. Thereafter generations alternate as 'grandparents' and 'parents'.

The Lozi thus tend to trace and merge relationships as widely as possible in the present living generations of immediate cognates, and not to trace relationship between kinsmen in one line who may be widely dispersed over the country, or generally to differentiate between lines of ancestry. They do emphasize generation differences and seniority within a generation. Thus brothers and sisters have a self-reciprocal term of address, *kaizeli*, but a man calls his elder brother *muhulwani* and is called by him *munyani*, and these terms are also used between younger and older sisters. Classificatory parents, uncles, and aunts are also distinguished by age in relation to a person's actual progenitors.

The merging of kin also extends to affines. Parent-in-law and child-in-law address each other by a term *mukwenyani*, defined by very respectful behaviour. The parents of two spouses recognize a common parenthood by calling each other 'the other parent'. Siblings of a spouse, irrespective of sex, are *balamu* (plural), or 'husband' (woman-speaking) or 'wife' (man-speaking), again irrespective of sex. Beyond that a man or woman takes over the terms of address which his or her spouse uses for kinsfolk.

Thus among the Lozi relationships in all lines of descent tend to be merged by generations. The actual importance of the different lines varies from individual to individual, with a general bias to the paternal. But the mother's immediate home is more important than the home of someone distantly connected in the patrilineal line. Nearness of cognatic relationship, and not membership of a unilineal kin-group, is emphasized. Even an affine may settle in a village where he has no rights in the land save that of working his wife's sites, and acquire by character a position of respect and authority, validated when he produces children for the village. This applies equally to the position of wives.

The corporate groups of kindred which in theory have lasted from the beginnings of Lozi history are the villages. Since people have constantly moved or been moved by the king between villages and neighbourhoods, the pattern of kinship links in local communities is constantly altering. No unilineal framework exists to which they can be referred; only royal people close to ruling kings can trace their descent from Mboo, the founder of the Lozi kingdom, son of God and His daughter. This agnatic line is the core of the whole nation's history. Nevertheless, for commoners too kinship links are all-important in defining membership of a village and rights in it, and denoting relationships with and claims in other villages. Descent-names provide the ultimate reference for common origin by blood. By whatever links cognates are united, they express their kinship by citing their descent-names. Correspondingly, strangers who find they share a descent-name feel that they are kin. The descent-names have this high value because they originated with the first Lozi who lived with King Mboo. They symbolize that kinship, relationship by blood as such, comes from the beginning of time, even though the Lozi can only remember their genealogical ties for a very few generations. They give historic depth to the shallow genealogical system. Every descent-name is related to some stage of Lozi history; the Lozi names are those of the first inhabitants of the Plain, those of foreign tribes date to the absorption of those tribes in the nation. The villages which are the corporate groups of kindred are built on mounds which provide the only site for homes in the Plain. Certain of the mounds are known as those of the Lozi's distant forebears, and each Lozi descent-name is referred to an ancestral village on one of the mounds. The possession of a Lozi descent-name enables a man to point to his ancestral village, and claim to be a true Lozi, a true inhabitant of the Plain, a descendant by blood of the original settlers related to the daughter of God, a kinsman of all Lozi.

The Lozi kinship system is thus largely consistent with their modes of residence and production. As people move constantly between seasons and associate with different kinsmen, and as the restricted size of mounds and their resources compels kinsmen to go to settle far away, or they are moved afar by the king, the people at each mound depend on their neighbours for help in prosecuting their many dispersed and contemporaneous activities. With these neighbours they intermarry and become related in a variety of ways. To all these ways they give equal weight. Cognatic relationships are periodically broken by marriages between people who can still trace relationship. These marriages establish new cognatic ties, and it is these marriages alone which are cursed with a ban on divorce.

The villages provide, as we have seen, the knots which shape the network of kinship ties. Only they can achieve this. The Lozi have an ancestral cult and sometimes in divination refer misfortunes, like good luck, to the ancestors. The ancestor cited may be in any line and of either sex. The ancestors have no fixed homes. Lozi bury their dead in cemeteries which serve neighbourhoods, or at the edge of a village, or in the gardens or bush, and do not make offerings at the graves. Offerings of beer or meal or a beast are made at one of the posts of the courtyard fence around the hut, by men or women, even by a wife in her husband's home to her ancestors. His ancestors may affect her: hers cannot affect him. A keen hunter may stake a forked branch in his homestead and place the skulls of the game he kills on it, and there make offerings to his ancestors. There are no local foci in the cult for kinship groups. In accordance with these rules, at a funeral all kinsmen and neighbours and friends attend, and any men among them can act as gravediggers and undertakers—son or father, brother or nephew, grandchild or grandparent, brother-in-law or son-in-law, or friend. Indeed, the ancestors are rarely referred to as the cause of happenings, or as sanctions on moral behaviour. The Lozi more commonly refer to God, Nyambe: 'it is as God wishes', 'if Nyambe pleases', &c. To Him many Lozi pray over dishes of water, each sunrise and sunset, at small altars at the edge of the village.

On the other hand, sorcery is commonly blamed for many misfortunes. Accusations of sorcery are sometimes made outside the village, but most frequently within it, or at least against kinsfolk, or co-wives. A particularly feared kind of sorcery, which is often accompanied by necrophagy, is where a person sells a kinsman or kinswoman in return for success in life. These beliefs are a reflex of the tensions in the village, within which kinship ties are commingled with political and other ties.

## Kinship between Royal Family and Commoners

The king and other members of the royal family are related to Lozi commoners and to members of certain subject tribes by marriage and by blood. Only ruling kings are freed from the normal bans on marrying kinswomen, and they normally observe them. At least one prince has tried to marry a princess and been told: 'You are not king.'

All royals therefore marry commoners, and have their commoner kin (*lineku lasitanga*, commoner side) as well as royal kin (*lineku lasilena*) in every generation. Royals and commoners are thus associated intimately in the web of kinship relationships, and to some extent observe kinship dues as commoners do among themselves. However, they cannot do so entirely. Commoner relatives help royals in their gardening and fishing; but though nowadays royals may work in their own gardens, no commoner expects a royal relative to assist him in his tasks, though he asks for material assistance in need. Moreover, he does not allow his relationship to trespass on the elaborate code of respectful etiquette which marks approaches to the royal family, and even extends that respect to kinsfolk who have married royals. Nevertheless the Lozi do not think of the royal family as cut off from commoners in the kinship system, and their intermarriages knit commoners and royals together.

The royals depend largely on their commoner kin for help in their own affairs and for support in political struggles. This is true even of the king. His commoner kin and affines acquire particular power as *likwanabi* in virtue of their relationship with him as an individual, and have no special relationship with the kingship itself. Therefore he relies largely on their advice and support.

Ordinary royals obey the normal rules of kinship in going to mourn, to attend weddings, &c., but ruling chiefs do not. The king must not be brought into contact with death; he does not attend a funeral, even of his own child or wife, and no bereaved person should enter the capital. The king does not marry in a wedding; his wives are merely installed. Nor does he go to a queen who has borne a child, or to the first menstruation ceremony of his daughters.

The king also becomes related to commoners in other ways. Some of the palace-women are not full wives, but *linalianga*. Should one of these women become pregnant by the king, the king may make her a queen, or he may give her to some commoner. The child is then the child of the commoner, though it is known to be of the king's blood. It is strictly *sikwanabi* (related to a royal), but may be addressed as *mwana'mulena* (child of the king). Commoners also had wives of similar status, in the past, among their serfs.

Commoners resent the way in which royal kin are set above them.

The only occasion on which I have heard commoners express hostility against the position of the royal family was when a number of them protested strongly that they would not allow a royal kinsman to become heir in their family. They argued that he would feel himself too much above them and that he would take their property into the kingship. They objected so vehemently to this that a prince who was sitting by the fire interjected ruefully: 'we too have mothers'. Actually there are many instances of royals inheriting thus, and even kings participate in the land problems of their kin. The late King Imwiko and ex-NGAMBELA Wina told me that the royal could not move property to the kingship, any more than a commoner can move property from his mother's to his father's family.

However, though members of the royal family thus have claims and rights in the villages of their commoner kin, important princes and princesses do not normally reside in these villages. Nor do grown-up princes and princesses, who are closely related, reside together in a single village (as similar commoners do) until they are only distantly related to the ruling kings. Princes and princesses close to the ruling line, when they grow up, are usually given one or more villages, either already established or newly formed with selected commoners. They have sites at the capital, but they hold land and people in these villages. As a royal line becomes more distant from the ruling line its members settle in villages allocated to them and become a group of kin, as there are groups of commoners; but in these villages there will also be the descendants of commoners attached to the royal ancestor. The royals and commoners are likely to be intermarried and therefore related by blood.

## The Instability of Marriages

Lozi marriages are extremely unstable. I consider this to be an attribute of all kinship systems other than those which are dominated by father-right.[1] A man's ties with his wife are strong, but easily snapped, and though the position of wives in their husbands' villages is important, it is extremely insecure. As mothers, sisters, aunts, daughters, nieces, granddaughters, women are held in great esteem and love, and speak with authority. Wives exercise important influence, but they are liable to easy dismissal, and as widows they have no rights in their dead husbands' homes.

[1] This is my main argument in my already cited comparison of 'Kinship and Marriage among the Lozi of Northern Rhodesia and the Zulu of Natal'. See also Radcliffe-Brown, 'Patrilineal and Matrilineal Succession'.

As in all African societies, though marriage is a vitally important relationship, the essential one for the proper begetting of children, there is only a limited field in which men and women can associate. They sleep together and produce children together, and their union founds an economic unit, but in general social and public life their contacts are limited. A man seeks companionship with his fellow men and a woman with her fellow women. Except in the intimacy of the marriage bed it is difficult for a man to enjoy the company of a woman. A Lozi may not touch his sister or a female affine without committing *sindoye* (a breach of the sexual ban), and he must not be alone with her in a hut. If he is, he is accused of sorcery. By Lozi standards, if a man walks along a path with another's wife who is not related to him, or gives her snuff or a drink of beer, he commits 'adultery', even if he does not sleep with her. Men are often afraid to work gardens for, or help, the wives of their brothers who are labour migrants, lest their brothers charge them with being lovers of their sisters-in-law. In this background Lozi marry for sexual satisfaction, to secure an economic partner, to obtain children, and not to find a companion.

Lozi men and women are strongly attracted to each other and will often persist in marrying despite the opposition of their kin. Also, they enter into adulterous affairs, and married women elope with other men, despite public disapproval and penal sanctions. Men are jealous of their wives and wives of their husbands. But if a man is too attached to his wife or favours one wife among all his wives, the Lozi suspect that she has corrupted him with medicines or that he is a bit crazy and a fool. Jealousy among co-wives of one man for his sexual and other favours is pronounced and is accepted as normal, though Lozi fear that if it is too great it may lead to sorcery.

Lozi society is polygynous, but it is obvious that because of the balance in numbers of the sexes, at any one time most men are monogamous. The emphasis here is on 'at any one time'. Very many Lozi women live in a state of serial monogamy, passing from one husband to another; men live in serial monogamy-polygyny, married to a series of different wives, sometimes one at a time, sometimes more. In modern conditions the divorce rate has probably risen, but there is no doubt that Lozi marriage was always extremely unstable.[1]

I begin this analysis of marriage from its dissolution and not from its contracting, because it is necessary to grasp the instability of Lozi

[1] See my 'Kinship and Marriage among the Lozi of Northern Rhodesia and the Zulu of Natal', Section III.

marriage in order to understand its whole structure. This instability explains why the Lozi disapprove of sororal polygyny, where 'jealousy will spoil the love of sisters'. Jealousy might easily lead to the break up of one's marriage, or the divorce of one sister to trouble in the other's marriage. Other incidents of the lack of durability in Lozi marriage are the absence of the leviratic and other forms of 'proxy-marriage' and of the sororate.

When a Lozi man and woman decide they wish to marry, the man approaches one of her senior kinsmen. As far as he is concerned this may be a kinsman in any line who is the guardian of the girl. He gives a small gift, of about 1*s*., to open the affair. He may do so himself or through one of his own kin. The affair is openly discussed, without oblique reference, but usually not closed on that day. A short time afterwards the girl's guardian is again approached, and if he consents the marriage is arranged and the marriage-payment fixed. At the appointed date the bridegroom may just take the girl to his home, or he may send kinswomen to fetch her with some of her own kinswomen to his home. There a beast may be killed of which one-half is taken to her kin to eat at their home. At the bridegroom's his kinswomen dress the bride in beads and clothes he provides, and both eat porridge off a stone to symbolize the hope that the marriage may endure. He sleeps with her, and if he is satisfied leaves a small gift at the door. If the girl takes this, she too is satisfied. Meanwhile his younger kin feast and may dance—his elders if they feast do so separately and not in public. The bride is now married if the marriage-payment has been made. Sometime later the bride's kin kill a beast and send half to the man's home.

For the Lozi the wedding is not necessary to constitute a legal marriage. For this there must be consent of the parties and consent of the bride's guardians, which is implicit in their accepting the marriage-payment. The last is the most important indicator of a legal marriage, at which a Lozi court looks to see if it will award adultery damages if another man sleeps with the woman. Should her parents have consented to the union but the man not have delivered the cattle or money, the court will not award him damages. It will say she is his concubine, 'a wife of the country'. Thus the marriage-payment gives a man the right to exclude other men from his wife and the right to control her. Though divorce is frequent, a woman has to sue for it, while a man can just send his wife to her home. She will obtain a divorce if she can prove that he did anything that can be construed as dismissal from the position of a wife, such as pushing her in a quarrel, telling her to go home, tearing her clothes, taking something away which he gave her, not giving her with her co-wives a fair share of his sexual and material favours. If she refuses to live with him neither he nor the courts can compel her to do so; but he can always take other wives or concubines and she can only sleep with or go to another man under penalty of damages and fining. If her lover desires her enough, she can force a divorce by eloping with him, and when he pays a certain amount of damages she becomes his wife.

When an ostensible virgin marries the husband gives two beasts (or £2) as marriage-payment. One only is given for a non-virgin. This beast, and one of those given for a virgin, is called 'the beast of shame' and is for the right of sexual intercourse. It does not return on divorce. The other beast given for a virgin is 'the beast of herding' and is for her untouched fertility. On divorce, it is returnable if she has not conceived; i.e. if she has miscarried or borne a child the husband loses his claim. Formerly nothing was returnable if husband or wife died before a child was conceived; since 1946, following a Northern Rhodesia High Court decision, the 'beast of herding' and its progeny return in these circumstances.

The marriage-payment does not give the husband absolute rights to the woman's children. In general, under Lozi law, the genitor is the pater. If an unmarried virgin has a child, the genitor pays a beast reckoned equivalent to the beast of herding as damages, since it comes off the marriage-payment when she does marry; but even if he does not pay, the child is his. Recently similar damages were attached to impregnating a non-virgin (widow, divorcee, unmarried mother, grown unmarried woman) where formerly no damages lay; but again the genitor claims the child even if he fails to pay. If a wife commits adultery and conceives, the child is her husband's if he has had access to her in the period of conception; but if he has been away it belongs to the genitor. In the former circumstances, the Lozi hold that the adulterer is a thief who mixed with the husband and therefore he has no rights.

Barrenness of the wife does not of itself entitle the husband to claim a fertile substitute for her from her kin or a refund of part of the marriage-payment.

Affiliation of the children is thus not primarily determined by marriage-payment or its equivalent, a legitimatization fee. I suggest that since children are not dominantly affiliated to the agnatic line of their father, i.e. since their mother does not move from her kin-group to produce for his kin-group, the main buttress of marital stability is removed, and divorce is frequent and easy. Further, I suggest that it is because of the high divorce rate that the Lozi did not make high marriage-payments from their large herds of cattle. Indeed it is only comparatively recently (1900–10) that King Lewanika fixed marriage-payments at one or two head of cattle. Before that, when a Lozi married he gave his wife's parents a few hoes or mats.

When a Lozi dies his kinsmen have no rights to keep his wives. These are free to go and marry where they please. If a wife marries her dead husband's brother or uterine nephew she will be approved of, as it will keep the children in the paternal home; but it is a new marriage for which a new marriage-payment must be given and its children are of the new husband, not of the dead man.

Lozi husband and wife constitute an economic unit. The husband must give his wife land for gardens, feed her from his own gardens, herds, and fishing, and provide her with a hut and clothing. The wife must work her gardens and do household duties. In Lozi law the husband and wife have equal rights in the crops she produces by her labour on his land; on divorce they share these crops equally; she takes half if he dies, and her heirs take half if she dies. Similarly, father and mother each have a right to half the marriage-payments given for daughters and each divides the share among his or her kin. The mother's own heirs inherit her rights, not the father or his heirs. A woman has rights in other property allocated to her by her husband, that is, in the gardens and cows given her for her sustenance, only during the subsistence of the marriage. She does not transmit these rights to her own children as against her husband's children by other wives, as among the Southern Bantu. On divorce or her death they return to her husband's power, or on the death of her husband to his heir, for redistribution as he pleases. Cattle allocated thus to a wife to nurture her and her children differ from 'the beast of the fire' which a husband may give his wife in reward for long service. This is hers, and she can take it to her own home; her own heirs, including her children, inherit it. On the other hand, though children do not acquire and inherit rights in their patrimony through their mother, through her they acquire and inherit rights in her own stock's property, which are equal to the rights of the children of her brothers.

In short, a woman does not pass rights to her children in her husband's village, but she passes to them rights in her own village. It is consistent with this that Lozi wives do not have strongly graded positions in their husband's home. Wives are graded as the first, second, third, &c., wife in order of marriage, irrespective of age or tribal status, but though junior wives should respect senior wives, all are more or less equal in status. The first wife has certain privileges such as the right to be given fish or meat first in a distribution, or the right to claim that her husband come to her hut when he returns from a journey, but she exercises no authority over other wives.

Though a wife thus remains a member of her own kin-group more than she enters her husband's, she occupies an important position in his household. A man confides largely in his mother, sister, or grown-up daughter, since their relationship is permanent and enduring. These women have great influence in his home and are indeed sanctuaries for his wives from his wrath. But his wife is head of his household. He must bring his catch and his earnings to her; he asks her to entertain his visitors, and if he is away she welcomes them. 'She too is a lord (*mulena*).' If he passes her over and asks his kinswoman to act with him, the wife can claim a divorce. These are the standards of Lozi marriage. Relations of husband and wife vary markedly from marriage to marriage; and in many marriages husbands depend greatly on their wives for advice. This dependence may continue after divorce, where the couple remain united through their children and these children's affairs.

*Growing-up*

Lozi children are thus born into a system of kinship relationships in which they have rights in a large number of villages and in which many of them will pass at different times of their life through several villages. Their birth is always welcomed, but is attended with little ceremonial. Friends and kinsfolk come to 'thank' the parents for their child. A name of some ancestor or ancestress is selected for the child. It will cry when the name is mentioned. The Lozi do not consider that the ancestor is reincarnated in the child, and a boy may get a woman's name or a girl a man's. The name and personality of a dead man or woman pass at the installation of his or her heir after the funeral.

Lozi infants are suckled for two or three years, and then are abruptly weaned.[1] The children as they grow older take an ever larger role in family activities. The Lozi had no initiation ceremonies for boys, nor age-sets, though most boys and girls served the king in his capital or other village for a time. Lozi also say that in the past boys

---

[1] See J. F. Ritchie, *The African as Suckling and as Adult*, who shows that this involves a severe emotional shock.

and girls above puberty used to go in charge of men to cattle-posts to herd cattle in the flood-season and that there they were hardened and taught morals and tribal law. Also they say that marriage-ages were higher then. Nowadays almost all Lozi boys, and most girls, go to school, for the Barotse Government has endeavoured to make education compulsory.

Girls too grow gradually into family activities, but they have a sharp break at first menstruation. Then a girl is secluded for two or three months, spending the day in a hideout in the bush in charge of older women, and returning in the evening to the village. I have been told by men that the girl enlarges her vagina[1] with a hoe-handle, and enlarges her labia minora. At the end of this period the girl is finely dressed and decorated and sits downcast and tearful surrounded by women. Later in the day, escorted by her male guardian and a substitute for her mother, she emerges under a blanket, which the man removes with a hoe and the woman with an axe. The girl fetches water and is abused, then she chooses a new name. The people present dance. The girl is now ready for marriage.

## Other Social Relationships

I mention briefly here a few other social relationships to complete this account of Lozi society. As the Lozi desire goods they do not make themselves, they barter and now also buy goods from many unrelated persons. They frequently have barter partners in the subject tribes with whom they establish *bulikani*, friendship, thus changing the transitory barter relationship into a wider one of mutual help. Often they make blood-brotherhood with their friends, who then become as kinsfolk to them and their own kin. The Lozi used to make these friendships both among themselves and with Kwangwa smiths, Nkoya hunters and honey-collectors, Lunda dugout makers, and other tribal specialists.

In these pacts the Lozi tend to extend the scope and duration of transitory associations to make them multiplex and permanent relationships, akin to the pattern of their kinship and political ties. Thus if a Lozi gives some of his cattle to another to herd, joins with others in herding cattle, employs a servant, ploughs for another, lends another land, joins people in working a fish-dam or net, his relationships with them are more than mere contracts. The pattern of all

---

[1] Most Lozi men denied knowledge of the hymen, so do not speak of this as deflowering.

social relationships for the Lozi is the multiplex ties which link them in subsistence units in which they and their fellow villagers and kin hold land, live, work, play, rejoice, and mourn together.

This establishing of wider ties extends to relationships in the supernatural realm, or is extended by mystical links to some apparently temporary associations. If a warrior kills an enemy or big game, he has to take ritual precautions to prevent the dead affecting him ill. If a Lozi is treated by a leech, he tends to become bound to that leech.

Leeches and diviners are among the most common important specialists of Lozi society. Many of them are Old Mbunda and Wiko. The longer I lived among the Lozi the more I felt that almost everyone was skilled in treating some disease. Certain of them are well known over wide areas.

Should a Lozi suffer a misfortune, he is likely to resort to a diviner to detect the cause. Some of these causes I have already mentioned: royal spirits, sorcerers, the ancestors. But many diseases are almost personified by the Lozi and are commonly divined: *liyala*, *maimbwe*, *mahamba*, *sisongo*, *muba*, and others. Some of these diseases are more clearly associated with demons; thus *muba* is related to *mwenda-ndjangula* and *mwenda-lutaka*, demons of the bush and the Plain respectively, which have half of human bodies and are fiery red. They are of both sexes. Should one of these spirits desire a man or woman, it will try to kidnap him or her, and can at least strike with severe illness. In all these diseases the treatment aims to produce, by smoking, drumming, and singing, hysteric symptoms: violent jerkings of the body in a state of seeming trance. When a patient is being treated, kin and neighbours come to attend. The drumming wakens the disease in all of them who have been ill of it before and they too will join in the violent dance of the sufferer. The disease links together all sufferers, and anyone who recovers from a severe attack has to become a leech treating it.

Most of these diseases are held by the Lozi to come from the subject tribes. *Liyala* only is Lozi and Kwangwa. *Maimbwe* is Nkoya. *Sisongo* and *mahamba* have been brought by the recent Wiko immigrants and in 1940–2 *sisongo* was sweeping through the land. Some Lozi held that the Wiko had planted it in the paths to get victims from whom they could make money. In 1947 *muba* had replaced it: most drummings were for *muba*. Despite *muba*'s association with the Lozi demons of bush and Plain, it is believed to come from the Totela. We have here the common ascription of mystical powers to subjected peoples.

This also appears in beliefs about a *mukushangu* or *mukubilu*. This is a person who eats medicines so that after his death he shall turn into a lion or hyena or other wild thing. Lozi believe other Lozi do this, but they particularly suspect the Wiko of it. Wiko lack cattle and fishing-sites, so when Lozi were plagued in 1942 with hyenas killing cattle, it seemed reasonable to conclude that these were Wiko *mikishangu* after meat.

## Conclusion

I have attempted in this compressed account to summarize those categories of social relationships and the relations between the categories which comprise the main structure of Lozi society. In doing so I have had to restrict detailed descriptions of the cultural content of those relationships. I am fully aware of the importance of that content, but I considered it better to concentrate on the network of ties and cleavages between offices, individuals, and groups. I hope my analysis of this network has brought out what was vividly impressed on me during my stays in Loziland: the extremely strong cohesion of the Lozi as a nation. This struck me because several things seemed to militate against it. The Lozi have absorbed many thousands of foreigners of several tribes of different culture; yet they are a people proudly conscious of the superior worth of their own culture, which indeed is distinctive from the cultures of the surrounding peoples. Their domestic associations are extremely unstable, and their kinship associations, like their descent-names, do not demarcate groups whose membership changes only with the generations, yet their inheritance of property and their knowledge of what are their 'homes' is precise. Their administration is a tangled skein of personal attachments to titles of offices in which no one seems to have clear-cut authority over any set of followers; yet the State organization is strong and works efficiently.

I have tried to show the bases for this strong cohesion. They are the land, the Plain as a marked geographical feature of the region, the nation that inhabits it, the king who owns it, and the councils of titles that administer rule in it, in the one set of relations, the political system. The Lozi and their subject tribes are knit together in another set of relations in the kinship system, and the villages enduring through the centuries on the mounds in the Plain provide for all Lozi permanent cores of corporate groups of kin. In these villages the political and kinship systems are firmly intertwined in local cores that persist in specific places on the land. Underlying both these systems was the comparatively high degree of economic cohesion, arising from differentiation of holding of types of resources, from differentiation of labour, and from the scattered distribution of each village's productive activities in every month. The cohesion of these systems of relations was not disturbed by economic cleavages, though struggles within them were set in economic terms; for the Lozi economy was primitive, possessing only primary goods and egalitarian standards of living. Chiefs and wealthy men used their riches only to attract dependants.

## APPENDIX

### Tribes of Barotse Kingdom, classified in Groups, with Notes and Population Figures

(I have taken population figures for the tribes from *Memorandum on the Native Tribes and Tribal Areas of Northern Rhodesia*, by J. Moffat Thomson, 1934. These are put in parentheses and are italicized when a large part of the tribe lives outside Barotseland in British Territory. 'Zone' refers to their classification by Doke.)

A. LUYANA GROUP[1]
  Lozi (67,193)
  Kwandi (2,510)
  Kwangwa (25,497)←———————Kwangwalima[3]———————→Nkoya (18,543)
                      (under Kwangwa?)
  Muenyi (4,018)                                    Mashasha (13,083)
  Mbowe[4] (5,336)                                  Lukolwe (9,351)
                      Kaonde[5] (37,952)            Lushange (9,349)
                                                    *Mbwela*[6] (4,052)

D. NKOYA GROUP[2]
  (CENTRAL ZONE)

[1] Doke does not relate their languages specifically, but they fall in his Central Zone with Luba as principal other tribe in it. Languages classed with Subiya in his Zambesi Group. Now some speak own languages, but all have Kololo (Sotho) as main language or lingua franca.

[2] The Lozi and Nkoya say they are akin, though they speak different languages. This agrees with Doke's preliminary classification.

[3] A small group living east of Kwangwa. They are of Kwangwa-Nkoya descent.

[4] Memorandum by Moffat Thomson classifies as Luba-speaking. But they are clearly related to Luyana.

[5] Melland (*In Witchbound Africa*) groups the Kaonde as a branch of the Luba, though they have not circumcision ceremonies and other customs which are characteristic of the Luba group. Doke groups them with Luba, on the basis of language, putting them in Luba Group of Central Zone, of which Nkoya is a sub-group. This agrees with Lozi grouping of Kaonde as related to Nkoya. The Kaonde are commonly related (as by Moffat Thomson) with the Bemba-Lala-Lamba peoples, whom Doke puts as another sub-group of the Luba Group.

[6] There are several groups of Mbwela. One described by Smith and Dale (i, p. 25)

B. Assimilated to Luyana[1]

Old Mbunda (?)
Nyengo (4,457)

Makoma (7,605)
Imilangu (Ndundulu) (21,962)
Mishulundu (?)
Simaa (9,109)
Yei (?)

Shanjo (7,910)
Mashi (4,500)

C. West-central zone
(Many outside British Territory)

(a) Lozi call Wiko

Luena or
    Lubale (68,943)

Chokwe (?)
Luchaze (5,323)
(b) Lozi do not call Wiko

Lunda[2] (82,044)
Ndembo (9,464)

E. Ila-Tonga group

Ila proper (Shukulumbwe) (18,653)
Tonga (82,586)
Subiya (2,950)

Totela (14,160)
Toka (9,458)

F. Others

Occasional Ndebele Tswana, Swahili. A few Bushmen.

in Ilaland is of Lozi descent; Serpa Pinto (i, pp. 303 ff.) encountered Ambuellas whom he related to Mbunda, west of Loziland; Moffat Thomson says they are probably Luba-speaking or Bemba-Lala-Lamba-speaking. Doke groups them with Nkoya, and White states that the Luena call the Nkoya 'Ambwela' (people of the South).

[1] These people are largely Lozi-ized and Kololo-speaking. I group them together because they form a group in the Lozi polity. Doke does not mention Nyengo, Makoma, Imilangu, Mishulundu, Simaa, who probably speak dialects of Angolan languages, or the Mashi. The Yeyi are in his Western Zone. Shanjo is an Ila-Tonga language.

[2] The Lozi distinguish the Lunda from the Wiko, but the Wiko regard them as similar 'because they have circumcision lodges and masked dancers, though they speak a different language'. Doke groups these peoples' languages in one zone.

## Population

The 1938 Native Affairs Annual Report estimated the population of Barotse Province at 295,741.

| Modern Administrative District | Estimated population 1938 (in above report) | Density per sq. mile (according to 1934 map) |
|---|---|---|
| Mongu-Lealui . . . . | 73,400 | 29·6 |
| Senanga . . . . | 47,065 | 4·05 |
| Kalabo . . . . . | 60,000 | 8·64 |
| Balovale (since independent) . | 61,276 | 5·84 |
| Sesheke . . . . | 20,000 | 2·55 |
| Mankoya . . . . | 34,000 | 2·52 |

Mongu-Lealui, Kalabo, and Senanga share the Plain, but all contain non-Plain areas. Balovale lies to the north of the Plain on either side of the Zambezi;

Sesheke occupies only the north bank of the Zambezi and is partly in the tsetse-fly belt; Mankoya is away from all big rivers and includes part of the fly-belt. I give the 1938 figures as those available when I did the bulk of my work. In 1948 the total population is given as 265,884, but it is not comparable owing to boundary changes.

## BIBLIOGRAPHY FOR THE BAROTSE

ARNAUD, MARTHE [nom de plume for a missionary]. *Manière de Blanc: Roman*, Paris: Éditions Sociales Internationales (1938).

ARNOT, F. S. *Missionary Travels in Central Africa* (1883).

—— *Garenganze, or Seven Years' Pioneer Mission Work in Central Africa*, London: James E. Hawkins (2nd edition, 1889).

BAKER, E. *The Life and Explorations of F. S. Arnot, F.R.G.S.*, London: Seeley, Service and Co. (1921).

—— 'Barotse Boundary Award', *Geographical Journal* (1905), pp. 201–4.

BEGUIN, E. *Les Ma-Rotsé: étude géographique et ethnographique du Haut-Zambèze*, Lausanne: Sack (1903).

BERTRAND, A. *Au pays des Ba-Rotsi: voyage d'exploration en Afrique*, Paris (1898); translated by A. B. Miall as *The Kingdom of the Barotsi, Upper Zambezia*, London: T. Fisher Unwin (1899).

—— 'From the Machili to Lealui', *Geographical Journal* (1897), pp. 145–9.

BERTRAND, MADAME. *Alfred Bertrand: Explorer and Captain of Cavalry*, London: The Religious Tract Society (1926).

BRADLEY, K. 'Statesmen: Coryndon and Lewanika in North-Western Rhodesia', *African Observer*, v. 5 (September 1936).

BRIOD, R. 'Rites d'Initiation, La Jeune Fille zambèzienne et sa préparation à sa vie de femme', *Nouvelles du Zambèze*, pp. 1–8.

BURNIER, TH. *Âmes Primitives*. Paris: Société des Missions évangéliques (1922).

—— *Chants zambiezens*, Paris: Société des Missions évangéliques (without date, about 1927).

CAKAHANGA, D. Diary in 'Uma viagem de Angola em direcção a Contra Costa pelo Sr. A. F. F. da Silva Porto', *Annales de Conselho Ultramarino*, Lisbon: Imp. Nacional (1857), Ser. I, pp. 273 ff.

CAMERON, V. L. *Across Africa* (2 volumes), London: Daldy, Isbister and Co. (1877).

CHAPMAN, W. *A Pathfinder in South Central Africa*, London: Hammond (1910).

CLARK, P. M. *The Autobiography of an Old Drifter*, London: Harrap (1936).

CLARKE, J. H. C. 'Nutrition of School Boys in the Mongu-Lealui District of Barotseland', *East African Medical Journal*, xxi (1944), pp. 164–70.

CLAY, G. C. *The History of Mankoya District*, Livingstone: Rhodes–Livingstone Institute (1945). (Cyclostyled.)

COILLARD, F. *On the Threshold of Central Africa*, London: Hodder and Stoughton (1897).

COLYER, S. *Sikololo, Notes on the Grammar with a Vocabulary* (1914).

COUVE, D. *Des monts du Lessouto aux plaines du Zambèze*, Paris: Société des Missions évangéliques (1926).

COXHEAD, J. C. C. 'Barotse and Their Country', *Windsor* (1924), pp. 77–83.

DECLE, L. *Three Years in Savage Africa*, London: Methuen (1900).

DENNY, S. 'Some Zambesi Boat Songs', *Nada*, xiv (1936).

DEPELCHIN, H., and CROONENBERGHS, C. *Trois ans dans l'Afrique Australe au pays d'Umzile; chez les Batongas; la vallée des Barotses; débuts de la Mission du Zambèze*, Brussels (1879, 1880, 1881).

DIETERLEN, H. *François Coillard*, Paris: Société des Missions évangéliques (1921).

DIETERLEN, R. *Les Barotsi* (thesis presented to the faculty of theology of Montauban), Cahors: Imprimerie Coueslant (1909).

ELLENBERGER, D. F. (written in English by J. C. Macgregor). *History of the Basuto, Ancient and Modern*, London: Caxton Publishing Co. (1912).

ELLENBERGER, MME V. *Silhouettes Zambèziennes*, Paris: Société des Missions évangéliques (1920).

FELL, J. R. 'Report of the Commission on Objectionable Native Marriage Customs', *Proc. Gen. Missionary Conf. Northern Rhodesia* (1922).

GIBBONS, A. ST. H. *Africa from South to North through Marotseland*, London: John Lane (1904).

—— *Exploration and Hunting in Central Africa, 1895–96*, London: Methuen (1898).

—— 'Journey in the Marotse and Mashikolumbwe Countries', *Geographical Journal*, ix (1897), pp. 121–45.

—— 'Marotseland and the Tribes of the Upper Zambezi', *Proceedings of the Royal Colonial Institute*, xxix (1897–8), pp. 260–76.

—— 'Exploration in Marotseland and Neighbouring Regions', *Geographical Journal*, xvii (1901), pp. 106–34.

GLUCKMAN, M. *Economy of the Central Barotse Plain*, Livingstone: Rhodes–Livingstone Institute, Paper No. 7 (1941).

—— *Essays on Lozi Land and Royal Property*, Livingstone: Rhodes–Livingstone Institute, Paper No. 10 (1943).

—— *Administrative Organization of the Barotse Native Authorities, with a plan for reforming them*, Livingstone: Rhodes–Livingstone Institute (1943). (Cyclostyled.)

—— 'Kinship and Marriage among the Lozi of Northern Rhodesia and the Zulu of Natal' in *African Systems of Kinship and Marriage* (ed. by A. R. Radcliffe-Brown and C. D. Forde), London: Oxford University Press (1950).

—— (with J. C. Mitchell and J. A. Barnes), 'The Village Headman in British Central Africa', *Africa*, xix. 2 (April 1949).

—— 'The Role of the Sexes in Wiko Circumcision Ceremonies', in *Social Structure: Essays Presented to A. R. Radcliffe-Brown* (ed. by M. Fortes), Oxford: The Clarendon Press (1949).

—— 'Notes on the Social Background of Barotse Music', in *African Music* by A. M. Jones, Livingstone: Occasional Paper from the Rhodes–Livingstone Museum, No. 2 (1943), reprinted in New Series, Paper No. 4 (1949).

—— 'Barotse Ironworkers', *Iscor Magazine*, Pretoria (1946).

—— 'A Lozi Price Control Debate', *South African Journal of Economics*, xi. 3 (September 1943); summarized in *Colonial Review*, March 1944.

—— 'African Land Tenure', in *Rhodes–Livingstone Journal: Human Problems in British Central Africa*, iii (June 1945).

—— 'Zambezi River Kingdom', *Libertas*, Johannesburg, v. 8 (July 1945).

—— 'Human Laboratory across the Zambezi', *Libertas*, Johannesburg, vi. 4 (March 1946).

GLUCKMAN, M. 'Prefix Concordance in Kololo, Lingua Franca of Barotseland', *African Studies*, i. 2 (June 1942).

GOY, MME M. K. *Dans les Solitudes de l'Afrique*, Paris: Société des Missions évangéliques (1901), translated as *Alone in Africa; or, Seven Years on the Zambesi* (1901), London: J. Nisbet (1901).

GIUGLER, —. 'Les conceptions des Marotsés décrites par un Zambézien', *L'Anthropologie*, xxxviii (1928), pp. 135–7.

HAILEY, LORD. *An African Survey*, London: Oxford University Press (1938), especially at pp. 456 ff.

HARDING, C. *In Remotest Barotseland: Being an Account of a Journey of over 8,000 Miles through the Wildest and Remotest Parts of Lewanika's Empire*, London: Hurst and Blackett (1904).

HOLE, H. M. *The Passing of the Black Kings*, London: Philip Allan (1932).

HOLUB, E. *Eine Culturskizze des Marutse-Mambundas Reich in Süd-Central Africa*, Vienna: Kaiserlich-Königlich Geographische Gesellschaft (1879).

—— *Seven Years in South Africa: Travels, Researches, and Hunting Adventures, between the Diamond-fields and the Zambesi (1872–79)* (translated by E. E. Frewer), London: Sampson Low, Marston, Searle, and Rivington (1881). (In two volumes; vol. ii. for Barotse.)

HUDSON, R. S., and PRESCOT, H. K. 'The Election of a "ngambela" in Barotseland', *Man*, xxiv (1924), No. 103, pp. 138 ff.

HUDSON, R. S. 'The Human Geography of Balovale District', *J.R.A.I.* lxv (1935).

*Human Geography Reports* (MSS.) by Northern Rhodesia District Officers for the Committee on the Human Geography of Inter-tropical Africa, British Association for the Advancement of Science, 1932. (On file at Secretariat, Lusaka, and at the Rhodes–Livingstone Institute.)

JACOTTET, E. *Études sur les Langues du Haut-Zambèze*, Paris: Ernest Leroux (1896).

JAKEMAN, E. M. *Pioneering in Northern Rhodesia*, London: Morgan and Scott (1927).

JALLA, A. and E. *Pionniers parmi les Ma-Rotse*, Florence: Imprimerie Claudienne (1903).

JALLA, A. *Dictionary of the Lozi Language*, Vol. I: *Lozi–English*, London: U.S.C.L. (2nd edition, 1936).

—— *Elementary Grammar of the Lozi Language*, London: U.S.C.L. (1937).

—— *Litaba za Sicaba sa Malozi* [History of the Lozi Nation], Sefula, Barotseland: The Book Depot of the Paris Missionary Society (4th edition, 1939).

—— 'Initiation Schools for Boys in Barotseland', *Proc. Gen. Missionary Conf. of Northern Rhodesia*, 1927.

JALLA, MRS. A. 'Initiation Schools for Girls in Barotseland', *Proc. Gen. Missionary Conf. of Northern Rhodesia*, 1927.

JALLA, L. *Sur les Rives du Zambèze: Notes Ethnographiques*, Paris: Société des Missions évangéliques (1928).

JAMES, FATHER. *African Adventure: Irishmen on Safari* [History of the Capuchin Mission in South Africa and Rhodesia]. Dublin: The Father Mathew Record Office (1936).

JENSEN, A. E. *Die staatliche Organisation und die historischen Überlieferungen der Barotse am oberen Zambesi*, Festschrift und L. Jahresbericht 1931–1932 des Württemberger Vereins für Handelsgeographie E. V., Museum für Länder- und Völkerkunde, Linden-Museum, Stuttgart, pp. 71–115.

JOHNSTON, H. H. *British Central Africa*, London: Methuen (1897).

JOHNSTON, J. *Romance and Reality in Central Africa*, London: Hodder and Stoughton (1897).

*Journal des Missions* (reprint from). 'The Death of Lewanika', *Journal of the African Society*, xvi (January 1917), pp. 149–54.

*Journal des Missions Évangéliques* (The Organ of the Paris Missionary Society). Paris: *passim*.

JOUSSE, T. *La Mission au Zambèze*, Paris: Société des Missions évangéliques (1890).

KUNTZ, M. *Terre d'Afrique*, Paris: Société des Missions évangéliques (1927).

—— *Ombres et Lumières*, Paris: Société des Missions évangéliques (1921).

—— 'Les Rites occultes et la sorcellerie sur le Haut-Zambèze', *Journal de la Société Africanistes*, ii. 2 (1932), pp. 123–38.

LAMBERT, J. C. *Missionary Heroes in Africa*, London: Seeley Service (1912).

LAWLEY, Sir A. 'From Bulawayo to the Victoria Falls: A Mission to King Lewanika', *Blackwoods Magazine* (December 1898), pp. 739–59.

LIENARD, J. L. *Notre Voyage au Zambèze*, Cahors: Imprimerie Coueslant (1899).

——*Lettres et Fragments*, Cahors: Imprimerie Coueslant (1901).

LIVINGSTONE, D. *Missionary Travels and Researches in South Africa*, London: John Murray (1857).

—— D. and C. *Narrative of an Expedition to the Zambesi and its Tributaries*, London: John Murray (1865).

LUCK, R. A. *Visit to Lewanika, King of the Barotse* (1902).

MACINTOSH, C. W. *Coillard of the Zambesi*, London: T. Fisher Unwin (1907).

—— *New Zambesi Trail*, London: Marshall (1922).

—— *Lewanika of the Barotse*, London: U.S.C.L. (1942).

MARTIN, J. D. *Report of Forestry in Barotseland*, Lusaka: Government Printer (1941).

MBIKUSITA, G. *The Paramount Chief Yeta III's visit to England*, Lusaka: Government Printer (1937).

—— *Some Impressions of a Visit to England*, Ndola: The African Literature Committee of Northern Rhodesia (1944).

McCULLOCH, M. *The Lunda, Luena and Related Tribes of North-Western Rhodesia and Adjoining Territories* [Ethnographic Survey of Africa], London: Oxford University Press for the International African Institute (1951).

MELLAND, F. H. *In Witchbound Africa*, London: Seeley, Service and Co. (1923).

*News from Barotsiland and Letters of Missionaries* (1898–1907) (5 Adamson Road, S. Hampstead, London).

Northern Rhodesia Government Reports on Native Affairs, Agriculture, Animal Husbandry, Health.

*Nouvelles du Zambèze*, Geneva: Imprimerie Kundig, *passim* (1898–1940).

OGILVIE, A. G. 'Cooperative Research in Geography; with an African Example', Presidential Address to Section E of the British Association for the Advancement of Science, 1934; reprinted in *The Scottish Geographical Magazine*, l (November 1934).

ORDE BROWN, G. ST. J. *Labour Conditions in Northern Rhodesia*, London: H.M.S.O., Colonial No. 150, 1938.

PHILPOTT, R. 'The Mulobezi–Mongu Labour Route', *Rhodes–Livingstone Journal*, iii (June 1945).

PIM, SIR ALAN, and MILLIGAN, S. *Report of the Commission to Enquire into the Financial and Economic Position of Northern Rhodesia*, London: H.M.S.O., Colonial No. 145, 1938.

PINTO, SERPA. *How I Crossed Africa: From the Atlantic to the Indian Ocean, through Unknown Countries, Discovery of the Great Zambesi Affluents, &c.* (translated by A. Elwes from MSS.), London: Sampson, Low, Marston, Searle, and Rivington (1881).

'PULA'. 'The Barotse People and some of their Customs', *Nada* (1926).

REID, P. C. 'Journeys up the Machili', *Geographical Journal* (1898), pp. 143–5.

—— 'Journeys in the Linyanti Region', ibid. (1901), pp. 573–88.

RICHTER, M. *Kultur und Reich der Marotse* (thesis presented at the University of Leipzig), Leipzig: Voigtländer (1908).

RITCHIE, J. F. *The African as Suckling and as Adult*, Livingstone: Rhodes–Livingstone Institute, Paper No. 9 (1943).

SCOTT, E. D. *Letters from South Africa*. Manchester and London: Sherratt and Hughes (1903).

SELOUS, F. C. *Travel and Adventure in South-east Africa*, London: Rowland Ward (1893).

——*A Hunter's Wanderings in Africa*, London: Richard Bentley and Son (1881).

SHILLITO, E. *Francois Coillard: A Wayfaring Man*, London: Student Christian Movement (1923).

SILVA PORTO, A. F. F. DA. *A travessia do continente africano*, Lisbon: Agência Geral das Colónias (1939).

—— *Viagens e apontamentos de um portuense em África: Excerptos de seu diário*, Lisbon: Agência Geral das Colónias (1942).

SMITH, E. W. and DALE, A. *The Ila-speaking Peoples of Northern Rhodesia*, London: Macmillan (1920).

STIRKE, D. E. C. *Baro.seland: Eight Years among the Barotse*, London: John Bale, Sons and Danielsson (1922).

—— and THOMAS, A. W. *A Comparative Vocabulary of Sikololo-Silui-Simbunda*, London: John Bale, Sons and Danielsson (1916).

—— —— *Sikololo Phrase Book* (1915).

STREITWOLF, HAUPTMANN. *Der Caprivizipfel*, Berlin: Wilhelm Süsserott (1911).

THOMSON, J. MOFFAT. *Memorandum on the Native Tribes and Tribal Areas of Northern Rhodesia*, Livingstone: Government Printer (1934).

—— *Report on the Native Fishing Industry, Northern Rhodesia*, Livingstone: Government Printer (1930).

TORREND, J. A. *A Comparative Grammar of the South-African Bantu Languages*, London: Kegan Paul, Trench and Trubner (1891).

TRAPNELL, C. G. 'Ecological Methods in the Study of Native Agriculture in Northern Rhodesia', *Kew Bulletin*, No. 1 (1937).

—— and CLOTHIER, J. *The Soils, Vegetation and Agricultural Systems of North Western Rhodesia*, Lusaka: Government Printer (1937).

TURNER, V. W. *The Luyana Peoples of Barotseland* (Ethnographic Survey of Africa), London: Oxford University Press for the International African Institute (1951).

WHITE, C. M. N. 'The History of the Lunda-Lubale Peoples', *Rhodes–Livingstone Journal*, viii (1949).

H

# THE PLATEAU TONGA OF
# NORTHERN RHODESIA
### *By* E. COLSON

## I. INTRODUCTION

THE Plateau Tonga, a matrilineal people, occupy a large portion of the Southern Province of Northern Rhodesia.[1] The following description is based on an investigation of the Tonga who live in Mazabuka District, north of Muzoka, and may not apply to Tonga living south of this point. The latter at one period were incorporated in the Barotse Kingdom, an experience not shared by their northern relatives, who in pre-European days were neither subjects of a foreign state nor creators of any large-scale political organization of their own. If it is necessary henceforth to speak of the Tonga living south of Muzoka, they will be referred to as Southern Tonga. 'Tonga' will be reserved for the northern branch with which we are directly concerned.

### Affiliations and Definition of the Tonga Group

Linguistically 'Tonga' has a wider meaning than that given above. Doke uses 'Tonga' as the name of one of his divisions of the Central Bantu Zone which includes Tonga, We, Totela, Ila, and Lenje.[2]

[1] From September 1946 to September 1947 I carried out investigations in four different sections of Tonga country: in Mwansa chieftaincy, close to the railway line; in Chona chieftaincy, on the edge of the Zambezi Escarpment Hills; in Monze chieftaincy, near the western boundary of the Tonga; and in Mwanacingwala chieftaincy, on the lower Magoye river near the north-western boundary. These intensive investigations of particular areas were supplemented by questioning Tonga from other sections of the country. The following description, which formed the gist of a series of four lectures given at the Institute of Social Anthropology at Oxford University during 1948, was revised after a further month of field investigation in July 1948. It is still in a sense a preliminary account, since further work among the Tonga was carried on during 1948–9, 1949–50.

Thanks are due to Professor E. E. Evans-Pritchard and Dr. M. Fortes of Oxford, and to my colleagues of the Rhodes–Livingstone Institute, Mr. John Barnes and Mr. Clyde Mitchell, and Dr. Max Gluckman, former Director of the Institute, for clarifying discussions and helpful criticism. I also wish to thank Benjamin Shipopa, my interpreter.

[2] Doke, *Bantu*, p. 31. Doke also distinguishes the Zambezi Group, which he regards as allied to Tonga. This includes Subiya, Luyi, and Leya.

People speaking these dialects inhabit a compact stretch of territory in south-western Northern Rhodesia and across the Zambezi into Southern Rhodesia to the vicinity of Wankie. So far as we know there are neither islands of alien speech within this territory nor outlying representatives of the linguistic group. The Tonga are surrounded by peoples speaking cognate dialects except on the north-east, where they are contiguous with the Soli of the lower Kafue river.

Written material on any of these peoples is lacking, except for the Ila and Tonga.[1] Generalizations are therefore risky, but my impression is that no sharp distinctions in culture or language set the Tonga apart from linguistically related peoples. Instead they tend to merge with them, while within the Tonga group itself slight changes accumulate until those who live at one end of the area are more closely akin to related peoples near by than they are to their fellow Tonga at the opposite end of the area.

In a sense it is probably false to regard the Tonga as a definite group or real unit which is set off by definite criteria from other peoples. Physically they are not distinctive. They lack tribal marks peculiar to themselves. The custom of knocking out the six upper front teeth is shared with Ila and other neighbours. In the days before the Europeans came the Tonga formed a stateless society with no political system which could weld them together into a common body. Apparently they have always lacked, as they do today, any system of trading associations, of tribal-wide age-grade sets or regiments, or other devices to form them into a common society.

Today the Tonga exist within one political unit, the Plateau Tonga Native Authority, but this is of recent origin and due to circumstances beyond their control. Government has placed them within the bounds

[1] The Ila have been described in Smith and Dale, *The Ila-speaking Peoples of Northern Rhodesia*. Until recently the only written references to the Tonga were to be found in travellers' accounts or in short papers in mission journals, which give only the vaguest information. Cf. Livingstone, *Missionary Travels and Researches in South Africa*, pp. 549–59 (1857); Selous, *Travels and Adventures in South-East Africa*, pp. 203–43; articles appearing in the *Zambesi Mission Journal*, 1903–25. Information on the soils and agricultural system of the Tonga was included in Trapnell and Clothier, *The Soils, Vegetation and Agricultural Systems of North Western Rhodesia* (cf. especially pp. 35–7). In 1945 a team of agriculturists, assisted by M. Gluckman, made a survey of Tonga land holding and usage. This was circulated first as a mimeographed report, and was published in 1948, as Allan, Gluckman, Peters, and Trapnell, *Land-Holding and Land-Usage Among the Plateau Tonga of Mazabuka District*. The report formed an invaluable background for my own work. It will henceforth be referred to as *Tonga Report*.

of a single administrative district and has organized them into the following chieftaincies: Moya, Siamaundu, Ufwenuka, Chona, Mwansa, Sianjalika, Naluama, Mweenda, Mwanacingwala, Chongo, Simuyobe, Monze, Mapanza, Macha, Singani, and Siabunkululu.[1] Monze is recognized, with many reservations, as senior chief. However, the Mazabuka District also administers people who are not considered Tonga and the chieftaincies represent Government policy and convenience, and not cultural, linguistic, or political distinctions among the Tonga themselves.

In general today the people in these chieftaincies refer to themselves as 'Tonga', but the name is not a common rallying point or symbol of unity. Tonga in the western chieftaincies are apt to say that those living but a few miles east of the line of rail are really We, while these eastern people regard themselves as Tonga.[2] Again, many of the people in the west, who are regarded by their eastern neighbours as Tonga, are likely to claim that they are really Ila, or at least are more Ila than Tonga. This is true in Simuyobe, Chongo, and Mwanacingwala chieftaincies. But this belief in Ila affinities does not form these people into a common block, conscious of their difference from other Tonga. In Chongo one hears comments that the people living to the north in Mwanacingwala are either Sala or We. Occasionally the western peoples are even referred to as Lundwe.[3] Despite this lack of unity, it is still possible to give a generalized description of the organization of the Tonga which holds true with minor variations for the area as a whole.[4]

### The Country

Tongaland is approximately 70 miles from north to south and 60 miles from east to west. At the present time it is divided into an eastern

[1] The Southern Tonga are largely outside Mazabuka District. District boundaries have changed often, and will probably be revised again.

[2] In accordance with accepted practice, I have dropped prefixes and speak only of Tonga, and not of Mutonga (singular), Batonga (plural), Butonga (Tonga country), and Citonga (Tonga language). In the few Tonga words which occur in this paper I have not attempted a true phonetic spelling. Tonga is today a written language and I have preferred to follow customary spellings.

[3] This name occasionally appears in printed references to the western Tonga. Cf. Smith and Dale, *The Ila*, i, p. xxvi; *The Report of the Native Land Tenure Committee*, Part II, *Mazabuka District*, p. 19.

[4] The Tonga probably should not be called a 'tribe'. They seem to lack even the 'consciousness of unity' which Nadel uses in his definition of the Nuba tribe. See Nadel, *The Nuba*, p. 13.

and a western half by a belt of European farm land and Crown land
which lies on either side of the railway line. The entire area is a part
of the Batoka or Northern Rhodesian Plateau, at an elevation well
over 3,000 feet. Though it lies only about 16° 50' south of the
Equator, the climate is tempered by the altitude. In some years the
coldest nights bring a slight frost which damages the fruit-trees on
the higher lands. The mean maximum temperature varies about
85° F.; the mean minimum, about 55–60° F.[1]

Throughout most of its extent the country is a flattened plain with
little relief save on the east where the monotony breaks before the
ridges and narrow valleys running westward from the Zambesi Escarpment. On the north-west the flood plains of the Kafue river and of the
lower Magoye again vary the landscape. Elsewhere the bush stretches
monotonously mile after mile, interspersed with occasional open
plains, or dambos, or with areas marked by the upthrust of great ant-
heaps, or by occasional changes in vegetation. A number of rivers or
small streams flow through the country, in addition to the Kafue
river which flows along a portion of the north-western border. None
of them, save the Kafue, are perennial at the present time, though the
Ngwezi and the Magoye were so within living memory.[2] The annual
rainfall varies from 18 to 30 inches from one part of the area to
another. Even within closely contiguous regions the fall is highly
variable. A brisk shower may be falling on the houses of the village
while the crops in the fields still wilt with drought; one village may
have sufficient rain while the next suffers drought and a total crop
failure. Such local variations are especially found in the Escarpment
country with its narrow ridges and valleys which divert the storms;
in a lesser sense it is true of all Tongaland. During the dry season
almost every section suffers from water famine except where a Government dam or well has been dug or along some of the rivers where
small pools occupy a portion of the river-bed though the stream itself
has ceased to flow.

The soil varies somewhat in fertility, with the more fertile strips
lying in belts running roughly east to west, separated from each other
by the poorer, sandy soils of the Plateau type. Transitions between soil
types are relatively abrupt. Under the old native system of agriculture
such variations were of minimum importance, for as the soil became
exhausted villages shifted easily to new sites and the old fields were
abandoned. Today they are coming more and more to the fore with

[1] District note-book.   [2] *Tonga Report.*

the development of cash cropping for maize, the use of the plough with the resultant desire to keep stumped land in cultivation, and the developing shortage of land which makes shifting cultivation impossible. Since maize needs a more fertile soil than do finger millet and sorghum, the principal crops under the old system, the effect of such soil variations is likely to be increasingly noticeable.[1] As a whole, however, the region has some of the best soil in Northern Rhodesia, and this, together with its proximity to the railway line, has led to large tracts of land being taken over for European farms.

Tsetse fly occurs only sporadically. Most of the area is cattle country, though cattle are most numerous to the west and north-west, and fewest towards the east in the Escarpment borders. There large numbers of goats are kept, while to the north-west these animals are few in number and rather despised. Chickens are numerous and universal. Today there is a lively trade in chickens and eggs to the European settlements on the railway. Within the last twenty years the Tonga east of the railway and those in Monze chieftaincy on the west have begun to raise pigs for the market, but the more strictly cattle people in the north-west speak disdainfully of this practice. Once the area was rich in game. Early travellers reported it a hunter's paradise. Today only a few small buck manage to survive except in certain protected spots along the Kafue where herds of zebra, wildebeest, and lechwe still exist. Lions and other dangerous carnivora have been destroyed over most of the country, and there is no longer any need to take measures to protect people or stock from their raids.

The Tonga area has the three seasons of the year characteristic of most of Northern Rhodesia: rainy, cold, and hot. The first begins towards the end of October or beginning of November and should last until March. Often it is interrupted by a period of drought in January or February which effectively blights the crops. In some years the whole country suffers from insufficient rains or from their delay. The cold season begins in April and lasts until the middle or end of August. Then within a few days there is an abrupt change, and the hot season descends upon the country. This lasts until the beginning of the rains offers some slight relief. Through both cold and hot seasons, almost daily dust-storms sweep across the level plains, whirl into dust devils, and roar off in tremendous swirls of flying sand and soil.

The rainy season and the early part of the cold season are the periods of most intensive activity. Planting starts soon after the beginning

[1] See *Tonga Report*, p. 27.

of the rains, about the end of November. From then until the
harvest there is usually some work to be done in the fields. Harvesting
begins about April and lasts well into June. This ends the real work
of the year for most of the Tonga, and during the remainder of the
cold season and through the heat people are free to visit or to rest unless they need to clear new fields or to build new houses. In the west,
however, the cattle must be driven to dry-season camps along the
Kafue where they pasture until the rains again restore the local
pastures and watering places. Such moves were once common to most
of the area, but they have been abandoned as the building of dams has
ensured the local water-supplies. Hunting and fishing are of relatively
little importance today. Along the lower Magoye, fish drives are held
at the end of the rains when the flood waters begin to fall, and elsewhere the women use scoop baskets to fish sporadically in the pools
left standing as the rivers dry. Game drives may be held towards the
end of the dry season, though over most of the country hunting is
unprofitable.

*Population*

No census has ever been made of the Tonga. Population estimates
are based on the tax registers kept by the district officials. In 1946
it was estimated that the total native population of the Mazabuka
District might lie anywhere between 85,000 and 110,000.[1] This figure
presumably includes We and other non-Tonga people who inhabit a
portion of the Mazabuka District as well as alien Africans who have
settled among the Tonga.

It seems probable that the population has increased fairly steadily
during the past forty years. Older Tonga say that sections of country
now crowded lay unoccupied forty years ago and point to this as
evidence of the increase. Early travellers speak of marching long distances through unpopulated country. This would be impossible today
unless the march were made through Crown lands. Still we know that
at that period the Tonga were hiding from Ndebele raiders in the less
accessible hills of the Escarpment, or in other corners of the country-
side, and such areas probably had a greater concentration of population than they do now. However, it is generally believed by both
Europeans and Africans that the Tonga have increased rapidly since
the European occupation. This is my own impression from genealogies
and census material I have collected.

[1] Oral communication from district officials.

Estimates of population density are presumably no more reliable than the figure for total population. In 1946 it was estimated that the reserve area as a whole supports a density of 50 persons per square mile. On the fertile soils in parts of Mwanacingwala chieftaincy it may rise as high as 137·7 per square mile, though over much of the chieftaincy it falls well below this figure. The density is partially a feature of the dispossession of the Tonga from some of their lands by the Europeans, with the resultant concentration of population within the area left to them. It has also been affected by immigration, especially from the Zambezi Valley where yearly famines drive the We to seek refuge with Tonga relatives. It has been affected by the settlement of peoples from other tribes who have been drawn to the railroad line by the economic opportunities offered to them there.[1]

## History

Almost nothing is known of the history of the Tonga before the middle of the nineteenth century when they first came in contact with European explorers. The Tonga have few traditions that go back that far, and none that tell of a former home or of any mass migration into their present area.[2] They must have entered the country some-time before 1800, since they were well established when Livingstone met them there in 1855.

During the nineteenth century the Tonga were badly smashed by the raids of Kololo, Lozi, and Ndebele armies. Such raids were usually for slaves and cattle and the pleasure of raiding, and not to gain land or to establish political domination. The Southern Tonga were controlled by the Barotse Kingdom, but the Tonga to the north sent only tribute and thus occasionally gained immunity from Lozi raids, but never from the Ndebele. Under the pressure of the raids the Tonga did not attempt to unite in a common defence of their country. During such respites as they had from external foes they continued their internal feuds and fought against each other. By 1890 they were a broken and a beaten people, their cattle stolen, many of their people enslaved in Barotseland or among the Ndebele. They were fortunate only in that they lived away from the main slave-routes followed by the Arab and Mambari slavers.

[1] See discussion of population and density in *Tonga Report*, Chap. ii.

[2] A lack of history is correlated with the amorphous character of the society which lacked institutionalized leadership. A similar lack of tradition is found among the stateless Nuba. Cf. Nadel, *The Nuba*, p. 93, 'evaluation of the past . . . tends to go hand in hand with the growth of hereditary power and prestige'.

The raids ended only with the conquest of the Ndebele by the British. Shortly thereafter the Tonga passed under European rule under the auspices of the British South Africa Company. Soon afterwards the country began to be opened up. Civil administration began in 1903.[1] Before 1910 the railway had been driven through the heart of Tongaland, and European traders were beginning to settle in the area. Already it was the site of several mission stations.[2] Today probably no Tonga lives more than thirty miles from the railway line and some European or Indian trading store. There are three small European settlements on the railway, and farmers scattered along the line of rail. By 1913 a portion of the land was alienated for European farms, and later reserves were set aside for the Tonga. The European section, including Crown lands, extends approximately 5 miles on either side of the railway. Tonga who lived within the area assigned for European development were ordered to move.

Many of the men and boys, as well as men and boys from the reserves, went off to Southern Rhodesia or the Union as labour migrants—a movement which had begun even before European rule was imposed.[3] Others went to work for local European farmers. Those who remained in the reserves, as well as many who returned there after a short period of work at European centres, adopted the use of the plough and began to raise maize to sell on the market that developed as the mines opened on the Copper Belt. Today the Tonga have a low labour-migration rate, due no doubt to the economic opportunities within their own area.[4]

The emergence of cash cropping disrupted the old agricultural system which provided for some rotation and rest of land. Finger millet was abandoned almost entirely save on the poorest soils which would not support maize; sorghum became a subsidiary crop used chiefly for beer. Maize became all important. Meantime other changes were taking place. The abundant game was killed out, while the cattle population increased rapidly. Returned labour migrants invested part of their savings in cattle. No longer preyed upon by raids or wild beasts, the herds grew steadily. Soon over-stocking in the

[1] District note-book. The Tonga accepted European rule quietly.

[2] A number of denominations have missions in the area today and also provide day schools or other services. The two oldest missions were founded by the Roman Catholics and by the Seventh Day Adventists in 1905. Other denominations represented are: Anglican, Pilgrim Holiness, Brethren in Christ, Salvation Army, Methodist.

[3] *B.S.A. Report, 1898–1900*, p. 94; *1900–1902*, p. 449.

[4] See *Tonga Report*, pp. 160 ff.

reserves, together with the use of the plough, created an erosion problem. Changes in agricultural techniques, increase in population, and
other features in the situation have steadily diminished the possibili-
ties for shifting cultivation. Land is no longer so readily abandoned;
village shifts are becoming difficult. The Tonga will soon be faced
with the problem of readjusting not only their subsistence techniques
but also their whole theory of land-holding. The Administration has
set up technical departments to work within the Tonga reserves to
try to meet these problems, and their activities have changed the face
of the country-side. Contour ridges or grass strips have been built, as
well as dams and wells. Roads have been pushed out from the railway
line through the reserves. Various restrictions have been laid on the
agricultural methods of the people.

   Government also has attempted to develop the region politically
and thus has touched many aspects of Tonga social organization.
Here the Europeans could not simply replace one authority by another,
one legal code by another, as they could in organized states; they had
to set to work to create political organization and authority from
whole cloth. As soon as the Europeans took over the country, they
seized upon the village as the administrative unit and ordered all
Tonga to live in villages. Furthermore, they ruled that no village
might consist of less than ten taxpayers, which meant not less than ten
adult males, and that no one in the village might live more than
approximately half a mile from the headman's hut. Soon the Administration was trying to mould the villages into larger political units on
a territorial basis, though the villages were still recognized as groups
of people registered under one headman, and thus they retained their
identity though they moved some miles from their previous sites. The
larger political units had boundaries, and included the people living
within these boundaries. At one time the Administration recognized
116 small chieftaincies, each one of only a few miles in extent. In 1918
it reorganized the system, consolidating the tiny chieftaincies into
a few larger ones, and one chief was recognized as the senior chief of
the Tonga.[1] This system still remains in force, though the power
of the chiefs has been increased under the Native Authorities Act of
1929. The chiefs have been given courts in which they hear cases and
pass judgement. They also are allowed to legislate and to change the
customary laws of the Tonga under the guidance of the Administration. They, with their councillors, clerks, and messengers, represent a

[1] District note-book.

focusing or canalizing of authority foreign to the traditional ways of the Tonga. In choosing the original chiefs the Administration picked prominent men from each area. Some of them had ritual status as officiants at a local rain shrine; others dominated their neighbours through their personal qualities. None of them had the type of prerogatives generally associated with chiefly status. Today they are referred to by the Tonga as 'Government chiefs'. The description which follows is not concerned with these modern developments in the political field.[1] Nevertheless they affect the working of the social system.

From the above sketch it should be plain that it is difficult to factor out a set of customs or a social structure which we can regard as Tonga apart from these various changes. We know nothing of the culture or social organization of these people from the time before it was receiving the smashing blows of Lozi and Ndebele. During this period it could hardly function efficiently—the Tonga did not have time to recuperate from one raid before they went down under another. Since then they have been swept up into the wider political unit of Northern Rhodesia which has taken over the duties of preserving order, and protection from outside enemies, which formerly vested in the Tonga themselves.

## II. TECHNOLOGY AND ECONOMIC LIFE

*Specialization and Co-operation*

The Tonga are farmers and herdmen. Each man aims at combining the tillage of his fields with the increase of his herd. Even under changed conditions they have been slow to develop into craftsmen or traders. This lack of economic differentiation and the low level of technological development is correlated with the relatively undifferentiated character of Tonga social organization.

*Division of Labour*

Crafts are primarily subject to the sexual division of labour, in which work with wood and metals is assigned to men, the making of pots, baskets, and mats to women. Within this broad division there is further specialization, for not all men and women are skilled in the crafts assigned to their sex. Only those who have been instructed by an ancestral spirit are considered to have the right to work at a particular craft, which in theory restricts the crafts to those whose ancestors

[1] See Colson, 'Modern Political Organization of the Plateau Tonga'.

had the skill, and within this group to those particularly chosen by the ancestors for the work. Since the ancestors are not restricted in their choice of an heir by either matrilineal or patrilineal descent, the theory does not establish a craft monopoly in particular lines. Moreover, a long-forgotten ancestor may decide to pass on his skill to one who has no claim to the craft through any known ancestor. In practice, therefore, the theory of inheritance allows any Tonga who cares to do so to practise any craft assigned to his or her sex, and removes any stigma of laziness from those who feel no such inclination. Moreover, the simpler forms of a craft are not encumbered with this restriction.

Almost every man is capable of doing some elementary work with metal, or of roughing out the few wooden articles needed by the Tonga—sledges, spoons, axe- and hoe-handles, spear shafts, and porridge-stirrers. Specialists make the wooden dishes, stools, drums, and big stamping-blocks in which maize is pounded into meal, and specialists handle the more difficult work in making axe- or spear-blades or cattle-bells.[1] Such men work at their crafts only in their spare time, and depend on their herds and cultivations for their livelihood. Working casually one or two specialists can fill the needs of the surrounding neighbourhood. The crafts assigned to women show the same specialization. Probably each village includes two or three who can make pots or baskets, and they trade their surplus articles in a casual fashion with their neighbours, though they do not produce deliberately for a market. A potter, indeed, is prevented from filling contracts by the belief that a promised pot will break during the firing.

This specialization results in only a small casual trade in handicrafts within the village and within neighbourhoods of villages. Even today, when Tonga are setting up as hawkers or traders they do not deal in Tonga crafts. There are no markets, and even ritual exchange is practically absent. The only ones I have recorded are gifts of spear- and hoe- blades as part of the bride-wealth transaction.

Even less specialization appears in other forms of production, though the sex division of labour is usually present. Men clear the fields, cut poles for huts, granaries, and storage platforms, and build these. They care for the cattle and today do the ploughing, and give an occasional hand with weeding and harvesting. They also hunt and fish, though these are very minor occupations at the present time. Women do the housework and have powerful positions as cooks and brewers. They also plant the crops, do most of the weeding and harvest-

[1] For hoes, ploughs, ox chains, &c., the Tonga depend on European manufactures.

ing, collect wild produce for relish, and gather firewood. They bring
the water, cut the thatching-grass, and after the huts are built are
responsible for plastering the walls. Once past puberty they are not
allowed to have any contact with cattle, even those they own, but
they usually care for the small stock owned by the family.[1] They
also fish with large scoop baskets.

In ordinary life the minimum unit is therefore one which includes
both a man and a woman, though the woman is less dependent upon
her co-partner than is the man. She needs his assistance only occasionally, for building her house or clearing and ploughing her fields; he is
constantly in need of someone to draw his water, work his fields, and
cook his food. Indeed, if he has no wife to brew beer for him he is unable to approach his ancestral spirits. Married couples, however, can
be relatively independent of the assistance of other people; and they
are usually expected to be so. Even headmen and modern chiefs get
little assistance from other people, and must rely on their own efforts.

On certain occasions, however, larger working units are necessary.
They are exceptional, and not all of them recur even annually. A man
may need help to clear his fields for the first time, though many today
prefer to do the work alone; again he needs help in making the roof
of his hut, though he can gather the materials and build the walls by
himself; he may need help in weeding or in harvesting if he has planted
large fields. Large numbers of men are needed for game or fish drives.
On the first three occasions it is left to the individual concerned to
mobilize additional man-power. He does this through a work-party.
Beer is brewed, and an announcement is made that help is needed.
Anyone may then come to work, and the work-party may be drawn
from several villages. Attendance is entirely voluntary, but those who
fail to turn up for the work-parties of others may find their own
poorly attended. However, this sanction has now faded in many areas
with the introduction of money and the use of hired labour, and many
Tonga prefer to hire their workers on the ground that work-parties
are inefficient. In a sense they are, for people who take no part in the
work may come to drink the beer.[2]

---

[1] The Tonga say they can give no reason for the rule forbidding women to approach
the cattle kraal, milking, or otherwise handling cattle. According to them, nothing
would happen to women, cattle, other people, or the crops if the rule were trans-
gressed. It is simply among the things 'which aren't done'.

[2] Members of the Seventh Day Adventist sect, which forbids the drinking of beer,
usually substitute a meal.

Work-parties are rarely large gatherings. An attendance of thirty to forty workers is considered large but not unusual. Work-parties of chiefs and headmen draw no larger attendance than do those organized by ordinary individuals. The work to be done is known in advance, and the party attacks the job without apparent guidance or leadership.

Some larger gathering is needed for game and fish drives, but again there appears to be an absence of formal organization or leadership. Usually one man has the right to announce the day on which the grass and bush in a particular section is to be burned and he lets it be known that a hunt is to be held. Men swarm in from the surrounding country-side. They take their stations according to the direction from which they come and begin to burn the grass where and as they please with no one having authority to give the starting signal or to direct their activities. After that it is each man for himself. The man who kills a beast and those two or three who are close enough to rush in and add a spear to the dying animal share the kill. Then as the men grow tired of the hunt they drift back to their homes or to the nearest beer-drink, taking their bag with them. The man who has announced the hunt receives nothing unless he has been fortunate enough to reach some successful hunter immediately after the kill; nor does he make any arrangements to feed the hunters who have gathered.[1]

I have been told that this same system operates during the fish drives along the lower Magoye, and that there is no arrangement for dividing the catch among the various people who co-operate in such an enterprise; nor do those taking part pass on a share to the man who announces the drive. In the past, game drives, at least, frequently led to fights between the different sections combining in the hunt, as men disputed the ownership of an animal which each claimed to have killed. At the present time, however, game and fish drives are of relatively little importance in the life of the Tonga.

A new form of co-operation has developed in recent years with the introduction of new agricultural equipment. When a man is unable to furnish his own plough, cultivator, and work oxen, he sometimes joins with neighbours in what the Tonga call a *company*. The men who form a company pool their equipment—ploughs, cultivators, oxen, and sledges. Each man has access to the pool, and often they join together and move from field to field until all are finished. Such companies may include men who live in the same section of the village, or a

---

[1] Thirty years or more ago the man who announced the hunt would perform ritual to help all who came to the hunt, and other hunters had to assist.

man may join with relatives or friends who live elsewhere in the village, or even with those living in neighbouring villages. Moreover, the composition of a company may change from year to year. It offers advantages to all concerned. Young men who as yet have little capital of their own have access to the equipment of older friends; established men are able to mobilize labour which does not expect a cash return. Other methods of sharing equipment are known. Some men rent out their ploughs and oxen after they themselves have finished planting. Others, especially men who are attempting to weld a following to them, will loan their equipment without demanding payment, though with a general understanding that when they need assistance it will be forthcoming.[1]

## Trade

Today many Tonga have started small trading stores or tea rooms in the reserves, where they sell trade goods in return for cash, maize, or eggs. Others tour the area buying chickens, eggs, and cattle, which they then sell at a profit on the railway line. Still others make trips to the Kafue river where they buy supplies of fresh or dried fish to peddle in the villages far from the river. These men still have their fields and regard hawking or trading as profitable side-lines. Even so, it is a new departure for the Tonga. In former days trade was largely non-existent, though there was some variation in production which might have made it profitable.[2] Areas adjacent to the Magoye and to the country of the Twa on the Kafue had plentiful supplies of fish at certain times of the year; other areas were good hunting-grounds; still others were primarily agricultural. In the escarpment the We raised a surplus of tobacco.

There are signs that an unorganized trading system spread into Tonga country from the We and the Twa, though it is difficult to say how widespread the trade was in pre-European days. The Twa on the Kafue traded dried fish into the Mwanacingwala country adjacent to them, and perhaps farther afield, along a system of friendship. The hawker would make a tentative trip during which he attempted to

---

[1] Money plays a large role in Tonga life. Men expect a fee for loaning their bicycles even to friends. A man who owns a wagon or a Scotch cart is paid for hauling the maize of his neighbours to market. Even a chief expects to cash in on his capital equipment. A youngster who helps his older brother expects a gift of cash or clothing.

[2] In pre-European days the Tonga were dependent on the Lozi for hoes and other iron goods. They seem to have paid with ivory and slaves.

establish friendship with some Tonga. In future trips he would go straight to this man, who was expected to buy his entire stock either with cattle or grain. He in turn would distribute it among his fellow Tonga. If the hawker ran into trouble in the country intervening between Twa country and the home of his Tonga friend, his friend was expected to bring pressure to bear upon the offenders. If his stock were stolen, his friend attempted to make the thieves pay for it. When either man died, the contact might be maintained by his heirs. Secondary ties might also grow up around the relationship, and it was common for the surviving partner to send a funeral gift to his dead friend. But it never became a ritually formalized relationship like the blood pacts which the Lozi used in similar circumstances.[1]

Distribution and exchange of goods through a tribute system did not occur. No one was in a position to exact tribute, until the Lozi instituted a tribute of leopard and other choice skins at the end of the nineteenth century. A number of chieftaincies still forward this tribute occasionally, though the Tonga say that they received nothing in return for it save immunity from raids. Beer and new grain taken to ritual leaders were immediately consumed on the spot by those attending the ritual.[2]

### Cattle camps

Another possibility for large-scale social cohesion to develop around subsistence requirements arose with the need for dry-season pasture to which the cattle could be driven. Most of the country suffered from water famines during at least three or four months of the year. The difficulty was met by building kraals in areas with perennial water, and when local supplies failed the cattle were driven to the alternative pastures. This system is still in force in the west, in Simuyobe, Chongo, and Mwanacingwala chieftaincies; elsewhere it seems to have died out with the development of Government dams and wells.[3]

---

[1] Traces of the system still remain, but on the whole the Twa find it more profitable to sell directly to middlemen who either ship fish to urban centres or hawk in the reserves.

[2] Some informants say that when an elephant was killed one tusk was given to the local leader; the other belonged to the hunter. Others maintain that the hunter presented one to his father's matrilineal group and kept one for his own group. Informants from the same area give contradictory information and therefore the discrepancy cannot be due to local variations.

[3] Cf. *Tonga Report*, p. 117. During much of the nineteenth century the custom

The Mwanacingwala people drive their cattle to the Kafue, into the country of the Twa. Young men and older boys in charge of the herds build a kraal somewhere along the Kafue margin. The owner of the cattle makes an arrangement with the headman of the nearest Twa village by which he establishes his claim to the site and the right to return to it year after year. He pays the Twa neighbour only a few sticks of tobacco. The Twa is then expected to tell all later comers that this site is reserved. It is not a yearly payment, but is made only once at the beginning of the arrangement. Any man who owns cattle may start such a dry-season kraal (*lutanga*). Later on his friends or relatives may ask to send their cattle with his. They make no additional arrangement with the Twa neighbour, for they are regarded as guests of the Tonga kraal owner. They apparently pay nothing to him, and there is no obligation on them to send their cattle to the same kraal year after year. Men who live in the same village may send their cattle to different kraals. While the cattle are on the Kafue margins most of the people remain behind in their villages. The men and boys take turns at the cattle camp, and occasionally parties of children or of women and girls will visit the camp to get milk. The herdsmen also bring home calabashes of sour milk when they are relieved of their duties by fresh contingents from home, and surplus milk is traded to the nearest Twa villages for meal or dried or fresh fish.

Important as this movement is, it has given rise to no large-scale organization to safeguard the herds at the camp or during their passage to them. Some of the Tonga have to drive their cattle many miles and send them trampling through the country surrounding intervening villages. In the Mwanacingwala chieftaincy the cattle of Munenga district are driven through the country of Chikaloma twice a year on their way to and from the Kafue. No payment is made to the Chikaloma people for this passage. Strangely enough, though formerly there was much bad blood between the two districts which at times exploded into pitched battles, neither side appears to have considered the possibility of this interfering with the yearly cattle drives. The same type of system was found in other parts of Tonga territory. In the foothills of the Escarpment country villages sent their cattle to sites on small rivers farther west or north, with apparently no complaints of trespass from those who lived either in the intervening areas or along the margins of the rivers.

must have been in abeyance over a large part of the country if early reports that the raiders had denuded the country of its herds are to be credited.

I

*Summary*

The technology of the Tonga in pre-European days and even at the present time is simple and on the whole unspecialized. It does lead to a small-scale exchange of goods within the community, but this has not found a reflection in the development of economic institutions which would regulate the exchanges within the group or over large distances. Instead it remains very largely an individual matter, aided only by the device of 'friendship'. Much the same is true of co-operation in subsistence activities. Work-parties may be organized for hoeing or building, and may include people from several villages; fishing and hunting drives occasionally involve some hundreds of people drawn from an even larger community. But devices for organizing and directing such large-scale parties are embryonic. Even the need to move cattle long distances to dry-season camps has not resulted in permanent alliances involving any large group of people.

The Tonga then, even in pre-European days, had at least occasional opportunities and needs for coming into contact with people who did not belong to his immediate village or his immediate neighbourhood, or even to his immediate kin group. Yet these opportunities and needs did not lead to any developed form of political or social organization which could regulate the contacts and safeguard those who took part in them.

## III. THE VILLAGE

*Description*

The Tonga live in villages, which only in post-European days have been placed within a larger political organization. Previously, and in some measure today, each village was an independent unit, recognizing the power of no superior political authority.

In parts of the country each village is separated from its neighbours by tracts of bush or field. Elsewhere the villages follow in a continuous stream across the country-side, often with huts of one village intermingled with those of the next. In the east, towards the Escarpment country, and in the north-west along the lower Magoye, fairly compact villages may be found, with the huts arranged in a long, slightly curving line or in two rows, or crowded in little clusters along a slope, though many are composed of widely dispersed hamlets or clusters of huts. Elsewhere there may be a central core to the village, consisting of from perhaps ten to a dozen dwelling-huts, but most people tend to build in little clusters of three or four huts, each separated from the next cluster by 50 yards or more. Occasionally some man builds by himself, but even then he chooses a site from which he can catch a glimpse of a neighbouring roof.[1]

A Government rule that no village may consist of less than ten tax-payers—i.e. ten able-bodied men—fixes the minimum size beneath which a village may not fall without risk of an order from Government to unite itself with a neighbour.[2] Most villages, however, are rather larger, with an average of twenty taxpayers, and a total population in the vicinity of a hundred individuals—men, women, and children.[3] These live in some thirty huts, none of which should be farther than one-half mile from the headman's hut. Many villages, including very small ones, have a greater radius. Government still attempts to check the scattering of the population, and if men are found building too far from their headman they are ordered to move back within the legal range. There are no real towns. In 1945 the largest village reported seems to have contained only about 500 inhabitants.

As far as physical features are concerned, a village consists of a number of huts, usually scattered in little groups and connected by a network of paths. In addition there are associated granaries and storage platforms, pigeon crofts, cattle kraals, and perhaps small pens for goats or pigs, though these are usually penned in abandoned huts if the people bother to pen them at all. Around some of the hut-clusters low hedges of euphorbia or other quick-growing plants roughly mark the limits of the dooryard kept clear of intruding grass or weeds by constant use and occasional sweeping. Few villages have any public buildings of any kind, and those which do exist have been built to meet modern needs. The villages of the chiefs have courts; many villages have a school or a church on their outskirts; a few have tea-shops or trading-stores owned by Africans. Very occasionally a village will have a central shelter where visitors may rest and where the men of the village may sit and talk. More commonly there is nothing of this

[1] Informants in some areas say that villages were formerly built in a circular shape with a cattle byre in the centre and a surrounding stockade as a precaution against wild beasts. The hut or huts of the unmarried boys were at the entrance to the village, while the hut or huts of the headman were at the far end of the circle, opposite the entrance. Today such an ordered arrangement has long since vanished.

[2] Formally altered in 1946, but still observed in practice.

[3] See *Tonga Report*, pp. 37 ff., for a discussion of the size of villages. The figures in the report are based on an analysis of the tax registers, checked by some village censuses.

nature, and those who come that way seek out some friend or find accommodation with the headman. The huts of the latter, however, have no distinguishing marks, nor are they likely to be larger or in better state than the dwellings of other members of the village.

## Composition

The population of a village consists of a varying number of people who owe allegiance to a headman recognized by themselves and accepted by Government as their leader. It is not a collection of unilineally-related people, nor do the clusters of huts within a village necessarily reflect divisions along the lines of kinship structure.[1] The families, and individuals, who comprise the village can trace their relationship to each other and to the headman in a variety of ways. Occasionally strangers who can claim no ties of kinship whatsoever are settled in the village. After all, according to Tonga rules, a man has the right to settle where he will and to change his residence as often as the spirit moves him—which may be as often as he quarrels with his neighbours or decides that the soil is more fertile some miles away. Usually he prefers to settle near someone to whom he or his wife can trace some tie of relationship, though this may be so faint that no one knows much more than that it exists, but he is not limited to any one set of relatives. On the other hand, while the Tonga are a matrilineal people, it is most likely that a man will take his wife to live with his relatives and that he will live with his father's people. If there is any regularity, then, in Tonga residence, it is likely to be a patrilocal one.[2]

The only restriction on a man's movements is the right of the headman to refuse to accept a new-comer—which he is not likely to do unless the man has a bad reputation from his previous home. Today the chiefs involved in the move must be notified also. Some headmen, seeking to build up big villages, attract new-comers by giving them food

[1] See *Tonga Report*, pp. 34 ff. and 42 ff.

[2] The following table shows the relationship to headman of the adult population of one village.

|                                   | Males | %    | Females | %    |
|-----------------------------------|-------|------|---------|------|
| Matrilineal tie                   | 5     | 17·8 | 6       | 17·6 |
| Patrilineal tie                   | 12    | 42·8 | 4       | 11·8 |
| Both patrilineal and matrilineal  | 2     | 7·1  | 3       | 8·8  |
| Other, including in-law           | 9     | 32·2 | 21      | 61·8 |
| Total                             | 28    | 100  | 34      | 100  |

PLATE V

1. Huts of a village are spread out in the bush

2. Feeding chickens, which are now an important source of money

TONGA

PLATE VI

4. Woman making basket

3. Woman making bark-rope

TONGA

to carry them through to the next harvest or by aiding them with equipment; others are beginning to worry about the growing shortage of land and the problem of finding fields for new-comers and no longer welcome the increase of their villages. As land shortages increase and become more general throughout the country, population mobility may well decrease and the internal organization of the village along kinship lines become more stable. At the present time, though the Tonga are organized in matrilineal clans and smaller matrilineal kin groups, villages rarely have even half their adult population of either sex belonging to a single matrilineal line. Usually, however, the matrilineal group of the headman contains more adult representatives than does any other one matrilineal group represented in the village.

### Role of the Village

The role of the village is difficult to understand. Today it represents an administrative unit, but it is possible that the small clusters which exist within it are more representative of the village of pre-European days. The word *munzi* seems to refer indifferently to the administrative village of today, to the clusters within it, or even to the dwellings of a single family, but the cluster may also be termed *katungu* or *matungu*. Clusters rarely contain as many as ten taxpayers, and thus usually cannot gain recognition by the Administration as a village.[1]

A cluster may be composed of the dwellings of one family group, which usually consists of a man and his wife or wives and their dependent children as well as sons or daughters who are newly married and have not yet set up their own households. To this group may also be attached older men and women, temporarily unmarried, who have come with their children to live with relatives. Some clusters, however, may include two or more such groups connected by a varied pattern of kinship ties.[2] The cluster is not a permanent arrangement.

[1] Of thirteen villages studied: one was compact and not built on the cluster principle; ten contained no cluster with as many as ten taxpayers; in one the cluster of the headman himself was the only one that could meet the taxpayer rule; and in one village where the headman's own cluster was small, another cluster existed which contained more than the requisite number of men. This cluster, however, was headed by the headman's older brother, so old that he had long before declined the responsibilities of headmanship and had passed the job on to his brother.

[2] Three typical clusters were composed as follows: (1) A man, his wife, and unmarried children; two married sons, their wives, and children. (2) A man, his wife, and unmarried children; his wife's mother, an old widow; his wife's brother, and wife, and children; his sister, her husband, and children. (3) A man, his wife and children; his wife's brother married to his classificatory sister, and their children.

On the whole, huts rarely last more than five or six years, and they may be abandoned at an earlier date. New huts may be built a few feet from the old sites, or they may be shifted 50 yards or more away, or perhaps half a mile or so from the old location. Such moves are constantly going on within the village. When the move is made, members of the cluster may stay together or a split may occur. Some people remain behind while others go off to build a new cluster by themselves or join with other friends. All may move, but in opposite directions. In the split two families will usually separate, but affiliated members may decide to join the other family or to move off to join other relatives. The hut sites are regarded as the property of the former occupants who now have the right to cultivate the patch of ground. But it is quite likely that the people will not return to build their huts on the same spot again, and that if new huts do rise there they will belong to other people.

In the nineteenth century villages were usually small. Livingstone, in 1855, found the Tonga living in scattered hamlets.[1] In 1888 Selous entered a village and was told that its headman was at the next village, which turned out to be only about a hundred yards away.[2] In 1903 villages were still very small, apparently tiny hamlets of two and three huts. According to one traveller of that date it was common to find three or four such hamlets in close proximity, then another hamlet about a mile away, and after that you might walk half a day before seeing another hut.[3] It is entirely possible, of course, that the travellers overlooked the existence of a larger village unit which included these hamlets. But village histories indicate that many present-day villages were originally tiny hamlets with only one or two adult males. A not unusual history is that of Shakaobile village, now located in the western part of Monze chieftaincy. It was founded by a man who escaped from his village at night under threats of violence. With him he took his wives and his sister's son, Shakaobile I. The tiny group fled to the Ila border, only to be driven out by a Lozi raid. They moved back into Tonga country, near the present site of the village. Here they settled near another village, but apparently regarded themselves as an independent unit though their village consisted of but the two men, their wives, and children. Soon the fugitive died, and his place was

[1] Livingstone, *Missionary Travels*, p. 554.

[2] Selous, *Travels and Adventures*, p. 216.

[3] F. J., 'A Visit to Monze Mission', p. 60; Prestage, 'From Bulawayo to the Victoria Falls and Beyond', p. 268.

taken by Shakaobile. At this point the Europeans came and began to develop the administration of the country. When officials came through registering the villages Shakaobile reported himself as a village headman, and was so recognized by Government. His village remained a tiny affair, smaller than many modern clusters. His uncle's children had moved away, but he had his own children growing up and also succeeded in attracting his own sister's son to his village. The latter, however, moved away before Shakaobile I died. Again the village lost population, for one of his wives moved away with her children. The other wife remained, and her son inherited the headmanship as Shakaobile II. Today the village still exists and consists of Shakaobile II, his wives, and one tax-paying son, two sisters of the headman with their husbands and three married sons. A son of a dead sister also lives in the village.[1] In recent years an unrelated man with his wives and a married stepson have come to live in the village, but they have their own cluster, as, indeed, do two of the headman's sisters' sons. The village has thus the bare minimum of taxpayers. At one point Shakaobile was ordered by Government to amalgamate his village with two small neighbouring villages since it was too small to receive official recognition, but as soon as it recruited sufficient members it again established its independence.

It is thus possible that many of the modern villages represent a Government-imposed alliance of independent local groups whose allegiance is to some leader within the cluster and not to the official headman.

Some villages, even those built on the cluster principle, seem to represent more than this. Tonga with whom I have discussed the point insist that all the people of the village, whether or not they live in separate clusters, have a particular relationship to the headman.[2] They represent his *lutundu*, which may perhaps best be translated as 'his village'. Only the headman may be said to have *lutundu*; a man who has a large number of dependants and builds with them in a separate cluster does not have a *lutundu*. He and his people belong to that of the headman. The various *matundu* are specified by the names of their headmen, and on certain occasions they must be dealt with as such groups. At funerals people of a village may go in a body to perform the mourning rite together. Even when they drift in one by one, at the time when the funeral feast is served, they are called to sit together as a village. Moreover, when beasts are killed for the mourning the

---

[1] Other siblings of the headman have moved away to marry or to join other relatives.   [2] This is the opinion in the Escarpment country.

meat is divided and portions of it supplied to the people to take to their homes if they do not wish to cook it on the spot. The division is made by villages, rather than by clusters or by individuals. At beer-drinks where large numbers are gathered the same arrangement is used. The hosts commonly serve the people by calling them to sit according to their village affiliations. Then the name of the headman is called and he sends a young man from his village to bring the pot assigned to his people and to divide it among them. This, however, may be a new custom, for some informants say that they formerly drank in age-groups and that only within the last thirty years did they decide to change when they found that the men from different villages who shared a common pot as an age-group fought too heartily over the division of the beer.

It is thus the position of the headman which apparently establishes the identity of the village and differentiates it from other groups of like nature.

There are numerous instances of villages having been founded by women who were then headmen, even in the immediate past. Today most, if not all, headmen are men. Some achieve this status by per-suading a sufficient number of followers to join with them in creating a new village. In some cases this means only that an existing cluster is registered formally with Government as a village under the name of the new headman. More commonly the headman inherits his position. He may be appointed during the lifetime of his predecessor, when the latter grows old and feels himself no longer willing or able to cope with the demands of Government. In other cases he is chosen on the death of his predecessor. An attempt will usually be made to find a suitable successor within the matrilineal group of the former headman, but the choice is not limited by any rules of seniority. The people of the village will try to find a man who will be able to look after them properly. If no suitable man is found within the matrilineal group of the former headman the choice then goes to someone out-side the group. Often a son of the headman will be chosen. I traced the history of the headmanship in seventeen villages from four chief-taincies. Two of the villages had been recently founded and were still under their original headmen. In seven villages the headmanship had remained in the matrilineal line of the original headman. In eight villages it had passed to a different matrilineal line.

The headman is therefore likely to be the real leader of his village, since the village itself has chosen him.

His position is emphasized by the fact that his name is also the name of his village, and his villagers refer to themselves as his people.[1] Officially this name is now permanent. On the death of the headman his successor takes the same name, and the continuity of the village through time is established. This, however, is a new custom brought in by the needs of European administration, and one which is not adopted whole-heartedly even yet by the Tonga. Names of villages whose history can be traced into pre-European days change with each change of headman. The present name is that of the man who first received his appointment from the European administration. This is true despite the fact that the Tonga practise the inheritance of names and the common term for inheritance or succession is *kulya izina*—'to eat the name'. But this does not mean that the heir is thereafter known commonly by the name of the dead man. A good case in point appears in the name of Chona village. The first Chona moved into the Escarpment country about 1840 or 1850 and either founded or inherited a village there. He was able to dominate the surrounding villages and soon controlled a rain cult affecting some miles of Escarpment country. He was succeeded by his sister's son, who died within a short time and was succeeded by one of the family slaves. The slave took this opportunity to escape to his own people, and again it was necessary to choose a leader. The choice went to Namukamba, a sister's son of the second headman. The village became Namukamba village, and the name of Chona fell into abeyance. The Europeans found Namukamba and named him as headman. When he died his brother succeeded and took the name of Namukamba, and the village continued officially to be known by this name as was now the custom. But when chieftaincies were being established the headman put in his claim to recognition as a chief, basing his claims on the importance of the original Chona. He was recognized and told to assume the name of Chona as this was the name which the Administration regarded as appropriate to the office. But today Tonga often refer to the village as Shameja, by the name the present headman and chief used before he succeeded to the headmanship of the village.

The position of the headman is further recognized by the contention that he is the owner of the cattle kraals of his village, whether or not he has had a hand in building them. Today any man who wants to

---

[1] Shakaobile thus gives his name to his village, which is known as *Shakaobile munzi*, and its people are known as *Bana Shakaobile* (Shakaobile's children) or *lutundu lwa Shakaobile*.

expend the labour may build his own kraal. It is not uncommon to find three or more associated with a village, and even a cluster may contain several. The people of the village may place their cattle where they will, and many send part or even all of their cattle to relatives in some other village. Probably in no village do all the people have their cattle in the same kraal, nor will the cattle in the kraal belong only to the people of the village. Nevertheless, the headman is regarded as the owner of the kraal. At least the courts have so far held this view in a long litigation between headman X and his brother-in-law Y who live in the same village. At one period they had their cattle in the same kraal but herded separately. One day Y's herdboy reported that a cow had joined Y's grazing herd. He took it back to the kraal, where it was kept for the owner to claim. No owner appeared. The cow and its increase now belong to X as headman and owner of the kraal. Y claims that he himself built the kraal and that X later began to use it with him. But the courts maintain that X as headman is owner of the kraal and therefore that all the cattle found by his people belong to him.[1]

The position of the headman is thus a recognized status with certain rights and privileges inherent in it. But these are of very limited nature. The headman does not appear to perform any ritual for his village as a whole; he is not entitled to first-fruits or to tribute or to labour from his people. Even his jural rights were formerly only those of any other elder, though today under the influence of the courts his position is strengthened. He has no recognized officials to help him administer his village, though the older men of the village often form an informal council. His authority over his people is largely determined by his personal qualities, and not by a norm of headmanship. Today with the increased demands made upon the headman to exert authority over the people to make them carry out Administration or Native Authority orders, his position is becoming more and more onerous as he is made to assume new duties not inherent in his status.

The village, then, exists as a real unit, but its role is a restricted one. It is a residence group, a 'social' group. It is not an economic unit. Work-parties are not confined to members of one village, and on most

[1] The Tonga laughed at the suggestion that this right was based on a theoretical ownership of the land by the headman or on any mystical relationship between headman and land which entitled him to claim all lost articles. Their view was that the headman must bear the brunt of the questioning about strayed stock and runs most danger of being accused of stock-theft. Ownership of untraced beasts lapses to him as payment for his difficulties.

occasions a man or woman is expected to work alone or with other members of the immediate family. In a sense a village does not even exist as a territorial unit, though it has a spatial distribution. It is not endowed with landed property, though it has a certain association with the particular area upon which its huts are built. In former days a headman and his people could not prevent a strange village from coming to settle near by unless they resorted to force. A land dispute originating some twenty to thirty years ago was recently heard in one of the Native Authority courts. A stranger started to build his huts and lay out his fields close to those of an existing village which tried unsuccessfully to order him off. The headman of the established village then told the stranger that he might stay there for the time being, but that when he shifted his fields and huts his right to the sites must lapse and he would have no right to return to them. In the course of some years the stranger proceeded to shift his huts and cultivate the old sites. Again the established headman protested, but with no effect. Apparently there was nothing that a village could do if faced with a determined adversary who cared little about good relations with his neighbours.

Ordinarily, however, when a village first moves into a new area it questions the previous inhabitants in the surrounding villages as to which sites are unclaimed. After a site has been decided upon, each man proceeds to build his own huts and to seek for fields which he obtains either by taking unclaimed bush land into cultivation or by begging cleared land from those who have previously settled in the area.[1] Thus, land may be transferred from the original user to someone living in another village, for the right to cultivate the soil is not vested in the residents of a given village. Those who join the village later will obtain their lands in the same way—by begging from those who first came with the village, by begging from those who live in neighbouring villages, or by clearing unclaimed land for themselves. The headman cannot allot land, for he possesses none save that which he has cleared himself; he can merely point out to the new-comer land which has no previous claim upon it, unless he can spare a few acres of his own fields. On the other hand, if a man dislikes his headman or his fellow villagers, he may transfer his allegiance to another village without being forced to shift his huts or to abandon his fields. This, of course, is true only of the areas where villages lie tangled together and the fields of the villagers may lie anywhere within the surrounding and intervening cultivation.

[1] Cf. *Tonga Report*, pp. 92 ff.

The system of land-holding is possible and gives rise to little trouble since land rights are of a very limited character. A man has a right to clear unoccupied land and to cultivate it and to harvest his crops; he may lend or give his cleared land to someone else; if he wishes to do so he may let it lie fallow through a period of years to recover fertility; he has a right to build his huts and other buildings upon it. But here the rights of private ownership end. Other rights to the use of land seem to be vested in all those living in the neighbourhood and not in individuals or in the inhabitants of one village. Pasture, the gathering of wild produce and firewood, the cutting of poles and thatching-grass, the digging of clay for pottery, and even the use of water-holes are open to all, though it is naturally assumed that a man will seek these as close to his dwellings as possible.[1] A man has a legal right to the maize he grows in his field which he can enforce even against his fellow villagers; he has no legal right to honey or wild fruit found in his field which he can invoke even against a stranger from a distant village. The use of rivers and water-holes seems to vest in the neighbourhood and not in a particular village. When wells have been dug they belong to the men who dug them and who keep them in repair. Someone who joins a village does not gain from his residence any right to use the wells, though the owners will usually as a matter of courtesy extend him an invitation to join in the use and upkeep of the wells.[2] Pasturage, including the cropped fields after the harvest, are open to the cattle from all the surrounding villages.

Hence the fact that adjacent fields may be owned by people from a number of different villages does not entangle the people in constant land squabbles, for individual ownership is of a very limited nature, and all residual rights are common neighbourhood property and not village property. This system of land-holding limits the position of the headman of the village, since he has no right over land as a symbol of village unity.[3]

Only to a very minor degree does the village represent a unit of

[1] This traditional system has been changed by new rules made by the Native Authorities.

[2] Wells which have been dug each year for several generations along the dry beds of streams, so that they are traditional watering-places, are for general use.

[3] He does appear to have certain rights to land which has been abandoned as people have moved away to such distant sites that it is no longer possible for them to return to cultivate their fields. Unless they make some disposition of their fields before they leave, the headman may give the land to someone who comes to beg for it. But he is not bound to give it to someone resident in his own village.

collective responsibility. Formerly a headman was not held responsible for the actions of one of his people unless this person belonged to his own matrilineal kin group. However, if a man offended against the taboos associated with the rain shrines or harvest festivals and was unable to pay the fine demanded by the elders of the community, they might order his headman to pay on the grounds that he should have prevented anyone living with him from being so foolish. Murder, theft, or other offences involving people of the same village were dealt with in the same way as when people from several villages were concerned. The people of a village did not feel called upon to defend or help an accused fellow unless he was a relative. To some extent this feeling still persists. In 1946 two unrelated men from Chobana village were visiting in We country where they chanced upon a man to whom one of them owed money. The We decided to do something about the matter and tried to hold them both. The companion announced, 'I'm not related to him. We just live in the same village.' And he cleared off home, leaving the debtor to face the music.

In former days, however, a village might unwillingly be involved in a case which it might well disavow. If a man committed murder, the victim's relatives proceeded to a village which contained some of his matrilineal kin and proceeded to raid it without much regard to the relationship of those whom they caught. This put a double pressure upon the matrilineal group of the murderer, who must now pay not only the original case but also the demands of the matrilineal groups of the captives, who could see no reason why their people should be taken to pay the case of the murderer just because of the accident of co-residence. On the other hand, if two men from a village who belonged to different matrilineal groups joined in a murder, the victim's relatives proceeded against both groups. Today, though self-help is no longer allowed, the murderer's matrilineal group is still expected to pay compensation to the victim's kin; but this is not a matter which directly involves the village of either murderer or victim.

## IV. THE FAMILY

*Composition*

Within the village the basic unit is the family. This consists of a man, his wife or wives, such of their unmarried children as live with them, and other attached individuals or incomplete families.[1] A young

---

[1] It is difficult to get informants even in one village to agree on a name for this unit. Some say that *mukwaashi* has this meaning or may also mean the tiny immediate

couple only gradually establishes its independence. As soon as a man marries he should build a hut for his wife and should provide her with fields and granaries, but for some years they continue to cook and eat with an established family which is said to be rearing (*kulela*) them. The established family may also have attached to it some older person —a widow or widower or a divorced person—who has come with his or her small children to live with relatives. Within the family there may also be young children who are being reared by the family— grandchildren, children of the siblings of one of the spouses, or children of even more distantly related people. A few of the wealthier men have been able to hire workers, usually unmarried, who live closely associated with the family.

Each such family, and often each household within the family— a household being composed of each wife and her own children— has a good deal of independence.[1]

Commonly a man builds the huts of his wives immediately adjacent to each other, and thus the dwellings of the family unit are grouped together, though they are not likely to be separated from the other huts in the same cluster by any barrier or mark. Occasionally a man finds such proximity of wives impractical for reasons of family peace and he builds a hut for one wife some distance away or perhaps even in another village. Each married woman has, or should have, her own hut which is shared with her small children and with her husband. He has no separate hut of his own. Those who have several wives divide their time and their belongings among the wives' huts. Unmarried women who have reached what is regarded as the age of discretion will have their own huts where they live with their young children or with a child borrowed from some relative. A single woman, however, never

family of a young man, his wife, and one child. Still others say that a man only establishes his *mukwaashi* when he moves with his dependants to establish his own cluster and that so long as he lives with another man he has no *mukwaashi*. Still others deny that *mukwaashi* has any such meaning and equate it with the matrilineal group. They, however, are able to give no alternative name for the family as described above, though they suggest that *balelwa*, 'those who are dependent', covers the group. Even the small unit of man, wife, and children has no generally accepted term. The closest approach to it is *Inganda*, which properly means 'house'. When a man is married to several wives and has children from all, informants can suggest no other word for the grouping than *Bana ba maali*, 'children of polygyny'. Torrend, *Bantu Botatwe Dictionary*, p. 199, gives *ciko* as the word for family; *ciinga* or *bana* as the word for household. My informants do not recognize this usage.

[1] My material indicates that only 21 per cent. of the married men have two or more wives, so the large majority of Tonga are monogamous. Cf. *Tonga Report*, p. 159.

builds any distance from other huts; she is always closely attached to a family group. Young unmarried women, even if they have borne a child or two, are not allowed the privilege of a hut of their own, but always live with relatives. This may not be true in the north-west where in at least one village all unmarried girls share a hut. Unmarried boys are much freer. Traditionally each village had its boys' house to which boys moved when they were ten or twelve. They moved out again only when they married or when they were adult and felt that the privacy of a small hut of their own was desirable. The institution still persists in most of the country. It is not associated with any age-grade ceremony or with initiation into a new age status. A boy decides for himself when he wants to enter a boy's house, and without more ado he proceeds to put his decision into effect. In some villages each boy when he nears his late teens will build his own house; more usually, siblings or other relatives will build and share a house, and it is not uncommon to find that all the boys in a cluster—whatever their relationships to each other—will share a hut. Boys of ten or eleven may move in to join the older boys; or they may prefer to sleep in the family hut until they are close to puberty, or they may take their blankets into the kitchen or to a dilapidated hut which the older people have abandoned and there sleep among the clutter of smaller brothers and sisters. The dwelling-huts of one family with its attached dependants may thus resemble a small hamlet.

## Co-operation

To the dwelling-huts are attached a number of other buildings which may be owned by the family as a unit, or by the individual households within the family. There may be kitchens. Often all the wives and other women attached to the family will share a single kitchen, but each wife may demand her own. How far the family represents a consumption unit is a matter of individual preference. Often all the women will cook together, or arrange among themselves to cook in turn. When the food is cooked, the men and boys group themselves around one set of pots, while the women and girls form a separate circle. In other families each wife prefers to cook separately, but the whole family will still assemble to share the meal together with each wife contributing a portion of the food. Still others find such an amicable arrangement beyond them, and each wife cooks for herself and her children and each sends a dish to the husband. The cooking and eating group may thus be narrowed to the individual household within the family. On the other hand, it may be widened to include several families which habitually cook and eat together.

Each family has its own granaries and storage platforms usually placed close to the dwelling-huts. The number and ownership depends upon the arrangements agreed to within the family, an arrangement which also affects the ownership and cultivation of fields.

A man usually provides a field for each wife and usually has a field of his own as well. In this case each one is likely to have a separate storage place. The woman stores her crop in her own granary and uses it to provide food for herself, her children, and her husband. If there is a surplus she may sell and is entitled to keep some of the money, or she may prefer to make it into beer. Her husband must be consulted, but it is not his immediate concern. A woman is under no obligation to share her crop with her co-wives, even though these have had a crop failure and are without sufficient food to last until the next harvest. If she is a 'good woman' she will help, but even then she is not expected to do so constantly. The husband is expected to provide for his unfortunate wife from his own field or by buying food. The husband in turn stores his crop in his own granary, and this he uses to help out any deficiencies in his wife's store, or sells to provide for cash requirements of his family and its dependants—tax, clothing, ploughs, and other agricultural equipment, &c. Before he sells he should consult his first wife and inform his other wives of his intention. Any surplus he may turn into cattle, which belong to him, though he may present cash or a beast to his wife if he cares to do so. In other families the problem of ownership of the crop and granaries does not arise. A man and his wives, though they each have their own fields, will store in one granary and any wife may go to the common stock for food. A family maize granary is common. Each wife, however, is likely to demand her own small granary for storing crops such as ground-nuts. More rarely a man and his wife or wives have but one field and cultivate this together. They will then store in one granary and use the stored food without the question of individual rights arising.

Adult dependants attached to the family also own their own fields and granaries, though I am not clear as to what obligation there is for them to contribute food to the common pot. Single men often prefer to sell their maize immediately after harvest, and thus avoid the necessity for a granary. Single women will almost always have a separate granary as soon as they have their own fields. Unmarried boys and girls are unlikely to own fields; those who do, sell their crop to pay for clothing or other expenses.

Small stock and fowls, although always individually owned, are left free to wander about the cluster. Individual members of a family put their cattle where they like, and often send them to be herded by relatives in some other village even at a distance. If a woman inherits, buys, or receives cattle, she customarily sends them to her relatives to herd so that at her husband's death there may be no confusion as to their ownership. Her husband may send part of his herd to his relatives. Cattle owned by children are usually sent to matrilineal relatives for safe keeping until the child is old enough to look after them. Family dependants are not required to place their beasts in the same kraal as the head of the family. On the other hand, the family and its dependants do co-operate in the use of herds and kraals. The family head may call upon his dependants to help him build the kraal. Small boys act as herdsmen for their fathers or guardians, and when several men from the same cluster use the same kraal either their sons will take turns in the herding duties, or each will herd the beasts of his own father or guardian.

## Stability

Family solidarity is affected by the counter-claims of the matrilineal groups to which its members belong. A marriage does not create a group having joint responsibility and outlawing legal claims against other members of the group. If a woman becomes involved in a case her husband is under no legal obligation to pay her fines or judgements against her, and may tell her to go to her own kin for assistance. This is true even where the husband has brought suit for damages because of his wife's adultery. If the accused can prove his innocence and demonstrate that the woman has accused him falsely, he may then begin a countersuit for false witness. This is a suit against the wife and not her husband, and the husband is praised if he helps her to pay it. A woman is under no necessity to help her husband pay his own damages, and if her husband uses her property she may sue him for restitution. Her sons are likely to join with her against their father in such a suit since they are her heirs and not potential heirs of their father. Equally a woman may sue her husband if he has endangered the lives of her children. In one case heard in a Native Authority Court a man was accused of having obtained medicine to bring him

K

luck. The medicine turned on him and killed two of his children. His wife demanded and received damages.

Men are not held completely responsible for the actions of their small sons and daughters even though the latter live with them, far from matrilineal kinsmen. When two small boys started a bush fire which burned a hut and its contents the court ordered the fathers to pay for the loss involved. The fathers sought and obtained permission to go to the matrilineal kinsmen of their sons and ask them to pay the damages.

The family, despite its importance, is moreover an unstable unit, as are all local units among the Tonga. It constantly loses and gains members. Suddenly it may be disrupted and fall to pieces with divorce or with the death of one of the spouses. At the same time new families are constantly in formation, a process which can only occur in conjunction with the dismemberment of some established family. For though a man and his wife remain together, through the years their children break away to form independent family groups of the same status as the parental family. This is done even during the lifetime of the parents, for with the payment of the final instalment of bridewealth a couple establishes itself as a separate family with a right to manage its own affairs and to appeal directly to the ancestors. Before this, however, the family ranks may be broken. Sons, as they mature, may go off to join maternal relatives, to relatives of their father, or perhaps to work and settle among strangers. If they remain with their parents, still they marry and after a few years of tutelage establish themselves as independent family heads within the circle of their own dependants. At any time they may move from their father's cluster. Usually daughters as they marry move away with their husbands; occasionally they settle matrilocally, but again it is but a few years before the young couple establishes itself as an independent entity. In the meantime the children of the siblings of the husband and wife may come to join the family for a few years and then to break away in the same manner as the children.

Eventually there may be a cluster of independent families under the nominal leadership of the original family head, but his authority is of a limited nature. His advice should be asked until he is so far in his dotage that his advice is useless, but his power to enforce decisions is limited by his lack of power to reward or punish, for the new families which have sprung up about him have their own fields, their own homesteads, and their own property which lies in their control and not in the control of the older man. If they have moved to another cluster or a different village, they are still less likely to accept his orders or recommendations, nor will they now be likely to assist him in any way.

Before this stage is reached the family may be disrupted by death. If a woman dies her family is under no obligation to replace her with a kinswoman, and it is exceptional for them to do so. Her children are allowed to decide whether or not they will stay with their father. If it is the husband who dies, an effort is made to prolong the life of the family, and the general heir chosen from among his matrilineal kin should assume his name and his position within the family, marrying his widows and fathering his children. Where this happens the family continues as before, though the widows are now the wives of the heir and henceforth children born to them are his legally as well as physically and not children of the dead man. But often the matrilineal kin prefer to name several men to take the widows, or the widows themselves may choose to marry different men from among their dead husband's kin. In this case, or even when there is but one general heir, the widows and children go off to join the new husbands who may live far from the original home, and the affiliated members of the family usually break away to join other relatives. A widow, however, may refuse to remarry into her husband's family and she will rejoin her own relatives until she marries again. Her children may accompany her, or they may stay with their paternal relatives. A woman who is past the child-bearing age when her husband dies frequently refuses to marry again and will either stay with her children or go off to live as an affiliated member in the family of some relative, even though this means moving to a strange and distant place. No matter what the decision, a person's personal belongings, including cattle, are inherited by his or her own kin, and not by the spouse. Where no substitute spouse is provided, the one who has married into the group usually leaves, and thus the land is left for any relatives of the dead who may live in the vicinity, though if the widow is old she may be allowed to retain her fields. Most of the stores of food are consumed during the mourning period, and there is thus no question of division. If something remains, the survivor may sell and keep the money, or remove some of the stores with him when he leaves or divide this with the kin of the dead spouse.

In case of divorce,[1] the person who has married into the village departs, taking the stores from his or her granary. When the divorce has

[1] Divorce is fairly frequent, but the Tonga marriage is more stable than the Yao.

been amicable the couple may make a division, or sell the lot and divide the money. Hut and lands are abandoned to the person who remains in the village. The children themselves decide where they will go,[1] and the family group breaks up. A woman who is past child-bearing may be persuaded by her children to leave her husband. She may then continue to live in the same village, perhaps in the same cluster, but the family unit has ceased to exist. Her husband is no longer expected to help her build her hut or to till her field. He is not expected to provide her with clothing or meet her other needs. Instead, she now turns to her children for help. She in turn no longer expects to cook for her husband or to work in his fields.

## V. CLAN AND MATRILINEAL GROUP

Membership in a local unit to the Tonga is largely a matter of free choice. Membership in clan and matrilineal group, on the other hand, is inherited through the mother, and cannot be changed except under exceptional circumstances which no longer occur. In former days when a person was enslaved, his head was shaved and at the same time he was given one of the names current within his owner's matrilineal group as a symbol of his incorporation into a new group. Henceforth he was a member of this matrilineal group and therefore automatically of his owner's clan. A woman slave passed this affiliation on to her descendants, who within a generation or so were no longer distinguished from other members. Nevertheless, for several generations the rules of exogamy which normally prohibited intermarriage within the clan and therefore, of course, within the matrilineal group, were suspended. A man might marry his woman slave though she now bore his clan name, or a member of the group might marry the child of such a woman though their clan and matrilineal group affiliation would now be the same and such a marriage would normally rank as incest.

The matrilineal group consists of people who share a fiction of

---

[1] Children have the right to decide, and their decision must be respected whether or not bride-wealth has been returned. Some men who had kept their children after divorce said they had not asked for the return of their bride-wealth because they had their children. Yet the Tonga maintain that a man cannot hold his children to him by leaving his bride-wealth with the relatives of the wife, and that the matrilineal relatives cannot regain possession of the child by returning the bride-wealth. The child must decide for itself and may at any time change its mind. It would consider itself treated as a slave if forced to stay where it did not wish, and would run away. Usually children accompany their mother.

PLATE VII

5. A deserted hut, where relatives are preparing final funeral beer for the dead

6. 'Spirit gate', showing two doors through which the ancestors of the matrilineal group and of the father's matrilineal group enter owner's homestead

TONGA

PLATE VIII

7. Praying for rain in front of the house of the 'owner of the country'

8. Asking for rain at one of the rain-shrines

TONGA

common descent through matrilineal links, though actual genealogical links may not be known and though some of its members may be known to be affiliated to the group through a slave status. The clan is a much broader group, including all those people who bear a common clan name. Ultimately, people assume, all those who bear this name have descended from one woman, whom they neither know of nor care about. The matrilineal group is distinct from the clan, though it is contained within it. The Tonga do not have a lineage system of a segmentary type in which minimal groups of unilineal kin combine into larger groups in contrast to other groups of like nature which in turn combine until a maximal lineage or clan is formed as a final capstone to the whole structure. Instead, each matrilineal group is an entity in itself which apparently recognizes all other matrilineal groups in the same clan as being of the same order as itself. Thus the clan lacks internal structure of the lineage type, and in turn the clans are not opposed to each other to form the framework of a political organization.

## The Clan

The clan is known as *mukowa*, a word which also seems to have the meaning of species, kind, type.[1] Clans as such have no corporate status. There are never occasions when all members of a given clan meet or join in some activity which would give evidence of their corporate nature. A clan owns no property; it controls no territory; it has no recognized leaders; it has no ritual centres or special ritual occasions. In the scanty literature on the Tonga we do find references to clan shrines or to clan areas, but this seems to be due to a confusion, only too easy, between the clan and the matrilineal group.[2] No one clan seems to have had any particular prestige higher or different from that of the rest, though informants are prone to stress that their own clans provided the leadership of the Tonga. The ritual leaders of the rain cults, who were the most important men in pre-European days, were drawn from many clans.

At the present time no peculiarities of dress or practice serve to distinguish one clan from another. Each clan has one or more animals said to be associated with it, but any totemic element which may have existed has disappeared. No one avoids or honours his clan animal. Some people say that formerly it was taboo to eat one's clan animal,

---

[1] Cf. Casset, 'Some Batonga Customs', p. 207.  [2] Cf. *Tonga Report*, p. 94.

but today this does not affect even the oldest people. Each clan does have special praise-names which are used by its members at funerals or at puberty rites. The ordinary name of the clan is used as a polite form of address, though a person may also be addressed by the clan name of his father or of either grandfather, or by the clan name of the father of the ancestral spirit after whom he is named.

Today clans are dispersed rather than local groups; most of them occur throughout Tonga country and also among neighbouring peoples of the same linguistic group. Twelve are common to most of the area; two seem largely confined to the western chieftaincies.[1] On the north and north-west the whole system changes. Only a few of the customary clans are found, and the number of clans is swelled by new clans which appear to be importations from Lenje, Sala, and Ila. Thus, in a few hours in Sianjalika I recorded a list of seventeen clans known locally, whereas five months at Cona brought to light only the customary twelve. But though these clan names are widely spread, it is possible that they do not refer to the same groupings.

Many clans have two or three names, any one of which may be used quite indiscriminately by the speaker. Again all clans have an association with some plant, creature, or natural phenomenon. Usually a clan has more than one. But these associations are not invariable, nor do the names always form the same cluster. In the east, for example, the Elephant clan is known indifferently as Batenda, Baungu, or Bakuli. On the western borders appear Baungu, who maintain that they are not Batenda or Bakuli and that they are associated with lechwe rather than elephant. The Pigeon clan of the east also has three names: Bafumu, Baganda, and Boono. This clan has another creature, frog, associated with it. In the west the Boono claim to be distinct from Bafumu and say their association is with cattle. In the east the baboon is assigned to the Balongo clan; on the north it is Bankombwe; and the Balongo are associated with buffalo; and elsewhere the baboon is associated with still a third clan. In view of this confusion it is amazing that

---

[1] These fourteen clans are listed below. The two found to the west are starred:

1. Bahyamba—hyena, rhinoceros, pig.
2. Batenda—elephant.
3. Baleya—goat, tortoise, vulture.
4. Bansaka—leopard, bee.
5. Bakonka—eland, jackal.
6. Bafumu—pigeon, hippopotamus.
7. Bansange—rabbit.
8. Bayuni—bird.
9. Bacindu—lion.
10. Beetwa—crocodile.
11. Bantanga—vulture.
12. Balongo—baboon.
*13. Banchanga—bush-baby.
*14. Bankombwe— ?

Only the commonest clan name and some of commonest animal associates are listed.

the Tonga seem adept at relating themselves to some clan no matter where they go and can fit strangers from other tribes into their clan system. I am not clear as yet whether they do this on the basis of the animal association or on the basis of the name, assuming that the two are not in agreement with the local system.

It is therefore difficult to estimate the average size of a clan, and clans probably vary considerably. Leaving aside the particular problems raised by the variation in name clusters and animal associates, however, it is probable that four or five clans contain about 8,000 members, two or three more between 4,000 and 5,000, and that the rest fall well below this figure. This estimate is based on a sample of 600 adult men and women from three chieftaincies. The Eland clan (Bakonka) found in all three areas had 94 members; Balongo, which also appeared in all three areas, was represented by only 10 individuals; the smallest clan seems to be the Bankombwe, which appeared in only one area and was represented by only 9 individuals.

Clan representation is widely but unevenly spread. Thus, in no village have I recorded fewer than six clans, and most villages include representatives from eight to ten clans. In Chona village the 61 adults belong to 10 different clans, the 26 men to 8 clans. At Sintuba village the 30 adults belong to 9 clans, the 13 men to 5 clans. This shows something of the clan dispersal and indicates that the clan itself is unlikely to form a stable local group. On the other hand, there is a slight tendency for a given clan to dominate numerically in particular areas. In each of the three different neighbourhoods where I have worked this tendency has appeared. In Chona neighbourhood the Eland clan contains slightly over 34 per cent. of all men in the neighbourhood, the next largest clan only about 14 per cent. In Mujika the Rabbit clan contained 21 per cent. of the men, the next largest clan 18 per cent. At Katimba the Goat clan predominated. In all three neighbourhoods, however, the clan affiliation of the women is more evenly spread than that of the men. This is to be expected since the presence of the women in a neighbourhood is likely to be due to marriage ties and not to ties of birth. Unless their children seek their matrilineal kin the clan composition of the village and neighbourhood must change from generation to generation and should eventually even out. Today there is no strong feeling for rejoining matrilineal kin. Therefore, clumping or clustering of clans in a given area at the present time is fortuitous and gives an appearance of stability which may well vanish within a few years.

In former days clans may have had some ritual or political function.[1] They enjoined hospitality for fellow clansmen and probably gave individuals some protection in the days before European administration outlawed the feud and the practice of enslaving strangers for slight offences, though there appear to have been no supernatural sanctions against despoiling a fellow clansman from a distant area. Today clans seem important chiefly for the regulation of marriage, and this seems to have been the case for the past fifty years or more. The founder of the first Catholic mission says that even at the beginning of the century the Tonga if asked about the origin and function of their clans swore, 'God gave them to us so that we could marry properly.'[2] This is still the Tonga attitude: the clans have been here from the beginning; their existence allows people to marry correctly. If this is the role of the clan, it is still performing it efficiently despite the changes in other parts of Tonga culture. A few cases of intraclan marriage do occur, but it is probable that most or all of these involve a slave affiliation to the clan. Even young people who have received a maximum of education for this group seem committed to clan exogamy. As a corollary, all Tonga know their clan affiliation. Even children of eight and nine can produce the information.

Indeed, the Tonga cannot conceive of a social system which lacks the clan. They are firmly convinced that the Europeans have clans and perversely conceal the fact from the Africans. Old men say they spent much time and thought on the matter when they worked in European centres and still were unable to discover just how the European clans operated or what they were. Even young people are convinced of the importance of the clan. A schoolboy assured me, 'The clan is the most important thing we Africans have.'

Yet today it lacks apparent function to the outside observer. I think we must look for its real value to the Tonga in two directions. It is partially confused with the matrilineal group which has a very real existence and a real role, and it is difficult to be sure that when an informant is stressing the importance of the clan that he is not thinking instead of the matrilineal group. Again, the clan—not as a body of people but as an institution—is the most permanent element in Tonga social organization. Villages and neighbourhoods are born, change completely their patterns of internal relationships, move freely through Tonga country, and vanish again. The matrilineal group itself

---

[1] Even today there is a joking relationship between certain clans.
[2] Personal communication from Father J. Moreau, S.J., Chikuni Mission.

has very little time-depth and gives the individual little reason to assume that he has a permanent group which will support him and give him a constant point of reference by which he can relate himself to the rest of society. Clan affiliation is a constant which survives changes of residence and the death of one's kin. By stressing the claim to clan hospitality a man can always reintroduce himself into some social group. Under special circumstances he may even be incorporated into a new matrilineal group; for the concept of relationship, vague and remote, persists, as evidenced by the fact that kinship terms are extended to include all clan members.

## The Matrilineal Group

The matrilineal group is composed of those people who have the right to inherit from each other, to choose one from among themselves to replace a dead member of their group by taking his name (*kulya izina*) and his spirit (*kwangwa muzimu*). It is the matrilineal group, and not the clan, which acts in inheritance, which provides and shares bride-wealth, which accepts responsibility for its members. The men of the group have a joint right to inherit each other's widows. If a widow remarries anyone in the group, no additional bride-wealth will be paid; if she marries outside the group, the bride-wealth must be returned. The children of the men stand in a special relation to the group as a whole, and are children of the entire group and not of just one man. Formerly, if a man was unable through illness to perform his duties as a husband, one of his matrilineal group might be substituted for him. That these arrangements may still be made is evident from a divorce case heard in a Native Authority court. A woman demanded a divorce on the grounds that her husband had leprosy, and the court granted the divorce only after asking the husband if he had no brother he could give to his wife to father children for her. On the other hand, abduction of wives or adultery is outlawed within the group. It is wrong, but an acknowledged practice, to run off with another man's wife; it is immoral but known to run off with the wife of a member of your group. According to Tonga thought, since you may inherit this woman after her husband's death, to take her while he is alive is to anticipate his death and thus to symbolize your wish for it. Equally, no man may be married to two women of the same matrilineal group simultaneously, though he may be married to two or more women of the same clan.[1]

[1] Informants also claim that two men from the same matrilineal group should not

The members of a matrilineal group share a common ancestral cult, since all may call upon the same spirits which are concerned with all members of the group. The matrilineal group is also the unit of joint responsibility, but this does not mean that retaliation is outlawed within the group. Witchcraft charges are frequently brought within the group; since those within the group profit most from an individual's death they are considered logical suspects. The accused witch may then be killed by his matrilineal kin without compensation. Formerly theft was not regarded as possible between matrilineal kinsmen. A man had the right to take and use the property of these kin, though someone who impoverished the group too greatly would be left in the lurch eventually. But in cases of adultery or assault, the offender was made to pay compensation to the injured person. No compensation was paid for murder within the group, since the same people would have to collect the fine and then receive it again.

To the outside world, however, the matrilineal group represented a single unit, and an actual offender was no more guilty than the whole of his group. Even at the present time a man may be haled into court to pay for an absent kinsman's debts, though today the Tonga feel that the group has only a limited liability for its members. One man was brought to court twice on different claims against his brother who had gone off as a labour migrant after borrowing money. On the first appearance the court forced him to pay the debt, on the grounds that he was responsible for his brother. On the second occasion the court again decided that he must pay and pleaded with him at length to do so, saying that this was the last time they would give such a decision and if a third borrower should appear they would refuse to press the claim against him. The defendant refused to accept the court's judgement on the grounds that he had paid once and that was enough; he finally won his point and was held to be no longer responsible in the matter. In many courts today when a man is unable to pay his fine or a claim immediately he is detained in the chief's village while some friend or kinsman is sent to collect the money from his matrilineal group.

In former days, when the feud was the ultimate sanction for enforcing public order, responsibility went still further. If a man from group A stole goods or killed a man from group B his people were held responsible. If they did not pay immediately, men of B would go to some village where people of A were known to live and would wait

marry two women who belong to the same matrilineal group. I have recorded cases where they have done so.

at the water-hole until women from the village appeared. The women would be seized, and one or two sent back to announce why the raid had been made. It then behoved A to mobilize its wealth with great speed and pay off the claim with no more ado before the women had their heads shaved and were sold as slaves. If this happened their troubles had but begun, for within a village there were women from many different matrilineal groups and it was improbable that only those of A had been captured. If women from C, D, and E had been taken, their kin took the not unreasonable view that A had used their daughters to pay off a case in which they were not concerned, and C, D, and E in turn would capture women to hold as hostages for the return of their daughters or to sell as slaves if these were not returned. And so from one case the whole group might be impoverished or even annihilated. If the women belonging to the group had been seized and could not be redeemed or if it had to pay its own women to redeem those from other matrilineal groups who had become involved, it might well vanish; for upon the women depended the continued existence of the group, and these had now taken on their owners' affiliations and their children would go to swell those groups.

The matrilineal group may be disrupted and members secede to found a new group. There is an obligation for those within the group to visit each other, especially in cases of illness. Those who fail to visit at such a time may be driven away when they come to attend the mourning with the angry words that they have already forgotten their membership within the group. The cleavage may become permanent, and those disowned by the group will no longer be permitted to inherit from it or to share in distributions of bride-wealth. In other ways those who feel themselves aggrieved may show their intentions of cutting themselves adrift from their group. If a woman feels neglected by her kin she will demand that they hand over to her the cattle they received from her bride-wealth. Or a man may demand the cattle from his mother's bride-wealth. I have heard two such cases in the courts. Though neither came to a decision—and later the counsellors said that the claimants had no legal claim under Tonga custom —they were regarded as most serious matters involving the death of the matrilineal group itself. The court pointed out that people who behaved in this way would lose their matrilineal group; they would be afraid to visit and to call upon each other for help; they would be unable to teach their children that these were kinsmen to whom they had the right to appeal; and the group would disintegrate.

The matrilineal group has thus a specific role in contrast to the much more diffuse role of the clan. But this does not make it easy to distinguish the two groups in actual practice. This is due partly to a linguistic confusion between the two concepts. The word for clan, *mukowa*, is also used for the matrilineal group. In the cases cited above, for example, the refrain was, 'If you act like this, you will lose your *mukowa*.' People composing the matrilineal group are commonly called *Bashimukowa* and *Bakwesu*, but both terms are politely extended to include fellow clansmen. English-speaking informants may qualify their statements if pressed, and refer to the matrilineal group as the 'real *mukowa*', but this is not invariable. Older people in some areas recognize a specific word *citiba* for the matrilineal group. The word literally means a wooden dish or plate, and refers to the dish around which members of the group gather at the funeral of one of its members. This is at least the explanation given by informants.[1]

Moreover, the various matrilineal groups usually have no specific name. If pressed, people may say that their group is called by the name of the woman who founded it, who is usually the grandmother of the oldest member, or that it is called by the name of the man who is regarded as its leader. Some groups seem to have no name at all. In any community, therefore, it takes much time and questioning to discover what the matrilineal groups are and who belongs to any particular one. The genealogical method is not always fruitful since Tonga memory for genealogical details is short and they are not concerned with remembering exactly how they are related to one another. The group therefore lacks internal structure of the lineage type, just as it fails to connect itself to the other matrilineal groups in the same clan through a lineage system. Since you and your siblings do not form a unit with specific rights and duties to each other setting you off from the children of your mother's sister, and since you and they do not form a unit in contrast to the descendants of your grandmother's siblings, there is little point in remembering genealogical details to assign you a position in relation to each other.

Kinship terms emphasize this point of view. A man calls all members of his matrilineal group who are of his generation 'brother' or 'sister'; all who are one generation younger than himself 'sister's child'; all two generations lower than himself 'brother' or 'sister'; all three

---

[1] In practice I have found them willing to extend *citiba* to include the clan. I have recorded a number of words which seem to have much the same meaning: *mukowa*, *cihuwa*, *mukwaashi*, *cikoto*, *cikombo*, *iciinga*, and *citiba*.

generations lower than himself 'sister's child'; and thus on in a continuous extension of the terms. All 'brothers' are debarred from taking the bride-wealth of their 'sisters', but share in the bride-wealth of those whom they call 'sister's child'.

DIAGRAM I

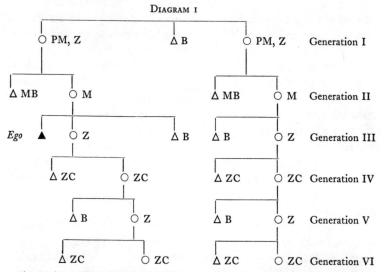

Generations are linked as follows: I, III, V; II, IV, VI. *Ego* may take bride-wealth of women in generations IV and VI, since he calls these women ZC. He is prohibited from taking bride-wealth of women in generations III and V, since he calls these women Z. He should not take bride-wealth of women in any generation above his own. These rules will be disregarded if there are no men of the appropriate generations to take the bride-wealth, but the bride-wealth should then go to a classificatory brother rather than to a full brother.

### Distribution of Bride-wealth

Thus, distribution of bride-wealth is spread widely throughout the group. Formerly a woman was not told what her bride-wealth was or how it was divided by her kin. She and her children could therefore only regard the whole matrilineal group as standing in a special relationship to them and not some particular section or individual within it. Those who did not share in one distribution might be given a portion from the next bride-wealth received by the group, or they might be given a share from the increase of the cattle. A person's chance of obtaining a portion of any particular bride-wealth, then, depends not so much on his relationship to the woman who is being married as it does upon his generation status.

In inheritance, again, the primary concern is not to guide the property through the genealogical table. When a man of wealth dies, a general heir is chosen who marries the wives and remains as custodian to a portion of the property. The rest is divided as widely as possible through the group. Anyone may be chosen as the general heir—with the emphasis always on finding the most suitable person among the whole group.[1] In former days a slave might be chosen, or perhaps even someone from outside the group. Wives are not necessarily inherited by the closest relative of the dead man. The matrilineal group is likely to nominate men who are not yet provided with wives, but the widows have the right to ask for any men they themselves want so long as the men belong to the group. The same choice is possible where the group controls a ritual office. At the present time the Chona group controls the rain rituals for its area. At a recent meeting held to choose a successor to the old ritual leader the choice lay between a man descended from his mother's sister and a man whose genealogical link to the group cannot be established, though the old leader has brothers, sisters' sons, and other close relatives living in his own village.

The ancestral cult is also consistent with this general lack of lineage structure within the group. Any ancestor may be reincarnated in any member of the group, who thereafter stands in a special relationship to this ancestor. The same ancestor may be incarnate in two or more members of the group. Even those who are affiliated to the group through a slave link may appeal to the ancestors and will find the ancestors reincarnating among their descendants. As the Tonga say, 'You can't tell such a child he is a slave. Nobody would tell him. You call him your sister's child. And he has only your ancestors to appeal to.' Since every adult man who has a wife to brew beer for him, and every adult woman is capable of appealing directly to the ancestors, every adult is independent of other relatives in relations with the ancestors, and you do not find segments of the group joining in common ritual under the guidance of some family priest. But if a man wants to call in attendants when he makes his offering or when he builds a shrine for the ancestors, anyone in the group is able to attend and to take part.

It is therefore membership in a group which is important and not membership in specified segments. In most matrilineal groups there

---

[1] Today there appears to be an increasing tendency to restrict inheritance to immediate relatives. Informants say that this is due to the increased wealth of the Tonga.

are people who cannot tell you how they are related to other people in the group, and they content themselves with the knowledge that the old people now dead probably knew. For the matrilineal group, then, to endure there must be a personal contact between its members, for a stranger cannot link himself into the group through reciting a genealogy and thus validating a claim to membership. Since residence is not fixed, and women tend to move off to their husbands' homes and often their children do not return to their matrilineal kin to settle but in turn move still farther away, the group tends automatically to shed its members, or rather gradually to split into smaller groups which lose contact with each other.[1] With land plentiful there was formerly no need to seek one's matrilineal kin to beg for a share in the ancestral acres. Until the present day the inheritance with which the group has been concerned has been movable property, which can follow the members in their wanderings. I have tried discussing segmentary lineage systems with the Tonga. They point out that it is impossible under their system where a woman marries into a distant village, her daughter marries still farther away, and soon all knowledge of her and her children is lost. In turn they do not remember the people in the original home. Genealogies bear this out, for few people remember the names of ancestors beyond grandparents, and often they do not know where their grandparents were born or if they had siblings.

Even where a tradition of kinship is preserved, distance may largely nullify its effects. Unless a man can attend the meeting at which inheritance is discussed, unless he is present to lay his claim to a portion of a bride-wealth, he has little chance to obtain a portion. In former days, moreover, he could get little protection from his group in case trouble started. His relatives were not likely to make a distant expedition into strange territory to stress the rights of a stray kinsman whom they thought would have been wiser in any event to have settled more closely to them. If they heard that he had been killed they would remember the matter and take vengeance upon the first person from the offending group who was injudicious enough to come within their reach. But such sanctions could be effective only

[1] Tonga say that in the unsettled days before the Europeans came they did not like to marry into distant villages or into families where marriages had not previously occurred. They also practised cross-cousin marriage—with mother's brother's daughter and father's sister's daughter—which tended to keep together cores of kinsmen. Actually, however, genealogies indicate that distant moves and foreign marriages have always been common.

over an area compact enough for there to be considerable visiting back and forth.

The effective matrilineal group therefore consists of those people who are near enough to exchange visits and services which will keep alive the recognition of their unity. Those who live outside this range may be able to re-establish contact with the group and be accepted within it again so long as the memory of the common kinship persists. Once this is gone, kinship disappears into clanship and even common residence does not necessarily convert it into kinship again.

## Clan and Matrilineal Group

The distinction between clan and matrilineal group appears in a case brought before one of the Native Authority courts—a case which gave me the necessary clue to start untangling the matter. Those involved in the case belonged to the Bird clan, yet the plaintiffs were demanding that the defendant return to them a beast he had inherited, on the plea that he did not belong to their *mukowa*. When I pressed for an explanation the court agreed that the defendant was a member of the Bird clan, and yet he was not. In the following discussion it appeared that two types of relationship were involved: the clan and the matrilineal group. Years before, A, the defendant, had settled with a fellow clansman, B. Though they could trace no relationship they were friends and B gave A some cattle to herd. When B died, A brought a beast to kill at his funeral; a gesture which might be interpreted as arising from friendship, from the economic relationship of cattle-owner and herdsman, or from kinship. B's matrilineal group met for the division of the property left by B. They gave one beast to A, and in the court they now claimed that they had given this to him as his share in the inheritance and not to repay him for the beast killed at the funeral. Later on they supplied A's brother with a beast to help him marry. They were acting as though A were a member of the group. Later, for some reason which did not appear in the court, B's heir, C, and others of the group decided that A was merely a fellow clansman and therefore had no right to inherit or to receive assistance. They demanded that he return the beast of the inheritance as a token that he recognized that he did not belong within the group. He had also received other cattle from them, but in the court they disclaimed all immediate interest in these beasts and said, 'We want only the beast he received from the inheritance. He must return it. He does not belong to our *mukowa*.' The court decided that A must return it.

During the hearing and in later discussions about the matter the implication was always that if the matter had been allowed to rest and possession of this beast gone undisputed, then A would have been in a strong position to regard himself as a genuine member of B's group and to put forward his claim to inherit from other members, to demand assistance in any emergency, and to have full status. It was this they were repudiating by their demands to regain the beast from the inheritance.

Informants say that this distinction between clan and group may be raised at a funeral, the time when the status of the group is most clearly demonstrated. A man who has settled with a fellow clansman might be turned upon at the funeral of his protector with the words, 'Now you must go away. You came only to settle with this man and you have no right to live with us. You cannot inherit our places.' On the other hand, there are indications that under some conditions people belonging to the same clan but to different matrilineal groups and settled in the same area may decide to regard themselves as a single group. Such a suggestion seems to offer the only explanation for some of my data.

In the Mujika area this seems to have occurred. Chepa, the headman of the largest village, belongs to the Hyena clan. He is surrounded by a large number of fellow clansmen. Some are his siblings and his sisters' children, one or two others are remote but traceable kin. Others count themselves as members of his group, though they can murmur only vaguely that the old people must have known how they were related but they themselves never bothered to learn. These people were born or grew up in the Mujika area, where their immediate ancestors moved from We country some fifty to seventy years ago. Chepa and his immediate relatives moved into the district about 1921. Chepa's mother was born in We country on the Zambezi and was married by an elephant hunter who after much wandering settled in Chona country, probably about 1880. She maintained some contact with her family on the Zambezi, and when Chepa formed his own village two of her sister's descendants came to join him. It is possible that the ancestors of the Mujika people and Chepa's ancestors formed one matrilineal group on the Zambezi; if so, I believe that the connexion had been forgotten and no tradition of kinship existed when Chepa moved to Mujika and formed his village. Yet today they have entered into the types of relationship which seem to imply a common matrilineal group. One Mujika woman was kept in Chepa's house for her puberty seclusion; Chepa shared in the bride-wealth of another. Chepa and older Mujika men claim that they will inherit from each other. Such a coalescence into one group is aided by a number of circumstances. Chepa is the wealthiest person in the vicinity; it therefore pays outsiders to be incorporated into his group. Chepa in turn is proud of having a large village and of his dominating influence in the neighbourhood. He has a better chance to stabilize his village about a strong core of Hyena clansmen if he can give them some permanent stake in the village. He does this by converting them into kinsmen. Since he has a strong personality and a strong position at the moment *vis-à-vis* his own immediate kinsmen he is able to get away with widening the inheritance group which they might well prefer to see narrowed. Moreover, he is probably one of the more emancipated of the Tonga. To the best of my knowledge he ignores the ancestors, and would probably feel no qualms at any possible resentment on their part. Moreover, he actively dislikes the system of matrilineal inheritance which prevents his own sons from succeeding to his property. He is therefore unlikely to feel any particularly tender regard for the interests of his siblings and his sisters' children or for the one or two other people who belong without question to his matrilineal group. If he should die, of course, these people might question the status of the group and repudiate the outsiders who have been incorporated into it. They may find this difficult to do since Chepa has taken a share of the bride-wealth of the women belonging to the outsiders.

In other cases close proximity over long periods has not given rise to any blurring of the matrilineal groups. At Chona the Eland clan is represented by two nuclei which remain quite separate and have succeeded in doing so for possibly seventy to eighty years. One was apparently founded by the first Chona and his sister, Naciteba, who moved into the area from Shamaundu country. Naciteba is regarded as the progenitrix of the group, whose oldest living members are her grandchildren. Today the group consists of about fifty adults, ten or twelve of whom cannot be fitted into the genealogy and who are assumed to represent some earlier link to Naciteba. A few others represent slave links. The majority live in the two villages of Chona and Chobana, a few live a good distance away, and this is not entirely due to recent dispersal. After Chona and his sister were established in the country a famine in We country drove Hanamoonga, another Eland, to settle near his fellow clansmen. He came with his mother and some of his siblings. Today his group is largely settled in three villages,

Hanamoonga, Simuzingeni, and Haluinde, and probably numbers about thirty members. Hanamoonga and Chona villages are closer together, only fifteen minutes' walk apart, than they are to any of the other three villages. At times in the past they have been in even closer proximity. Visits, exchange of labour, &c., link the two matrilineal groups. At the present time four members of the Chona group live in Hanamoonga village. But Hanamoonga does not share in the inheritance if a member of Chona dies, and vice versa. They do not share in the distribution of bride-wealth, nor must the marriage of a Chona woman be announced at Hanamoonga. When a Hanamoonga girl is secluded for puberty she would not be sent to Chona people for her seclusion (unless there were a patrilineal link), and during the final rite when the girl emerges from seclusion, a member of Hanamoonga would kill the beast provided by the matrilineal group. When a member of Chona brews beer to make an offering to the ancestors, Hanamoonga people may come for the public beer-drink as may anyone else, but only the Chona people may help with the offering. Hanamoonga people have no right to look to Chona for help in paying claims against them, nor will Chona call upon Hanamoonga. Informants explain that they have remained distinct groups because each contains many people, but that they will coalesce if either appears about to die out.

## The Linking of Matrilineal Groups

While the matrilineal groups are not linked into a lineage system, there is an intricate interlocking of groups which cuts across the clan lines and which is created by intermarriage and the birth of children. The link is through individuals, but the relationships involve groups of people organized on kinship principles.

This linkage is supplied by the incorporation of the individual into the matrilineal group of his father. Though his primary group and clan affiliation, his *bashimukowa*, are from his mother, he has what might be termed an honorary life-membership in the clan and group to which his father belongs, his *bashanaushi*. He may use either clan name, though if asked he will specify that one is his own clan, the other the clan which 'bore' him.

For the individual there are always two blocks of kin to which he owes allegiance, to which he has special obligations, and from whom he can expect support. He is a child of one; he is an integral member of the other. From the point of view of any one matrilineal group, there is the solid core of people who compose the group itself and there is a periphery of people who are the children of the group and to which it as a body has obligations. Unlike the matrilineal group itself, the periphery has the span of but one generation. It is extinguished with

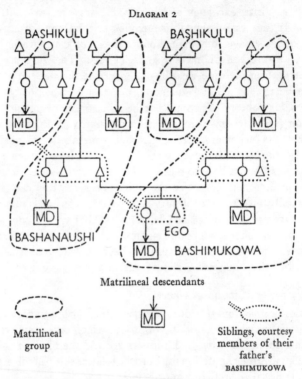

DIAGRAM 2

*Descent in the four matrilineal groups*

The diagram shows the four groups, each of which is surrounded with a broken line. The names *Bashimukowa* (people of the mother), *Bashanaushi* (people of the father), and *Bashikulu* (grandparent groups) are all shown relative to Ego. The dotted lines link sibling groups to their respective *Bashanaushi*. The squares marked MD represent the matrilineal descendants who remain members of each outlined matrilineal group.

the death of the original holder of the right, and in the next generation gives place to the relationship of *bashikulu* which an individual has with the matrilineal groups of his mother's father and his father's father. This is a joking relationship in which there is no direct responsibility for a person's actions or direct claims upon him or his property.

Each individual has thus four distinct matrilineal groups to which he stands in stereotyped relationships: the two groups of his grandfathers who are not directly concerned in his affairs, and the two groups of his grandmothers who are immediately interested in his welfare.

DIAGRAM 3

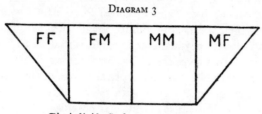

*The individual's four matrilineal groups*

Through marriage he acquires new relationships which are also to groups.[1] In every marriage four groups are immediately concerned. If you also consider the *bashikulu*, there are eight groups which have some interest in the affair.

The immediate interests of the groups are shown in the institution of bride-wealth. The *bashikulu* participate to a very minor degree; the other four groups are primarily concerned, two as contributors and two as recipients. The bride-wealth is divided into five payments, only one of which appears to be essential to make the marriage legal.[2] This is *muyumusho*, which is given during the marriage negotiations. Traditionally it consists of a spear and a number of hoes; today a money payment of about ten shillings is often substituted. This should be divided between the matrilineal group of the girl and the group

---

[1] When a member of the matrilineal group dies, the work of killing and cutting up the cattle brought for the funeral, the cooking of the porridge, and other such duties fall upon the men who have married the women of the group.

[2] This is only a preliminary legality. If the husband delays too long in making the final payment of *ciko*, his wife's family may refuse to recognize the marriage further. The courts uphold them and inform a delinquent husband that he has used up his initial payment, that he is now to be considered as a lover and not as a husband, and that if the wife commits adultery he cannot collect damages. If awarded they are due to her parents. A reasonably satisfactory son-in-law, however, should have nothing to fear for four or five years, and the point appears to be stressed only if the family is dissatisfied for other reasons. For a couple to live together, however, before the first payment is made does not represent marriage. The man will be made to pay if the woman conceives, and to pay heavily if the child is born dead or the mother dies in childbirth.

of her father, though frequently the father's group keeps the entire payment. At the same time two additional payments should be made, though these are regarded as recent innovations and seem to represent the immediate interests of the parents themselves. One is *cilezu*, given to the girl's father and named for his beard with which she played as a child. The other payment is *muumiya*, which goes to the girl's mother or to her mother's sister, and is named for the rope which women wear around their waists after childbirth. When the bride is taken to her husband a fourth payment, *mafwenesya*, is made. The bride should be accompanied by two young girls—one from her father's group and one from her mother's. The two representatives of the husband, one from each of his groups, bargain with them and finally present them with money. This is divided as widely as possible through the bride's two groups, with small payments reserved for the two *bashikulu* groups. Such payments establish the legality of the marriage and entitle a man and his matrilineal group to share in the bride-wealth of the daughters of the marriage. This is true, at least, if the marriage endures and the father contributes to the rearing of his daughters. But if a man dies at this point in the payments his matrilineal group is not allowed to appoint a new husband for the wife. For this *ciko* must be given, which is conceived as the final instalment which creates the new family, for the wife may not brew beer at her own house nor may the couple invoke the ancestors by themselves until *ciko* is paid. Over most of Tonga country this was once paid in hoes or goats; today it is paid almost always in cattle or money. The normal *ciko* consists of from two to four cattle, but there are signs that the amount is being steadily increased as the Tonga gain in wealth. It must be repaid in case of divorce, or if a widow refuses to marry again into her husband's family. Its return does not seem to affect the father's rights in the children of the marriage, though the courts today urge him to leave at least one beast with his wife's family to provide for his children. If the wife dies no refund is made.

This last instalment is handed to the girl's father or to his representative. He in turn hands a share to the representative of the girl's matrilineal group. The two men then divide within their own groups. Usually the matter of distribution has been partially settled at the time of the girl's puberty ceremony when usually two beasts or two goats are killed, one by her father's group, one by her own. Any individual belonging to the group may be asked to supply a beast for this occasion, and he has a presumptive right to receive at least one beast from her bride-wealth.[1] If the girl is impregnated before marriage, the two beasts paid in compensation are given to the men who killed their cattle for her ceremony, who represent her two groups.

The bride-wealth of the woman is thus held by two groups, and she has the right to look to either one for help. Both groups have an interest in seeing that her marriage endures and therefore in maintaining good relations with the two groups represented by her husband. However, the woman holds only a life interest in the cattle given to her father's group. She herself may approach her father's people on the grounds that they hold cattle given for her. Her children may not do so; they may follow only the cattle assigned to her own matrilineal group.[2] In turn her father's matrilineal group has no right to share in the bride-wealth of her daughters except for the token payment from the *mafwenesya*. They are now only *bashikulu*.

Meantime a man looks for help in marriage both to his matrilineal group and to his father's matrilineal group, though his rights in the two directions are of a different nature—the one unquestioned, the other hedged with reservations. Thus after he has been married for some years and the cattle of his bride-wealth have begun to bear, one cow with its calf should be returned to him. If the major portion of his bride-wealth came from his own group he keeps the beast himself and that ends the matter. If it has come from his father he must give the beast to his father and may be fined if he fails to do so. The father, however, may then present it to his son again to help him build up his herd. Again, if the father's group has provided all or the majority of the bride-wealth, it may refuse to let his matrilineal group inherit his widow. Before his group may retain her it must pay bride-wealth to the group of the father. Finally, though a man's father's group helps with his bride-wealth it has no rights over his children or over the bride-wealth of his daughters. Again this has become a *bashikulu* relationship.

With the birth of children a new alinement of groups comes into being. The Tonga symbolize the relationship of an individual to his two groups by saying that the left hand and body belong to the mother, the right hand and head belong to the father. Today, however,

---

[1] Today some of the Tonga are attempting to ask for an extra beast with the *ciko* to cover this payment and then to hold that it is not returnable in the case of divorce. So far this is not general.

[2] If a man can get no assistance from either of his groups he may approach his *bashikulu* and ask for help to marry. They should give a token payment, such as a hoe, but any other assistance is given not as his right but as a sign of generosity or friendliness.

those who resent the matrilineal system argue that the entire child belongs to the father since he pays a large bride-wealth. Just what beliefs about conception may underlie the traditional saying I do not know. Some Tonga say that the father makes the child. But it is not a purely physiological relationship. A child conceived by a married woman belongs to her husband whoever the physical father may be. This point has been raised in the courts, as in a case involving two children born to a woman who had left her husband and lived with her lover for several years. The husband said he wanted to know what to do since his wife refused to allow him to give names to the children born of her lover. The court turned to the lover and said: 'You're not a father. You just stole the womb. The children belong to the husband.'[1]

The claims of the two groups are clearly demonstrated in this matter of naming. Within a few months of its birth the father gives the child one of the names current in his group. This is symbolized by a circlet of beads placed around the child's right arm. Thereafter the mother's group gives one of its names and places a wristlet on the left arm. Each name symbolizes some ancestral spirit who is now thought to reincarnate in the child. When an individual dies his father's group comes to take back the name which it gave him, while the name given by the mother's group remains and is inherited by the person chosen by the group to succeed him.

The same symbolism of right and left is retained throughout life. When a man marries, his first house is called 'the house of the father', and here he places his father's spirit as a special guardian of this wife and her children. His father's kin stay at this house when they come to visit him. The house of the second wife is placed to the left and this is the house of the matrilineal group. Here a man places the spirit of some ancestor of his own group. It is at this house that his matrilineal kin will stay.[2] Since only about 21 per cent. of Tonga men are married polygamously, this balancing of the kin groups is not always possible. But if a man has only one wife the right side of the door belongs to

---

[1] To the north-west, formerly, when an unmarried girl conceived, her lover was not allowed to establish his paternity. When the woman finally married, the child went with her and belonged to her husband. Today the north-western people have accepted the custom, always general elsewhere, that the man must pay compensation, a portion of which gives him the right to name his child. When it is weaned he may even take it to live with him. In either case the child's rights in the group of its legal father are identical with the rights of the child whose paternity cannot be questioned.

[2] This assignment of visitors appears to be true only of the north-west.

his father's group, the left-hand side to his own. When he makes offerings to the ancestors he calls someone of his father's group to pour the libation on the right side of the doorway, and he himself makes the offering to the left. Some men still build a special shrine for the ancestors. This is the *ciilyango*, which consists of three groups of poles in a straight line, with a cross-bar on top, forming two doorways. This is the gateway through which the spirits enter his homestead. The right-hand gate belongs to the ancestors of his father's group, the left-hand to his own group.

Throughout his life the individual has to acknowledge the claims of both groups. In the old days when Tonga country teemed with game a boy or man divided his larger kills between the two. But his first kills went to his father's group. Later on, when labour migration became important, the returned migrant was expected to share with his group the goods and money he brought back. But his own group could not dictate to him what its share would be. It was otherwise with his father and his father's group. When he returned he was expected to hand the key to his locked box to his father or his father's representative. His father opened the box and took what he would before he returned it to his son. In addition, he had the right to demand a certain fixed sum of money. This practice has now been abandoned. A man also has claims on his father's group. If he gets into difficulties he can demand help from this group. This is still acknowledged. His own group may even declare in the court that they are tired of paying for his misdeeds, that he has broken them, and that his father's group must be called to help pay the damages. Formerly, if trouble arose within his own group a man counted on his father's group for support. If his group accused him of witchcraft against them, for instance, and the case fell through, his father's group would demand compensation for the insult paid to them.

A man or woman cannot inherit from the father to any extent. If there are many cattle one beast is assigned to the children from each wife. Or one beast may be given to all the children collectively. But certain rights are passed on to the children which enable them to follow the father's group and to join in its inheritances long after the father's death. A man may attend the funeral of his father's sister's son, for example, and beg for a beast on the grounds that he is a child of the group. It may be given to him, although he could not enforce his claim in court. Half-brothers by the same father might in this way inherit from each other by a claim upon their father's group.

At all important moments of the individual's life-cycle—the naming, when a girl comes to puberty, at marriage, and at death—there is this balancing of one group against the other. But the relationship of the two groups is most clearly shown at the death of the individual who relates them. At the final mourning ceremony the two groups assemble in the hut of the dead. Two pots of beer are brought in, one for each group. All other people are sent out. The two groups exchange pots, and while they drink they rise alternately to bemoan

DIAGRAM 4

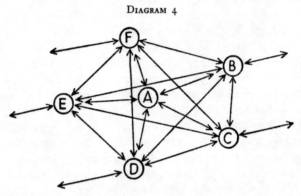

*The interlocking of the matrilineal groups within a neighbourhood*

their loss. Then, immediately, they begin quarrelling over the property left by the dead. The father's group say that they are following the head of their child and claim their share in his estate. If it is a large one, perhaps a quarter of the cattle herd may be turned over to them, and they in turn divide among themselves. The matrilineal group retains the rest of the estate and makes its own division. Once the primary division is made neither side has the right to question the subsequent division within the other group, nor does it have the right to come to make fresh claims on the cattle. The matrilineal group has the obligation of purifying the spouse of the dead person and the right to appoint a successor. With this the direct affiliation of the two groups ends.

New balancings are now in order. The matrilineal group must now pay over to the father of the man chosen as heir a beast in compensation for having taken his child to take part in their succession, unless, of course, the heir is a full sibling of the deceased. If a woman dies, and her kin wish to supply her husband with a new wife, they will waive their share in the bride-wealth. But the husband must compensate the father's people for the loss of their daughter.

Thus, a matrilineal group, through the children of its male members, has claims on the property held by perhaps a dozen or more such groups. And in turn they have claims against it for assistance for their members who are directly linked to it. Since intermarriage soon results from common residence in an area, every neighbourhood is soon embroiled in an intricate linkage of matrilineal groups which unite in common interests and are bound to mutual helpfulness.

This is probably a mechanism by which order is maintained within the Tonga community. A general neighbourhood quarrel involving the rupture of these innumerable ties would probably involve much more trouble than it would be worth to any one group.

## VI. THE DISTRICT

### Neighbourhoods and communities

In most parts of Tonga country no larger territorial unit intervenes between village and modern chieftaincy, save for the community organized around a rain shrine.[1] In some parts of the country even this is lacking. One can, however, speak everywhere of neighbourhoods. For these the Tonga appear to have no word, and neighbourhoods are not definite entities each distinguished from the other. In Katimba area, for instance, there is a constant stream of huts across the countryside which compose a number of villages. The neighbourhood of village B will include A to the south and C to the north; C's neighbourhood will include B and a village D farther north; and so on for mile after mile. Thus each village is in a sense a link in the chain. Even though a village moves into a new area, it quickly sets up social links which establish a neighbourhood and through intermarriages these are reinforced by kinship links.

Such neighbourhoods are given no backbone of consistency by the domination of any one clan or matrilineal group. A neighbourhood does not develop through the fissions of a lineage structure, but is created by the moving into unoccupied spaces of foreign villages, through the budding off of foreign elements once incorporated in the local villages, through an occasional proliferation of kin. At Katimba, for example, there are five villages, each under a headman

[1] Cf. Kendal, 'A Visit to Chikuni', p. 307: 'The villages are small and own no Paramount Chief, the principal man among them being the rain-maker. . . .'

of a different clan. Shaciobeka cannot trace its history out of the immediate area; Sicaambwa was founded by a man moving in from the west; Shakaobile was founded by a fugitive from the east; Simwaami by a man from the north-west; and Monze has recently brought his village here from a site some 20 miles to the east. At one time the first four villages were united in a common rain ritual under the leadership of Simwaami, but since Monze has moved in among them they have transferred their allegiance to the rain rituals of the Monze. The villages acknowledge no overlordship save that of the chief at the present time, though when pressed the headmen said that the country might be said to belong to Chiyumu, who had his village some six miles away. But when their villages were founded they had not consulted Chiyumu; they had not asked him for land or for permission to build in the country. And they could not instance any way in which his authority had impinged upon them.

Elsewhere the country is divided into tiny districts known as *cisi*, *kasi*, or *katongo*.[1] These have boundaries and are usually named from some natural object which dominates the landscape of the area. At the present time some of them contain as many as six or seven villages, which give a very nominal allegiance to a man known as *ulanyika* or *sikatongo* or *mupati wa cisi* (terms which may be translated as 'owner of the country' or 'big man of the district'). Such men are said to derive their authority because they or the men from whom they inherited were the first to settle in this particular area, and other people have come to live with them. Their authority is nebulous, save where it rests on a further status as guardian of the local rain shrine. Even then it appears to give the 'owner of the country' no real powers over his people save that which he can exercise through his personal domination. If he does not have a strong personality some newcomer will take the leadership from him. Thus, in the Mujika area eight villages acknowledge their special relationship to the village which was first founded in this area. About 1850 Chima built his village on what is now European farm-land near a good hunting territory. This attracted others, apparently complete strangers, who came to settle with Chima. With some of these he established further bonds by marrying to them his kinswomen or his slaves. When the strangers had had time to gather a few friends or perhaps some of their own relatives around them, they would announce to Chima that they wished to move out and found their own villages. He would in-

[1] *Cisi* is commonly used today to refer to the modern chieftaincy.

dicate an unoccupied area for them to build in. In this way the area was gradually populated with villages which continued to recognize their original ties to Chima. Nevertheless, while today the matrilineal kin of Chima claim to lead the district, the most important and influential man within it happens to be a foreigner who moved in fairly recently.

The existence of a *cisi* receives some recognition in ritual, particularly in the rain ritual which will be dealt with below. If a man from outside the district dies in one of its villages, his relatives must bring a beast which is killed in a ceremonial cleansing of the neighbourhood. All the elders of the district have the right to attend and share in the distribution of the meat. This is a cleansing of the whole district and not of the village where the death occurred.[1] When cattle are killed at ordinary funerals the villages of the district should each be allocated a portion. This is a custom known as *kasiasia* or *cisiasia*, terms which also apply to the custom at beer-drinks of reserving certain pots for the consumption of members of the district. A man who moves from one district to another joins the rites of his new district and is now regarded as a stranger in his former home and would not be entitled to join in its purification rite. Indeed, if he died there, his kin would have to produce a beast for purification of the district.

The district is also mobilized as a unit to eat together of the new maize, though many districts no longer observe this custom. Most of them still make a beer to celebrate the harvest. Each woman who brews sends one pot of beer to the 'owner of the country', and he in turn distributes it among the people who attend. Formerly, before the harvest beer or the beer for the rain ritual could be made, the district had to be purified of any human blood spilled on its earth since the last ritual. Today this is not always observed, even in cases of murder.

## The Rain Shrine Community

The *cisi* districts seem generally to have been coterminous with rain-shrine communities.[2] Today these still operate, but they were

---

[1] Formerly, at least in certain areas, the beast killed for this purification was not killed in the village but at some spot chosen for this purpose by the entire *cisi*. Informants say that this was so that the people would be sure that the purification was not for a particular village but for the *cisi* as a whole, and so that the spirit of the dead man would not be confused and think the beast was killed as part of the mourning.

[2] Cf. Colson, 'Rain Shrines of the Plateau Tonga of Northern Rhodesia'. The editor of *Africa* has very kindly permitted the use here of sections from the article which appeared in that Journal.

undoubtedly more important in the days before European administration spread a new form of polity across the land. The rain cults organized small groups of villages for corporate activities and were able to impose sanctions on offences against their rules, but there was no hierarchy of shrines organizing the various separate cult districts into a country-wide system which could integrate the whole of the Tonga people. The district over which a particular cult held sway usually contained only a few square miles and four or five villages. One or two, such as the cult of Monze, had a wide reputation and drew people far more widely.

For the few days each year when the rain rituals or the harvest ceremonies were being enacted, a general district peace was imposed in the name of the shrine. This overrode the customary rights of the matrilineal groups to exact compensation for offences against their members' persons or property. In some districts this peace was instituted through a ritual licence at this period, and the district refused to recognize any offence save murder or some violation of the cult rules as culpable. In other districts the customary code of behaviour remained in effect, but fines were payable to the shrine or to the community. The floor of the Monze shrine is covered with hoe-blades paid as fines. Adherents in other districts were fined a fowl, a beast, or tobacco, which was then distributed among the elders of the area. The ritual peace has now disappeared, and breaches of peace or civil cases arising during the period find their way into the Native Authority courts, where they are treated on the same plane with cases arising at other periods of the year.

Today a man who fails to attend the ritual is not fined, but once the ritual was coercive upon all who lived within the cult area. Therefore a man knew that at least twice a year he must co-operate with his neighbours in a ritual for their common good. If feuds split the community so badly that its members could not co-operate in the ritual, one of the dissident sections would have to move into another district, or the whole area might expect the visitation of drought, famine, epidemic, or other pestilence. The shrines were therefore effective in keeping the internal differences in the communities which they served within reasonable bounds.

At non-ritual periods the community of the rain shrine might be called into existence and its integrity reaffirmed. Disrespect towards the shrine at any time might bring general disaster upon the community unless the offenders were punished and a ritual cleansing performed. The immediate area around a shrine is sacrosanct, and no one may cut wood, dig roots, or burn the bush in that area save on pre-scribed occasions. An offender is ordered to pay a black chicken or a goat, which is killed and eaten by assembled elders. In 1946 a fool-hardy youth burned the bush on a hill-side which ranks as a rain shrine, and came to announce what he had done when the local headmen were assembled for another purpose. They had him soundly beaten and threatened to make all the men of the district who belonged to his approximate age pay chickens for a general purifying feast. His act had endangered the whole community. In the Mwanacingwala area the chief discovered a pile of firewood at the base of a very large, hollow fig-tree associated with the shrine of Luanga. He marched into the nearest village, which had immigrated into the area a year or so before, and threatened the inhabitants with a fine of a beast. They were let off with a warning when they apologized profusely and protested their ignorance of the sacred nature of this tree. The same shrine of Luanga figures in the last big feud in this area. About 1910, women from a village perhaps three miles from Luanga, but belonging to the cult district of Chiboya, were found cutting grass near Luanga. When Luanga men warned them of their trespass the women cursed them heartily in a manner which left no doubt as to their opinion of Luanga and its people. The leader of Luanga demanded an apology from his peer at Chiboya, who promptly spat in his face. The next step was an armed raid by the Luanga people in which several men were killed and the followers of Chiboya were driven from their home.

This incident illustrates a number of aspects of the rain cult. Those who live outside the cult district owe a shrine no reverence as a holy place for all Tonga; adherents to the shrine, however, regard any insult to it as an insult to the whole community. Moreover, once people move within the cult area they are expected to observe the rules which surround the particular shrine of the place.

Since the largest social groups ever mobilized by the Tonga are not of impressive size, we cannot expect that the shrines which symbolize the groups will be pretentious structures. They are not. They consist of two general types, both called *malende*.[1] One type consists of natural objects which have become sacralized. Large hollow fig-trees are often sacred, and are regarded as dwelling-places for the spirits responsible for the rain. Hills, springs, and pools of water may also be sacred, though I have not discovered that such shrines are

[1] Cf. Syaamusonde and Shilling, *Naakoyo waamba caano cakwe*, Lesson 16.

connected specifically with any spirit, nor could I determine what was the mechanism of their power. At Chona the same spirits are supplicated at both natural and artificial shrines, and the people claim they visit the spots at the present time because the first Chona visited them when he was alive. But they do not seem to hold that the spirit of Chona dwells there. The other general type of shrine is man-made, and consists of small structures called *kaanda* (*twaanda*, in the plural) or 'little hut'. They consist of a circle of upright supports capped by a thatched roof. In the north-west they are tiny affairs which vanish completely from one year to the next; elsewhere they are slightly larger, and those at Monze's shrine are large enough to admit an adult, though no one does enter the shrine once it is built. The contents, clearly in view, usually consist of a couple of pots placed upside down near the doorway.

The hut-shrines are connected with definite spirits who are thought to have the power to control the rain through their intervention with Leza, the god who controls all things.

Shrines come into existence in several ways. When an *ulanyika* ('owner of the country') died his relatives and other neighbours might decide to honour him by building a shrine at his grave. This did not necessarily become a cult centre. It might soon decay and be forgotten as the community which he had collected about him was dispersed. If, however, the area suffered from drought or other disaster within a few years of his death, a diviner might announce that his spirit was angry because the people had forgotten him though he had looked after the community during his lifetime. The people would then rebuild the shrine, and thenceforth carry out the rites there each year at the beginning of the rains simply to be on the safe side. Or they might return to it only in another period of emergency. Other shrines were initiated by people whom we may call rain-makers, though there seems to be no specific term for them in Tonga.

Rain-makers are subject to possession by spirits, who through them make demands on the people, lecture them for their misdeeds, and demand the institution of new rituals or the better conduct of the old. Such spirits are called *basangu*[1] and they are regarded as distinct from the *mizimo* or ancestral spirits, though there are cases where the same spirits are addressed as *basangu* at the rain shrines and as ancestral spirits at the private household rituals. This is true if the *musangu* is a former member of the community. Such a man is honoured as an

---

[1] Cf. Myers, 'A Religious Survey of the Batonga'.

ancestral spirit by his matrilineal group, which approaches him as it does any other ancestor, in private rites. He is honoured as a *musangu* by the community, which may include members of his matrilineal group, but as a *musangu* he is concerned with community affairs and not with the narrow sphere of individual or private matters. While the ancestral spirits can affect only their own kin, the *basangu* can possess anyone they choose to enter without regard for the proprieties of kinship regulations, and they can affect communities with drought, cattle epidemics, disease of epidemic proportions, or any other disaster which is of a general nature. *Basangu* do not send sickness to one individual or one family, or crop failure to the fields of one person. For such misfortunes one accuses either the ancestors or the witchcraft of one's enemies. The only exception is that the *basangu* punish with illness individuals who violate their shrines and do not make restitution.

When the rain-maker is first possessed by his spirit, if it is a foreign one which has no local shrine, he calls upon the people to build a hut-shrine for it and to participate in ritual on the spot. If it seems effective in producing rain, the rites become institutionalized. When the rain-maker dies, the shrine continues to be visited under the leadership of some member of his matrilineal group. Another shrine may be built at his grave, for he, too, is considered to have become a *musangu* and to have power over the area. Occasionally the original shrine and the shrine of the dead rain-maker will coalesce, and both *basangu* will be appealed to at the same time and place. The rain shrine of Monze represents such a coalescence.

In some cases rain-makers in different districts have been possessed by the same *musangu*, but this results in no connexion between the resulting shrines.

Once the original figure is dead, the cult passes into the hands of his matrilineal group. The shrines to local leaders are in the hands of their matrilineal groups; the shrines of foreign spirits are in the hands of the matrilineal group of the rain-maker whom they possessed. While the shrine affects the entire local community, this matrilineal group is regarded as the proper medium through which appeals may be made to the indwelling spirit. As officials of the cult, members of this group are the living representatives of the community itself, but their power and responsibility begin and end in the ritual sphere. They choose one of their group to decide when the rituals will be held and to direct the activities of the ritual period. He himself may be possessed

M

by a *musangu*, but often he is an ordinary person without supernatural assistance. If he wishes to do so, he may delegate his work to some more energetic person. His role is that of director and chief participant, but he can do nothing by himself. He visits the shrine only on public occasions and never by himself. He can invoke the *basangu* only for the public good.

The ritual itself is simple and usually is performed but once. If the rains fail to come or do not last, however, the shrines are visited again. In 1946–7 the Chona community visited the shrines five times. In desperation they consulted diviners. A woman was possessed by the spirit of the first Chona and ordered an innovation in the ritual, the presentation of a black cloth to the shrine. On another visit an ox was killed. Finally, on the last appeal to the *basangu*, when no rain clouds had appeared, one of the women turned as they left the shrine and announced, 'Look, your children will all starve and we will all die. You don't care for us. Now we are through with you.'

Participation in the rite is general. At the Chona shrines the leaders urged all the people, not only members of the matrilineal group controlling the shrines, to dance and pray for rain. They said, 'The rain falls on your fields as well as on ours. You must all dance.' In this area, moreover, there is a widening of participation which is brought about by sharing the control of the shrines with the matrilineal group to which the father of the person to whom the shrine is dedicated belonged. Thus for the full ceremony at all five shrines of this district six matrilineal groups must co-operate. This custom, however, does not appear to be typical of all of Tonga country. But everywhere, whether the control of the rites is vested in one matrilineal group or in several, the whole community should participate in carrying them out —men, women, children. Women take a prominent part in the rites. Women as well as men have been possessed by *basangu* and become rain-makers, and some of them have shrines dedicated to them.

If you press the Tonga for an explanation as to why they perform the ritual, they say they are carrying out the instructions of a particular *musangu*, or of a particular rain-maker, and that if they do as their predecessors did at this spot, then they can expect the desired results. Yet, strangely enough, none of the shrines are regarded as deriving their sanctity from great antiquity, and myths concerning the first establishment of rain ceremonies in the land are absent. None of the shrines I have traced can be said to have been in existence prior to 1850, although we know that the Monze who apparently instituted one particular rain cult was alive in 1855.[1] The shrines which seem most important today are all associated with the cults of men and women remembered by those now living, or who lived only a generation earlier.

Since it is impossible that the rain ritual and the associated shrines are recent innovations, we must assume that shrines as well as their originators are mortal, and that in each generation some disappear while new ones are created. One can only guess at the cause of their extinction: their adherents may have been dispersed through epidemics or through the wars which devastated this area during the nineteenth century. Or the casual shift of villages over the land as fields became exhausted may have scattered the original village members to such an extent that they no longer represented a local community, and the shrines were too distant to be visited. Since rainfall is extremely localized, those who moved some distance might well have good reason to doubt the efficacy of the rituals they had formerly joined. It may be noted that only in one area do the shrines tie even the ritual leaders to their immediate vicinity. The group controlling the Chona cult believe that the leaders would be punished by illness if they moved as much as four miles from the shrines. Elsewhere people laugh at this idea and say they can move where they will, though they should return each year to celebrate the ceremony. Thus in general the shrines imposed their peace on those who lived within their vicinity, but had no effect in building up a permanent group tied to one area.

In other cases shrines probably disappeared as they were eclipsed by rivals instituted by new men, who were possessed by new *basangu*. Over a series of good years the older shrines might be so neglected that they vanished. But so long as they were remembered it was always likely that in times of desperation the diviners would call upon the people to go back to the sites, rebuild the huts, and perform the rituals again. Or through a series of bad years the attitude of 'You don't care for us, and we won't care for you' might swell into a general disgust and the shrine be abandoned as useless.

Many districts at the present time have a number of shrines integrated into one cult. My data are not entirely satisfactory, but it is possible that this proliferation of shrines is characteristic today only in the cults controlled by the matrilineal groups of the chiefs appointed by Government and that other cults centre in only one shrine, or at

[1] Cf. Livingstone, *Missionary Travels and Researches in South Africa*, p. 554.

least only one hut-shrine. This would suggest that the growth of such complexes is due to conditions imposed by European rule. When the Europeans began to develop the administration of the country they tended to recognize the rain-makers or other such leaders as the Tonga authorities and to vest in them the status of chief, and thenceforth to make this status hereditary in the matrilineal lines of the chiefs. Thus several successive members of the same matrilineal line have been recognized and supported as leaders in a particular area, whereas in pre-European days it was quite possible, as it is today, that the next rain-maker to speak with the voice of the *basangu*, and not merely as a shrine custodian, would appear in some other matrilineal line, in a different clan, and in a slightly different area. His appeal would be to those who lived around him, and his influence or that of his shrine after his death might well serve to detach some of his neighbours from their allegiance to an older cult centre and to draw them into a new community. Since the Tonga population was a shifting one, the new shrine which would represent the particular concatenation of population at this particular time could more truly represent the community than could the old. Control of the two cults would be vested in two different matrilineal groups and there would be little chance of their being integrated into a common complex unless the two communities which they represented were one and the same.

The system described above, overlaid though it is by the creation of hereditary chiefs, is still a fundamental element in Tonga social structure. Authority in the last analysis rests on personal qualities, but some continuity is given to the society through the recognition that a man who has led the community continues after his death his interest in its welfare, and that his matrilineal group is the proper channel through which to approach him. But this recognition is only a sea-anchor in the society, which slows the drift but does not stop it. It creates a small community within which the rudiments of community law can be discerned, and which forces its members to remember occasionally that they belong to a wider unit than the village or the matrilineal group. Such communities endure for only a moment in time and then reform themselves into new units.

Unsatisfactory though it may seem to us, it appears to be the only guise in which the Tonga could visualize authority. Indeed, at the present time, battered as the rituals are by the attacks of the missions, most modern chiefs tend to identify themselves with the rain shrines, using this as a prop to their authority. Monze, the titular Paramount, refuses to admit that any rain shrines save those of the Monze line exist in all of Tonga country. Other chiefs refer only to those in the hands of their matrilineal groups and ignore completely other shrines of nearby neighbourhoods. They maintain that villages in all directions and in great numbers attend their rituals, though the influence of their cults seems to be but a fraction of their claims.

Since Government pays little attention to the rain rituals, and seems largely unaware of their role in Tonga life, this attitude must reflect a deep-seated tendency among the Tonga to equate rain rituals with political integration.

## BIBLIOGRAPHY FOR THE PLATEAU TONGA

ALLAN, W., GLUCKMAN, M., PETERS, D. U., TRAPNELL, C. G. *Land-Holding and Land-Usage among the Plateau Tonga of Mazabuka District: A Reconnaissance Survey*, Cape Town: Oxford University Press for the Rhodes–Livingstone Institute (Paper No. 14) (1948). (*Tonga Report.*)

*British South Africa Company Administrators' Reports.*

CASSET, A. 'Some Batonga Customs', *Zambesi Mission Record*, vi (1919), pp. 207, 208.

—— 'Funeral Customs among the Batonga', ibid. v (1916), pp. 407–8.

CIPRIANI, L. 'The Anthropological Investigation of the Batonga of Northern Rhodesia', *South African Journal of Science*, xxvi (1929), pp. 541–6.

COLSON, E. 'Rain Shrines of the Plateau Tonga of Northern Rhodesia', *Africa*, xviii. 3 (October 1948).

—— 'Modern Political Organization of the Plateau Tonga', *African Studies*, vii. 2–3 (June–September, 1948).

—— 'Possible Effects of the Right to make Wills upon the Plateau Tonga', *Journal of African Administration*, ii (1950).

—— 'Every Day Life among the Cattle-keeping Plateau Tonga', *Rhodes–Livingstone Museum Papers*, N.S. No. 9 (1953).

—— 'Marriage among the Plateau Tonga' (forthcoming).

ENGELS, F. 'Records of Missionary Travel in South Africa', *Z.M.R.* i (1899), pp. 160–1.

FELL, J. R. 'Native Reserves', Appendix to *Proc. Gen. Missionary Conf. Northern Rhodesia* (1922).

—— 'Report of the Commission on Objectionable Native Marriage Customs', ibid.

F. J. 'A Visit to Monze Mission', *Z.M.R.* iii (1906), p. 60.

*Folk Tales of the Batonga*, London: Holborn Publishing House (1922).

GIBBONS, A. ST. H. *Exploration and Hunting in Central Africa*, London: Methuen (1898).

HOLE, H. M. 'Notes on the Batonga and Bashukulumbwe Tribes', *Rhodesian Scientific Association*, v (1905).

HOPGOOD, C. R. 'The Future of Bantu Languages in Northern Rhodesia', *Rhodes–Livingstone Journal*, ii (December 1944).

HOPGOOD, C. R. *Tonga Grammar*, London: Longmans (1940).

HORN, H. 'A Holiday in North-west Rhodesia', *Z.M.R.* vi (1919), pp. 183–90.

JOHNSON, C. E. *Agriculture for Africans in the Maize Belt of Northern Rhodesia*, Lusaka: Government Printer (1945).

JOHNSTON, H. H. *British Central Africa*, London: Methuen (1897).

JONES, N. CAREY. 'Native Treasuries in Northern Rhodesia', *Rhodes–Livingstone Journal*, ii (December 1944).

KENDAL, J. 'A Visit to Chikuni', *Z.M.R.* iv (1911), p. 307.

LIVINGSTONE, D. *Missionary Travels and Researches in South Africa*, London: John Murray (1857), pp. 549–59.

LIVINGSTONE, D. and C. *Narrative of an Expedition to the Zambesi and its Tributaries, 1858–1864*, London: John Murray (1865), pp. 219–64.

MACNAMARA, C. J. 'Natives of the Zambezi Valley, North Side', *Rhodesian Scientific Association*, xii (1912), pp. 60–7.

MOREAU, J. 'Survey of Social Conditions in the Native Church', *Proc. Gen. Missionary Conf. Northern Rhodesia* (1927), Appendix.

MYERS, J. L. 'Religious Surveys of the Batonga', ibid.

NORTHERN RHODESIA GOVERNMENT: *Report of the Native Land Tenure Committee, Part II. Mazabuka District*, Lusaka: Government Printer (1946).

PRESTAGE, P. 'From Bulawayo to the Victoria Falls, and Beyond', *Z.M.R.* ii (1903), p. 268.

SELOUS, F. C. *Travels and Adventures in South-East Africa*, London: Rowland Ward and Co. (1893), pp. 203–41.

—— *A Hunter's Wanderings in Africa*, London: Richard Bentley and Son (1881).

SMITH, E. W., and DALE, A. *The Ila-speaking Peoples of Northern Rhodesia*, London: Macmillan (1920).

SYAAMUSONDE, J., and SHILLING, P. *Naakoyo waamba caano cakwe* (*Old Naakoyo tells her story*), *with Monze Mukulu* (*The Great Chief*), Ndola: African Literature Committee (1947).

TORREND, J. *An English-Vernacular Dictionary of the Bantu-Botatwe Dialects of Northern Rhodesia*, London: Kegan Paul, Trench, Trubner, and Co. (1931). (*Bantu-Botatwe Dictionary*.)

—— *A Comparative Grammar of the South-African Bantu Languages*, London: Kegan, Paul, Trench, Trubner, and Co. (1891).

—— *Bantu Folk-lore from Northern Rhodesia*, London: Kegan Paul, Trench, Trubner, and Co. (1921).

—— 'Likenesses of Moses' Story in the Central African Folklore', *Anthropos*, v (1910).

—— 'A Mysterious Visitor to Tongaland', *Z.M.R.* iii (1909), pp. 548–9.

TRAPNELL, C. G., and CLOTHIER, J. *The Soils, Vegetation and Agricultural Systems of North Western Rhodesia*, Lusaka: Government Printer (1937), pp. 35–7.

*Zambesi Mission Record.* Various anonymous and editorial articles on Tonga and on mission and other modern influences.

# THE TRIBES OF
## —NORTH EASTERN RHODESIA—

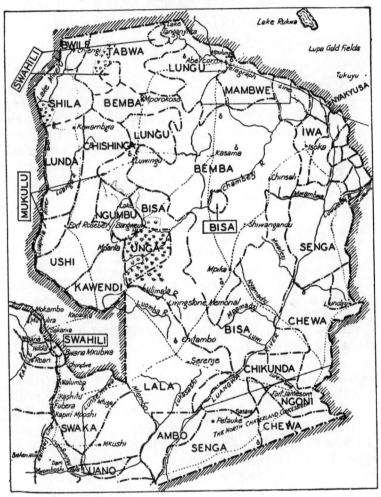

(By permission of the Government Printer, Lusaka)

# THE BEMBA OF NORTH-EASTERN RHODESIA[1]

## By AUDREY I. RICHARDS

### The Tribal Area

THE Bemba occupy the high plateau land of North-eastern Rhodesia stretching from Lake Bangweulu on the west to the Nyasaland border on the east, their empire formerly including the territory between the four big lakes, Tanganyika, Nyasa, Bangweulu, and Mweru. The tribe numbers now roughly 150,000, sparsely distributed over an area roughly equivalent to the size of Scotland and Wales, giving a population of about 3·95 per square mile.

### Origins

Bemba tradition is unanimous that the tribe reached its present territory from the west, being an offshoot of the Luba tribe east of the Kasai river. They thus form one of a successive series of invasions of Northern Rhodesia and even Nyasaland from the Congo area, and may on this ground be classed with such kindred peoples as the Bisa, the congeries of tribes occupying the swamps of Lake Bangweulu (Ushi, Unga, &c.), the Lala, Lamba, and even the Kaonde farther to the south-west. Whenever the Bemba invasion took place it seems at any rate certain that the Lunda, now ruled by the Kazembe, accompanied them, and that both these tribes were found occupying most of their present territory by the Portuguese traveller, Lacerda, in 1784. From our point of view it is worth noting two points: first that the Bemba state that they found the country empty on their arrival, although later, during the end of the last century, they enlarged their territory by pushing back the Bisa to the south-west and south-east, and the Lungu and Mambwe to the north. This means that we are dealing here with a uniform culture and not with one kingdom super-

[1] Reprinted from *Bantu Studies*, ix. 3 (September 1935). Material collected in two field expeditions from 1930–1 and 1933–4 made possible through the generosity of the School of African Studies of the Cape Town University, The Percy Sladen Trust, and The Rockefeller Foundation. The text has been altered in places to make it clear that the statements made were true in 1934 but are not necessarily correct now.

imposed on another as is the case among other Northern Rhodesian peoples. Second, we must class the Bemba among the tribes which have been, comparatively speaking, immune from the influence of northward migrations of Southern Bantu, such as penetrated Southern Rhodesia, Barotseland, and Nyasaland. This divides them off sharply from the peoples on their eastern border who have been subject to Ngoni influence.

I myself took no physical measurements in this area, and it is doubtful whether our knowledge of other Bantu areas would enable us to classify the Bantu peoples by this means. Suffice it to say that the Bemba are a tall, spare, muscular people of very mixed type, as is natural in an area where so much tribal movement has taken place. The skin colour varies from dark chocolate to light brown, and the features from a definitely negroid type, prognathous and with thick everted lips, to a face with fine features and a thin, almost semitic, type of nose. The reigning chiefs come of a very tall family averaging over 6 feet, and with the negroid type of face.

The Central Bantu can also be grouped according to the type of contact they have had with different races, European or not. The Bemba are among those tribes which stood on a direct trade route of the Arabs, exchange of guns and cloth for ivory and slaves having apparently lasted from 1865 to 1893,[1] such contact here, as among other Central African peoples, having led to the centralization of government and the increased power of the chief, who had the monopoly of ivory and hence of guns.

The type of European contact is even more important to define, both as regards its length and scope. The first administrative centre was established on the borders of the district by the British South Africa Company in 1897 and missionary posts were built from 1898 onwards. There are now six Government stations and over twelve missions in or near Bemba country. But the chief form of European contact takes place outside the area rather than within. The poverty of the soil and the absence of railway communications has prevented European settlement and farming, and the Bemba country can therefore be classed as a typical labour reserve for the industrial and mining developments of Northern and Southern Rhodesia. Forty to sixty per cent. of adult males are away from the villages at work at different periods during the year, such a situation leading to a special set of problems from the anthropologist's point of view.

[1] J. C. C. Coxhead, *The Native Tribes of North-Eastern Rhodesia*.

*Economic Life*

The preliminary classification of the Bantu peoples must obviously be based on their type of economic life. Are they predominantly pastoral or agricultural? What are the chief differences in environment, and what is their staple crop?

I mean by this type of grouping one that can be made at a surface glance without a deeper sociological analysis of the varying attitudes of different tribes towards their cattle and without committing the anthropologist to any theory of migration of peoples, the tracing of Hamitic influences, or to any hypothesis as to the association of economic life with some special social feature such as patrilineal organization. Such a rough classification is not only useful practically, but gives us the necessary background for any description of the social organization of the tribe, economic life affecting as it does the type of grouping, the relation between individual members, and the whole concepts of value and status in tribal life.

Of the environment of the Bemba, suffice it to say that they occupy high plateau land of poor agricultural soil. Rainfall is usually ample and the country is open and well watered, allowing for the free movement of villages about the district. Except on the banks of one or two rivers, there is no conglomeration of natives in one particular spot.

The Bemba are not a pastoral people. Not only is the country tsetse-ridden, but the people have no tradition or knowledge of handling cattle as have the contiguous tribes such as the Mambwe to the east. Cattle introduced by Europeans usually die. Goats exist in small numbers but are not cared for. Chiefs formerly possessed herds of cattle taken as a result of raids over the eastern border, but these perished in the Rinderpest at the end of the century. Sacrifices of cattle are made at the accession and burial ceremonies of chiefs, but this rite may be of recent origin, for it seems that all objects of value, such as china plates brought by the Arabs, or European goods, have been used from time to time to put on the graves of the chiefs. The body of the chief is also wrapped in the skin of an ox for burial.

As regards agriculture, the staple crop of the natives is finger millet (*Eleusinium coracanium*) but there is evidence that *sorghum*, which is still grown, was formerly a staple food. Maize, pumpkins, beans, peas, ground-nuts, and a number of subsidiary crops are grown. Manioc, which is extensively cultivated by the Bisa near Lake Bangweulu, is becoming more common lately with the destruction of millet by locust raids, and the planting of sweet potatoes has been encouraged by the Government for the same reason.

The Bemba follow a shifting system of cultivation. They make gardens by lopping off the branches of the trees according to the characteristic *citemene* system, this type of tree-cutting being the centre of the most important religious ceremonies of the year. The piled-up branches are then fired, and seeds are sown in the patch of ashes thus formed. Weeds are thus burned, and no further hoeing is needed during the year. Gardens once made are planted for four or five years according to a definite system of rotation of crops. Characteristic of the Bemba is their lack of interest in agriculture or ambition to do well in this line. By tradition they are warriors. Formerly they lived largely from tribute brought by other peoples. Under modern conditions there is no market for the sale of vegetable produce, which would act as a stimulus to agricultural development.

Hunting, on the contrary, is the great delight of the Bemba. They hunt with nets, spears, and dogs, muzzle-loading guns and, formerly, bows and arrows, and the digging of pits. Elephant hunts, under the direction of the chief and with specialist elephant-hunters, formed one of the main sources of the wealth of chiefs.

Fish are caught by the method of poison, by the setting of nets across streams and backwaters, and by means of conical fish-traps set in weirs. But fishing is an important industry only for the villages along the Chambezi river, from which there is a certain traffic in dried fish.

Characteristic of the Bemba is their lack of instinct or aptitude for trade. Exchange of ivory for Arab guns and cloth was formerly in the hands of the chiefs, and these also had the monopoly of the salt trade from the deposits around Mpika. No markets for the exchange of goods among commoners exist, and with the introduction of a money currency these natives have shown themselves particularly inefficient at commercial transactions of a European type.

The lack of skilled handicrafts is also characteristic of this warrior people. A little pottery is made by some women, mats and baskets of the very simplest type by the men, and native smiths can forge axe-heads and spears. The smelting of iron was mostly done by the Lunda to the west, though a few iron furnaces are still found in the Bemba country. Wood carving is almost non-existent. Houses are made on the circular pattern with conical thatched roofs with overhanging eaves supported on posts to form verandas. Bark cloth used to be made and worn, but has almost entirely given place to European cloth.

*Chieftainship*

Turning to the social structure of the Bemba we must start with an outline of what we may call its key institution. The most characteristic feature of the tribal system is undoubtedly its centralized form of government under a hereditary Paramount Chief, the *Citimukulu*. In this respect, the Bemba are typical of the Central African peoples which have produced so many large kingdoms, such as those of the Congo or Lubaland, while they differ from the contiguous tribes such as the Bisa or Lala which they have dispersed and conquered, from the scattered tribal units of Southern Rhodesia, and again from the more democratic Bantu societies of East Africa with their characteristic age-grade structure.

I call chieftainship the dominant institution among the Bemba because the belief in his power, both political and religious, is the main source of tribal cohesion throughout this scarcely populated area. The worship of the dead chief's spirits is the essential element of Bemba religion: war under his leadership was formerly the dominant ambition of each individual: and, in a community without any storable form of wealth such as cattle, rank and social status were determined, not by the number of a man's possessions, but by his kinship with the chief or by the services he had been able to do for him.

The political machinery includes the Paramount Chief himself, drawn from the royal clan—the *Benang'andu* or crocodile totem—who traces his descent in the matrilineal line from more than twenty-five holders of the title. The *Citimukulu* rules over his own district—the centre of the country (Lubemba)—but acts also as overlord to a number of territorial chiefs who succeed similarly to fixed titles and are drawn from the immediate family of the *Citimukulu* himself, the *Mwamba* and *Nkolemfumu* in 1934, for instance, being own brothers to the Paramount Chief himself. These close ties of kinship between the chiefs give them a very strong grip over the country. On the death of the *Citimukulu* he is succeeded by the next chief in order of precedence, it thus being possible for one man to hold several chieftainships in the course of his life. A number of sub-chiefs are responsible to the territorial chiefs, these being again drawn from the royal clan, but in some cases from more distant lines localized in some particular area. Some of the sisters and uterine nieces of the Chief are reckoned as chieftainesses, and rule over villages, while the chief's mother, the *Canda-mukulu*, has a territory of her own and plays quite an important part in tribal councils. The heirs of the chief, his brothers, or uterine nephews or grandsons may rule over villages and, when a vacancy occurs, territories of their own, while the sons and paternal grandsons of chiefs have special privileges. Relationship to the chief, and indeed even membership of the crocodile clan, can in fact be said to constitute a definite rank.

The tribal council consists of thirty to forty hereditary officials—the *bakabilo*—many of royal descent, and each responsible for some special ritual duty kept secret from the ordinary members of the tribe. The *bakabilo* are in charge of the chief's relic shrines (*babeni*), advise him on all religious matters, perform tribal ceremonies, act as regents at his death, and form a corps of hereditary buriers at the mortuary rites of the biggest chiefs. They also act as a council dealing with matters of tribal importance, such as questions of succession and legal decisions of any magnitude.

Each chief has also his own councillors (*the bafilolo*)—officials with executive and judicial functions, resident at his court, and appointed by him from the old men of his village. Formerly the office of *Mushika* or captain of the troops was important.

The sanctions behind the chief's authority are:

(*a*) *Supernatural.* The people believed in his descent from the original tribal ancestress and his inheritance of the guardian spirits (*mipashi*) of chiefs. These *mipashi* not only act as guardians of the chief himself but may also enter the womb of the pregnant mothers of the dead chief's territory, and act as guardian spirits to the children they bear. By virtue of his succession to the name and *mupashi* of the dead chief, each holder of the office is believed in his person to influence the prosperity of his whole land. His good or ill health affects the welfare of his peoples. His sex life has similar tribal importance, and for this reason is hedged with taboos. Of particular importance are the regulations for the protection of the chief's sacred fire from sexual impurities, which adversely affect the whole tribal welfare.

Besides this general influence over his country's prosperity the chief is able to invoke the tribal *mipashi* at the relic shrines, sacred objects, mostly stools, believed to have been brought by the first Bemba chief from Lubaland. To his possession of these relics the chief owes much of his power, those of the *Citimukulu* being of course the most important.

(*b*) *The organization and number of his followers.* The chief, as we have seen, is backed by a number of hereditary officials: his kinsmen have special rank and are expected to act as his loyal supporters; while other followers are attached to him by the rewards he is able to give them. In old days his power was largely based on his command of warrior bands under the control of the *bamushika*, who raided the surrounding districts, exacting tribute, and held new territory for him. Other executive officials apprehended criminals within the district, carried out sentences of mutilation on those who offended him, and enforced the payment of tribute in labour or kind, although apparently such payments were always made without question. Nowadays this situation is altered and the chief has hardly enough food from his diminished gardens to feed even the necessary tribal officials, and certainly not enough money to pay them.

(*c*) *His wealth.* The real wealth of the chief lay in the number of his villages, which provided the labour for his gardens and the young men for his army. But he also had slaves taken in war or given as compensation for some crime, and the monopoly over ivory and elephant meat. The possession of ivory gave him, with the coming of the Arabs at the end of the last century, a supply of guns and of trade goods, and so greatly increased his power. In 1934 tribute labour had very much decreased. The Paramount Chief had a Government subsidy of £60 a year, and the territorial chiefs smaller sums in order of decreasing importance, and their whole economic position was therefore changed.

(*d*) *His judicial powers.* The Paramount Chief acts as head of the supreme court of justice, and he with the three or four chiefs immediately below him had formerly alone the right to administer the *mwafi* or poison ordeal. His judicial powers were and still are important sanctions for his authority.

The duties of a chief towards his subjects were thus (*a*) to carry out religious ceremonies both at the relic shrines and the spirit centres throughout his district; (*b*) to exercise political powers in the appointment of sub-chiefs, officials, and headmen of villages; (*c*) to administer justice; (*d*) to initiate economic enterprises, such as the firing of the fields preparatory to sowing, or the organization of elephant hunts; (*e*) to lead in the case of war (the last two functions being no longer performed); (*f*) to provide food for his followers, and often to arrange for their marriages, and to support his villagers in time of famine.

The duties of a commoner were to serve his chief in garden work or war, to give him tribute of beer and food when required, and to give him every kind of ceremonial respect.

It will be noted that the power of the chief to allot land among his subjects, an important sanction for the power of some Bantu chiefs in South Africa, is here of little importance. Land is so plentiful that the chief is not asked to exercise this right of distribution.

## Territorial Grouping

Next to the problem of chieftainship, the form of territorial grouping is the most important background to our study of Bantu social organization. Among the Bantu we find every variation of local unit, from the small individual farm of the banana-growing Ganda or Chagga to the hedged kraals of the Southern Bantu, including the huts of a patrilineal group of kinsmen—father, wives, and married sons. Elsewhere, again, we find regular towns, such as Serowe, Kanye, Molepolole, and Mochudi in the Bechuanaland Protectorate, numbering 10,000 or more inhabitants. I believe the type of territorial unit with its profound effect on social institutions is one of the most important factors to study in the classification of the Bantu. We have to deal with the following in this case: (a) the size of the community, (b) the functions of the unit, and (c) its composition and leadership.

Bemba villages number from thirty to fifty huts, rising, in the case of a chief's village, to 300 or 400. Formerly chief's villages were even larger, but the security brought by British rule has made for the splitting into smaller and smaller units. The life of a village is four or five years, when the community moves to a new area to find new trees to cut.

As compared with the typical kraal of the Southern Bantu, the varied composition of the Bemba village is striking. Headmen are appointed in three ways: (a) by inheritance, (b) by the individual initiative of the man who has collected a following of relatives and receives the chief's permission, and (c) on the nomination of a chief who may give a village to one of his own relatives. The functions of the headman are to maintain law and order, to decide small disputes, and to act as intermediary between his people and the chief. Formerly the prayers of the headman to his ancestral spirits—before tree-cutting, the burning of branches, sowing, and first-fruits—gave him the leadership in economic pursuits, but these rites are now becoming rarer. Gardens are grouped together on kinship principles, and, unlike the Southern Bantu, ground for cultivation is not allotted by the headman; it is not scarce enough to make rules of distribution necessary. Fishing and hunting are communal village activities, and joint labour is performed in the clearing of paths and the paying of tribute in labour or kind to the chief. Moreover, the village is a small enough unit for recreational and social activities, dancing, beer-drinks, and games to be open to all. The old and the young men build themselves separate shelters (*nsaka*) in which they eat and spend the day, and the members of each *nsaka* remain close friends throughout life. However he may subsequently wander, the Bemba reckons that he belongs to his original village (*cifulo*), or more properly the village of his mother or maternal uncle, and he speaks with sentiment of the deserted sites of old villages (*fibolya*) of the group to which he belongs. The ceremony of inaugurating a new village is very important in native eyes even at the present day.

The core of a Bemba village is an extended family composed of the headman and his married daughters with their husbands and children, since marriage is initially, at any rate, matrilocal. This group is not divided spatially from the rest of the village but forms a domestic unit, since a mother and her married daughters tend to cook together, work together in the gardens, and to pool supplies of food. But there are a number of other principles governing residence. A headman may be joined by members of his own matrilineage, that is to say, by widowed, deserted, or divorced sisters and their married daughters, by uterine nephews who have been married some years and have won the right to remove their brides to some community of their own choosing, or by maternal grandsons. He may also be joined by his married sons, since a man may remove his bride to his father's village as well as to that of his maternal uncle. It will depend on individual choice and, that important factor in Bemba society, the question of the relative rank of the two. From figures collected in 1934 I find that in the case of the villages of two of the territorial chiefs, 51 per cent. and 58 per cent. of the headmen respectively had succeeded to their titles whereas the remaining 49 per cent. and 42 per cent. were new villages of the kind described above. In the case of the Paramount Chief, where communities were of older standing, as many as 71 per cent. of the headmen had succeeded to their titles. Within the group of hereditary headmen the following figures show the age of the community concerned:

|  | Citimukulu | Mwamba | Nkula |
|---|---|---|---|
| Villages with 1 previous holder of headmanship | 16 | 26 | 9 |
| Villages with 2 previous holders of headmanship | 10 | 14 | 18 |
| Villages with 3 previous holders of headmanship | 40 | 10 | 13 |

(See my *Land, Labour, and Diet in Northern Rhodesia*, Table D, p. 412.)

In the case of old villages it is, of course, common to find a number of combined father/married-daughter families as well as that of the headman's own family group. There may be, for instance, the families of the late headman's brothers or even those of their sons, for a temporary period at any rate. Lastly, the power of the chief to appoint his own nominees as heads of different villages means the possible intrusion of outside elements into the original kinship group. The shifting and rebuilding of the Bemba village every four or five years gives a constant opportunity for such grouping and regrouping. Moreover, in general these people are great travellers, visiting relatives in distant areas; while the children, according to tribal custom, move freely from relative to relative, especially when their parents are divorced.

This variety in the composition of the Bemba village, greatly increased as it is under European rule, naturally affects the whole nature of kinship sentiment, the educational influence to which the child and adolescent is subject, and the whole question of authority in the group. It is for this reason that I believe the study of the local unit is so important from the comparative point of view. In Bemba society status was formerly reckoned by the number of a man's followers and slaves, but under modern unstable conditions to build and hold together a village has become an absolutely dominant ambition for the average middle-aged man.

The larger territorial unit is the *calo*, which is the district ruled over by a chief. Each *calo* has more or less defined boundaries within which the chief has hunting and fishing rights as against the neighbouring chief, and he will not allow the latter's subjects to make gardens in his territory without permission. He performs religious rites for the benefit of the whole *calo* and provides for its inhabitants a court of law.

## Kinship

The Bemba have always been grouped with the matrilineal, matrilocal tribes of Central Africa. It is therefore important from the point of view of the classification of the Bantu peoples to define rather exactly what we mean by the terms as applied in this particular area. In doing so I shall concentrate on such legal aspects of the kinship system as descent, succession, inheritance, and authority in the household, as I have already dealt with the subject more fully elsewhere.[1]

Descent among the Bemba follows the matrilineal line. A man takes his mother's clan (*mukoa*), traces back his ancestors on his mother's

---

[1] A. I. Richards, *Mother-right among the Central Bantu (see bib.)*.

side, and speaks of his village of origin (*cifulo*) as the place where his mother and matrilineal uncles were born. In the case of the royal clan this tracing of descent is particularly important as determining status. With a man of chiefly rank it is typical to find ancestry traced back thirteen generations on the mother's side and only two on the father's. As against this fact we must remember that children of both sexes take their father's name as a sort of surname added to their own, and this even in the case of the children of a chieftainess by a slave husband. A father's ancestral spirit (*mupashi*) is honoured as well as a mother's, and may enter the womb of a pregnant woman of the family and act as a guardian spirit to the new-born child. Formerly also a man would stress his father's clan if this were more honourable than his mother's. Rank, all important among the Bemba, thus had a tendency to cut across the regular matrilineal kinship pattern. Nowadays the patrilineal elements have been still more stressed by European influence. Young men believe it to be more English, and therefore fashionable, to claim their father's clan instead of their mother's, and some missions have definitely encouraged this change.

Succession is also matrilineal. In the case of a chief, office passes first to the dead man's brothers, next to his matrilineal nephews, and then to his grandsons, i.e. the children of his sister's daughters. A chieftainess is succeeded by her sisters, maternal nieces, and granddaughters. In the case of a commoner, the question of succession is also important, since by the characteristic *kupyanika* system of the Bemba and kindred tribes a man's heir succeeds to his name, his guardian spirit, his social status and duties. Succession in this case is also matrilineal, but even here we have to note some patrilineal features. Chiefs are able to favour their sons as well as their uterine nephews, the rightful heirs; and sons of chiefs—*bana bamfumu*—hold definite rank in the community (cf. 'Chieftainship'). Certain territories acquired by the Bemba by conquest were originally given to the sons of the chiefs, and to this day appointments to these chieftainships are made from among the Paramount Chief's sons, not his nephews.

Inheritance is not an important factor among these peoples, as there are few forms of inheritable wealth. A man received the hereditary bow on the death of his maternal uncle, but nowadays money is often divided between a man's own children rather than his nephews. In the case of a woman, her girdle (*mushingo*) is handed on as a symbol of inheritance.

The question of authority in the household and over the children is difficult to deal with shortly. The father is the head of the household, but this term does not imply a large kraal or set of huts which we find among the Southern or some of the Eastern Bantu. A man lives in his hut with his wife and small baby, children over three being sent to their maternal grandmother to be brought up under her charge and later building huts of their own. Further, according to the rules of matrilocal marriage, invariably practised formerly, the father naturally occupies an inferior position in the village during the early years of married life.[1] As they grew up the children were formerly in the power of the maternal uncle, who had the right to their services and could even offer them as slaves in compensation for some injury done by the family.

But even in these early days the father had certain rights over his own children. He had to be consulted as to the marriage of his daughter and the right to distribute the marriage payment received for her (cf. 'Marriage'). The son-in-law worked for him and not for the maternal uncle. The father's sister (*Nyina senge*) played an important part in the marriage ceremony of the girl and could bless or curse the fertility of the union, while the father himself had an essential function to perform in the *kupyanika* ceremony of his son. Moreover, there were other factors that gave increased power to the father's family. A father's rank and position could establish claims to the children superior to those of the maternal uncle of lower social status. The freedom of movement allowed to children made possible constant visiting of both the paternal and maternal relatives. These ties were maintained even in the case of divorce of the parents.

Nowadays the authority of the father is immeasurably increased. The wage-earner naturally acquires rights over the children under modern economic conditions, and direct European influence supports the position of the father.

It can be said that a characteristic of the original Bemba kinship system was its bilateral nature, the father and his family having certain rights over the children which rank could considerably increase. The change of residence from the mother's to the father's village half-way through married life and the constantly shifting village system of the Bemba allowed for much change in the kinship composition of the local unit as compared with those of South Africa (cf. 'Territorial Groups'). Modern conditions have altered the position further,

---

[1] He was allowed to move to his own village after two or three children had been born.

greatly increasing the power of the father, and diminishing the practice of matrilocal marriage.

The bilateral nature of kinship is reflected linguistically. The kinship group to which the native constantly refers in common parlance is the *lupwa*, a bilateral group of the near relatives on both sides of his family who join in religious ceremonies, matrimonial transactions, in mortuary ritual and inheritance. This group is more important to the Bemba sociologically than his matrilineal clan.

Another important group of relatives are the *bukwe*, or relatives by marriage. In a primitive community the attitude to the relatives-in-law depends largely on the nature of the economic ties which bind the two. Many writers on South African society have emphasized the sentiments of watchful suspicion between the groups united by marriage which is inherent in the *lobola* system of passage of cattle before and after marriage. The relationship is associated here with a strongly developed system of in-law taboos and avoidances, among them the famous *hlonipa* taboos of the Zulu and kindred tribes. Among the Bemba, the passage of goods at marriage is unimportant (cf. 'Marriage'), and the tension between the two groups seemed to me to be *ipso facto* lessened. A man keeps taboos on eating with, or speaking to, his near relatives-in-law, but these are ended gradually after the birth of one or more children by the *kuingishya* ceremony, or 'the entering-in of the son-in-law'. Bemba do not speak of their in-laws very usually as a hostile group, and in some cases where matrilocal marriage has lasted for many years a man seems to identify himself very largely with the interests of his wife's village.

According to the Bemba system, kinship terms are never used as forms of address. A child is first called by the name of the guardian spirit (*mupashi*) he acquires through a rite of divination at the time of his birth. As a young boy he gives himself another name, or acquires a nickname. As a man he is called after the name of his child, or later his grandchild (e.g. ShiCilufya, 'the father of Cilufya'; Shikulu Canda, 'the grandfather of Canda'). It is only a very small child who will use the kinship terms of address, and then only in the case of his parents and grandparents.

Other characteristics of the system are:

(a) *The declension of the kinship terms* for the near relatives, i.e. grandfather, grandmother, father, mother, maternal uncle, and brother: e.g. father = *tata* (my father), *wiso* (thy father), *wishi* (his father), *shifwe* (our fathers), *shinwe* (your fathers), *shibo* (their fathers). Mother = *mayo, noko, nyina*, &c. Maternal uncle = *yama, nokolume, nalume*, &c.

(*b*) *In the generation above ego* the use of a classificatory term, *tata* (my father), for father and father's brother, with distinction made between the latter according to age, i.e. *tata mukalamba*, 'my father's eldest brother'; *tata mwaice*, 'my father's youngest brother'; and of a term *mayo* for 'my mother' and mother's sisters, with the same distinctions made as to age, i.e. *mayo mukalamba*, 'my mother's eldest sister', and *mayo mwaice*, 'my mother's youngest sister'. The father term is also applied to the husbands of my mother's sisters and the mother term to the wives of my father's brothers.

In the same generation there is also a distinctive term for ego's mother's brother (*yama*) and father's brother (*tata*), and similarly between mother's sister (*mayo*) and father's sister (*mayo senge*).

(*c*) *In ego's generation* the use of classificatory terms for ortho-cousin (*munyinane*), with distinction as to age, particularly important in the case of ego's own brothers, e.g. *mukalamba wandi*, 'my eldest brother'; *mwaice wandi*, 'my young brother': the use of classificatory terms for cross-cousins of both sexes (*mufyala wandi*): and the use of separate terms for siblings according to the sex of the speaker, e.g. *nkashi yandi*, 'my sister'; *munyinane*, 'my brother' (man speaking); *ndume yandi*, 'my brother'; *munyinane*, 'my sister' (woman speaking).

(*d*) *In the generation below ego* the use of a classificatory term—*mwana wandi*, 'my child'—for children of either sex of ego, ego's brothers, and ego's male cross-cousin and ortho-cousins (man speaking); and of ego, ego's sisters, and ego's female ortho-cousins and cross-cousins (woman speaking).

The use of a distinctive term, *mwipwa wandi* (my maternal nephew or niece), for children of both sexes of ego's sisters, ego's female ortho-cousins and cross-cousins (woman speaking).

(*e*) *In the generations above and below ego* the use of one classificatory term (*shikulu*) for both grandfathers, paternal and maternal, and the latter's brothers; and the use of a similar term (*mama*) for both grand-mothers and their sisters. In the generation of ego's grandchildren, one term—*mweshikulu wandi*—is used for the grandchildren of either sex, and equally for the children of ego's maternal nephews and nieces (*bepwa*) and children (*bana*).

Characteristic of the Bemba system is the complete reorientation of kinship terms which may take place later in a man's life when he succeeds, by the *kupyanika* system, to the position of his maternal uncle or his grandfather, i.e. a man either one or two generations above him; in the first case, he will call sister (*nkashi*) those women whom he previously called mother (*mayo*), while those whom he formerly called sisters or cross-cousins he will now speak of as *bepwa* or *bafyala* respectively, similar changes being made as regards the male relatives. In the case of the man who succeeds his grandfather, it will be seen that an even more complete reorientation of the kinship system as regards ego will have to be made.

The Bemba are divided into about thirty clans (*mikoa*). The names of these, some animal, some vegetable, and some of non-organic phenomena such as rain, are found widely spread over Northern Rhodesia, the Bisa of Lake Bangweulu in particular having practically identical clan names. Clan membership consists in the common use of a name by which a man is addressed as, for instance, *mwina mfula*, 'member of the rain', and by the reckoning of descent usually from one ancestress, but sometimes from the head of some localized branch of a clan. Each clan has usually a legend of origin, dating from the time of conquest of the present territory, such legends being often associated with archaic forms of greeting, used now only by old men or at the chief's capitals. Totemic food taboos are not kept, nor would this be possible since some clan names are those of important foodstuffs such as mushrooms or porridge.

The localization of different clans is only found in out of the way regions where little movement has taken place for many years, and certain dominant clans are now recognized. The heads of clans do not recognize rights over any clan lands, such as are claimed, for instance, among the Ganda, and indeed clan heads do not exist except in so far as the *bakabilo* or hereditary priests and councillors of the Paramount Chief are appealed to occasionally as the oldest or most eminent members of their respective clans.

As regards its sociological functions, the matrilineal clan is in effect an exogamous unit, but the bilateral emphasis on kinship among the Bemba makes a man count his descent from his father's clan as well as his mother's, and he will therefore describe a cross-cousin marriage on his father's side as a marriage within the clan (*mu mukoamukoa*). He himself describes the rule of clan exogamy as a prohibition on marriage with women he calls *nkashi* (his own sisters and parallel cousins) as distinct from those he calls *mufyala* (his cross-cousins on both sides).

Mutual aid is still practised among clan members to a certain limited extent. Clan membership confers rights to hospitality in out of the way districts and I have met cases of substitution within the clan in the case of ritual duties.

In ceremonial life the clan is still an important unit. Certain hereditary offices about the chief's court or connected with the guardianship of shrines must be held by members of specified clans. Moreover, it is characteristic of the Central Bantu that clans should be arranged in opposite pairs, known as *banungwe*, each performing reciprocal ceremonial functions for the other, particularly at funeral and marriage rites. In daily life the two stand in regular joking relationship, and may steal each other's possessions at the new moon. The pairs are arranged according to the complementary nature of the two totems, e.g. the Mushroom clan are *banungwe* of the Rain clan, since mushrooms come with the rain. The Crocodile clan, the royal totem, are *banungwe* of the Fish clan, since the latter are the food of the former.

To conclude, the clan does not perform such important social functions among the Bemba as we find in a number of South and East African societies, and the bilateral nature of kinship makes the *lupwa* a more significant unit in everyday life. The *mukoa* of the Bemba survives as a means of tracing descent and fulfils an important part in the ceremonial life of the tribe.

Widely differing economic environments shape the characteristic form of Bantu marriage. The typical *lobola* system of the pastoral peoples of South and South-east Africa divides them off sharply from the agricultural Bantu of Northern Rhodesia and Nyasaland, where the marriage contract is fulfilled very largely by the performamce of a period of service by the son-in-law.[1] So also the introduction of money currency and European economic values account for certain typical recrystallizations of the marriage institutions wherever contact with the White races has been prolonged. For this reason I shall preface my account of Bemba marriage with a description of the type of economic contract between relatives party to the union, and shall then consider the rules governing the choice of marriage partners, and finally the wedding ceremony itself.

In the marriage contract of the Bemba, as distinct from that of

[1] Cullen Young uses the existence of this type of marriage by service, which he describes as 'symbol-transfer-marriage', as the basis for his classification of Nyasaland peoples: 'Tribal Mixtures in Nyasaland', *J.R.A.I.*, lviii, 1933.

South and East Africa, the transfer of goods is relatively unimportant. It consisted formerly in:

(a) An initial present (the *nsalamo*)—a small trifle such as a bangle—constituting betrothal.

(b) The main marriage payment (*mpango*)—usually two bark cloths or a hoe.

(c) A further present at the initiation ceremony (*cisungu*) of the girl.

It is characteristic also that the transfer of goods among these people is more or less completed with the termination of the marriage ceremony, unlike some of the tribes of East Africa where payments between the in-laws groups last throughout life. Among the Bemba it is merely food and beer that are exchanged between the relatives united by the marriage on various ceremonial occasions in the life of the young pair. Moreover, in the old days bark cloth was quickly worn out and quickly remade. Thus the question of the return of the marriage payment in case of divorce did not occur. The whole *lobola* psychology, if we may so describe it, with its effect on the relations between man and wife, and their respective kinship groups, was non-existent and is so still today.

The essential element in the contract consisted formerly in service—the making and fencing of gardens principally—performed by the son-in-law. This he started soon after betrothal and continued for four or more years, and sometimes indeed for the whole of his life. As the Bemba chief regards his wealth in terms of the number of his followers rather than the number of his cattle and possessions, so also the Bemba father counts his assets in terms of the number of sons-in-law whose services he can command, such a system being correlated with the institution of matrilocal marriage.

Nowadays the whole nature of the contract is being altered by the institution of money payments, both as *mpango* and also as a means of commuting for agricultural labour. The *mpango* in 1934 was anything from 5s. to £3 with 10s. a year given the father-in-law in lieu of labour, the higher the sum paid the stronger the claim of the father as against that of the maternal uncle in a matrilineal society. There is a tendency too to demand the return of the *mpango* in case of default of the wife. Hence natives feel that a higher marriage payment gives them a greater hold over wife and children in these days of the break-up of family life.

PLATE IX

1. Man climbing tree to lop off the branches. The piled-up branches are fired and millet, the staple crop, is planted in the ash-bed

2. Village scene. Children dancing round a drum. Granary with the roof off in order that grain may be taken out

BEMBA

PLATE X

3. A councillor rolls on his back in salutation to his territorial chief—the common Bemba greeting to a chief

4. The chief (Mwamba) is carried shoulder high on ceremonial occasions. A hereditary councillor with plumed head-dress precedes him carrying his hereditary bow

BEMBA

The money *mpango* is distributed by the father between the relatives, the maternal uncle and paternal aunt being most important.

The preferential marriages among the Bemba are as follows:

(*a*) Cross-cousins on both the father's and the mother's side of the family, i.e. those women whom a man calls *mufyala wandi*.

(*b*) Classificatory granddaughters, or the women whom a man calls *mweshikulu wandi*. In the case of a chief, a man may marry the daughter of his own son, but in the case of a commoner this is regarded as bad, and he may only marry the daughter of his brother's son. The daughter of a daughter is taboo in both cases because 'the daughter of a daughter is a sister'. So also a woman may marry her grandson (*mweshikulu wandi*), although this is not common.

(*c*) In Bemba society a woman has definite rights over her brother's daughter, and may demand this girl as an additional wife for her husband or a substitute wife if she herself is tired of married life. This marriage, known as the *mpokoleshi*, is characteristic of the Bemba.

Marriage within the matrilineal clan is not permitted, although the people themselves express this taboo in terms of incest rules (see 'Clan'). Inter-tribal marriage is now exceedingly common, but Bemba say that they were formerly only allowed to marry kindred tribes, such as the Bisa and Lunda, and not the Nsenga or the Lumbwe.

Polygamy is, relatively speaking, rare. In the old days chiefs were said to have some sixty or seventy wives, but at present the Paramount Chief has only twelve. It is rare to find more than one man in a village with two wives, and the Bemba women have never accepted the institution of polygamy after the fashion of some of the Southern Bantu. Except where the two are related, they ignore the existence of the second wife and refuse to co-operate with her in any way.

Infant betrothal is exceedingly rare. Girls are usually bespoken at the age of ten or eleven, while boys are affianced rather later.

Formerly slave wives were common. Chiefs had many wives taken from conquered peoples; and men of rank had slave wives bestowed on them by the chief or given in compensation for some injury done to a member of the family, particularly in case of murder.

The surviving partner of a marriage must perform an act of ritual intercourse with a man or woman respectively who is the potential successor to the dead husband or wife. Unless this custom, known as 'kubula mfwa, 'to take back the death', is carried out, it is believed that the *mupashi* of the dead man or woman cannot return to its own family, and that it will avenge itself on the surviving partner if he or she subsequently marries someone else. After the rite has been performed a widow may either remain as the wife of the dead man's heir or, if she prefers, return home and live in her brother's care.

The marriage ceremony actually starts with the betrothal of the pair by the acceptance of the betrothal present (*nsalamo*), the beginning of the period of service of the son-in-law, and the first marriage payment (*mpango*). After this the girl may be handed over to her husband. She then sweeps his hut and draws water for him, while her mother provides him with cooked food. At night the girl sleeps with her husband, although partial intercourse only is allowed. This form of pre-puberty intercourse, characteristic of a number of Northern Rhodesian tribes, is believed by the people to produce the best and most stable marriages. It is not correlated, as in East Africa, with the institution of age-grades and a period of experimentation and promiscuity among the young people. It is associated rather with the matrilocal system of marriage, by which a girl is kept under her parents' tutelage and handed over to her husband by degrees. The son-in-law is first gradually admitted to the privilege of eating foods cooked by his mother-in-law by a separate ceremony for each.

After the marriage ceremony, the girl is not allowed her own fireplace for a year or so, and her husband does not build his own granary until later, the whole period being one of probation for the son-in-law. If he is lazy or quarrelsome during this time, he will not be allowed to remove his wife to his own village should he desire to do so later on.

When puberty seems to be approaching, the girl is taken back to her mother's hut to wait for the performance of her initiation ceremony, as it is considered exceedingly dangerous for the whole community if a girl should become pregnant before this rite has been carried out. The *cisungu*, or initiation ceremony, characteristic of many of the Central Bantu, is found in a particularly complex form among the Bemba. It used to last for six weeks to three months, but is now practised, if at all, in a very attenuated form. Its essential elements are: (*a*) The seclusion of the girl, or girls, who sleep in a separate hut, keeping taboos and remaining out of sight by day. (*b*) The mimetic representation of the woman's future work as a wife by songs and dances showing her agricultural work, domestic tasks, and her correct attitude towards her relatives-in-law and the bringing up of her children. (*c*) The revelation of secrets to the girl who is shown various objects, known as *mbusa* or 'things handed down', consisting of pottery images, made especially for her, representing tribal legends, domestic objects, salt, flour, &c.; designs painted on the walls of the initiation hut; or pottery models made each day on its floor. All these have archaic names which are now revealed to the girl. (*d*) A rite of purifying the girl from the stain of the menstrual blood by bathing her in the river and covering her with white clay. (*e*) The exchange of food and beer between the families of the bridegroom and the bride. (*f*) A final ceremony consisting in the showing of the *mbusa* to the bridegroom, who has to shoot with bow and arrow at a mark on the wall of the hut below which the bride sits. Then after singing through the night till the first cock crows, a chicken is ritually killed and eaten by all the women present, the girls are bathed in the river, and emerge next day to make formal obeisance outside each hut in the village.

This ceremony does not admit the girl to a new age-grade, but is definitely part of the marriage ceremony, or was so, and without its performance a girl was formerly despised. The gathering of women for the ceremony under the direction of the *nacimbusa*, or mistress of the ceremonies, showed all the women of the district graded with elaborate rule of precedence, according to a hierarchy of age.

Some days after her *cisungu* rite the girl is given to her husband, that is to say, she is carried to his hut on the back of her paternal aunt. After the consummation of the marriage the bridegroom should throw out a smouldering brand to the waiting relatives. Next day the pair must stay inside the hut, keeping taboos and avoiding talk with their fellows. Early next morning the paternal aunt brings the ceremonial marriage pot, and the rite of purification is first performed (cf. 'Religion'). The ceremony concludes when the bride and bridegroom, bathed and oiled, are brought out before the village, where, seated in silence, they receive congratulations, advice, and small gifts, the bride's father presenting his son-in-law with an arrow with which he is commanded to kill anyone who tries to seduce his wife.

The characteristic elements of this ceremony, as far as they can be summarized here, are, therefore, the rites gradually admitting the son-in-law to the community of the matrilocal village, the handing over of the ceremonial marriage pot, and the symbolism of the bow and arrow which occurs throughout Bemba ritual.

*Religion and Magic*

The religious and magical conceptions of a people are particularly difficult to summarize in a few words. I cannot do more than stress certain distinctive features of Bemba religion as compared with that of the other Bantu tribes best known to us, and describe certain of their most characteristic rites.

As compared with the typical form of ancestor worship practised by the Bantu, the chief characteristic of Bemba religion is the place it accords to the worship of the spirits (*mipashi*) of dead chiefs—those of the *Citimukulu* himself and the territorial chiefs under him—this ritual attitude being of course correlated with the dominant position of the chief in the whole tribal organization.

The spirits of the chiefs are worshipped

(1) *Annually at the chief economic events of the year*—tree-cutting, sowing, and first-fruit rites.

(2) *At times of disaster or before special undertakings*—such as war in the old days.

The rites performed are of two kinds: the addressing of prayers to the dead chiefs (*kulumbula imipashi*), and the offering of objects of value such as beer, cloth, sacrifice of cattle at the spirit shrines, &c. Such rites are known as *kupepa imipashi*, and take place at irregular intervals according to the prosperity of the Paramount Chief, who himself initiates the rites that are subsequently carried out at all the shrines throughout the territory.

Rites are carried out (*a*) *at the spirit shrines* (*nfuba*), small shelters of branches supposed to be remade each year after the forest fires have swept the country. The most important of these are shrines on the sites of the villages of the chief's first ancestors, and an essential part of the mortuary ritual of a chief is the final ceremony by which his hut is destroyed, an animal tied to the lintel posts and sacrificed, and a new shrine built on the site (*kutoba itembwe*). Other shrines commemorate important events in the lives of dead chiefs, each being in the charge of an hereditary priest (*shimiapepo*), who can only perform the rites there at the order of the reigning chief of the territory.

Small *nfuba* used to be made to the spirits of territorial chiefs in each village as well as those to the headman's ancestors, but this practice is now dying out.

(*b*) *At the burial groves* of the chiefs, and particularly that of the

*Citimukulus*. Here the hereditary priest, the *shimwalule*, performs important ritual functions, including sacrifices made in the event of failure of rain.

(*c*) *At the relic shrines* (*babenye*) in the chief's villages, only the most important chiefs having relics of this kind. These shrines contain stools and other objects handed down from dead chiefs. They are housed in small huts in the centre of the chief's village; kept with the utmost secrecy; hedged with taboos, and guarded by old women, descendants of the first chief's wives (*bamukabeni*). At these shrines the reigning chief is able to invoke the ancestral spirits guarding that particular territory, or, in the case of the Paramount Chief, of the tribe itself. The most important religious rites of the Bemba are those ceremonies by which a new chief acquires the *babeni*, and so the right of access to his ancestral spirits.

At the death of the Paramount Chief the *babenye* are placed under the care of hereditary priests (*bakabilo*) while the body of the dead man is dried and partially preserved with a sauce of beans for a period of a year. After this the body, wrapped in an ox-skin, is carried a four-days' journey to the burial grove, formerly with the killing of victims *en route* and the sacrifice of the chief's head wife and other near officials to line the grave.[1]

Besides the all-important chiefs' spirits, the Bemba also carry out rites at certain waterfalls, high rocks, or unusual objects in the landscape, believed to be inhabited by spirits known as *ngulu*—mythical beings with names and legends attached, but specifically stated not to be chiefs. *Ngulu* is also the name given to certain individuals who believe themselves to be possessed by spirits and who prophesy and heal their fellows.

Shrines are also put up to a hunting deity known as *Mulenga*, and his mother and wife, and to *Kampinda*, the mythical forerunner believed to have taught the art of medicine to the Bemba.

Formerly the headman of each village would build one or more tiny shrines (about 2 feet high) outside his hut to his own *mipashi* as well as one to those of the chief of that tract of land. Nowadays the building of shrines has been discouraged by missionaries and prayers are offered either on cleared spaces outside the village, at the base of a tree, or inside the owner's hut where objects to be blessed, such as seeds or axes, are

---

[1] It should be noted here that the mortuary ritual of commoners is entirely different and extremely simple, consisting merely in the burial of the body a few hours after death.

laid under the head of the bed in certain rites. The ceremonies performed here are a simplified version of those that take place at the chief's shrines and consist of words addressed to the spirit, with the spraying of saliva into the air (*kupala amate*).

Characteristic of Bemba dogma is the belief in the return of the *mipashi* of dead ancestors or of the chiefs of the territory to act as guardian spirits to new-born children, the arrival of the spirit being indicated by the first stirring of the child in the womb, and its identity revealed by divination rites. Otherwise *mipashi* are acquired by the succession or *kupyanika* rite (cf. 'Kinship').

Another belief which affects very deeply the moral codes and behaviour of the people is the dogma of the dualism of ancestral spirits, good and bad. Good spirits (*mipashi*) are those that die contented and honoured and return to help their relatives. Bad spirits (*fiwa*) are the spirits of those that die neglected, injured, or wrongfully accused, and return with the permission of *Lesa*, the High God, to afflict their descendants with disease or death. Fear of their vengeance is so powerful that it still acts as a constant sanction for the keeping of Bemba kinship obligations. Bemba constantly say, when performing some arduous duty for a relative, 'lest he return'.

The ritual attitude to the use of fire is one of those traits, supposedly Hamitic, of which the distribution has been mapped throughout Africa. Among the Bemba this ritual is too complex to describe in full. The essence of their belief is that fire can be contaminated by sexual impurity and when so contaminated can bring harm on members of the household who touch it or eat food cooked upon it. A person who is sexually impure is one who has committed adultery, or who has touched the fire without previously performing a rite of purification with the ceremonial pot which each woman receives at her marriage. Hence the importance of this rite in the life of the ordinary householder, and more especially in the case of a chief, who may bring disaster upon himself and his whole land if he allows his fire to be contaminated. Hence also the complex taboos regarding the use of fire at a chief's capital, the rites of extinguishing and relighting in case of death or the building of a new village, and the double sacred fire in the Paramount Chief's village—his own and a supplementary fire guarded by a hereditary fire-keeper from whom alone he can borrow a glowing ember for his own household.

It should be added that the taboos protecting fire are also applied to the protection of all sacred objects. The relic shrines of chiefs can be similarly contaminated by sexual impurity, and rites of purification must be performed by the participants in any religious rite of whatsoever kind, this whole belief throwing a light on the Bemba attitude towards fire itself.

It is impossible to summarize clearly the magic beliefs of the Bemba. As among the Bantu generally, the typical magic rite consists in the use of a medicine (*muti*) which is almost invariably part of a plant or tree, the word *muti* itself being the common term for tree. A leaf or a twig of the tree is either worn by its owner for magic or curative purposes or a decoction is formed from it to be drunk or applied externally. The Bemba also believe in the importance of certain activating principles (*fishimba*), charms such as a bone of a bird or animal, which act as catalytic agents increasing the efficacy of the medicine itself. Words are sometimes used, but there is no fixed spell with definite rites of possession as is the case in Melanesia. The witch-doctor who procures the medicine must call upon the name of *Lesa*, the High God, without whom the magic is believed not to work.

The knowledge of medicine is in the hands of witch-doctors (*ŋanga*), some of whom acquire the secrets as a heritage from father or maternal uncle, others by right of purchase. Certain of their more valuable medicines are kept secret, while others may be sold to invalids and those in trouble; while a number of simple cures for ordinary diseases are known to most old people in the community. The *ŋanga* also possess most forms of magic of divination (e.g. rubbing an axe head or an inverted pot on a skin; the boiling-water test; balancing of small horns in a vessel of water; the rattling of a seed under an inverted pot; the smoke test, &c.), although the characteristic Bemba form of divination is the hunting test, by which results are decided according to the sex of the victim first killed at the hunting nets, and these can be performed by any member of the community.

Another characteristic of the magic system of the Bemba is the complete absence of communal magic rites. There are no tribal rites for rain, such as we find among the Swazi, for instance, since the ceremonies the chiefs perform to their ancestral spirits are considered efficacious in this case. Economic magic, in fact, consists chiefly in the very widespread use of charms to increase the lasting power of food (*cibyalilo*) of which many individuals own their separate brand. The protection of property by means of a conditional curse is almost unknown among the Bemba, although very commonly practised by the Bisa for the protection of manioc gardens.

Destructive magic is supposed to be performed by sorcerers (*baloshi*), individuals who acquire their evil magic hereditarily, who start their career by performing some outrageous act, such as father–daughter incest, and who possess supernatural attributes such as invisibility and the power to kill at a distance; but unlike some of the neighbouring tribes no Bemba will admit that he practises bad magic, and it cannot technically be bought or sold. The *ŋanga* will only admit that he sells protective magic for those who have already been attacked by the sorcerers' arts.

## Conclusion

I began these preliminary notes with a query as to the possibility of classifying African tribes from a scientific point of view. Classification necessarily means the enumeration of the outstanding features of a culture, and the more we know of the complexity of the social organization of any one primitive people the less feasible does it seem to classify such societies by the arbitrary selection of specific culture traits. The range of cultural forms far exceeds the possible morphological modifications, say, of animal organisms, which can, of course, readily be classified into species and genera. It is the interrelation of the different institutions of a human society which stamps its essential pattern, and our problem is, therefore, to find some mechanism by which we can compare such different cultures as wholes.

To this end I have given this very cursory outline of the social organization of the Bemba, analysing the material from a general comparative point of view. For practical purposes we can make some rough estimate of tribal affinities through our knowledge of historic and environmental features. We saw that the Bemba must be classed with those Bantu tribes which migrated eastward from the Congo Basin to the Tanganyika Plateau of Northern Rhodesia during the last two hundred years. Although there is no geographical area exactly corresponding to the territories of this migrating group, we can look for the greatest concentration of tribes of the Luba-Bemba type along the Congo border and in north-eastern and north-western Rhodesia. Of these the Bemba were the most successful as warlike colonizers, forming one of the typical large Bantu kingdoms, but the problem of tribal mixtures is simplified in this case since the Bemba method of warfare was to push back other tribes into the empty country to the south and east, or to exact tribute from them. A joint kingdom of two

PLATE XI

5. The installation of a titled chieftainess—the Mukukamfumu. A hereditary councillor and a father's sister throw gifts of money before her

6. Making a hunting net from bark-rope

BEMBA

PLATE XII

7. Setting up the nets for a ritual hunt

8. Iron forge: man hammering out an axe-head while children blow the goat-skin bellows

BEMBA

racial or tribal stocks such as we find among the Lacustrine Bantu elsewhere was not created.

The original cultural forms in this area were subject to influences from northward migrations of Southern Bantu, and the resultant displacement of peoples on the Nyasaland and Southern Rhodesia border; of Arab trading caravans crossing the district during the latter end of the nineteenth century; and of European contact in the form of administrative and educational influences throughout the country during the past thirty years. We noted also the powerful effects on social organization of the exodus of the males of the tribe as wage-labourers in European industrial concerns to the south. A comparison of the effect on different Bantu cultures of these three types of contact remains to be made.

Those who put faith in large-scale reconstruction of tribal migration will no doubt be able to mark the Bemba on such distribution maps as show the range of belief in chiefs with supernatural powers, the burial of chiefs with human sacrifices after a process of desiccation lasting a year, the preservation of relics, chiefly in the form of stools, a ritual attitude to fire, the use of the *mwafi* poison ordeal, the presence of puberty rites for girls and not for boys, matrilineal organization, the general use of round huts with conical roofs, and the absence of iron-work and weaving. But I have only indicated the tribal affinities of the Bemba within the limits of ascertainable historical fact.

From a more general comparative point of view I have tried to analyse my material in three different ways. First, I outlined the dominant morphological features of the society in question, thus determining the essential structure of the group and the chief values and beliefs of its individual members. Secondly, I described certain fundamental aspects of the culture, such as its economic system, the type of kinship or territorial grouping or political organization, so as to enable us to group the culture first with this and then with that other society according to these main sociological features. Thirdly, I mentioned certain peculiarities of the Bemba tribal system, due either to environmental or historic factors, which make it atypical in any respect.

To turn, then, to the dominant pattern of Bemba culture, we have seen that its key institution is a well-marked political system, a hierarchy of hereditary rulers, supported by hereditary councillors, and a series of executive officials, military and religious, the whole organization centred round the fundamental objective of the tribe—military conquest. The whole political system produces, and is itself a product of, the well-marked attitude to authority developed throughout the group, whether it be from youth to age, slave to commoner, son-in-law to father-in-law, commoner to man of rank, headman to sub-chief, and sub-chief to Paramount Chief—an attitude reflected in religious belief and practice, and directly correlated with an economic system in which wealth consists in the power to exact services either in war or cultivation, and social status is entirely determined by a man's relationship to the chief, whether by blood or otherwise. Dependent on the Bemba attitude to chieftainship is the importance of rank in social structure, and the hypertrophy of ceremonial centred round the chief's person, his accession and burial ceremonies, and the protection of his sacred relics.

Turning to the question of environment, we must reckon the Bemba among those African tribes living sparsely distributed over poor soil in bush and savannah forest country. The different methods by which social cohesion is maintained by such peoples, and their whole attitude to the question of land tenure, would make an interesting comparative study. We are dealing, too, with a millet-eating people, millet sometimes being used as a staple crop, as among some of the Central Bantu, and sometimes for beer alone, as among the natives round Lake Bangweulu. We have as yet no comparative knowledge of the different methods of cultivation of millet and the effect of these on social organization, but here the system is connected with the constant moving of villages characteristic of many of these prairie-dwelling Bantu. An economic system largely dominated by the military ambitions of the tribe makes Bemba society of further interest from a comparative point of view. We have as yet no study of the war organization of the Bantu peoples and the different types of warrior age-grades, or chief's armies. A connected problem is the almost complete lack of aptitude for arts and crafts among these people, or skill in trade.

The kinship system of the Bemba enables us to class them with the matrilineal, matrilocal peoples of Central Africa, although we have very little knowledge of some of these latter. The bilateral nature of kinship in this area, and the growing predominance of paternal authority which has resulted from the changed economic conditions of today, makes this question exceedingly interesting from a comparative point of view. We saw that kinship is the basis of territorial grouping among the Bemba, although in this, as in other aspects of Bemba tribal life, rank cuts across the typical kinship pattern. The clan among the Bemba does not fulfil such important functions as among some of the Southern and Eastern Bantu, clan leadership being completely subordinated to the institution of chieftainship, but characteristic of this area are the ceremonial functions carried out by members of different clans in court ritual, and the division of the clans into complementary pairs (*banungwe*), each performing reciprocal ritual functions.

The marriage contract of the Bemba groups them with those Central African tribes in which the son-in-law performs service for his bride instead of handing over cattle or other forms of wealth. The effect of the introduction of European economic values among matrilineal and marriage-by-service peoples is a problem of real practical importance. In this case, the service of the son-in-law is associated with matrilocal marriage during a preliminary trial period, and characteristic of this, as among other Central Bantu, is the pre-puberty intercourse allowed to a girl with her bridegroom. The girl's initiation rite, *cisungu*, which forms a part of the marriage rite, achieves a complexity in this tribe that we do not find among the neighbouring peoples.

Bemba religion is dominated by the worship of spirits of dead chiefs associated with their sacred relics, deserted village sites, and graves. Long and elaborate burial ceremonies for the dead chief, and the role of the latter in ritual observances connected with household and village fires, are also characteristic.

## BIBLIOGRAPHY FOR THE BEMBA

ANON. 'Les Soirées littéraires des Babemba. Fables', *Journal African Society*, xix. 3 (October 1903), pp. 62–73. (Fables in French, by a Father of the Roman Catholic Mission, NE. Rhodesia.)

BRELSFORD, W. V. 'The Bemba Tridents', *Nada*, xiii (1935).

—— 'Some Reflections on Bemba Geometric Art', *Bantu Studies*, xi, 1 (January 1937).

—— 'Babemba Animal Medicines', *Nada*, xviii (1941).

—— *Some Aspects of Bemba Chieftainship*, Livingstone: Communications from the Rhodes–Livingstone Institute, No. 2 (1944).

—— *The Succession of Bemba Chiefs*, Lusaka: Government Printer (1944); 2nd edition with additions, 1949.

—— 'Shimwalule: A Study of a Bemba Chief and Priest', *African Studies*, i. 3 (September 1942).

—— *Fishermen of the Bangweulu Swamps*, Livingstone: Rhodes–Livingstone Institute, Paper No. 12 (1946).

—— 'Insanity among the Bemba of Northern Rhodesia', *Africa*, xx (1950).

CLARKE, H. S. 'Rough Notes on M'wembe Customs', *Man*, xxxi (1931), pp. 274–5.

—— 'Ba-wemba Initiation', *Man*, xxx (1930), p. 148.

COXHEAD, J. C. *The Native Tribes of Northern Rhodesia*, Royal Anthropological Institute, Occasional Papers No. 5 (1914) and articles in *Journal of the African Society*, xiv, xv (1915), and xvi (1916).

GIRAUD, —. *Les Lacs de l'Afrique Équatoriale*, Paris (1890).

GOODALL, E. B. H. *Some Wemba Words*, London: Oxford University Press (1921).

GOULDSBURY, C. 'Notes on the Customary Law of the Awemba', *Journal of the African Society*, xiv, xv (1915); xvi (1916).

—— and SHEANE H. *The Great Plateau of Northern Rhodesia*, London: Edwin Arnold (1911).

LABRÈQUE, E. 'Accidents de la naissance chez les Babemba', *Anthropos*, xxv (1930).

—— 'Le Mariage chez les Babemba', *Africa*, iv (1931).

—— 'Le Tribu des Babemba', *Anthropos*, xxviii (1933), xxxi (1936).

—— 'La Sorcellerie chez les Babemba', *Anthropos*, xxxii (1938).

MELLAND, FRANK H. 'Some Ethnographic Notes on the Awemba Tribe of North Eastern Rhodesia' (and on some portion of the Wabisa), *Journal of the African Society*, xi. 3 (1904). Also continuation in *Journal of the African Society*, xv. 4 (April 1905).

MOLINIER, LUD. 'Croyances superstitieuses chez les Babemba', *Journal of the African Society*, ix. 3 (October 1903).

MOORE, R. J. 'Industry and Trade on the Shores of Lake Mweru', *Africa*, x (1937).

—— 'Bwanga among the Bemba', *Africa*, xiii (1940), and *Bantu Studies*, xv (1941).

MUENYA, AARON, H. 'The Burial of Chitimukulu Mubanga', *African Affairs*, xlvi. 183, App. (1947), pp. 101–4.

MURSAN, —. 'Sépulture du Grand Chef chez les Babemba', *Ann. de la Propagation de la Foi*, Lyon, Paris, xcviii, 585 (1926), pp. 81–5. (Within Tanganyika and Bangweulu.)

NORTHERN RHODESIA GOVERNMENT. *Census of Northern Rhodesia*, Lusaka; Northern Rhodesia (1946).

OGILVIE, A. G. 'Co-operative, Research in Geography; with an African Example', Pres. address to Section E, Brit. Ass. for Adv. of Science, 1934.

ORDE-BROWNE, G. St. J. *Labour Conditions in Northern Rhodesia*, London: H.M.S.O., Col. No. 150 (1938).

PIM, SIR A., and MILLIGAN, S. *Report of the Commission to enquire into the financial and economic position in Northern Rhodesia*, London: H.M.S.O., Col. No. 145 (1938).

QUICK, G. *Arts and Crafts in the Training of Bemba Youth* (1935).

RAGOEN, J. 'L'Idée de Dieu d'après les proverbes et les dictons des Babemba', *Grands lacs* (July 1935), pp. 477–9.

RICHARDS, A. I. 'Anthropological Problems in North-eastern Rhodesia', *Africa*, v (1932).

—— 'Mother-right among the Central Bantu', in *Essays Presented to C. G. Seligman*, edited by E. E. Evans-Pritchard, R. Firth, B. Malinowski, and I. Schapera, London: Kegan Paul (1933).

—— 'Tribal Government in Transition', Supplement to *Journal of the African Society*, xxxiv. 3 (October 1935).

—— 'Preliminary Notes on the Babemba of North-Eastern Rhodesia', *Bantu Studies*, ix. 3 (September 1935).

RICHARDS, A. I. 'The Village Census in the Study of Culture Contact', *Africa*, viii (1935).
—— 'A Modern Movement of Witchfinders', *Africa*, viii. 3 (October 1935).
—— 'From Bush to Mine', *Geographical Magazine* (October 1935).
—— 'The Life of Bwembya, a Native of Northern Rhodesia,' in *Ten Africans*, edited by M. Perham, London: Faber and Faber (1936).
—— 'A Dietary Study in Northern Rhodesia' (with E. M. Widdowson), *Africa*, ix. 2 (1936).
—— 'Reciprocal Clan Relationships among the Bemba of North-eastern Rhodesia', *Man*, xxxvii (December 1937).
—— *Land, Labour and Diet in Northern Rhodesia*, London: Oxford University Press (1939).
—— 'The Political System of the Bemba of North-Eastern Rhodesia', in *African Political Systems*, edited by M. Fortes and E. E. Evans-Pritchard, London: Oxford University Press (1940).
—— *Bemba Marriage and Modern Economic Conditions*, Rhodes–Livingstone Institute, Paper No. 4 (1940).
—— 'Variations in Family Structure among the Central Bantu', in *African Systems of Kinship and Marriage*, edited by A. R. Radcliffe-Browne and C. D. Forde, London: Oxford University Press (1950).
—— 'Huts and Hut-building among the Bemba', *Man*, l (1950), 134 and 162.
ROBERTSON, W. G. 'Kasembe and the Bemba (Awemba) Nation', *Journal of the African Society*, **v.** 3 (1903, 1904).
—— *An Introductory Hand Book to the Language of the Bemba People*, London: L.M.S. (1904).
SHEANE, J. W. WEST. 'Some Aspects of the Awemba Religion and Superstitious Observances', *J.R.A.I.* xxxvi (1906).
—— 'Wemba Warpaths', *Journal of the African Society*, vii (1911–12).
THOMSON, J. MOFFAT. *Memorandum on the Native Tribes and Tribal Areas of Northern Rhodesia*, Livingstone: Government Printer (1934).
TRAPNELL, C. G. *The Soils, Vegetation and Agricultural Systems of North-Eastern Rhodesia*, Lusaka: Government Printer (1943).
WALLER, H. *The Last Journals of David Livingstone in Central Africa*, vol. i, London: John Murray (1874).
WILSON, GODFREY. *Economics of Detribalization in Northern Rhodesia*, Livingstone: Rhodes–Livingstone Institute, Papers No. 5 (1941) and No. 6 (1942).

# THE FORT JAMESON NGONI

## By J. A. BARNES

*Historical and Ecological Background*

THERE are about a dozen groups of peoples in different parts of Africa who call themselves Ngoni, and others not using that name have also been classified as Ngoni on the basis of common origin. They are found in Tanganyika Territory, Portuguese East Africa, Nyasaland, and Northern Rhodesia. The name Ngoni is derived from Nguni, the designation applied to themselves by the Zulu and Xhosa peoples. The Ngoni have a common history of emigration from the vicinity of Zululand, in Natal, in the 1820's, and of subsequent migration northwards. This common heritage they share with the Ndebele of Southern Rhodesia. These migrations were occasioned by the rise to power of the Zulu chief Shaka, whose defeat of his chief rival, Zwide of the Ndandwe, led to the flight northwards of parties of Ndandwe refugees. At least two parties travelled as far north as the River Zambezi, one of them led by Zwangendaba, whose party crossed the river in 1835.[1] This Ngoni group reached the vicinity of Lake Tanganyika in about 1845, and there Zwangendaba died. His people split into several segments, led by his sons and other followers. One of these segments went on farther north, others turned towards Lake Nyasa, while one segment led by Mpezeni, a son of Zwangendaba, struck south-westwards towards the Bemba country in what is now the Northern Province of Northern Rhodesia. Here, in about 1856, they fought unsuccessfully with the Bemba, retreated southwards, and in about 1865 crossed the River Luangwa into Fort Jameson District. In 1868 they moved westwards into Petauke District, and a few years later moved eastwards to their present habitat in the vicinity of Fort Jameson.[2] It is with this group of Ngoni that we are concerned.[3]

[1] Poole, *Date of the Crossing of the Zambesi*, pp. 290–2.

[2] Cf. Bryant, *Olden Times in Zululand and Natal*, pp. 459–70; Chibambo, *My Ngoni of Nyasaland*, pp. 1–36; Decle, *Three Years in Savage Africa*, p. 151; Elmslie, *Among the Wild Angoni*, p. 28; Fraser, *Winning a Primitive People*, pp. 312–15; Hodgson, *Notes on the Achewa and Angoni*, p. 123; Kapunzah, *Angoni, Uzimba ndi Miyambi*, pp. 1–11; Lancaster, *Tentative Chronology*, p. 86; Poole, *Native Tribes*, pp. 5–10; Read, *Tradition and Prestige*, p. 464; Stigand, *Natives of Nyasaland*, p. 126; Werner, *Natives of British Central Africa*, p. 281; Wiese, *Geschichte . . . der Angoni*, pp. 181–6; Winterbottom, *Angoni Paramountcy*, pp. 126–7; Young, *History of the Tumbuka-Kamanga*, pp. 108–17.

[3] I worked among these people for a year in 1946–7 as an Assistant Anthropologist

The present-day population of the tribe is about 85,000, of whom about 60,000 live in Northern Rhodesia and 25,000 in the Fort Manning area of Nyasaland.[1] In Northern Rhodesia the tribe is largely confined in two demarcated Native Reserves. In 1938 the density of population in these two reserves averaged 68 persons to the square mile,[2] but in some congested or very fertile areas it was 90 or more.[3] Since 1941 the density has been reduced in some of the more congested parts by controlled resettlement in areas outside the reserves.[4] The density of population of the Nyasaland section of the tribe was about 46 persons to the square mile in 1945.[5]

The region in which the Ngoni live consists of a fairly flat plateau about 3,500 feet above sea-level, with massive granite outcrops rising another 1,000 feet or more. The soils of the region are principally of the types suitable only for shifting or partial cultivation, but there are also belts of more valuable soils.[6] In relation to the customary mode of agriculture, in which maize is the principal crop, the critical density of the land has been calculated to be about 22 persons to the square mile.[7] The annual rainfall at Fort Jameson varies from 27 to 48 inches, averaging about 35 inches. The region contains the meeting of the Luangwa–Nyasa and Luangwa–Zambezi watersheds. Most of the streams that flow down into the Luangwa dry up in July, while the Zambezi and Nyasa streams continue to flow somewhat longer.[8]

The natural vegetation of the region consists principally of *Brachystegia–Isoberlinia* woodlands, with larger trees along the lines of streams. The mean maximum temperature for the region is about

---

of the Rhodes–Livingstone Institute. This account was prepared at Oxford, and I am very grateful to Dr. Max Gluckman for criticism of this paper in draft.

[1] In the 1945 Nyasaland census many of the people living in the two Ngoni counties were classified as Cewa. Hence the figure of 5,531 Ngoni in Fort Manning does not represent the total population of these two counties. Cf. *Report on the Census*, Table 4.

[2] Calculated from the figures given in the *Pim Report*, p. 364. These two reserves contain Cewa chieftainships as well as Ngoni, but the average population density of the two tribes is probably of the same order.

[3] Trapnell, *Ecological Survey*, p. 72.

[4] Fraser, *Land Resettlement*, pp. 47–9.

[5] *Report on the Census*, Table 8. The Fort Manning District contains a Cewa chieftainship as well as the two Ngoni. The figure given above is the average for the whole district.

[6] Trapnell, *Ecological Survey*, p. 72.

[7] Allan, *African Land Usage*, p. 14.

[8] Poole, *Human Geography*, pp. 1 and 2.

84° F. and the mean minimum 61·5° F.[1] Three seasons are distinguished: the wet season, from the beginning of November until about April; the cold season, from May until July; and the hot season, from August until the rains begin again. Most of the planting takes place in the first half of the wet season, and the harvest comes after the rains have ceased. There is very little fishing, but antelopes, leopards, wild pig, and buck are hunted for their meat, and lions, leopards, hyenas, and monkeys on account of the damage they do to crops and livestock. The greater part of the region is free enough from tsetse fly to permit cattle-keeping, and for the tribe as a whole there is approximately one head of cattle to every two people. Pigs, sheep, goats, and chickens are also kept.

The material culture of the tribe is similar to that of their neighbours. They live in one- or two-roomed huts of bamboo or pole and mud; some women make pottery and some men make reed mats; all buy their clothes and their hoes from the shops.[2]

Three languages are used in the region: Ci-Ngoni, a language akin to Zulu, is now heard only in songs and royal praises; Ci-Nyanja is taught in the schools and is used for communication with Europeans and Indians; while the normal language used every day in the villages is a dialect of Ci-Nsenga.

# I. THE STATE

## Old Administrative System

The Ngoni think of themselves as different from their neighbours because of their chieftainship. The other tribes do not, in the eyes of the Ngoni, possess the same kind of pyramidal and centralized organization which was characteristic of the régime of Mpezeni I and which persists in a modified form at the present time.

The important positions in the old political structure were occupied by members of the royal lineage, their queens, the regional governors,[3] and the lieutenants.[4] The political system was at the same time the territorial system, residence being determined by political allegiance. The pattern of residence and allegiance persisted despite the movement of the tribe as a whole from one region to another and despite

---

[1] Trapnell, *Ecological Survey*, pp. 2–3.
[2] See my *Material Culture of the Fort Jameson Ngoni*.
[3] *Mulumuzana*, pl. *alumuzana*.                    [4] *Nduna*, pl. *nduna*.

the absence of any definite internal land boundaries between the territories of one political segment and another. The constant elements were the residential groups that we now know as villages,[1] and we may liken them to ships of different sizes and importance that preserve a loose formation while the fleet sails from place to place. Villages, discrete clusters of dwellings in comparative proximity and separated from one another by uninhabited stretches of garden-land and bush, were internally divided into divisions,[2] and from time to time these divisions broke away from one another or from their parent village to form new villages of their own. This process of divisional fission was characteristic of the commoner villages. Royal villages were usually formed by a parallel process by which an important member of the royal lineage established a new village for one or more of his queens by recruitment from his own natal village. The eldest son by the senior queen in that village then became the head of the segment of the royal lineage associated with the village. Thus the segmentation of the royal lineage was reflected in a proliferation of royal villages.

In the period immediately prior to the conquest of the tribe by British forces in 1898, there were four important royal villages, with populations of probably several thousands each. One belonged to a brother of Mpezeni, and the other three were controlled by groups of Mpezeni's own queens and their sons. Associated with each royal village were several regional governors, each of whom was responsible for the well-being of a group of lesser villages, and who resided among them in a village of his own. These lesser villages were commoner villages, each under its own headman. Each large royal village had also a number of lesser royal villages attached to it, and also many commoner villages were attached to a royal village of some sort directly, and not through a regional governor.[3]

Each important person, chief, member of the royal lineage, regional governor, or headman was assisted by a number of lieutenants, trusted subordinates who were usually not patrilineal kinsmen of their principal but who were sometimes related affinally. These lieutenants were ranked in order of the creation of their posts by their principal and assisted him in the control of his unit of administration. In the case of Mpezeni himself, however, there were two kinds of lieutenants. Those people known as the lieutenants of Mpezeni were

[1] *Munzi*, pl. *minzi*.
[2] *Cigaŵa*, pl. *vigaŵa*.
[3] Cf. Kuper, *An African Aristocracy*, p. 66, for a similar system among the Swazi.

charged by him with specific functions relating to the State as a whole, and appear to have exercised general jurisdiction. Other lieutenants were known as the lieutenants of such-and-such a royal village, and were appointed by Mpezeni to look after the queens of the village and to be responsible for the internal ordering of the village.

In addition to these lieutenants each important person had a deputy,[1] who was a patrilineal kinsman of the same generation. Each new holder of the principal office selected his own deputy. The deputy's task was to act for his principal in his absence and to serve as an intermediary between the principal and his lieutenants.

All these posts were hereditary in the agnatic line, except for that of deputy, but new posts were continually being created and the holders of other posts fell into disgrace. Some of the lieutenants of Mpezeni were also headmen of their own villages, while other lieutenants were promoted to be regional governors.

Increase in population led to increase in the number of villages and of recognizable divisions within villages, both by divisional fission and by the setting up of separate establishments for groups of wives. This process, operating in response to population pressure from below, was assisted from above by the need to give newly created lieutenants and governors their own dependants and their own recognizable residential cluster.

The relative position and importance of a segment of the political structure might alter if its leader was killed in battle or if he offended the Paramount. For example, a certain lieutenant who had a village of his own committed adultery with one of Mpezeni's queens. He was put to death, and all his followers were made to come and live in a royal village. But in addition to the natural increase in the population of any segment, new members were added by capture in war. There was never any distinct class of slaves or captives in the Ngoni State. Apart from the aristocratic families which traced their history back to the pre-migration period in Natal, the rest of the tribe had been either captured at one time or other on the way north, or had joined the Ngoni of their own volition. On capture, people were assigned to some or other important person, and after a while acquired a certain autonomy of their own. The men were all enrolled into the age-set regiment appropriate to their age, and it was possible for them to rise to high positions in the State. No distinction of ethnic origin was

[1] *Mnawa*, pl. *anawa*. Cf. the Zulu term *umnawa*, younger brother who is next to the heir.

made in the regimental system, which was organized on a national basis. A person of low ethnic status, that is, of comparatively late incorporation into the tribe but of senior regiment, was considered to be, in most circumstances, as good as a man of more aristocratic family but of a junior regiment. New regiments were formed about every four years.

## Development of Minor Chieftainships

The defeat of the Ngoni army at the hands of the British in 1898 and the subsequent establishment of British control led to the partial breakdown of this system. The population was dispersed by the fighting and by the unsettled conditions that followed, and part of the kingdom was cleared for European occupation. The Administration recognized the grandson of Mpezeni I as the chief of the tribe, and also worked through a number of men known as Divisional Headmen, who were made responsible for small areas. Some of these divisional headmen were regional governors, some lieutenants of Mpezeni, some members of the royal lineage, and others were upstarts. It is not clear from the rather meagre records that remain or from the statements of informants exactly what happened between 1898 and 1914, but we know that by the latter date the Administration had come to recognize six men as local chiefs, apart from Mpezeni, and that four of them were said to be sons of Mpezeni I.[1] In 1929, when the term Native Authority was introduced, nine minor chiefs were appointed, of whom four were descended from Mpezeni I and one from the father of Mpezeni I. Two of the other minor chiefs have the descent-name *jere* that belongs to the royal lineage, and may be regarded as belonging to assimilated lineages. One is descended from a regional governor, the other from a policeman. Two minor chiefs do not have this descent-name, one being descended from a lieutenant of Zwangendaba and the other from a regional governor. This arrangement of one Paramount Chief and nine minor chiefs persists to the present day. With each of the ten chiefs is associated a more or less defined area within which most of the villages are said to belong to the chief of the area. What appears to have happened during the thirty years after the conquest is that the central power declined and that certain political and territorial segments achieved a degree of autonomy. The ten areas belonging to the different chiefs, which I shall refer to as counties, represent

[1] Coxhead, *Native Tribes*, pp. 22 and 24.

ten units of different orders of segmentation in the old system and are now regarded as ten homologous territorial segments in the new. Thus one village founded for a group of queens by Mpezeni I has given rise to two royal chieftainships, another to one royal chieftainship, and a third to a royal chieftainship and a non-royal one. On the other hand, there is no chieftainship corresponding to the son of Mpezeni I who was next in succession to the main heir.

There are royal villages in every county. The oldest royal village in a county is now the capital of the county, and the lieutenants in the capital are responsible to the county chief. The minor chiefs have continued the process of making new villages for their queens, so that in each county the chief lives in a recently formed royal village, founded either by himself or by his father, and not in his capital. The capital is often the biggest village in the county, while the chief's village is more frequently quite small. It is the name of the capital village rather than that of the chief's village that serves as the name of the county itself. Thus, while in the old days the national capital changed with each new Paramount, the county capitals do not alter. The new royal villages founded since 1898 have not the same importance in the political structure as had the pre-conquest royal villages. This change is reflected in the fact that there is now no real national capital in the old sense.

Disputes in the old days were settled in the village by the headman, or were taken to the regional governor, or to the lieutenants of the royal village, for settlement. If the matter could not be settled there it was taken to the assembly of the senior lieutenants of Mpezeni, whose decision could be set aside only by Mpezeni himself. Now each chief has a court, and there is an appeal court on which representatives from each of the ten counties sit in turn. In the old days important decisions were taken by the senior lieutenants, in consultation with Mpezeni, although the four large royal villages were to some extent independent of one another. Sections of the army, for instance, appear to have been sent out on raids from a royal village without reference to the Paramount.[1] Under the present régime meetings of the tribe as a whole are held at Mcumo, a centre established by the Administration at which there is a school and a dispensary. These are attended by the chiefs and such people as choose to come. These meetings are usually sponsored by the Administration, and meetings to discuss affairs that arise independently of the Administration are

[1] Cf. Genthe, *A Trip to Mpezeni's*, p. 1.

sometimes held at the Paramount Chief's village. Each minor chief holds meetings for the people in his own county to discuss matters of common interest.

Quarrels among the chiefs are mainly in terms of the traditional norms rather than of the new differentiation between them in the Native Authority system. The Paramount Chief may abuse the minor chiefs for not coming to visit him on his return from a journey, or for not bringing beer with them when they come to visit him. In each county there are villages which claim to belong to the chief of some other county, on the ground that they originated from the capital village of that county. These interloping villages increase the pressure on the land of the county in which they are, and friction between the two chiefs concerned may ensue. The chiefs like to be able to offer new land for gardens to the people of their own villages, yet at the same time each chief likes to have as many villages as possible apparently under his sway. Hence there is competition both for the allegiance of the villagers as well as for the land that they occupy. These struggles may be resolved by the Paramount Chief or by the Administration with a redefinition of boundaries or by moving the interloping villages to some other region. The Administration has from time to time placed one county under the tutelage of the chief of another, on grounds of administrative efficiency or the inexperience of a young chief. These moves are interpreted as attempts by one chief to incorporate the county of the other into his own, and allegations of killing by sorcery may be made against one minor chief on the death of another. Attempts have also been made to usurp the paramountcy, but this cannot be done openly under the present régime.

Efforts are also made by members of the royal lineage to achieve the creation of new chieftainships by asserting the traditional autonomy of the rural districts into which the counties are divided for certain purposes. Seen in relation to the old system, these attempts are efforts to increase the segmentation in that branch of the royal lineage which corresponds with the modern county in which they live. It is unlikely that such attempts will be successful, as the policy of the Administration is opposed to the creation of new chieftainships.

## Sanctions

The principal check on the power of the minor chiefs is that exercised through the Paramount. The Administration, which is always sensitive to suggestions that a chief may be oppressing his people, usually works through the Paramount. One minor chief was sent to the Paramount's village for a period of instruction in order that he might learn how to rule wisely. On another occasion a chief who had abused the Administration was fined one month's salary by the Paramount. In both these instances the Administration was the initiator of the Paramount Chief's action, but he may also act without reference to it. It was reported to the Paramount that a certain minor chief had struck one of his subjects who had been slow to offer him beer. The Paramount warned the minor chief that he might kill someone this way, and that he ought to fine people, not to strike them. In a dispute between a minor chief and his court clerk over some new court furniture, which the chief wished to use in his own house, the Paramount intervened and ordered that the chairs be put in the courthouse.

The Paramount himself is subject to social constraint, and may be criticized by his senior lieutenants. He is advised on how he should behave by these men, and if his behaviour is unsatisfactory they may rebuke him. At county meetings, headmen and others can voice their complaints against the royal house as a whole, and have from time to time protested successfully at such a meeting against too many of the Native Authority posts being filled by members of the royal lineage.

*The Native Authority*

Under the Native Authority system, introduced by the Administration in 1929, there are a number of paid officials, apart from the chiefs, whose salaries are met by the Native Treasury. They include councillors, assessors, clerks, police, postmen, school attendance officers, and others. The most important of these, and the most highly paid, are the councillors and assessors. They sit once or twice a week in court and hear cases brought before them. Each of the chiefs has a court, and for the most part the cases that come before a county court are brought by people living in the county. When litigants from two counties are involved there is no definite rule as to which court will hear the case and it largely depends on the wish of the instigator of the proceedings. Cases come before the Paramount Chief's county court that concern people from other counties and a litigant may take his case from one chief to another, including the Nyasaland chiefs, in an attempt to obtain a favourable and enforceable decision. The Appeal Court sits at the Paramount Chief's village and is held once a month.

The councillors and assessors are nominated by the chiefs on the advice of their lieutenants and some of them are in fact lieutenants or their sons. The court clerk acts as secretary to his chief if he is illiterate, and he assists the chief in his contacts with the Administration. These clerks are also sometimes sons of lieutenants or brothers of chiefs. One of the tasks of the court clerk is to issue licences of all kinds, for guns, beer selling, bicycles, dogs, and so on. This brings him into contact with many people and he does a certain amount of touring looking for unlicensed dogs and bicycles. Owing to this interest in licences and the running of the court, he is the person who takes the initiative in the few public prosecutions that are brought. Civil actions are initiated by paying sixpence for a summons, which is usually issued by the court clerk. He is thus well informed of quarrels in advance before they come up for hearing in the court. He is well known throughout the county and exercises a great deal of influence.

## Chiefs and People

Whenever beer was brewed in a village, there was an obligation to carry one pot to the chief, and this obligation persists. Apart from this, however, there does not seem ever to have been any organized system of sending tribute to the chief. Mpezeni is said to have had a monopoly of all prisoners of war, but those who had taken the captives were frequently allowed to keep them themselves. This is mentioned as a specific privilege of regional governors. Nowadays the chiefs expect hospitality when they enter the villages, but they have little call on the services of their people. The little assistance they get locally is probably less valuable than the presents they are given by men who are away working or who have just returned. When the chiefs visit the mining towns they are offered money and clothes by Ngoni working there.

The chiefs own a number of guns and lend these to people they can trust. All the chiefs organize their own hunts, which differ from the hunts of ordinary people in that all the animals killed belong to the chief, who should, however, give a leg to the killer of each animal. Attendance is compulsory for adult men in the villages that are called out on the hunt, although in practice there are always many absentees. These royal hunts do not usually involve a whole county, but only part of the county. They are useful in keeping down the number of predatory animals, and damage done to crops by wild pigs and baboons is sometimes attributed to the failure of the chief to organize enough hunts.

*Royal and Commoner Villages*

Nowadays most of the villages in the kingdom are commoner villages, under the charge of headmen. From such evidence as is available, it seems likely that in the pre-conquest period there were fewer villages than there are now, and that they were bigger than are most modern villages.[1] It also appears that the process by which a division of a village broke away to become a separate village was a gradual one, so that at any one time there would have been some doubt in deciding how many distinct villages there were. This is seen at the present time in the histories of what are now distinct villages; the people relate how the first time they made a village of their own it was done only a little distance away from the parent village. Pairs of villages of common origin still tend to occupy sites in comparative proximity to one another, and may arrange their moves from one area to another, in search for new garden land, simultaneously.

In general, however, there is little difficulty in observing the village as a discrete spatial residential group. We may distinguish five types of village,[2] according to the status of the person in charge of the village. The capital villages and chiefs' villages have already been mentioned. Intermediate between these two categories are the regal villages. These have been formed from older royal villages to accommodate a group of wives of a chief or other member of the royal lineage, but do not now have a chief living in them. All these three kinds of royal village, capital, regal, and chief's, are controlled in the same way, by lieutenants appointed to the task in the first instance by a member of the royal family. There is another kind of village which I shall call a cadet village. The junior members of the royal lineage, that is, younger sons and sons by unimportant wives, did not have sufficient following to carry on this process of forming large new villages and merely lived with their wives in their natal villages or founded small villages of their own. Such villages are now similar in form to commoner villages, except that the headman of the village belongs to the royal lineage. All other villages we may class as commoner villages.

---

[1] 'The Angoni villages are about five times the size of an average Achewa village . . .' (Genthe, p. 1). Cf. Read, *Tradition and Prestige,* p. 475.

[2] All types are known in the vernacular by the same descriptive term, *munzi,* and there are no classificatory terms. It is possible to tell whether a village is royal or commoner by its name. A village with a male personal name is a commoner or cadet village. A village with a female personal name, or a descriptive name in the Ngoni language, is a royal village.

Table i. *Village Types*

| Type of village | | Senior resident |
|---|---|---|
| Royal | Capital | First lieutenant |
| | Regal | First lieutenant |
| | Chief's | Chief |
| | Cadet | Royal Headman |
| | Commoner | Commoner Headman |

This process of village formation may be illustrated from Mpezeni's own county. The capital of the county is the village founded by Mpezeni I for his chief wife and one or two other wives. His heir Singu was born in this village, and when he married he founded two villages of his own which are now regal villages. In the senior of these two Mpezeni II was born, and in about 1925 he founded a new village which is still the chief's village of the county. There are other regal villages in the county founded in a similar manner.

This formation of royal villages would, other things being equal, lead to a dispersal of the population. It seems, however, that the major factor in dispersing the population since 1898 has been the formation of independent commoner villages. Many of these villages have histories that go back to the foundation of the village as an independent unit immediately after 1898, and it seems likely that the unsettled conditions of those days and the burning of villages did much to bring about the breakdown of the old system in which the royal villages were more important than they are today.

The royal villages are more closely connected with the chieftain-ships than are the commoner villages, and the chiefs visit in them more frequently than in other villages. A dispute in a royal village is usually settled by a meeting in the village itself attended by the local chief, whereas in the case of an ordinary village dispute the matter would be taken to the chief for him to settle in his own village or court. A chief may be called to a royal village to drink beer. The royal herds of cattle are kept in the royal villages, and the chiefs look to the first lieutenants of their royal villages for the well-being of the royal cattle as well as of the inhabitants of the royal villages. All the cattle in the country are held to belong in one sense to the Paramount Chief himself,[1] but in as far as the cattle held by most people are concerned, there is no more to this statement than in the parallel expression that

[1] Cf. Coxhead, p. 27.

P

Mpezeni is the owner of the land, or of the world. The cattle kept in the royal villages are held to have belonged formerly to Mpezeni I or to Zwangendaba, and therefore still belong to the Paramount Chief. Chiefs and other members of the royal lineage who have cattle inherited in this way, in fact dispose of them as they please when the Paramount Chief is not in their village, but if he appears and a beast is killed in his honour, it is the Paramount who is praised as the owner of the beast and not the local owner. In the capital and chief's villages the lieutenants are more under the control of the chief of the county, who may intervene to depose a lieutenant if he thinks that his cattle are not being well looked after.

The Administration does not distinguish between one type of village and another, and gives the same title of headman[1] to the man in charge of the village, whoever he may be. It tends to act on the assumption that all headmen are of equal status and have the same amount of authority in their villages. Combined with the decline in the power of the royal lineage, this policy may lead to the assimilation of the different types of village to a common form.

## II. THE VILLAGE

*Material Setting*

Ngoni villages, which form the principal units of administration in the country, contain from half a dozen to 120 huts. It is seldom more than a quarter of a mile from one edge of a village to the other. There is a rough arrangement of huts into parallel lines, with the doors all facing the same way at right-angles to the direction of the lines. Kitchen huts, which are similar in appearance to dwelling huts, are included in these lines, while in front of a line of dwellings may be a line of storehouses and sties for small stock. On the edge of the village are the cattle byres. There are seldom any fences marking off courtyards within the village, so that it is possible to sit on the veranda of a hut and look along at all the other verandas. If there are well-established divisions within the village, the boundaries of the divisions may be indicated by lines of aloes.

Most people, except polygynists and some children, may be said to live in one hut, in which they keep most of their belongings and where they usually sleep. A single hut may be occupied by up to about ten

---

[1] Usually *hediman*, pl. *mahediman*; otherwise *mfumu yamunzi*, pl. *mafumu waminzi*. The specific term for headman of a cadet or commoner village is *mwinimunzi*.

children, but it is unusual to find more than two adults living in the same hut. These may be either man and wife, or two women who are unmarried or whose husbands are away. Adolescent boys sleep in dormitories containing a number of boys, and there are similar huts for girls. Smaller children sleep with whoever is responsible for their upbringing, parents, grandparents, or other relative, as the case may be. Children in fact sleep in a variety of huts, sometimes with their elders and sometimes with one group of playmates, sometimes with another. Polygynists divide their time between their several wives, although they may tend to keep their belongings in the hut of their chief wife. Men do not as a rule possess huts of their own apart from those of their wives.

The hut is said to belong to the man or woman living in it. There is a tendency to refer to the man as the owner if the marriage is patrilocal and to the woman if it is matrilocal, but this is not an invariable rule, and the builder of the hut, who may be living elsewhere, may be referred to as the owner. About half the dwelling huts have kitchens near by, separate huts of similar construction which are used for cooking and as sleeping-places for children and visitors. When there is no separate kitchen, cooking is done inside the dwelling hut or on the veranda.

The village, then, is a collection of buildings of different types, in which people sleep and keep their possessions, animals are sheltered, and food stored. We must now consider how the inhabitants of the village are organized.

### Structure

Royal villages have names in the Ngoni language that were given by their founders. For example, there is a regal village founded by Singu, the eldest son of Mpezeni I, called Ngalaweni, meaning 'dormitory', as it was there that he put his wives. These villages are also sometimes referred to by the name of the senior queen for whom they were founded.

Most commoner villages, however, do not possess names of this type, and are known only by descent-names or by the names of individuals. These are usually the name and descent-name of the founder of the village, the man who first established the village as a separate unit. It is this individual name that is used to refer to the present headman of the village, the man recognized by the chief and the Administration as responsible for the village. This office is hereditary, usually in the male line, and, other things being equal, it is the eldest son of the chief wife who succeeds his father. However, if the heir is a minor, the job of running the village may be undertaken by a brother of the deceased or by the first lieutenant of the village, and in this case difficulties may be placed in the way of the rightful heir should he claim his heritage on maturity. The usurper or his successors may take the name of the founder of the village as though there had been no break in the succession. There is among the Ngoni little of the importance attached to the inheritance of names that is reported from other tribes of the region. Anyone may use the name of any of his patrilineal ancestors, so that, for example, most of the members of the royal lineage, men and women, use the name of Mpezeni on formal occasions in addition to their other personal names.

To assist him in his work a headman may nominate a deputy, and there may be in the village one or more lieutenants. The office of lieutenant in a large and prosperous village tends to be hereditary, but if there is no suitable successor the headman may appoint a man from another family to succeed. Many headmen have no deputy and some have no lieutenants.

In pre-conquest times the small residential group appears to have consisted of the men of an effective minimal patrilineage,[1] their wives, and the families of their prisoners of war. With the passage of time some of the senior captives became lieutenants of the head of the lineage and there was intermarriage between the aristocratic lineage and the captured families as well as between one captured family and another. This process of intermarriage has continued and I found, in every village I examined in the Northern Rhodesia counties, that each person is related to everyone else in the village, affinally and cognatically, in at least one way, while many people are related to each other by a number of different paths. In the Nyasaland counties this process of affinal assimilation has not been going on for so long, and here I encountered families of former captives who have not yet been linked by marriage to the family of their aristocratic captors.

## Movement

A village is likely to stay in the same place for a dozen years or so. During this time some of the huts will have fallen down and have been

---

[1] Fortes, *Dynamics of Clanship*, p. 192: '. . . the effective minimal lineage, that is, the lineage of smallest span which emerges as a corporate unit in economic, jural, and ritual activities and is differentiated from other units of a like sort.'

PLATE XIII

1. Storing finger millet. The untidily thatched building on the right is a dormitory for boys

2. A queen brewing beer. It is only important people who own oil drums

NGONI

PLATE XIV

3. Boys crushing ground-nuts. The expressed oil will be used in a bird trap

4. Boy playing with a toy motor-car made from maize stalks

NGONI

replaced by new ones, but the village as a whole may be regarded as stationary. The exhaustion of garden land in the vicinity of the village is the principal reason for moving, as with the passage of time a man has to go farther and farther from the village to find new land. Sooner or later it becomes more convenient to move the village to another locality where there is plenty of regenerated land on which gardens can be made. The death of the headman is sometimes followed by a move to a new site, while quarrels within a village may cause a portion of the inhabitants to go off and live on their own, usually after the matter has been referred to the chief. Since 1898 many villages have been moved off land alienated to Whites, or away from congested areas.

When the Administration is the instigator of the move, the new village site is a matter for discussion between District Officer, county chief, and village headman. In moves made on the initiative of the villagers, the various possible new sites are reconnoitred by the headman and other important people in the village and the site chosen is notified to the chief for his approval. The first people start to make their gardens in the vicinity of the site, and work is started on the new village. For this a recently abandoned garden site may be chosen, as it is easier to clear. The first structure to be built is usually a cattle byre. Making a byre is very hard work, and I was told that if it was left till later it would be difficult to get people to tackle the job. Rattray, writing of Gomani's Ngoni of central Nyasaland, relates how the headman's hut is built before the others, but this custom appears to be unknown in Fort Jameson District.[1]

Building is begun by the more industrious before the rains end, and is completed after the harvest. The transition from the old site to the new one is gradual, as, unless the distance between the sites is too great, people will continue working the gardens in the old area until they are exhausted. New gardens are indeed opened up on the old site of the village, and it is quite common to see the ground dug up between the huts at the end of the rains while there are people still living there.

---

[1] Rattray, *Folk-Lore Stories*, pp. 109–11. Fraser, *Winning a Primitive People*, pp. 203–5, gives an account of the building of a new village among Mombera's Ngoni of northern Nyasaland, in which the cattle byre was built first, but it must be remembered that this was a village built round a central byre, after the fashion of the South-Eastern Bantu, whereas the cattle byre in a Fort Jameson village is nowadays a smaller affair placed on the outskirts of the village.

Huts sometimes become infested with ticks, or the site itself may prove to be intolerably damp. New huts are then built a short distance away or even contiguously to the old site, and no new gardens are made apart from those made among the deserted huts.

## Internal Segmentation of the Village

We have already seen that the divisions within the village are embryonic new villages. These divisions are most formally indicated in the Nyasaland counties, where there are large villages divided into a distinct number of divisions, with the spatial boundaries between the divisions indicated by a greater interval between the huts, and with each division named and under the charge of a lieutenant or of a patrilineal kinsman of the headman. On the Rhodesian side, however, it is more usual to find that certain small clusters of huts within a village are regarded as being the division of such-and-such a person living in one of them. The bulk of the huts in the village do not belong to any particular cluster but merely to the village as a whole. These clusters do not have any name apart from that of their senior inhabitant, whose close relatives occupy the huts of the cluster. The leader of a cluster may be a lieutenant of the headman or merely some important person with a comparatively large body of dependants. Such clusters, which are often on the periphery of the village, sometimes originate from the grouping together by a polygynist of the huts of his various wives, and grow as their children marry and live alongside their parents. Another mechanism for the formation of clusters is that of immigration into the village at about the same time by a number of persons related to each other more closely than to the other inhabitants of the village, as, for example, on the break-up of some other village. The immigrants tend to build together if there is room. In this case the leader of the cluster may have little standing in the village. The boundaries of clusters are not always plainly indicated, while a man who is ambitious to make his own village may as a first step try to increase the clarity with which his cluster is defined spatially.

## Land Utilization

We may divide gardens into three types: main, old village, and moist. The moist gardens are made near streams, and are fenced to keep out cattle. Tomatoes, cabbages, onions, and other vegetables are grown, and maize is planted during the hot season so that it can be harvested in December or January. These gardens are cultivated only by the more industrious and usually with a view to sale of vegetables in Fort Jameson. The sites last for many years and are usually abandoned because of the removal of the owner's village to a distant place rather than because of exhaustion of the soil.

Old-village gardens are made on the site of former huts and byres, in order to take advantage of the high fertility of the soil. These gardens are not usually fenced, except when they are made on the outskirts of some existing village on the site of an old byre. Tobacco is sometimes grown, but for the most part they are cultivated in the same way as are main gardens. The site belongs to the former owner of the hut or byre, so long as the garden continues to be worked.

Main gardens are made from bush clearings, and are chosen with some regard to the type and quantity of the natural vegetation. Land that has been abandoned for long enough, say twenty-five years, regains its natural cover, and if the ownership of former gardens has been forgotten, it is treated as though it were virgin woodland, that is, it is permissible for anyone who wishes to come and cultivate it. A new village site is chosen to be near, if possible, an ample amount of such regenerated land, and at the first selection of gardens the headman of the village may go round the area and see where the new gardens are being made. Gardens tend to be within 2 miles of the village, but there is no one definite area that is associated with a particular village, so that if there are a number of villages in proximity, the gardens of their inhabitants will be intermingled. A man exercises a lien on the area of uncleared land round his garden, and may take up this land himself as he enlarges his garden. Hence at first there are considerable belts of bush left between one garden and the next. With the passage of time, these are cleared, and gardens become contiguous, with boundaries between them that are almost imperceptible at first glance. At the same time as enlargements are made, the least productive parts of the gardens are neglected, so that, as the years go by, the area cultivated by one man may gradually change its position, and fresh areas of resting-land will appear between the gardens. Main gardens vary in size from about 1 to 3 acres.

If a man moves into a village and wishes to start a garden, he is usually given part of the garden of the person to whom he is attached in the village. A son returning from the mines may be given part of his father's garden. Conversely when someone leaves the village, his garden passes to his relatives. In particular, when a man dies, his widows continue to cultivate the gardens they had before his death. When a man opens up a new garden he may hand over his nearly exhausted old garden to some relative who does not wish to go to the labour of clearing new ground himself. Rights in land cannot be sold, but only given away, and no presents are given to the donor by the recipient of a garden or garden site. They can only be sustained by continued residence in the locality, either by the owner of the rights himself or by his relatives. There are very few court cases concerned with rights in land, and in the courts the only attempt I saw in which a man tried to enforce what he thought to be his rights was met by the statement from the bench that no one had any rights in land, for did not all land belong to the chief?

Maize is planted at the beginning of the rains, and the garden is usually weeded twice over before the maize has grown high enough to surmount the weeds. When the rains end, the stalks are felled and put into large stooks to dry. The cobs are then taken off the stalks and carried back to the village to be stored. Finger millet is grown in ash-fertilized patches scattered through the main garden, and in between the maize ground-nuts, pumpkins, and other crops are grown. Sorghum, bulrush millet, and rice are also grown. Most of the work in the garden is carried on in the rainy season, and after the harvest the garden is more or less deserted until the next season, although a certain amount of new land may be cleared as a garden extension.

## Dwellings outside the Village

There are two types of settlement outside the recognized villages that require mention. These are permanently occupied settlements consisting of two or three huts which I shall refer to as hamlets and temporarily occupied huts in the gardens. The hamlets usually arise as a result of quarrels within a village that are resolved by the breaking away of one of the parties to the quarrel. The activities of the Agricultural Department have also led to the formation of hamlets of similar size, both of hamlets of persons accepting agricultural control whose co-villagers have all moved off, and the other way about. These hamlets are all attached to proper villages for registration purposes, and participate in many of the collective activities of the villages near by.

The damage done to crops in the latter part of the rainy season necessitates the keeping of a continuous watch, particularly at gardens that are on the edge of a cultivated area, in order to drive off the monkeys by day and the wild pigs by night. Shelters are erected on the edge of gardens, and some people spend most of their time there, returning to the village only to fetch food. Beer parties are held in the gardens, and the villages, particularly in the middle of the week, are largely deserted during the day. One or two boys or old men may stay behind to look after the cattle. Streams are in spate at this time of year, and some men build garden byres to which they move their cattle to avoid the risk of the animals or their herdboys being taken by the water.

This life in the gardens is important from the point of view of inter-village action in that it provides an opportunity for new residential groups to form, albeit temporarily. People without garden shelters of their own may share the shelter of a neighbouring gardener, who may be from another village. People may site their gardens so that they are adjacent to those of kindred from other villages, with whom they will be united for this period of garden residence. Thus, for example, a woman who lives in her husband's village has a widowed mother still living in *her* dead husband's village a mile away. The gardens of the mother and daughter are adjacent, and they both possess garden huts which are built alongside one another. They co-operate in much of the work of their gardens.

With the completion of the harvest, the need for living in the garden ceases, but some people delay their return to the village for a month or so. The explanation given is that immediately after the end of the rains and the harvest, there is much activity by the Administration and the Native Authority in organizing public works, and that by staying on in the gardens people hope to avoid becoming involved in these projects.

### Cattle-keeping

The circular village cattle byre, with the dwelling huts built round it in a great circle, as occurs among the South-Eastern Bantu and as reported by Elmslie[1] from Mombera's Ngoni of Nyasaland, is not found at the present time among the Fort Jameson Ngoni. Most villages now have two or three separate cattle byres, and they are placed on the periphery of the village area. They consist of fenced enclosures open to the weather, with a single entrance blocked with poles, and may be up to 20 yards across. Calves are kept in smaller enclosures or in deserted dwelling huts whose owners have gone away or are dead. Where there are well-defined clusters of huts within a village, each cluster may have its own byre, but this is not always the case. Cattle

[1] Elmslie, p. 37.

are out at pasture all day under the charge of herdboys, and may be brought in for milking in the early afternoon, later returning to the bush. Alternatively they are not milked until they come in just before sunset to be put in their byres for the night. These activities are organized by the herdboys, who range from five up to about twelve years in age. All the boys in a village take part in herding, whether or not their parents own cattle. A man keeps all his cattle in the village in one byre, although he may also have cattle in other villages under the care of relatives. The boys attach themselves to definite byres, and the senior boy of the group becomes responsible for all the cattle in the byre. He sees that the cattle do not stray into gardens during the season when they may damage the crops, and he checks that all the cattle return at night. He instructs the younger boys in the art of milking, and supervises the allocation of the milk, which is his perquisite. Cattle from all the byres in the village may be herded together. After the harvest the cattle are often left to wander where they please and the boys occupy themselves in the village or hunting for rabbits until it is time to round up the cattle for milking.

There are no definite pastures associated with one village rather than with another, so that the herds from one village may come into contact with those from another. This may lead to fighting between the two groups of herdboys, and also, if it can be managed, between the bulls of the villages. Boys take pride in the fighting ability of their bulls, and sometimes seek out other herds in order to demonstrate the superior strength of themselves and their animals. It is significant that informants referred always to fights between bulls of different villages, and not of fights between bulls from different byres in the same village, although these do occur.

In the past, herding was carried out by older boys, and life as a herdboy was terminated only by enrolment into a regiment. Inter-village fighting went on partly to demonstrate that the boys concerned were now strong enough to join the army. At the present time boys of twelve and younger are employed on tobacco farms, and many attend school. Some cattle owners have to pay boys to come from other villages to herd their cattle as there are no boys available in the village itself, while others obtain the services of young girls.

## Inter-village Relationships

Villages are grouped together into counties, under a minor chief, and in some counties there are recognized subdivisions that I shall call rural districts. By virtue of their membership of rural districts and counties, villages have certain formal relationships with each other which we may regard as mainly political, and which we have discussed in connexion with the organization of the state. But there are other inter-village activities that are not related directly to the tribal political structure. These include hunting, dancing, drinking, trading, and some co-operative economic activities.

Hunting takes place for the most part in the dry season, but hunts may be organized at any time to deal with predatory animals which are causing damage to crops and livestock. Only men and boys hunt. Any man who chooses can organize a hunt, but it is usually a man of middle age with some experience and of some standing in his village who sends out word to the neighbouring villages that he proposes to hunt in such-and-such an area on such-and-such a day. The organizer is referred to as the owner of the hunt, and he is in tactical command. He nominates two men to be in charge of the two wings of the hunt, and himself stays in the middle of the single line abreast in which the hunters arrange themselves. Instructions are shouted from the centre and passed out to the wings. Any animals seen are attacked with knobkerries, spears, dogs, and, if there are any, guns. The owner of the hunt has no special privileges over the animals killed, which are divided between the men who actually kill them and the people who carry them back from the hunt to the village. Attendance at such hunts is not enforced, and if the chase is unsuccessful, people tend to drop out half-way. In the main, people distribute themselves along the line of the hunt in village groups, and the leaders of the wings usually bring with them a large band of hunters from their own villages. There are usually about sixty people on a hunt, coming from perhaps ten different villages.

Dancing is an activity that brings people together from many villages. Although girls, and sometimes boys, hold dances in their own villages in the evenings, these dances are thought of as practices rather than as proper dances. The latter take place in connexion with ceremonies of various kinds, and indeed wherever there is beer to drink there is the probability of some sort of dancing. Dances are also held for their own sake, without reference to other forms of social activity. Of these, two are important in promoting inter-village ties. The first, *ngoma*,[1] the most formal of all dances, was danced by regiments in the days when the regimental system was still operative, but

[1] Cf. the Zulu dance *ingoma*, and Read, *Tradition and Prestige*, p. 52.

is now danced by villages. The important men in one village suggest to another village that this dance should be held in the latter village. If this is agreed, beer is brewed in the second village and on the pre-arranged day many people from the first village come in procession from their village to the dance. The visiting dancers enter the cattle byre and start to dance. They are joined by people from the home village. The dancers are arranged in two lines, men on one side and women on the other, and the dance consists of a series of virtuoso performances by two or three men and women at a time in the space between the two lines, to the accompaniment of clapping and antiphonal singing. The dance is followed by drinking and more dancing. Later in the year, or in the next year, the host village goes to the home of the visitors, and the performance is repeated.

Of more frequent occurrence are dances involving girls only. These are usually held on Sunday afternoons, and as at the *ngoma* dances, at least two villages are involved. Here the initiative is taken not by the important men but by the senior unmarried girl in the village. She invites a girl of similar status in another village with whom she is acquainted, or whom she has seen dancing, to bring a team of girls to dance in her village. This kind of dance is competitive in that the visitors are opposed by a similar team of girls from the home village, who dance separately from the visitors until, at the end of the session, the two teams combine. That team which has danced best is held to be the winner, although there is always great doubt as to which team this is. The girl who invited the visitors is responsible for seeing that the visiting team is fed, although beer is not provided. No work is done in the gardens on Sundays, so that these dances always attract a large number of onlookers. As with *ngoma*, a return match is danced at some later date. The pairs of villages that are linked in these dance exchanges are not always those that contain many people related to one another. One girl may ask an acquaintance in another village to find a team; in one case the girl who made the invitation did not know the name of the girl she was inviting.

### Beer-drinking

Beer, water, and tea are the three main drinks of the Ngoni. The ordinary rules of hospitality govern the drinking of water, which is provided for the traveller whenever he asks for some. Tea is sold in the roadside stores known as hotels. Beer is more important socially than either of these two drinks, and the drinking of it is essentially a social event. The kind of beer brewed is made from maize, sorghum, and finger millet. It is brewed by women, the process lasting about a week. The beer can be drunk at any time during the week, but it is not regarded as truly beer until after the brewing process has been completed. It remains good to drink for about three days, after which it becomes too sour. About 20 to 30 gallons of beer are brewed at a time. The beer can be sold, used to provide refreshment for participants in some ceremony or other, offered in return for labour or other services, or else just drunk for its own sake. In each case the presence of beer in the village acts as a magnet attracting people from other villages. Beer that is sold is of economic importance as it is the principal way in which women raise funds for themselves. In connexion with a ceremony of some kind, the attraction of the beer is secondary in general to that exerted by the ceremony itself. The provision of beer in return for utilitarian services we shall discuss later. It is in the pattern of behaviour adopted when beer is drunk for its own sake that we can see reflected the structure of social action at the village level.

Beer is stored in earthenware jars of about 7 gallons capacity. A calabash-gourd cup is used to ladle the beer into earthenware bowls holding about 4 pints; from these the beer is drunk. When the beer is ready for drinking, the friendly fellow villagers of the man whose wife has brewed come to the beer-hut, which is usually the woman's kitchen, and the owner of the beer drinks the first jar with them. The procedure with each jar is that the owner of the beer gives the jar to someone, almost invariably a man, who becomes known as the divider of the beer, and who calls on someone junior to him to act as the dispenser of the beer. The dispenser sits on the ground and fills up the bowls from the jar under the instruction of the divider of the beer, and then takes them, or points them out to, the people to whom the divider wishes to give the beer. Thus the beer is given away in jars by the owner of the beer to the dividers of the beer, and is then divided into bowlfuls, and given by the dividers to yet other people. The owners of the bowlfuls drink some and pass on the bowls so that other people may drink. Each time these gifts of beer of different quantities are made they are acknowledged by the recipient in the form of a praise, consisting of the syllable *yo* followed by the descent-name of the giver. This is also done when a bowl or a jar is finished, so that when the last bowl of a jar is finished the owner of the bowl is praised, then the divider of the beer, and finally the owner of the beer. The recipient usually takes the lead in praising, and his praise is chorused by the rest of the people in the hut.

The first jar, then, is divided by the owner himself and the bowl-fuls are given to his village neighbours. The next jar is given to the headman or lieutenant of the village for division, and it is with the drinking of this jar that the party is held really to begin. The first bowl of this second jar is given by the divider of the beer back to the owner of the beer, who praises the divider before drinking. The second bowl goes to some other lieutenant or, if there is no other village lieutenant, to some important woman. Successive bowls go to other important people in the village. Subsequent jars are usually given to important visitors from other villages, who will allocate the bowls to their com-panions and to people in the host village. The first bowl of each jar goes to the divider of the jar, and the dregs, which are usually taken as the two last bowlfuls in each jar, and which are poured out after the jar has been tilted on its side, go to the dispenser of the beer, and to anyone who has been helping him.

There is a great deal of freedom in the allocation of beer in this way, and the complaints of people who hoped to be given beer and who were unfortunate are an invariable aftermath of any beer-party. It is important to note that the quantity of beer consumed by any indi-vidual is to some extent independent of the allocation of the jars and bowls. There are usually two or three bowls in use, and these are all filled up at each round. This means that most people in the hut drink each time. But what is remembered is not the beer drunk, but the method of allocation. Even if a man becomes intoxicated, he may yet complain the next day to his friends that the owner of the beer was miserly and lacking in generosity if no jar or bowl was specifically allocated to him. There is an obligation to return gifts of beer made in this way, so that a man can ensure a favourable reception for himself in other villages where there is beer, by his generosity and sagacity in distributing when there is beer in his own house.

The importance attached to beer-drinking is well brought out in some essays written by schoolboys on the topic 'What I want to do when I leave school'. One of the boys wrote: 'Beer and cattle are the food of the Ngoni. . . . If your friend comes and he doesn't get beer and meat, then although he gets porridge, he still says that there was hunger in the house.' Another said: 'I will brew beer very often. Our life depends on drinking beer.' The small importance attached to beer by the neighbouring Cewa tribe is well known to the Ngoni, and one sophisticated informant remarked: 'The Cewa are just slaves, they merely eat. The Ngoni are like the Whites; they eat little and drink much.'

## Economic Co-operation

There are other activities which entail inter-village ties. Cattle seek their own fodder, but small stock, pigs, goats, and sheep, are fed on husks and other scraps. A man whose animals have increased beyond his ability to feed them will farm out some of them to his friends, either in his own village or in some neighbouring one. The tender of the animals then exercises some control over the disposal of any natural increase and at the end of the arrangement he is entitled to be given one of the animals. The friends whom a man selects for this task are not always close relatives, and may sometimes be people to whom he can trace no genealogical relationship at all, but whom he may have met, for instance, in Southern Rhodesia. Other people acquire a reputation for integrity, and may be given animals to look after by their acquaintances. Cattle are not disposed of so widely, and there is more often a kinship connexion between the owner and the tender. On the other hand, cattle are more susceptible than small stock to tsetse fly, and in consequence there are many people in the new areas that have been recently resettled who have to keep their cattle in the village of a relative or friend who lives in an area free from fly.

Harvesting of crops is carried out by members of the household except in the case of the aged, who will call on their relatives to help them. Hut-building, making a new section of a garden, clearing the ground prior to planting, and, in particular, weeding the garden during the wet season, are activities that are often carried out by collective effort. Women, particularly pairs of widows, may work together in each other's gardens turn and turn about, and a man may be able to call on relatives, particularly his sons-in-law, to help in his garden without paying them for it. Most of the outside assistance that may be required in a garden is raised by means of a beer-party. The man's wife brews beer, and it is made known in the village and round about that on such-and-such a day there will be a party to hoe in their garden. A dozen or so people go to the garden in the morning, and work until the task set by the owner of the garden is completed. They then move to the village, and are refreshed with beer. Attendance at the beer-party is not restricted to those who have worked in the garden, and at some such parties a jar of beer may be specifically allocated to those who have not been working. Some people choose to do their work in the garden on the day previous to the party, on the theory that working and drinking do not go together. A few people offer baskets of ground-nuts or other crops or meat in return for a day's labour, and monetary payments are also known.

## Craftsmen

There are a number of specialized occupations which give rise to inter-village trading. Pots are made by women. Some villages have no potter and their inhabitants are dependent on pot-makers in neighbouring villages. Sometimes a woman may acquire a reputation for pot-making sufficiently high to attract custom even from villages where there are already pot-makers. Pots are sold in return for their own volume of maize, or for money, or the customers may be required to provide sufficient clay for twice the amount of pottery that they wish to obtain.

Basketry is a man's craft, and at the end of the rainy season, when it is necessary to watch all day in the gardens for monkeys, men with this skill spend their time at it. Baskets are sold for money or for maize, and, as with pottery, there is a certain amount of inter-village sale.

Herbalists draw their clients from a wider area than do the pot- and basket-makers, and their contacts with their patients are more intense. If a man falls sick, the remedies known in the family are tried first, but if these are unsuccessful he may go to someone who is known for his wide knowledge of medicines. Patients will travel up to 15 miles or so to consult a herbalist, who may require them to live in his village to receive treatment. Payment for medical treatment is sometimes demanded part in advance, but other practitioners ask for a fee only when a cure has been effected. Since the establishment of medical services by the Administration the way has been open for the medical orderlies to operate in opposition to the herbalists, using misappropriated European drugs.

# III. THE FAMILY

## Principles of Descent

The Ngoni are traditionally a patrilineal patrilocal people paying bride-wealth with cattle. This tradition is reflected in modern practice only to a limited extent. Many of the men and women who were incorporated after Zwangendaba had crossed the Zambezi came from matrilineal matrilocal tribes, and the values associated with these systems of organization were not entirely forgotten. With the decline of the central power of the chieftainship after the conquest, cultural diversity within the tribe increased, so that at the present time we have a wide range of variation in the kinds of family found between one village and the next, and even within the same village. In particular, the irreconcilable difference between the organization of unilineal kin-groups on patrilineal and matrilineal principles appears to have led to a condition in which, for most of the tribe, the only groups of relatives that emerge as corporate groups are stocks, people with a common ancestor from whom they are descended through sons or daughters or both. These stocks are not mutually exclusive, and a man may think of himself at one time as belonging to one stock and at another time to another stock. Frequently alongside the true members of a stock there are other people who claim to belong to the same 'family'[1] who are in fact related affinally to the members of the stock. The organizing factor in domestic affairs is not kinship by itself but common residence combined with genealogical connexion. A stock, with its affinal accretions, emerges as the core of a corporate group of kindred only when its members live near one another and meet each other frequently. The strongest groups are those people of a stock who are living alongside one another in the same part of a village.

The use made of double affinal links in establishing attachment to a stock is noticeable. For example, a child will call a man who is his mother's divorced husband's wife's divorced husband by the term *father* (see Diagram 4 below). A man may bring into his village a wife from outside who may come with her children by a former husband. When grown up, the sons may also bring in wives accompanied by their children from former marriages. These children grow up to regard the village as their own and to think of themselves, in certain contexts, as belonging to the 'family' of the headman of the village. Informants in a village with a most complicated kinship structure will say 'We are all one family here'.

## Kinship Terminology

The variation in the kinship systems of the different tribes from which the Ngoni recruited their members has led to some confusion in the use of kinship terms. Most of the terms now used are in the

---

[1] *Banja*, pl. *mabanja*.

Nsenga language,[1] but Nyanja and old Ngoni terms are also heard. The rules of application of these terms, as formulated by the people, are not always adhered to, and I found that when I challenged the accuracy of some of the kinship terms I heard being used, the speakers were quite ready to admit that the terms had been incorrect by their own rules. Here I propose to give only the Nsenga terms, in the way in which they are used when people are discussing other families, and in which to a lesser extent they are used as forms of address. It is with this meaning that the terms can be used to describe the operation of exogamy. A full account of their use must await further inquiry.

There are ten terms of wide application, and three more used in restricted contexts. These three may be translated as *husband, wife,* and *cross-cousin. Cross-cousin* is used of mother's brother's child and father's sister's child: usually the child referred to is of the sex opposite to ego. *Wife* refers to own wife, brother's wife, and brother's wife's sister, and similarly *husband* refers to own husband, sister's husband, and sister's husband's brother. Thus *husband* and *wife* are reciprocal terms, and *cross-cousin* is self-reciprocal.

The remaining terms may be grouped as follows.

1. *Father, mother,* and *mother's brother,* with a common reciprocal *child.*
2. The reciprocal pair *grandparent* and *grandchild.*
3. Four self-reciprocal terms, *sibling, sibling-in-law, affine,* and *child's parent-in-law.*

These have the meanings implied in their translation, but are also applied more widely, as is indicated in the diagrams. Throughout, the marriage sign is used to indicate any marriage, whether extant or terminated by death or divorce. The symbols used for vernacular terms are shown in Table II.

The way in which these terms are applied can be seen from the diagrams. In the more distant applications the genealogical connexion to ego ceases to be important, and indeed may be unknown. A man may have been told that he should call such-and-such a woman *mother.* He will then apply kinship terms to her close relatives in a systematic manner which is independent of his genealogical connexion to them. The same procedure is followed with the relatives of people called *father* or *sibling.*

[1] The same Nsenga terms seem to be used differently by the Ngoni and the Nsenga. Cf. Ranger, *Chinsenga Handbook,* pp. 68–9, 108–9.

TABLE II. *Principal kinship terms in Nsenga language*

| Symbol | Vernacular term | Basic referent used as translation | Reciprocal term |
|--------|-----------------|-------------------------------------|-----------------|
| F | *atata* | father | child |
| M | *amama* | mother | child |
| C | *mwana* | child | father, mother, mother's brother |
| PP | *ambuya* | grandparent | grandchild |
| CC | *mzukulu* | grandchild | grandparent |
| G | *mkwasu*[1] | sibling | sibling |
| EG | *mulamu* | sibling-in-law | sibling-in-law |
| EP | *mpongozi* | affine | affine |
| CEP | *sewele* | child's parent-in-law | child's parent-in-law |
| H | *mulume* | husband | wife |
| W | *akazi* | wife | husband |
| FZC | *mvyala* | cross-cousin | cross-cousin |
| MB | *malume* | mother's brother | child |

[1] *mkwasu* means 'our sibling'. The terms for 'your sibling' and 'his or their sibling' are *mkwanu* and *mkawo* respectively.

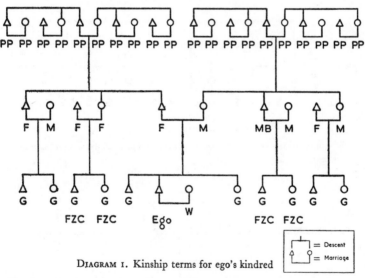

DIAGRAM 1. Kinship terms for ego's kindred

The terms for the generations after ego follow from the rule that *grandchild* is the reciprocal of *grandparent*, and *child* of *father*, *mother*, *mother's brother*. The term *sibling* is often used in place of *cross-cousin* when referring to a cousin of the same sex as ego.

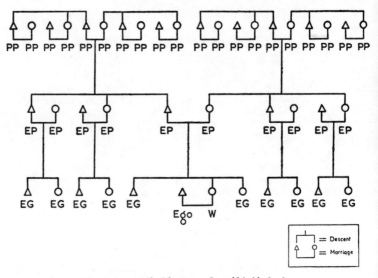

DIAGRAM 2. Kinship terms for wife's kindred

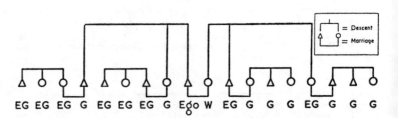

DIAGRAM 3. *Sibling* and *sibling-in-law*

The use of *sibling* to describe ego's spouse's sibling's spouse is more common by men than by women.

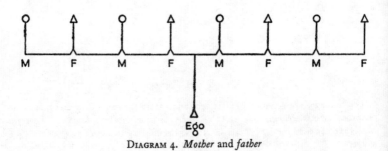

DIAGRAM 4. *Mother* and *father*

PLATE XV

5. Girls dancing *Citelele* in competition with another village. The girl in the centre has a whistle in her mouth

6. Young man drumming for a *Jimi Roja* dance at an installation ceremony. This dance, named after an American band leader, is allowed only on important occasions

NGONI

PLATE XVI

7. Drying a cow-hide at a funeral. A beast from the herd of the dead man has been killed for the mourners. The skin will be buried on top of the coffin

8. Later, at the same funeral. The body has been interred and the mourners are sitting round the grave, near the cattle-byre, listening to a sermon by a local preacher of the Dutch Reformed Church Mission

NGONI

In all the diagrams ego is shown as male. There is no difference in the way these terms are used when ego is a woman, except that she calls her spouse *husband* and not *wife*. There is no consensus as to what great-grandparents should be called. Sometimes *father*

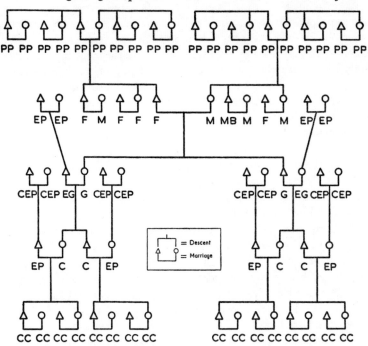

DIAGRAM 5. Extended use of kinship terms

or *mother* is used, according to sex, while others use *grandparent*. Similarly, great-grandchildren are sometimes called *child*, sometimes *grandchild*.

### Exogamy and Descent-names

A man may not marry anyone whom he calls *mother, father, mother's brother, child, affine, child's parent-in-law*, and, except for his *cross-cousins, sibling*. Marriage with his brother's wife's sister, whom he calls *sibling-in-law*, is allowed, but is thought to be not very satisfactory. As we have seen, these terms can be applied widely, with no theoretical limit to the extent of application. Little interest is shown, however, in tracing genealogical relationships accurately, and the sex and age of the relative referred to may affect the term used. If a proposed marriage appears to conflict with these rules of incest, because of some distant relationship between the couple, the connexion may be conveniently forgotten by the parties concerned. Incestuous liaisons between people whose parents are still alive are hampered from becoming proper marriages by the refusal of the woman's parents to accept any marriage payments from the man. Similar liaisons between older people may alter the relative kinship status of other couples so that their marriages become incestuous, and they will appeal to the courts. For example, an old man married his son's wife's mother, whom he called *child's parent-in-law*. In consequence, his son and his son's wife became *sibling* to each other. The young woman refused to go on sleeping with her husband, who appealed to the court. The old man was then ordered to give up his newly acquired wife, so that his son's marriage might continue.

At its widest extension, the term *sibling* is applied to any person of the same descent-name as ego and of approximately the same age. The other kinship terms are then applied to the relatives of this nominal sibling in the usual way. However, there is no rule of exogamy applying to these nominal relatives. These descent-names have been referred to by other writers on the Ngoni as clan-names and the aggregate of people with the same descent-name as a clan. The Ngoni term for such names, *vi-ẇongo*, is related to the Zulu *isi-bongo*, and many of the Ngoni descent-names are the same as the names of the clans described for the South-Eastern and Central Bantu.[1] However, among the Fort Jameson Ngoni at the present time, the category of persons formed by all those holding the same descent-name does not have any of the attributes generally attributed by modern writers to the clan. There are no clan heads, no clan exogamy, no clan taboos, no beliefs in a common origin from a legendary ancestor, no clan totems, and no correlation between clan and territory. In these conditions it seems better to use the term descent-name, as has been done for the Lozi.[2] Informants state that even in the old days, when there was a closer approximation to a clan system, there was no clan exogamy. These names are normally inherited by the child from its father, and some of the names are not very common in the tribe, so that it happens that all the people bearing the one name may be the patrilineal descendants of one man. Such groups are exogamic, but this is

[1] Cf. Young, *History of the Tumbuka-Kamanga*, p. 143, for a classification of some of these names, on the basis of ethnic origin.

[2] Gluckman, *Economy of the Central Barotse Plain*, pp. 84–5.

said to be due to their definite knowledge of common patrilineal descent rather than due to the common name. At the other extreme are names such as *tembo*, *lungu*, and *phili*, which are derived from the neighbouring tribes of the region and are very common and have no connotation of exogamy.

Prior to the arrival of the Ngoni descent-names were inherited in the matrilineal line by the Cewa, Nsenga, and other tribes of the Eastern Province. Under Ngoni influence, the rule was reversed and the great majority even of recently incorporated Ngoni now bear the same names as their fathers. Some people do take the descent-names of their mother, as, for example, a child born in adultery who is not accepted by its mother's husband, or one whose father dies young so that it is brought up by a relative of its mother. As with the Tonga of Mazabuka, some descent-names have locally alternative forms, and in one instance men and women take different names.[1]

Appeal is sometimes made for protection and help on the basis of a common descent-name, but this is not a very strong tie and is invoked only when no closer link can be found. The principal uses of descent-names are in polite forms of address and in connexion with beer-drinking.

## Marriage Payments

The initiative in choosing a spouse usually lies with the man. A woman who takes too much initiative in this matter is regarded, usually correctly, as likely to be unfaithful. In the old days marriages were more frequently arranged by the parents of the couple concerned, but now this happens only when the man is away. Men who are on the farms or in the mines send money home to brothers or fathers with instructions to find them suitable wives, and to offer the money as the legalization payment. During the 1939–45 War this arrangement was continued by soldiers who were away.

The most important payment in connexion with marriage is that made by the bridegroom to the bride's father which I shall call the legalization payment.[2] This payment is the one that establishes unequivocally the right of the husband to damages should his wife commit adultery or be allowed by the court to divorce him. It must be observed, however, that damages may still be awarded to the husband under certain conditions where no legalization payment has

---

[1] The name *zulu* for a man becomes *mvula* for a woman in certain areas.
[2] *Cimalo*, no plural. Cf. Young, *Customs and Folk Lore*, p. 61.

been made. It is the legalization payment that is recorded on the marriage registration certificate when one is issued.

Often this payment is postponed until some years after marriage and sometimes it is never made at all. It is generally £1. 10*s*., and is normally provided by the bridegroom himself out of his savings, although in the old days a man would have been helped by his father. The money goes to the bride's father, and there is no legal obligation on him to share the money with his relatives, although he may do so. Marriage ties can be reinforced by a whole series of ceremonies and ceremonial exchanges and payments between the man's people and the woman's people, and a marriage in which all these ceremonies have been performed is regarded as being 'well fixed'. In such a marriage the parents and siblings of the couple have come to know each other, have collaborated in ritual activities, and have probably had occasion to deliberate together as a court of conciliation in settling quarrels between the couple. This line of development is seldom taken in a marriage in which the legalization payment has not been made. If the husband refuses to pay, then the wife's people will not brew beer for him and his parents, and will not use their influence with his wife to maintain the marriage. We may say that in a well-fixed marriage the two families are linked together, and that in one that is not well fixed it is only the two individuals who are linked. Indeed when no payments have been made it is common for the bride's relatives to profess ignorance of the name of the husband, or at least of his parents' names. No action can be taken in the court to enforce marriage payments, although in an adultery or divorce case the court may order the legalization payment to be made.

The ceremonies of marriage should not be thought of merely as occasions for harmonious co-operation. They may also become the vehicle for the expression of aggression between the two families involved. This is particularly true of the obligation on the man to bring a party of his friends to hoe in the garden of his father-in-law. The hoeing party may do more harm than good to the crops if the present offered them by the father-in-law is considered inadequate.

Prior to the conquest of the tribe the principal marriage payment was bride-wealth,[1] consisting of so many head of cattle. In those days, according to informants, no legalization payment was made. Nowadays bride-wealth is paid only in a small proportion of marriages, and rarely until after several children have been born. In the old days

---

[1] *Malowolo*. Cf. the Zulu verb *uku-loɓola* and noun *iloɓolo*.

marriages in which bride-wealth was paid were patrilocal, and those in which it was not paid, except for marriages with slave wives, were matrilocal. The matrilocal marriages were made only by recently incorporated Ngoni. The payment of bride-wealth is now significant only in relation to the residence and affiliation of the children of the marriage and does not affect the residence of the couple themselves. It frequently happens that a man goes and lives in the village of his wife when they are first married and that after a year or so he takes her back to his own village. This practice is fairly common among the matrilineal tribes of the region. A small payment[1] of five shillings or so may be made instead to enable a man to take his bride to his own village without first completing a period of matrilocal residence. Sometimes the legalization payment is considered sufficient to exempt from matrilocal residence. Indeed it is indicative of the wide range of variation in the different payments made and not made and in the significance attached to them that some informants were unable to state with certainty what payments had been made in their own marriages, although they knew the amount of money or animals that had been handed over.

This wide range of variation in behaviour in relation to marriage is one instance of the high measure of cultural heterogeneity of the Fort Jameson Ngoni. While present-day conditions are relevant to a study of Ngoni marriage, at the same time the effect of the combination of people with very different conceptions of marriage into a single state must not be overlooked. Among families that are powerful and claim to have migrated with Zwangendaba from the south, patrilocal marriage and the payment of bride-wealth are more frequent than they are among families of more recent incorporation. Cross-cousin marriage is noticeably more frequent in villages with people of Bisa descent than in the population as a whole. In Nyasaland, where there is a sharper cleavage into old Ngoni villages and conquered Cewa villages, the old Ngoni are characterized by a greater, and the Cewa by a lesser, incidence of patrilocal marriage.

### Divorce

In the old days there was no way in which a woman could divorce her husband. A man could divorce his wife at any time by sending her back to her own people. The usual procedure nowadays, except in cases of adultery, is for the man to give his wife sixpence or a shilling

[1] *Nthakula.*

and inform her that she is divorced. If the wife has committed adultery, the husband can take the case to court. If the adultery is proved he is usually awarded £3 damages against his wife and £3 against the co-respondent, and the woman is divorced. On the other hand, a woman can seek a divorce in the courts on the grounds of desertion or cruelty. The court will award a divorce if the desertion or cruelty is proved, but may also rule that the woman must pay £3 to her husband's family.

If a man does not wish to divorce his adulterous wife, the court will award him damages of £1. 10s. against his wife and £1. 10s. against the co-respondent. In adultery cases in which a divorce is granted the damages awarded against the woman are often met by the co-respondent, who then marries the woman, but where there is no divorce the woman will appeal to her father or brothers to help her pay her husband.

If a woman runs away from her husband there is nothing that the husband can do to force her back, and if methods of conciliation fail, he has little hope of redress, except in cases of seduction or abduction. If the woman refuses to rejoin her husband the court may award damages against her, but such a marriage usually ends in adultery on the part of the woman and a divorce on that ground.

It has been observed by District Officers that divorce is not so frequent among the Ngoni as compared with their Cewa neighbours. Nevertheless, divorce must be considered as a frequent occurrence among the Ngoni, and is so regarded by the people themselves. There is a maxim that a man ought to rely on his brothers, not on his wife, and one informant remarked: 'Never trust your wife; perhaps to-morrow you will divorce her.'

## The Wife's Mother

The tensions between the two groups linked by a marriage find their most formal expression in the attitude prescribed for a man to his wife's mother. While a woman can speak to her parents-in-law and enter their house, a man cannot do so. In his contacts with his father-in-law he must be quiet and reserved, and although face-to-face contact is not considered shocking, it should be as rare as possible. But a man must go out of his way to avoid his mother-in-law, and this injunction is in the main observed in practice. The avoidance is usually phrased in terms of a prohibition on the entry into the hut of the mother-in-law. A man who has to pass by this hut will normally go round the back of it.

It is therefore appropriate that, when a man has proved himself to be a good son-in-law by fulfilling his obligations to his parents-in-law and by treating their daughter well, he is invited to make a formal entry into the house of his wife's parents. This is the occasion for much dancing and speech-making. The salient features of the ceremony[1] are as follows. The married couple come in procession with their relatives and neighbours from their village to the village of the woman's parents. The procession is led by the eldest child of the couple carrying a knobkerry. They dance in the cattle byre and then enter the hut of the woman's parents. Here after some drinking and dancing, during which the visitors keep themselves more or less to one side of the hut and leave the other side for the relatives of the woman, there is a ceremony in which a gift is offered by the man's people to the woman's people, and in which a female relative of the man takes a spoonful of boiled maize from a dish and then spits it out again. She is followed by a female relative of the woman, who does the same. The two people who do this are close relatives of the couple, sometimes sisters. The knobkerry stays in the hut overnight, and the next day the man's parents come and they formally enter the woman's parents' hut. The couple also come into the hut with their friends and the woman's mother offers beer to the man in the usual way by kneeling at his feet and drinking to him. He then drinks from the bowl, and it is passed round for everyone in the hut to drink.

The completion of this ceremony marks the setting aside of the avoidance taboos to the greatest extent allowed. The man may still not sit on the same mat as his mother-in-law but he can now talk to her and can come into her hut. It is, as it were, the final reward of the good son-in-law and marks the end of the series of adjustments in relative status that began with the small gifts that the man made before the legalization payment was fixed. The hostility between the two families has been reduced by carrying out through the years their reciprocal rights and duties, and their common interest in the children of the marriage is symbolized by the eldest child who leads the procession from one village to the other.

Even on such a family occasion as this, village, as distinct from kinship, ties remain important. At one ceremony I attended the leader of the first delegation from the man's village was described as being just an important woman in the village and not related to him.

[1] *Mngeniso.* Cf. the Zulu verb *uku-ngenisa,* to enter another person's house (Colenso).

## Grandparents

Children on weaning are often sent to their grandmothers to be brought up. The payments made in the marriage do not seem to influence either the choice of grandmother or whether or not the child stays with its parents. A child is sometimes sent to an old woman not its grandmother but related in some other way who lives in the same or a nearby village and who already has a brood of children to look after. This separation from the parents may occur whether the grandmother lives in the same or in a different village from the parents. Grandparents, and in particular that grandmother by whom a child was brought up, become confidants in later life. It is to her husband's grandparents that a wife complains if her husband does not fulfil his sexual obligations, while it is through the bride's grandparents that the groom should approach her parents when arranging the marriage. The husband must avoid his wife's mother, but his wife's mother's mother and his wife's father's mother can sit on the same side of the house as he does, as though they were themselves married to him. When he is drunk a man can fondle the breasts of his grandmother, whereas to attempt to do this to his mother would be regarded as shocking.

While it is the grandmothers who intervene in the beginning of a matrimonial quarrel when the dispute is still an affair of the village, it is the parents of the couple, or if the parents are dead or senile the brothers, who will go to court to support them when the dispute has moved to the judicial zone of activity. Women seeking divorce on grounds of desertion get their fathers to speak in their favour, while the absentee husband, who may be lost in Southern Rhodesia, will be represented by his father or his brother. Occasionally a father may give his support to his daughter-in-law rather than to his son if the son has annoyed his father as well as his wife.

Outsiders cannot intervene in the disputes within a family, although they may be called in to give their support to one side or the other. In particular the family of a man will not themselves take the initiative in bringing an action against his wife, however strongly they may rally to his support in a dispute where the initiative is taken by the wife's people. This principle applies even in cases of incest. For example, a woman whose husband was away in Southern Rhodesia slept with her father. The husband's brothers wrote to Southern Rhodesia to tell him what was happening, but as in his reply he did not instruct them to take proceedings in the matter, nothing more was done about it.

# IV. WIDER CONTACTS

*Other Local Groups*

We have so far in this account been concerned with delineating the main outlines of political and village structure and the kinship system. We have examined the internal constitution of the tribe and have only been concerned secondarily with the external relationships by which the Ngoni are connected with the wider world. But in the Fort Jameson District there are, and have been for many years, people who do not fall within the tribal framework but with whom the Ngoni interact. These include people from the British Isles and South Africa, Indians, and Coloured persons, as well as Africans from other tribes. The Europeans are there as administrators, missionaries, farmers, and traders. Indians are traders and farmers, while Coloured persons are farmers and foremen. Africans from other tribes are, like the Ngoni, labourers on the farms and in the township, as well as subsistence cultivators in their own tribal areas.

The land of the District is divided into Native Reserve and Trust land, farm-land, township, and Crown land. Almost all Ngoni villages lie on Reserve or Trust land, and it is in this zone that most of the activities described so far take place. On the farm-land Ngoni participate not as headmen or lieutenants or chiefs, but as labourers and foremen. They still fill the roles of husband, wife, sibling, parent, and child, and sometimes other kinship positions, but the family in the farm compound is on a smaller scale than in the village. In the town of Fort Jameson the range of activity open to them is greater, and there are Ngoni butchers, drivers, clerks, shop assistants, Native Urban Court assessors, and so on. All these roles on farm and in the town are shared with Africans from other tribes in the Eastern Province and from more distant regions.

*The Churches*

The influence of the non-African groups extends out beyond the areas in which they live into the reserves. We have already seen how the Administration has affected the life of the tribe. The Christian Church has also had a profound influence. By 1910 there were three denominations at work in Ngoni country: the Dutch Reformed Church Mission,[1] the White Fathers,[2] and the Universities' Mission to

[1] Algemeente Zending Commissie der Nederduitsche Gereformeerde Kerk in den Oranje Vrijstaat.

[2] Société des Missionaires de Notre Dame d'Afrique, a Catholic Order.

Central Africa. The U.M.C.A. subsequently concentrated its activities in another part of the District, so that the two main denominations are now the Dutch Reformed Church and the Catholic Church. There was for a time a branch of the Livingstonia Mission (Free Church of Scotland) in the area, while more recently a Seventh Day Adventist Mission has begun work. Since 1924 there have been some adherents to the Watch Tower[1] amongst the Ngoni, but this movement did not become important until some years later.

Primary education is carried on in mission schools subsidized by the Administration, but there is also a Native Authority school over which the chiefs exercise some influence and which is to some extent supported by Native Treasury funds. The teachers in the elementary schools live in the villages, but they do not exercise very much influence outside their classrooms. This does not appear to have been the case in the past, when there was greater hostility between the different missions and when the missions tended to disregard the tribal authorities. The teachers then seem to have set themselves up as headmen on their own, and schools were built without the permission of the local headmen. In many cases where the issue between the missions was undecided, there were two schools in the same village. In the middle 'thirties many of these so-called schools were closed on the initiative of the Administration and the teachers who remain are now more interested in education than in politics.

A village school serves more than one village, so that the children of a neighbourhood containing, say, half a dozen villages get to know each other and visit in each other's villages. Certain dances and songs, known as *konsert*, are performed by parties of schoolchildren going from one village to another, and this leads to similar inter-village dancing in the evenings organized by groups of boys. At the end of term a number of schools of the same denomination combine to perform a rather more elaborate programme of songs and dances, and these displays are attended by many adults.

The deacons and evangelists are of greater importance in the political life of the tribe than are the school teachers. Deacons take a certain initiative in settling disputes in the village, and they report to their missions deaths and serious sins that affect their people. They arrange for religious instruction for catechumens and may on occasion organize opposition to some practice that has been declared wrong by the mission. Evangelists are responsible for a number of villages and

[1] The Watch Tower Bible and Tract Society.

may often be heard in the afternoons blowing their whistles to call their flock to prayer in the local school.

Meetings of all deacons and evangelists of one denomination within the tribe are held every year or so. Permission to hold these meetings has to be obtained from the chief, who may sometimes attend. Food is provided by the local church members and a levy to raise funds for buying a goat or sheep may be made. The initiative at these meetings is taken by the senior deacons and decisions reached are passed on to the members by the deacons. Church services, which are attended by people from many villages, are not only meetings for worship but are also occasions when instructions for collective action are given. For example, a lieutenant was recently suspended by his mission for helping to find another wife for his chief. Church members in his county were then instructed at a church service that they must not attend the funeral of this man or of any of his children.

The tribal area is divided into two zones controlled by the two main denominations, with some overlapping, and this division cuts across the county boundaries, so that people from more than one county have a common interest in a church serving them all. This interest is reinforced by attendance at funerals and prayer meetings in the villages.

The Watch Tower, also known as Jehovah's Witnesses, or in the vernacular, as The Society, is now the third sect of importance in the area. This organization has had a rather chequered career, and has been the target of much adverse criticism from missions, Administration, and chiefs. From the point of view of social structure, it is significant because its organization within the tribe cuts across the county boundaries, because it holds that the teachers of the other denominations are wholly false, because its membership is drawn largely from people who previously belonged to these other denominations, and because no local Whites and few persons of importance in the tribe are members of this sect. In the past, members of the Society opposed the chiefs on principle, but this attitude is not held now, and opportunities are taken to demonstrate their loyalty to the existing order. Meetings are held in different parts of the country every month, and members from other parts are housed and fed by the local members.

Not every person in the tribe has been baptized as a Christian, but the initiative in religious affairs has passed to the functionaries of the different denominations. While the indigenous practices of the people

have affected the content of their Christian beliefs and their utiliza-
tion of Christian institutions, there is now little religious activity that
can be called pagan.

## The Nyasaland Counties

The Fort Jameson Ngoni maintain strong connexion with the two
counties under Ngoni chiefs in the Fort Manning division of Lilongwe
District, Nyasaland. When the border was drawn between North-
Eastern Rhodesia and Nyasaland, about a quarter of Mpezeni's tribal
area fell within Nyasaland. The two countries have been administered
separately, so that the ties that have persisted have done so despite the
formal division of the area and are in the main derived from sentiments related to pre-conquest times. These ties are seen in operation
in the attendance of the Nyasaland chiefs at Mpezeni's village on
various formal occasions, as at the ceremony ending the mourning for
Mpezeni II and beginning the reign of Mpezeni III. In 1920 a delegation from the Nyasaland chiefs visited Mpezeni, and in 1922 Mpezeni
took a party across into Nyasaland to visit the two chiefs, apparently
with the idea of discussing the possibility of moving his capital into
Nyasaland[1] where there was more land available than there was for
him in Northern Rhodesia. From time to time Mpezeni has called on
the Nyasaland chiefs to send him maize when his own supplies have
run low, and these requests have been met. The Nyasaland Administration has also tried to keep alive the connexion with Mpezeni. In the
past the Magistrate at Fort Manning brought the Nyasaland chiefs
into Fort Jameson to meet Mpezeni there on such occasions as the
King's Birthday, while in 1932 when there was a dispute between the
two chiefs as to which was the senior, the District Officer informed
them that the question did not arise as they were both only lieutenants
of Mpezeni. On the other hand, the Nyasaland Administration has
intervened to prevent tribal levies for the benefit of Mpezeni.

There are also relationships across the border that arise principally
from the mere territorial contiguity of the two areas. The border,
which is the Luangwa–Nyasa watershed, is not easy to follow and
there has sometimes been doubt as to where it runs. The villages
stretch without interruption across the watershed and there is much
coming and going from one village to another. Some villages have
moved from one country to the other and many people have relatives
on both sides of the border. The Catholic Missions were for a long

[1] Mpezeni I had the same idea. Cf. *British Central Africa Gazette*, 1 August
1897, p. 2.

time controlled from a mission station just inside Nyasaland, so that many people crossed to attend religious services and receive instruction. From Mpezeni's own county it is easier to get to the hospital at Fort Manning than to the one at Fort Jameson, so that people wanting European medicine tend to go to Nyasaland for treatment rather than to Fort Jameson. Nyasalanders are for their part attracted into Northern Rhodesia by the market for foodstuffs among the urban population, White and Black, of Fort Jameson and by the greater variety of goods on sale there.

## Other Ngoni Groups

The Fort Jameson Ngoni are conscious of their links with the other groups of Ngoni scattered over Central Africa, and of their similarity with the Ndebele and the Swazi and Zulu. The Paramount Chief is sometimes praised by the recital in the Ngoni language of the past exploits of the Ngoni, how they crossed the Zambezi, and how they conquered one tribe after another. On one occasion I heard someone who cannot speak Ngoni praise the Paramount by repeating, in Ndebele, which is similar to Ngoni, a praise of Mzilikazi[1] which he had learnt by rote. This oration was accepted without comment by the Paramount. Lancaster has recorded a legend that Lobengula[2] fled to Mpezeni after the second Matebele War, and that he died in the country.[3] Some years after his installation Mpezeni II was visited by a delegation from Mombera, chief of the Ngoni of Northern Nyasaland, which, it is said, came to ratify Mpezeni's position as Chief of the Fort Jameson section of the Ngoni. An important headman in Mpezeni's county, who bears the same name as Chief Chiwere of the Ngoni of Dowa District, still claims from time to time that because his namesake and alleged relative is a chief, he too ought to be a chief.

## Nsenga and Yao

The Ngoni are on more friendly terms with the Nsenga of Petauke District than with the other matrilineal tribes of the region. Some of the kinship ties that were formed as a result of intermarriage between the two tribes in the 1870's can still be traced, and their languages are similar. Mpezeni III went in 1944 with his first lieutenant and twenty-five followers to visit the Nsenga Chief Manjawanthu, and he is expected to return the invitation.

[1] The first Ndebele king.    [2] Son of Mzilikazi, defeated by the Whites.
[3] Lancaster, p. 83. Cf. *British Central Africa Gazette*, 15 May 1896, p. 2, and Posselt, *Upengula the Scatterer*, pp. 112–24.

R

The Yao are mistrusted more than any other tribe, and some of the decisions taken by the courts are harsh on Yao. For example, a Yao man who was married to an Ngoni woman had, it was alleged, caught venereal disease from his wife. His wife then applied to the courts for a divorce, which was granted, together with the custody of the children. No bride-wealth had been paid in the marriage, but the husband now offered to pay in order to retain the children. This bride-wealth was refused by the woman's parents. The Yao appealed, but the judgement was upheld, and in addition he was ordered to go back to Nyasaland at once. He asked for permission to return to the woman's village in order to collect his belongings, and this was granted by the court, after first securing agreement between the couple as to the extent of his possessions, to wit, four plates and two beds. This deportation order was made despite the fact that the Yao had been living with his wife for twenty-one years. If a man of some other tribe had been involved, it is unlikely that he would have been ordered to leave the country, nor would the court have been so suspicious of his trying to take away more than his rightful share of the household possessions.

A Yao, who had a good job in Fort Jameson, once offered 30s. to the Paramount Chief when he was in the town as the legalization payment for a woman of the royal lineage whom he wished to marry. The Paramount Chief refused the money on the ground that the man was a Yao and he was not going to permit Yao to marry into the royal lineage, despite the protest of one of his lieutenants that the Yao was just a man like anyone else.

The reason that is given for this dislike of Yao is that they are sexually very virile, due to the medicines that they possess for increasing potency. It is perhaps significant that the same is said of Indians, who are also disliked. The Yao are known among the Ngoni for their great knowledge of medicines of all kinds, and the allegation of unnatural sexual vigour may be a rationalization of the fear that the Yao may practise sorcery among the families into which they marry. Another factor that may operate is that the Yao are the only tribe in the region that the Ngoni cannot claim to have conquered.

### Political Relations with Other Tribes

Before the European conquest relations between the Ngoni and other tribes were principally those of raiders and raided. The great season for raiding was after the harvest, when the surrounding tribes could be raided for their crops, as well as for captives, and when the rivers did not form such an obstacle to rapid movement as they did during the wet season. Some of the early reports of travellers suggest that there was some sort of alliance or working arrangement between the Ngoni and Mwasi Kasungu, whose territory acted as a buffer-state between Mpezeni's Ngoni and Mombera's Ngoni of Nyasaland[1] but this alliance does not seem to have been very stable.

The British Administration restored or created Cewa chieftain-ships that now completely encircle the Ngoni except where the Ngoni area reaches to the edge of the waterless and uninhabited Luangwa escarpment. The Administration did not recognize any right of the Ngoni over these Cewa areas, and it is now difficult to discover how much control was in fact exercised by the Ngoni over the Cewa at that time. The Ngoni certainly continued to hold that they were entitled to control the Cewa. In 1913, when the formation of reserves was being discussed with the Administration, the Ngoni chiefs are said to have been disappointed that the scheme would give the Cewa land of their own and later in the same year they tried to ensure that the Cewa to their south, who were to be granted a reserve separate from those of the Ngoni, should be formally placed under the control of Mpezeni.

At the present time the principal institution in which Ngoni co-operate with other tribes under the aegis of the Administration is the Eastern Province African Provincial Council. This body meets once a year for three days, and is attended by delegates from all the Superior Native Authorities in the Eastern Province, as well as by representa-tives of the Administration. It discusses matters of common interest and it elects two members to represent the Eastern Province on the African Representative Council of the whole Territory, but it does not have any legislative or executive powers. Its meetings are open to the public,[2] but as yet few people attend and the recommendations reached are passed on to only a small section of the tribe. The dele-gates to the Council are chosen by the Paramount Chief on the advice of his lieutenants.

There are also other political relationships that unite Ngoni with other tribes. Some of them arise from common residence in an area outside the Ngoni country. Representatives are stationed at the

---

[1] Money and Smith, *Explorations in the Country West of Lake Nyasa*, p. 152.
[2] Except on the first day, when the African members of the Council meet by them-selves in Committee.

principal urban centres on the railway line in Northern Rhodesia who represent the Ngoni Native Authority in the various Native Urban Courts. These representatives are appointed by the Superior Native Authority, that is, by the Paramount Chief and his lieutenants. These posts are regarded in much the same light as those of the minor chiefs except that the tenure of office is not so stable, and the same struggles to gain them take place. There are Ngoni members of the Fort Jameson African Urban Advisory Council, but they are elected by urban Africans and are not appointed by the Native Authority.

### Rural and Urban Status

The relatively privileged position of certain individuals in the urban order may raise their status in the life of the tribe. We have already seen how the initiative in religious matters is taken by the deacons and evangelists, and these people are also called upon to lead the prayers that precede all county meetings. The orderlies in the hospitals in Fort Jameson are able to establish private practices and number chiefs and other important people among their clients. The senior shop assistants may find it possible to entertain important people by offering them European spirits. The clerks of the Administration, as part of the protective screen around the District Officers, can exercise their discretion in allowing pleas to go forward to them.

There seems to be very much less bribery and corruption than has been reported from other parts of Africa. The Ngoni are in the main more interested in and more able to make effective use of medicines and other material goods than they are of advance information. But the fact remains that the African Civil Service and the various commercial undertakings are institutions within which a man of no importance in the village and tribe can rise to a position of influence which will affect his dealings with other tribesmen. The only Ngoni on the African Representative Council, which meets yearly and includes representatives from the whole of Northern Rhodesia, was in 1946 not a headman or lieutenant but was the most prominent African businessman in Fort Jameson.

To some extent this association of high status in the urban community and low status in the rural one is inevitable, since it is only by absence from the district for many years that a man can advance himself sufficiently and acquire sufficient skill and seniority to reach this high urban status. The member of the African Representative

Council mentioned above spent some twenty years of his life in Johannesburg. Fort Jameson itself is not a sufficiently big town for this process to take place within it, and yet it is only in Fort Jameson or on the tobacco farms that a man can live with a leg in both camps, going home to the village at the week-ends and probably keeping his wife in the village during the wet season to tend her crop.

On the other hand, there is some rivalry between the traditional leaders and the comparatively prosperous townspeople. The well-clad and well-housed Ngoni of the township are sometimes described scornfully by village people as 'merely White'. There is a feeling that the leading African traders are trying to monopolize the economic opportunities in the villages. Recently the same prominent Ngoni businessman proposed that he should take over the delivery of mail to the Native Authorities, which he claimed he would be able to do more efficiently with a car than can the present postman on a bicycle. The Paramount Chief did not answer this proposal but wrote instead to the Administration to complain against the danger of one man being allowed to earn so much more than anyone else while there were so many people who needed money. At the same time, men whose lives are led principally in the towns complain that in the villages there is 'nothing but jungle', and that the chiefs are old-fashioned and obstructive.

## The Administration

The relationship between the Provincial Administration and the Ngoni is characteristically one of superordination and subordination. The District Officer can send for any Ngoni, but not even the Paramount Chief can send for the District Officer. This characteristic arises from two sources, from the premiss which we find held all over Southern Africa, that any White is superior to any Black, and from the supervisory role allotted to the Administration in the Native Authority scheme. These two facets of the same relationship are not always seen separately by the Ngoni, and in many contexts their behaviour towards the Administration is governed entirely by the fact that the District Officer and those above him are all White. Official reports by the Administration during the reign of Mpezeni II repeatedly remarked on the Paramount Chief's distrust of Whites, and this attitude still persists. Any kind of trouble at all, particularly when it is seen as a characteristic of the present times as opposed to the glorious trouble-free past of the days of peace, before the Whites came, is attributed to the Whites. I was told that the high incidence of divorce, the disappearance of wooden plates, the frequent breaches of the mother-in-law avoidance, were all due to the Whites. The District Officer is seen primarily as a member of this White tribe, and only secondarily as a member of the Administration as opposed to being a farmer or a missionary. An Administration official was once described by an admirer as 'a man whom the Ngoni trusted, although he was a White'.

In practice, it is the Administration, through the person of the District Officer, which supplies the stimulus to maintain the Native Authority structure in being in its present form. As far as many of the tasks allocated to it by the Administration are concerned, the Ngoni Native Authority falls into the class mentioned by Davidson as having 'still to be continually stirred into activity by the local District Officer'.[1] It is the Administration which calls the meetings of representatives of the whole tribe to discuss questions relating to land, agriculture, schools, labour migration, ex-soldiers, and the like. It is the Administration which supplies the forms to the Native Courts, the ubiquitous books that are the symbol of White power, which informs the Native Authority what taxes and licence fees to collect, which supplies land for resettlement, organizes the building of wells and roads, and so on.

Mistrust is certainly the principal characteristic of the Ngoni attitude to Whites, a mistrust which is based as much on what are felt to be past wrongs as on an inability to understand the motives for present administrative actions, however well intentioned these may be.[2] At the same time there is considerable admiration for White material achievements, and to a lesser extent for the large-scale political and economic developments of which they are aware. Sentiments such as 'the British Empire means peace for everybody' are not at all uncommon.

It is in relation to the farmers that the Administration is seen in the kindliest light, and it is from the Administration that Ngoni seek redress for infringements of their rights by Whites and Indians. The District Officer also acts as an agent for some of the smaller Ngoni traders, obtaining supplies for them from the urban centres. The Administration attempts to protect the rights of Ngoni by seeing that they are not cheated of their wages by planters or overcharged by traders.

[1] Davidson, *N.R. Legislative Council*, p. 29.
[2] Cf. Read, *Tradition and Prestige*, pp. 473–81.

The tribe is represented to the Administration in the person of its chief, and the fact that it is through him that the Administration articulates with the tribe is realized by thinking people. In a wider sense, he represents the tribe to the White community as a whole. When I first started work in the area there were many formalities at my meetings with the Paramount Chief, so that I should understand the importance of his position. Mpezeni II is said never to have allowed a White to see him dancing, because of the mystical and social dangers involved. At a county meeting, held while the Paramount Chief was away in Livingstone, the court clerk reminded headmen that the month of May was approaching, and that he would soon be wanting people to hoe the Native Authority roads. When the time came, he did not want headmen to say they had no people. He continued: 'If the people do not obey the laws, then Mpezeni will not be well regarded by the Whites. Then when the Administration wants to make bad laws, Mpezeni will not protest, as he will want to punish his own people.'

If the chief is too attentive to the requirements of the Administration, then his standing with his own people is likely to suffer. A chief's court was once described as 'just a White court' because of its alleged bias in favour of the Administration's interpretation of native custom. On the other hand, this identification with the White Administration is not accepted by the chiefs and their advisers. In an adultery case, in which the husband did not want to divorce his wife but she refused to go back to him, Mpezeni, who was present, ordered the woman to return to her husband. A councillor asked the woman what she had to say. She said she loved the co-respondent. The councillor was annoyed, and asked her, 'Do you know who Mpezeni is?' The woman said, 'He's a chief', using the usual word for chief, *mfumu*, current all over north-eastern Rhodesia. The councillor replied: 'No, Mpezeni is not just a chief, everyone is a chief nowadays.' The woman then said, 'He's a White.' The councillor answered: 'No, Mpezeni is not just a White whose orders can be sometimes obeyed and sometimes ignored. Mpezeni is *nkhosi*, the great chief of the Ngoni, whose commands must always be carried out.'

## V. EARNING A LIVING

*Intertribal Trade*

There is little trade between the Ngoni and the neighbouring tribes, whose products are largely the same as their own. Fish is brought up from the Luangwa valley by Kunda and some of it is sold to the Ngoni of the Cipalamba, through whose villages the hawkers pass on their way to Fort Jameson. Bracelets are sometimes brought from Portuguese East Africa by Chikunda. The main attraction for these hawkers is Fort Jameson itself, and it is the fact that the town is encircled by the Ngoni that gives rise to trading with them. The geographical location of the town has also led to the growth in Ngoni country of many stores and what are known in the vernacular as hotels, where tea and buns can be bought and where sometimes there is shelter for the night.

Of greater importance in the life of the tribe than these intertribal links are those arising from White and Indian economic activities. We may distinguish three zones of interaction, the shops both in Fort Jameson township and scattered throughout the district owned by Whites and Indians, the local tobacco farms, and the mines of Southern Rhodesia. The Ngoni have come to need cloth for clothes which they cannot produce themselves, and it is doubtful if there would be enough animals to provide skins for the tribe even if they did not insist on cloth. The need to earn money with which to buy clothes, soap, and other necessities can be met only by seeking employment on a farm, in Fort Jameson township, or farther off. A few people earn enough by selling vegetables in Fort Jameson, and there is a certain amount of maize and other cereals sold. These sales, however, do not provide sufficient income to reduce materially the extent to which people go out to work.

*Control of Movement*

To the White traveller, Fort Jameson District is an island of tobacco in a sea of bush. To the Ngoni, the island is not so sharply demarcated, and its characteristic property is cattle, not tobacco, yet it still remains an island, surrounded by a sea of other tribes whose traditions are different from their own. The ships that cross this sea are the lorries. In time past, men used to walk to their destinations, going by Feira to Southern Rhodesia, or across the Luangwa to Broken Hill. A few used to go down to Lake Nyasa, and thence to the

Lupa goldfields and Dar-es-Salaam. Nowadays almost everyone goes by lorry, but now as then a man has to go a long way before he can arrive at an island of friends in one of the urban centres. This means that, for the Ngoni, emigration is a definite event, and does not occur as a result of a gradual drifting farther and farther away from the tribal area. Lorries run from Fort Jameson to Lusaka and to Lilongwe, and from Missale to Mtoko in Southern Rhodesia. There is also a lorry service from Lundazi to Fort Jameson, but this does not lead anywhere else, and is not used by Mpezeni's people except locally. Lusaka is on a railway line, Lilongwe is connected by bus and train to Blantyre, while Mtoko is on the way to Salisbury. It is these lorry routes which now provide the links with the outside world, and along which people and goods travel, the people in both directions, and the goods, apart from tobacco, mainly inwards. Use of these routes is controlled by the chiefs, the Administration, by economic factors, and by the weather. This last has been less important of late, and the roads are seldom impassable for more than a week at a time, however heavy the rains. In order to travel on the lorries from Fort Jameson a man must have a ticket, which costs £1 for the journey to Lusaka, and less for the trip to Lilongwe. The lorry service from Missale to Mtoko is free.

The Administration exercise control by insisting that no man shall leave the Territory of Northern Rhodesia unless he is in possession of an identification certificate endorsed by the Administration permitting him to do so. In practice, such endorsements are not usually made unless the man can produce written permission from the chief that he is free to go. This working arrangement is intended to ensure that men do not flee the country when there are cases pending against them, and to prevent unjustifiable desertion of wives and children. In fact men are sometimes given permission to go while cases in which they are involved are still unheard.

The emigration of women and children is further controlled in that there is a law[1] forbidding a woman to leave the tribal area except in the company of her husband, or with a pass to leave from the Native Authority. Sucking children are allowed to accompany their mothers, but other children under the age of sixteen are not allowed to leave the province without permission of the Native Authority,[2] while boys

[1] Ngoni Native Authority Order 24.
[2] Ngoni N. A. Order 39. The child must be either accompanied by its parents or else accompanied by a guardian on the way to join its parents.

over sixteen are not allowed to leave without a pass from their Native Authority until they have paid tax for one year at home.[1] These laws are quite energetically enforced, principally by the placing of Native Authority police at strategic points along the lorry routes. These police inspect the passes of all passengers on the lorries, and bring offenders before the nearest Native Court.

The devices adopted to evade these restrictions are much as one might expect. The drivers of the lorries may be won over, particularly by women. A woman may get a lorry driver to say that she is his wife, or even enter into a temporary marriage with him, if she wishes to run away without a ticket. Some people walk to the far side of the police point and then attempt to get on the lorry after the search has been completed. A woman who has a ticket but no pass may pose as the wife of some unaccompanied male passenger.

The motives for leaving the area are many. Most of the men go to look for work, although a few go away to visit their urban relatives and friends for a holiday. Others go to buy goods that may be unobtainable locally for the time being, such as tools or window-panes, or which they think they can get more cheaply elsewhere, such as bicycles. Many of the women go to join their husbands, but some are fleeing from them, or have grown tired of living at home married to men who live permanently in Southern Rhodesia, and are out to try their luck in the towns.

Whereas the outgoing lorries are comparatively empty of goods, the returning passengers are well loaded with belongings. The fares are higher, and the Mtoko–Missale service is not free on the northward trip. One of the most important commodities brought in along these routes is the mail. Men working in Southern Rhodesia and elsewhere write home to keep their wives and brothers informed of their whereabouts, and send postal orders to enable their families to buy clothes.

This movement to and from the outside world must be seen in its relationship to the opportunities that exist for employment within the District on the tobacco farms.

### Farm Labour

No village in either of the reserves occupied by the Ngoni is more than 12 miles from a farm. This means that it is possible for a man to work as a labourer on a farm and yet retain a large number of his contacts with his village and chief. In particular, his wife and children

[1] Ngoni N. A. Order 37.

can live in the village and cultivate a garden. The maintenance of contacts is facilitated by the fairly general cessation of work on the farms at the week-ends. Apart from two periods of tobacco slump, the local demand for labour has exceeded the supply ever since the earlier period of European settlement. As early as January 1900 the manager of the North Charterland Exploration Company complained to the Administration that the lack of local labour was very serious, and attributed this to the large number of people who were going away to work in Southern Rhodesia. This theme has been repeated over and over again ever since. The practical effect of this chronic local shortage of labour has been that work on the farms has always been a more easy-going affair than work away on the mines or in the big towns. Men have been able to absent themselves from work to attend to their affairs at home very much as they have pleased. Payment has been either for piece-work or for the number of days worked, so that at one time it was not unusual for a man to take two or three months to complete thirty days' work, for which he had contracted.

Prior to about 1930, there were a few villages located on farm-land, whose inhabitants undertook to work for so many days, with pay, in return for permission to remain on the land. With the completion of the move into reserves, this became rare, and at the present time the bulk of the people who live on farm-land are accommodated in compounds provided for them by the farmer. These people are the labourers on the farm for the time being, their families, and friends. The compound is under the charge of a foreman who is usually an employee of long standing on the farm. On some of the farms there are small gardens, but none of them, as far as I know, permit the keeping of cattle by the labourers. This means that a man with cattle must continue to keep them at home in his village or in the village of a relative. Cattle are still the principal form of investment, particularly for people who cannot spend their capital in building a brick house, so that it is common to find in a village that many of the cattle in the byre are being tended for the benefit of an absent owner who spends the majority of his time away on a farm and who may not even have a hut in the village.

The demand for labour on the tobacco farms varies considerably with the time of year, being greatest from about Christmas until about June. At the same time, the calls on a man to tend his own garden are greatest from about November until May. Farmers therefore try to get labour for a few days at a time from people who live in villages near their farms, who go home every afternoon after work and come back the next morning. Others employ women and children, and most boys work intermittently on the farms to earn enough to keep themselves in clothes until they are old enough to go away to Southern Rhodesia. Other boys work in their holidays from school.

To some extent people from the same village tend to go to work together in groups on a farm. This is particularly true in the case of the short-term labourers who sleep at home, since the choice of farm is restricted to those in the immediate vicinity of the village. Here sometimes the majority of the inhabitants of a village will turn out under the leadership of the headman of the village and work for three or four days on the same farm. Longer-term labourers may be attracted to a farm by the presence of a foreman from their own village.

Girls also go to work on their own, and many marriages are made as a result of encounters on the farms. Marriages made in this way are not always recognized by the parents of the girl until the man has brought her back to her village and formally approached her parents.

The villages near the farms, and to a lesser extent those near the township, sell beer to the labourers, while the farms themselves buy up most of the maize and other cereals that villagers have to sell.

The continual demand for labour on the farms leads to their serving as a sanctuary for fugitives from social pressure of one kind or another. For example, a native policeman was going round the villages obtaining labour for the Administration for essential public works. He adopted the normal practice of imposing a quota of labourers to be supplied upon each village and made the headman responsible for seeing that his village quota was met. If the headman did not do this, he enlisted the headman as a labourer. At one village the headman told the policeman that his people had all run away to the gardens when they had heard of the arrival of the policeman in the area. The policeman warned the headman that either he must exercise his authority over his people and order them back into the village so that he could enlist them, or else the headman would be enlisted. He came back the next day to see what had happened, and found that the headman had gone off to work on a farm. There is machinery for recovering such people, but it does not work easily or quickly, and by the time a man has been located and brought back, the reason for which he was wanted may have fallen away.

Disputes between Africans on farms can be dealt with at the nearest Native Court, but if the farmer wishes to enforce his rights under the

Labour Ordinances, he can only do so through the District Commissioner's court at Fort Jameson, which may take up more of his time than he thinks the matter worth. In consequence, few actions are brought by farmers against their African labourers and if a man breaks his contract and deserts, no action may be taken against him.

It is not surprising that the efficiency of labour operating under these conditions is low, and that the wages are also low. These two conditions react on one another, and it is misleading to regard the low wages as the only cause of the inefficiency, or the inefficiency as the only cause of the low wages. The practical effect is that men who wish to earn more money than they can get as labourers on the farms at 14s. a month with food go away to Southern Rhodesia. It must be observed, however, that men started going to Southern Rhodesia long before the tobacco farms were opened up to their present extent.

### Labour Migration

Prior to the European conquest, the only men who had worked for Whites were those employed as carriers by the handful of travellers who passed through the country before 1896, and as carriers and labourers by the North Charterland Exploration Company from 1896 onwards. But immediately after the end of the fighting in 1898, recruiting started among the Ngoni for police work in Southern Rhodesia, and there has been a continual flow of labour migrants south ever since.

There have been considerable fluctuations in the number of men going south since that time, particularly during the two world wars, when the military requirements of the Territory exercised a greater claim. The latest figures for the Eastern Province as a whole show that, in 1946, 23 per cent. of the taxable males registered in the province were absent from the province. Another 17½ per cent. were at work within the province.[1] In May 1947, in two Ngoni counties with a combined total of 1,739 registered taxable males, it was found that 30 per cent. of them were at work in the Eastern Province and a further 42 per cent. were away elsewhere, a total of 72 per cent. away from their villages. Half of those living outside the Eastern Province were classified as 'lost', in that their present whereabouts were unknown to the people at home.[2] These figures exclude all men who have been 'lost' for more than five years.

[1] Labour Department, *Annual Report, 1946*, p. 12.
[2] These figures were given me by the District Commissioner, Fort Jameson.

Looked at from the point of view of the individual, we find that all adult men have at some time or other been away to work, and that the majority have been to Southern Rhodesia once or twice.

## Conclusion

In their lives on the farms and in Fort Jameson, Ngoni mix with men from other tribes, and their position is largely subsumed under the conditions common to all African labourers on all European-controlled farms. The Administration does not support the Ngoni more than the Cewa, or one chief more than another. As the content of the relationship becomes more and more related to the world-wide polity and economy, so the nature of the relationship becomes common to a wider group. Ngoni living in Fort Jameson Compound live lives that are closer to the lives led by other tribes in compounds in other towns than they are to those led in the villages 5 miles away. The phenomenon of labour migration greatly affects Ngoni social structure, but is not a distinctively Ngoni institution in the same way as the Ngoni village is distinctively Ngoni. When Ngoni ex-soldiers complain that when they were recruited they were promised that after the war they would get good jobs, and now find they do not get them, their sentiments derive more from their status as ex-soldiers, which they share with some millions of others, than they do from their status as Ngoni.

## BIBLIOGRAPHY FOR THE FORT JAMESON NGONI

ALLAN, W. 'African Land Usage', *Rhodes–Livingstone Journal*, iii (1945), pp. 13–20.

BARNES, H. F. 'The Birth of a Ngoni Child', *Man*, xlix (1949), 118.

BARNES, J. A. *The Material Culture of the Fort Jameson Ngoni*, Occasional Papers of the Rhodes–Livingstone Museum, No. 1, Livingstone: Rhodes–Livingstone Museum (1948).

—— 'Some Aspects of Political Development among the Fort Jameson Ngoni', *African Studies*, vii. 2–3 (June–Sept. 1948).

—— *Marriage in a Changing Society*, Cape Town: Oxford University Press (1951).

—— (with Max Gluckman and J. C. Mitchell), 'The Village Headman in British Central Africa', *Africa*, xix (1949), pp. 89–106.

BRYANT, A. T. *Olden Times in Zululand and Natal*, London: Longmans Green (1929).

CHIBAMBO, Y. M. *My Ngoni of Nyasaland*, London: United Society for Christian Literature (1942).

Colonial 145. *Report of the Commission appointed to enquire into the Financial and Economic Position of Northern Rhodesia* [A. W. Pim & S. Milligan], London: H.M.S.O. (1938).

COXHEAD, J. C. C. *The Native Tribes of North-Eastern Rhodesia*, London: Royal Anthropological Institute (1914).

DAVIDSON, J. W. *The Northern Rhodesia Legislative Council*, London: Faber & Faber (1948).

DECLE, L. *Three Years in Savage Africa*, London: Methuen (1898).

ELMSLIE, W. A. *Among the Wild Angoni*, Edinburgh: Oliphant Anderson & Ferrier (1899).

FRASER, D. *Winning a Primitive People*, London: Seeley Service (1914).

FRASER, R. H. 'Land Settlement in the Eastern Province of Northern Rhodesia', *Rhodes–Livingstone Journal*, iii (1945), pp. 45–9.

GENTHE, H. 'A trip to Mpezeni's', *British Central Africa Gazette*, 1 August 1897, pp. 1 and 2.

HODGSON, A. G. O. 'Notes on the Achewa and Angoni of the Dowa District of the Nyasaland Protectorate', *J.R.A.I.*, lxiii (1933), pp. 123–64.

KAPUNZAH, W. A. *Angoni, Uzimba ndi Miyambi*, Ncheu Nyasaland: Zambezi Mission (1941).

KUPER, H. *An African Aristocracy*, London: Oxford University Press (1947).

LANCASTER, D. G. 'Tentative Chronology of the Ngoni, genealogy of their chiefs, and notes', *J.R.A.I.*, lxvii (1937), pp. 77–90.

MONEY, R. I., and SMITH, S. K. 'Explorations in the Country West of Lake Nyasa', *Geographical Journal*, x (1897), pp. 146–72.

Northern Rhodesia. *Labour Department Annual Report 1946*, Lusaka: Government Printer.

Nyasaland Protectorate. *Report on the Census of 1945*, Zomba: Government Printer.

PIM, A. W. See Colonial 145 of 1938 (Pim Report).

POOLE, E. H. L. 'The Date of the Crossing of the Zambesi by the Ngoni', *Journal of the African Society*, xxix (1930), pp. 290–2.

—— MS.: 'Human Geography of the Fort Jameson District', on file at Rhodes–Livingstone Institute.

—— *The Native Tribes of the Eastern Province of Northern Rhodesia*, Lusaka: Government Printer, 2nd edition (1938).

POSSELT, F. W. T. *Upengula the Scatterer, or Lobengula and the Amandebele*, Bulawayo: Rhodesian Printing & Publishing Co. (1945).

RANGER, A. S. B. *Chinsenga Handbook*, London: Sheldon Press (1928).

RATTRAY, R. S. *Some Folk-Lore Stories and Songs in Chinyanja*, London: S.P.C.K. (1907).

READ, M. 'Tradition and Prestige among the Ngoni', *Africa*, ix (1936), pp. 453–84.

—— 'The Moral Code of the Ngoni and their former Military State', *Africa*, xi (1938), pp. 1–24.

STIGAND, C. H. 'Notes on the Natives of Nyasaland, North-East Rhodesia, and Portuguese Zambezia,' *J.R.A.I.* xxxvii (1907), pp. 119–32.

TRAPNELL, C. G. *The Soils, Vegetation and Agriculture of North-Eastern Rhodesia: Report of the Ecological Survey*, Lusaka: Government Printer (1943).

WERNER, A. *The Natives of British Central Africa*, London: Constable (1906).

WIESE, C. 'Beiträge zur Geschichte der Zulu im Norden des Zambesi, namentlich der Angoni', *Zeitschrift für Ethnologie*, xxxli (1900), pp. 181–201.

WINTERBOTTOM, J. M. 'A Note on the Angoni Paramountcy', *Man*, xxxvii (1937), No. 158.

YOUNG, T. C. *Notes on the Customs and Folk-Lore of the Tumbuka-Kamanga Peoples*, Livingstonia: Mission Press (1931).

—— *Notes on the History of the Tumbuka-Kamanga Peoples in the Northern Province of Nyasaland*, London: Religious Tract Society (1932).

# THE NYAKYUSA OF
# SOUTH-WESTERN TANGANYIKA[1]

## By GODFREY WILSON

### Country and People

THIS paper is an attempt to give an outline of the pagan culture
of the Nyakyusa people of Tanganyika[2] in relation to the three
fundamental groups into which their society is articulated—
the family, the age-village, and the chiefdom. Every Nyakyusa belongs to some family, to some age-village, to some chiefdom; and in
his membership of these three groups is comprehended most of his
behaviour.

The Nyakyusa live in the Rungwe District of the Southern Highland Province of Tanganyika in the Rift valley at the head of Lake
Nyasa. The valley is here dominated and closed at its north end by
the recently extinct Rungwe volcano, from whose foot the land,
starting as an upland plateau 5,000 feet above sea-level, tumbles
southwards for 25 miles in a broken cascade of hills, to level out in a
plain 15 or 20 miles from Lake Nyasa. The lake is 1,537 feet above the
sea.[3] The east wall of the Rift rises to 10,000 feet or more in the peaks
of the Livingstone Mountains, but the west wall is 2,000 or 3,000 feet
lower. The climate is very wet, for over 100 inches of rain fall each
year, and, at 9° south of the Equator, is also very hot. The rain and the
sun together make the land extremely fertile; the district is thickly
populated (over 80 to the square mile), famine is rare, and the Nyakyusa are far better fed than most of their neighbours. Rice was introduced into the plain by Arabs, coffee by the German missionaries
in the hills, and these two crops today[4], under the enthusiastic care
and guidance of the Government Agricultural Department, bring to
many Nyakyusa a small but steadily increasing cash income.

Their main foods are bananas, maize, beans, sweet potatoes, and a
variety of greenstuffs, together with meat and curds from their cattle.

---

[1] Reprinted (with certain amendments) from *Bantu Studies*, x (1936).
[2] I am greatly indebted to the Rockefeller Foundation for the Fellowship which
makes my investigation possible.
[3] *Geographical Journal*, Nov. 1935, p. 453. This is the minimum height recorded.
[4] i.e. in 1936.

Millet is extensively grown and is used both for making beer and for eating in the form of porridge.

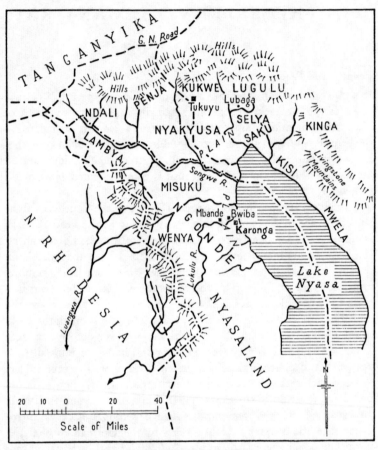

NYAKYUSALAND

The name Nyakyusa is nowadays used by themselves as a general name for all those who have similar speech and customs and who live in Tanganyika; but formerly it only covered those who live in the south of the district, in the plain and up in the hills as far north as the administrative capital, Tukuyu, and it is still thus used to distinguish this group from others. This group will here be referred to as 'Nyak-yusa proper'. Those in the north of the district to the west and east of

Mount Rungwe call themselves *Kukwe* and *Lugulu*,[1] respectively; to the east, under the Livingstone Mountains, is a group of chiefdoms called *Selya*, and farther south, on the north-east corner of the lake, are the *Saku*. All these five groups share a common culture, distinguished by minor local peculiarities of dialect and custom. Immediately bordering the Nyakyusa to the south-west are the *Ngɔndɛ* (Europeanized as 'Konde') in Northern Nyasaland; they belong to the same cultural group, but are distinguished by greater differences of custom and speech than the others.[2]

In the hills to the west of the Rift live the *Ndali* and *Lambya*, who are included in this administrative district; on the plateau under these hills to the west of the Kukwe live the *Penja*, and on the shore of the lake live the *Kisi*, famous as fishermen and potters. These small groups have languages of their own which, though related to that of the Nyakyusa, are more or less unintelligible to them; and they have equally distinct cultures. But they are now rapidly being assimilated to the Nyakyusa both in speech and in law.

I use the name Nyakyusa, in accordance with modern usage, to include the Nyakyusa proper, the Kukwe, Lugulu, Selya, and Saku groups, but to exclude the Ndali, the Penja, Kisi, and Ngɔndɛ. The Nyakyusa together with the Ndali, Penja, and Kisi in Rungwe District number 150,000, the Ngɔndɛ of Nyasaland 40,000.

Frederick Elton, His Britannic Majesty's Consul at Mozambique, was the first European to visit the country; he passed through in 1877.[3] After Elton came Scottish missionaries and traders, who established themselves at Karonga in Ngɔndɛ; then in 1891 members of the Berlin and Moravian missions settled among the Nyakyusa. The German administrators followed them closely, and later came a few planters. During the First World War many Nyakyusa were impressed as porters, but pronounced economic change is a matter of the past five to ten years,[4] during which time the Lupa goldfields of south Tanganyika have been opened up and have employed increasing numbers of Africans on the diggings. During the past few years the young men of the Nyakyusa have developed the habit of going for a

---

[1] The Lugulu are called *Mwamba* by the people of Selya; the application of this term, which may be translated 'the hill people,' varies from place to place, as also does the application of *Ngɔndɛ*. Cf. Wilson, *The Constitution of Ngonde*, p. 7.

[2] Godfrey Wilson, *The Constitution of Ngonde*.

[3] J. F. Elton, *Travels and Researches among the Lakes and Mountains of Eastern and Central Africa* (1879). [4] Written in 1936.

few months, now and again, to the goldfields to earn money for tax
and clothes. They seldom stay more than six months at a time, often
only one or two, so that their absence does not cause the same difficulties in their own community that are found in other areas where
the men spend longer periods away from home.

### The Family and Wider Kinship Groupings

The relationships of husband and wife, parent and child, sibling
and sibling are continually visible in the culture of the Nyakyusa.
The holding of land and the economics of life in general, the rules and
procedure of law, the emotional forms of ceremony, the dogma, rite,
morality, and symbol of religion, the forms of knowledge and opinion
—all are interpenetrated by these relationships.

The word 'family' is here used to mean the organized group of a
man, his wife or wives, and their children of any age, but not to include any other relatives. A married man is thus a member of two
families, his own and his father's. A Nyakyusa family, as we shall see,
does not become extinct when the father dies; his younger full-
brother or his senior son steps into his place, and the group continues
very much as before. In this society families are sometimes monogamous, sometimes polygynous; and, in consequence, two more relationships with which we are not familiar in our own culture are included in the Nyakyusa family; one is the relationship of co-wives and
the other is that of half-siblings. Within a polygynous family the
different wives and their respective children form groups to some
extent distinct from one another; and the term 'individual family' is
here used to denote the group of a man, one wife, and their children,
whether that group is part of a polygynous family or forms a complete
monogamous family by itself.

The Nyakyusa themselves have no separate word for either of
these small groups; the word *ekekɔlɔ* is occasionally used in the restricted
sense to which we have here confined the word 'family', but more
usually means the whole of any single person's recognized blood
kindred, living or dead, both in the male and female lines; and it is
here variously translated as stock, genealogy, kindred, kinsfolk, or
kinsmen. They also have a word *ovokamu* which includes the whole of
any one person's *ekekɔlɔ* together with all his recognized affines, and
this is here translated 'relatives'. The term 'affines' is used to translate
the Nyakyusa word *avako*, which is identical in meaning with it.

Marriage is legally effected by the handing over of four to thirty

PLATE XVII

1. Homestead with Ndali hills in the distance. Two huts are hidden in the bananas. Both rectangular and circular huts are traditional styles

2. A boys' village

NYAKYUSA

PLATE XVIII

3. A woman greeting a man politely. She must crouch and look away from him

4. A woman hammering bark-cloth in the shade of the bananas

NYAKYUSA

cows, together with one or two bulls, by the groom to his wife's father. And this transfer of cattle is the key to the whole Nyakyusa system of blood and affinal relationship. Cattle have a very high value because of their production of milk and meat, which are the most highly prized foods, and because of their scarcity; they are in constant circulation, and by their movement from one man to another they for ever create and maintain the bonds of kinship and affinity. Cattle circulate rapidly; few except chiefs have more than ten cows in their herds at any one time; more often each man has paid out, for his own and his sons' marriages, five, ten, or twenty times the numbers of cattle that he at present possesses. A young man is given cows by his father and sends them to his father-in-law; his father's income in cattle is derived partly from the increase of his own stock, but chiefly from the marriages of his own and his brothers' sisters and daughters, for it is the custom for full-brothers and half-brothers to give one another cows as their daughters and sisters get married; the young man's father-in-law gives the cows which he receives, some to his brothers, some to his sons, and some he keeps himself. And thus, continually, the cattle are driven down the paths of human relationship.

The passage of cattle makes the children of a marriage members of their father's family; the sons can inherit from their father, and the daughters, when they marry in their turn, bring cattle to him. But if a woman bears a child to a man who has given no cows for her, the child has no right of inheritance anywhere, and belongs either to her husband or father, not to its own biological sire.

Getting married is not a single event; the marriage-cattle are seldom handed over all at once, but in ones, twos, or threes over a period of years; and a girl very commonly goes to visit and sleep with her betrothed husband, from time to time, for several years before she finally sets up house with him and begins to bear his children. There are three ways of getting married: (1) by negotiation with the girl's father, (2) by running off with an unmarried girl, and (3) by running off with a married woman. The first is the ideal, socially approved, method and is not uncommonly followed. The negotiations often begin while the girl is still an infant, sometimes even before she is born; the man or his father sends one or two cows to her father to bespeak her (*okosingela*). These cows are counted as part of the marriage-cattle (*eŋgwɛla*) and the girl is henceforth called his 'wife', but she lives at home with her parents. Sometimes a boy is betrothed by his father while he himself is still young, but always, I think, to a girl several years his junior. Such betrothals are determined by the friendship of the two families. A girl who is bespoken in infancy does not, ideally, go to live altogether with her husband till after she has reached puberty and passed through the elaborate initiation which then takes place. But there is an intermediate period when, from the age of ten or earlier, she is allowed to visit and sleep with her husband from time to time. The man sends a hen to her father to ask for his wife (*okwasima*) and the old man agrees to let her go on occasional visits. But she is seldom allowed to go until at least three cows, in all, have been received for her. She is often not deflowered before puberty, and she and her husband always, at first, practise limited intercourse without penetration. Not infrequently, however, full intercourse takes place on some occasion and her parents usually find out when it does. If the girl has been forced against her will, or generally ill treated, her father sends back the cows he has received for her and breaks off the marriage; more often, however, there is no question of ill treatment, and he sends his daughter to live with her husband, saying: 'You have made her a woman yourself, you must pay the rest of the marriage-cattle quickly.' Occasionally the father does nothing at all.

We have no evidence to suggest that the girls in any general way dislike sleeping with their husbands before puberty, rather the reverse; and the men say: 'It is good, it accustoms a girl to her husband.' But some girls dislike the particular men to whom they are betrothed.

The initiation of a girl at puberty lasts for some months and includes several exchanges of food between her family and that of her husband, and a number of rites and ceremonies in which both her girl friends of the same village[1] and her husband's friends from his village participate. If a girl is not bespoken before puberty the initiation is still carried out in a modified form, but its full significance is lost.

Soon after her initiation a girl, if she has been bespoken, goes to live altogether with her husband, to play her part in his economy and to bear him children. If only a few cows have been received for her, her father insists on one or two more being handed over before she is allowed to go. At some time, perhaps during the girl's initiation, perhaps years later, the *okokwa* ceremony takes place. The bulk of the marriage-cattle are brought to her father by the husband and his village neighbours; her 'mothers' prepare a great deal of food for the guests to eat; there is dancing, feasting, and great excitement.

The number of cows handed over varies with the wealth and social

[1] See below, 'The Age-village'.

status of the two families concerned. Six to ten cows is now the most usual number, but sometimes as few as four or as many as thirty change hands. The number has been going up steadily; before the coming of the Europeans, marriages with only one cow were common.

The second method of marriage is adopted when a man falls in love with a grown girl, who is not bespoken, and cannot find the cows to satisfy her father at once; he runs off with her and regularizes the position later by sending cattle. The third method is adopted when a man falls in love with a married woman and has cows available; he runs off with her and then returns to her first husband the cows he had given for her, with two in addition as adultery fine. But this return is usually made only after the first husband has brought a lawsuit against him.

Adultery is extremely common nowadays; when a man runs off with, or is discovered seducing, a married woman and has not enough cows to marry her, he is legally compelled to pay two cows for the adultery to her husband. In pre-European days an adulterer, if caught, was usually killed by the husband and his brothers, and adultery was then a rare event.

The extent to which a girl is allowed to choose whom she will marry is difficult to gauge and varies in different circumstances. Opportunities of meeting and flirting with young men at dances and ceremonies are frequent; and owing to the abolition by the Europeans of the death penalty for adultery, and the new legal rights of women, girls are freer now than they used to be, for their lovers no longer fear to run off with them if they are married or bespoken (which is in Nyakyusa law very much the same thing) and the girl's submission can no longer be enforced by beating. The custom of betrothing infant girls is less common than it used to be; they are now more chary of pledging their daughters, 'for when they grow up they just run off with someone else'. A girl's choice is, however, limited by the necessity of finding a lover who has cows, and not all young men have enough to secure her if she is already married, though they may have enough to pay an adultery fine.

Owing, in part, to the laws of inheritance, by which a man's full-brother inherits before his son, it is the older men who control the cattle. Every bachelor is largely or wholly dependent on his own father (or his father's heir) for the cows for his first marriage, and he must hoe his father's fields for many years before he is given enough to secure a wife and to set up a family of his own. Economic reciprocity is an element in most human relationships, and it enters into the Nyakyusa relationship of father and son. It is well understood, in this society, that after a certain length of time spent hoeing his father's fields a young man is entitled to some cows, if his father has any; and if his father delays too long the young man either stops hoeing for his father or runs off with a girl to force his father's hand, or else he takes legal action and enforces his claim. Between father and son such law cases are rare, but they are frequent between a young man and the brother of his father who has inherited his father's wives, property, and position in the family.

Normally a bachelor is given cows one by one, over a period of years, and, as we have seen, he sends them, as he receives them, to the father of the girl he wants to marry. One cow is sufficient for betrothal, but not until he has given three can he begin openly to sleep with her. And he cannot usually set up his own economy until he has given at least three cows and she has reached puberty and been initiated. He may, of course, bespeak an already grown girl, but if he engages himself to a young one he is expected to bring at least one bull as well, during the course of her initiation.

If he chooses to spend his cows in adultery fines, he may, but he will then have to wait longer to get married.

Thus the system of marriage by a transfer of cattle is, in this society, directly linked with a late marriage age for young men and with a privileged position for older men. When a boy gets cattle he at once gives them to an older man in order to secure his daughter as a wife; the labour of every bachelor helps to increase his father's wealth in food; it is in general the older men alone who can afford more than one wife. And there is an average difference of ten years or more in the initial marriage age of men and girls. The tax registers show in part of the district, among 3,000 adult men,[1] 34 per cent. bachelors, 37 per cent. monogamists, and 29 per cent. polygynists; and investigation proves that, generally speaking, it is the young men who are bachelors, the men over forty-five years of age who are polygynists.

Though cattle are their most valued form of wealth, it is on agriculture that the economy of the Nyakyusa is primarily based. Meat and milk are luxuries, but daily bread comes from the fields. Hard work in a fertile country provides food for each family, and the millet beer which is the ordinary material of hospitality, and employment of labour. Hospitality brings a man prestige and authority among his

[1] Presumed to be eighteen years of age or over.

fellows; on the possession of sufficient food largely depends the contentment of his wives. And in the production, preparation, and eating of food the relationships of the family, and of the individual family within it, are clearly visible.

Hoeing is normally the work of men; planting, weeding, reaping, and cooking are the work of women. The men, young and old, hoe for four or five hours on most mornings of the year; in the lower altitudes they begin well before sunrise and finish about 9–10 a.m., on the upland plateau they begin later and continue till noon or beyond. The energetic ones sometimes hoe again for an hour or two in the late afternoon. Different crops are planted at different seasons of the year, so that there is always some hoeing to be done. Nowadays some women whose husbands and/or sons are away hoe for themselves, but this is an innovation.

In a polygynous family each wife has her own fields (*embaka*), hoed by her husband and his sons, which she plants, weeds, and reaps with the help of her own daughters, and the produce of which she uses to cook for her husband, her own children, and herself. The relative rights of husband and wife to dispose of produce vary with different crops, but no co-wife has any rights over a woman's food. She may, and often does, ask her co-wives to help in her fields and sends them presents of cooked food from her own fire; she may help them and receive presents in return; but they have no rights over her fields or her food, only her husband and herself.

Each wife has either a hut to herself or else a separate alcove in a large hut, and there she has her fire for cooking. She fetches her own firewood and water, or sends an unmarried daughter for them.

At meals the ages and sexes eat separately; in some polygynous families each wife sends a dish to the husband, in others the wives take it in turns to cook for him. The husband eats alone or with neighbours of his own age[1] to share his dish, the older boys and their friends eat separately from the younger children, and each mother again usually eats with her own daughters, apart.

In the relationship of husband and wife the chief elements are sexual intercourse, co-operation in work, the procreation of children, and factors of personal inclination, character, and temperament. By men women are praised for sexual skill, cleanliness, and beauty, for regular cooking and hard work, for their fecundity, and for gentleness of speech and behaviour, and those with opposite qualities are

[1] See below, 'The Age-village.'

criticized. Among women men are praised for sexual skill and attentiveness, for vigour in hoeing and skill in house-building, and for kindness; while sexual neglect, laziness, impotence, and cruelty are disliked, and may cause a woman to leave her husband for another man.

The birth of children is a most important factor in the marriage relationship, for children are greatly desired both by men and women. They are desired for themselves and also because they bring their parents wealth and prestige; a boy will one day work in the fields of his father and mother, a girl will bring in cattle from her marriage. And the possession of children brings compliments and respect both to man and woman. Impotence and barrenness are well-known facts, and magic is much used to cure them; but apart from their operation it is believed that each conception directly depends upon the frequency with which a man visits his wife. And thus the bearing of children is, for a woman, a demonstration of her husband's great affection for her. People adduce the number of children that a woman has borne to prove, in conversation, that she is her husband's favourite.

Polygyny is the ideal of every pagan Nyakyusa; a plurality of wives is necessary, in this society, for full sexual satisfaction; wives bring a man wealth, prestige, and authority; the more wives he has the more children, he thinks, will be born to him.

It is believed that any contact with the sexual fluids is dangerous to a young child's health, and so, after a woman has borne a child, her husband is supposed wholly to refrain from intercourse with her for some months until the child is old enough to play by itself and allow its mother time to wash in the mornings before touching it. Then he may begin to visit her again, but still she must not become pregnant until the child is of an age to be weaned, 'if she does her breasts become rotten' and the first child is harmed. As children are not weaned for two or three years, this rule involves the couple in two years or more either of *coitus interruptus* or of infrequent intercourse (which also is believed to avoid conception). These taboos on intercourse after a child's birth are usually observed in practice, and are one of the reasons for polygyny among the Nyakyusa.

Another reason is the absence of hired labour. With a few exceptions the only way a man can increase the supply of labour permanently at his disposal is by marrying more wives. Polygyny is the mark of a wealthy man, conditioned by his control of cattle, conditioning his supply of food. And the cattle spent in marriage come back again with interest as the polygynist's daughters begin to be betrothed and married.

It is extremely common for a man to take as his second or third wife the sister, half-sister, or brother's daughter of his first or second wife. By doing so a man pays a great compliment to the wife whose sister, or niece, he takes and to her family; his action implies complete satisfaction with her and friendship with her family. He sends his wife home 'to fetch out (her kinswoman) into the open' (*okosakola*); but she will not agree to do so unless she approves of him as a husband, and so, if she does agree, her action likewise compliments him. I know of one case in which a man wished to take his second wife's younger sister in this way, but his wife refused to go and fetch her on the ground that he was a bad husband.

The children of one man and two close kinswomen have almost the relationship of full-siblings, but not quite, and I propose to call their relationship that of *linked half-siblings* (see below).

In a polygynous family the first wife married, the chief wife (*oŋkasi-kolo*), is in a privileged position; she is entitled to the respect of her co-wives and her eldest son is her husband's ultimate heir. A man cannot lightly divorce his first wife, for while the other wives he obtains by his own efforts, with his own cattle, she is married with cattle given him by his father, who must be consulted before she is divorced and who is offended if she is sent away without very good cause.

Besides the chief wife there is, in most polygynous households, a favourite wife (*oŋkondwe*), who in fact has greater privileges. Ideally a man is supposed to be fair to all his wives and to distribute milk, land, and sexual attentions equally between them, with perhaps a slight bias in favour of his chief wife. But usually one wife is her husband's favourite and is given by him an undue share of the household's milk supply, and sometimes he hoes more land for her than for the others as well.

Divorce is legally effected by the return of the marriage-cattle. No pagan woman in this society ever desires to live single, and so when a wife leaves her husband it is always with the intention of marrying some other man. Usually she has a particular man in mind who has been making love to her and who has cows enough to redeem her, but not always. A woman may, as we have described already, run off with a lover and then, as soon as he has returned the marriage-cattle and the adultery fine to her former husband, she becomes his legal wife, and her children by him are legitimate. If she has no lover to run off with, or if her lover wishes to avoid the adultery fine, the woman goes to court[1] (before 1926 she went to her own chief) and publicly refuses to

[1] See below, 'The Chiefdom'.

live with her husband. She may or may not give a reason for leaving him, but if she persistently refuses to go back to him there is now no way of compelling her to do so. The judges say to her: 'Well, you must find the cattle', and so she stays, either with her father or in the charge of a court official, until some man comes to marry her. Then the cows are returned to her first husband and the divorce is effected. In pre-European times a woman could only appeal to her own father, who would never agree to a divorce unless for violent ill treatment. A man has the right to divorce his wife, that is to send her away and demand back his cows, if she is dirty or lazy in housework or if she commits adultery, but men do not often demand a divorce for adultery unless it is persistent. If a man sends his wife away for some such reason she returns to her father and he, if he has cows available, sends back to her husband his marriage-cattle; if he has not got the cows the husband must wait until the girl is remarried.

Into the relationship of mother and daughter economic co-operation and reciprocity enter. The care of young children is largely in the hands of their elder sisters, and the girls also help their own mothers in field-work and in fetching and carrying. In return their mothers cook for them, teach them how to cook, and how to make mats.

Each mother is responsible also for her own daughter's virginity. One of the bulls which a young man brings during the initiation of his betrothed wife is only given if the girl is found on examination to be still virgin, or if he has deflowered her himself. If it is given, this bull belongs to the girl's mother to eat with her own friends. But in spite of her mother's responsibility for her, a girl learns nothing positive from her mother about sex, but from her own slightly older friends; with them she discusses the technique of love-making in detail, but never with her mother.

The relationships of siblings are, in general, closer than those of half-siblings, and the eldest son in each individual family is privileged above his brothers. A boy's claim for cattle is, as we have seen, partly based on the time and energy he has put into hoeing his parents' fields; but it also depends, in part, on having full-sisters of his own. When a girl marries, the cows come to her father, but her own full-brothers expect to receive these cows, in time, for their own marriages, in the order of their age. Though the father controls the cattle the brothers speak of them as 'our cows' and they have an ultimate legal claim to them which only gross laziness or insult to their father can altogether vitiate. The eldest of a group of full-brothers is the first to draw on these cows and to marry; his juniors wait longer. Full-brothers are bound together in many ways; the eldest, who is privileged, is bound to help his juniors in any way he can, and they in turn respect him and in time give to him some cows from the marriages of their own daughters; and each makes the others' quarrels his own. What chiefly unites them is the law of inheritance, for though the eldest has first right to the cattle from their sisters' marriages, and though the younger ones, later in life, give cattle from their daughters' marriages to him, yet they are his heirs, and all his privileges in time pass to them. When the eldest dies his next full-brother steps into his place, takes his wives, huts, land, and cows and looks after his children; after him the next full-brother inherits and so on, until, when all are dead, their property and wives pass to the next generation.

The heir has exactly the same obligations to his predecessor's children that the dead man had himself while alive, but frequently he has less will to perform them; and his conformity is often only assured by the pressure of legal, conventional, and religious sanctions.

This rule of inheritance is part of a more general fact, which is that, in Nyakyusa society, death does not break a family and its relationships, but simply alters the particular people between whom these relationships obtain. Only rarely does death leave a man or woman widowed, or a child orphaned; nearly always someone is at once substituted in place of the one who has died. When a woman dies young her parents are bound, if her husband requests it, either to give another daughter to him or else to return part of the marriage-cattle so that he can obtain another wife; when a man dies his wives and children are not left alone but taken by his heir. If the heir is a brother he takes all the women as his wives; if a son, he builds a separate hut for his own mother and takes the others. And the heir is now 'the father' of the dead man's children. Even when a man and all his full-brothers are dead, the families of each are still united for some purposes under the leadership of each one's senior son (eldest son of chief wife). The senior son is now called 'father' by his siblings and half-siblings, he is religiously responsible for them all (see below), he normally exchanges cows with the eldest brother in each individual family (see below), he is entitled to their respect and obedience.

Half-brothers may, or may not, be linked especially closely together. They may, as we have seen, be linked by blood when their two mothers are either sisters or close kinswomen; they may also be linked by an exchange of cattle, by 'milking each other's cows' (*okokamanela*). Each group of full-brothers regards the cows that come in from the marriages of their sisters as their own cattle, but the father disposes of these cattle as he wishes. If he gives some of their cows to a half-brother, he thereby creates between the eldest of the group and this man the special relationship of 'milking each other's cows'; and it is expected that the cows given will in time be returned by this half-brother from the marriage-cattle either of a full-sister or of a daughter of his own. And the exchange once begun goes on; as their sisters and daughters marry they continually give each other cows; between their respective sons also the exchange usually continues, but between their grandsons it lapses. Reciprocity is expected and can be legally enforced, but it is not insisted upon so long as the two men concerned are friends, and its full legal enforcement at once breaks the relationship. If two such half-brothers (or their sons) quarrel, one may take legal action for 'separation' (*okolɛkana*) against the other. The cows that have been handed over by both sides since the beginning of the relationship (perhaps twenty or thirty years before) are counted up, and one or the other is ordered to pay over the balance to make the numbers equal. After this the two are 'no longer kinsmen'; they have no mutual obligations and do not attend each other's funerals.

It is usual for a father to create this relationship between his senior son and the eldest of each group of full-brothers, so that by this exchange of cows the family is held together. The linkage of half-brothers by 'milking each other's cows' is important in inheritance. If a man with no full-brother, or half-brother linked by blood, dies and leaves no sons, or sons too young to inherit, then the inheritance passes to a half-brother linked by exchange of cows.

Religion enters continually into family life and helps to maintain wider kinship bonds also. The Nyakyusa religion falls, broadly, into three intimately related parts: the ancestor cult, witchcraft, and magic. Taken as a whole their religion, as they believe, secures for them many of the most important values of life—health, good crops, and success in various enterprises; it provides an intelligible explanation of death and misfortune by tracing them to the ill will either of the ancestral spirits or of living men acting through witchcraft or magic; in its rituals it resolves the emotion of fear and replaces it by hope and confidence; while the believed destructive action of the ancestors and of men is generally, though not entirely, linked with morality.[1]

[1] Cf. Godfrey Wilson, 'An African Morality', *Africa*, ix. 1 (Jan. 1936).

The commonest explanation of misfortune is that some wrong done by the victim, or by his close kinsman, has provoked the spirits or his fellow men to anger.

As long as a man has alive a father, a father's full-brother, or senior brother or half-brother,[1] of his own, this senior kinsman deals with the ancestral spirits, not only on his behalf, but also on behalf of his wives and children; and health is the chief value which his prayers are believed to secure for them. In the absence of sickness or misfortune appeal is seldom made to the spirits, but when some member of a lineage or his wife or child falls sick, the anger of the spirits is often suspected as a possible cause. There are usually other reasons suspected as well, and so the sickness is taken to a diviner for diagnosis. Various causes are suggested to the diviner and he, by means of a magical technique, selects one among them. If the anger of the spirits is selected, then this senior kinsman must pray for the one who is sick, if he is to recover. When half-brothers live at a distance from one another, after their father and his brothers have died, then each may pray to the spirits to cure a little sickness in his own family, but if the sickness persists, then a message must be sent to the senior kinsman. And, as the anger of the spirits is due to wrongdoing, the sinner must reform his ways as well.

The wrongs which rouse the spirits to anger are usually breaches of family morality. If a son does not respect his father or insults him, if an heir neglects to feed and provide for the dead man's children, then, when sickness falls on him or his own children, it will probably be traced to the anger of the spirits at his behaviour.

Space does not allow any full analysis of religion in family life and in the relationships of kinsmen and affines. Not only the ancestor cult but witchcraft and magic are factors in them. A man's neglect of a wife or his cruelty to her may, it is believed, lead to his falling sick through her witchcraft and that of sympathetic neighbours; his relations with his father-in-law are affected by the fear that if he offends him, his father-in-law may, by magical means, kill his children, and so on.

Wider kinship groupings than the family gather at rites and cere-monies and are recognized in the rules against incest. But there are no clans; there is no descent group continuous down the generations with a common name and definite membership. Each individual family has its own penumbra of kinsfolk; the effective kindred of a

[1] Provided the relationship between them has not been legally broken (see above).

man and his son, or of two half-brothers, are not all the same, while each single person is especially related by respect, affection, and mutual obligations to particular kinsmen beyond his own family. Descent, as we have seen, is patrilineal except in the case of illegitimate children. A man asked for his *ekekɔlɔ* always recites first the names of his paternal forebears as far as he can remember. But if he is related through mother or grandmother to a chief he usually volunteers this fact as part of his *ekekɔlɔ*; and questions always elicit some knowledge of his mother's paternal kinsfolk and a statement that 'they are my *ekekɔlɔ* too'. Descendants of a common grandfather (either paternal or maternal) are forbidden to marry, and no case of infringement has come to my notice; descendants of a common great-grandfather are supposed not to marry, but they sometimes do so before the relationship is discovered, and then simply drink a protective medicine but do not break the marriage.

The bond between a man and his mother's brother (*omwipwa*) is mainly constituted by the passage of cattle. 'My real mother's brother', they say, 'is the one who took the bulk of the marriage-cattle which my father gave for my mother', and it is between this particular brother and a woman's eldest son that the bond is strongest. Because this brother of his mother has taken 'our cattle' and married with them, the young man has a certain right of making free with his property during his life, the right to receive from him one cow to set up a herd of his own with, and a residuary right of inheritance if this uncle dies childless and leaves no brothers. If his mother's brother does die without other heirs, it is only the particular wife obtained with and the particular progeny of his father's marriage-cattle that the young man can claim.

Ceremonies, and particularly funerals, are the occasions on which the effective relatives of any one family meet all together, both kinsmen and affines. I have even heard kinship defined by attendance at funerals. One man argued that he was not related to another because, though they were admittedly genealogically related, they did not attend the funerals in each other's families and were not therefore really kinsmen at all.

Known blood-kinship is a common occasion of friendship, but it does not necessarily produce it, while the absence of friendship can render many of the normal kinship bonds quite inoperative. We have seen already that quarrels may destroy the relationship between half-brothers and lead to a judicial separation. On the other hand, I have observed two men meet for the first time, discover a common great-grandfather, and at once become friends. A few months later the sister of one of them died and the other went to the funeral and behaved there like a close kinsman.

Proximity is another factor of great importance in the relations of kinsfolk, for while nearness of dwelling does not always make for friendship, yet a considerable distance tends to lessen it and to make attendance at funerals impossible.

One of the most stringent taboos in Nyakyusa life is that which separates father and daughter-in-law. A woman may never speak to, approach, or look at her husband's father. If she does it is believed that she will die, through the 'breath' of indignant neighbours, a painful and lingering death. And the taboo is extended from her own father-in-law to all his classificatory brothers. The normal routine of life is constantly interrupted by women's avoidance of these men: they crouch and hide and make wide detours to avoid them, a man comes into a room and a woman runs out hastily, a father cannot enter his son's house while his son's wives are cooking there, ceremonies are duplicated to avoid bringing them in contact. Few people seem to realize the meaning of this taboo, but occasionally a man is found who tells a story which makes its function abundantly clear. It is said that an old chief, long ago before the taboo was instituted, fell in love with his son's wife and took her, and such was the horror of everyone at what he had done that this taboo was instituted. This story expresses the necessity, in a society where the old men are accustomed to take the young women as wives, of guarding in some way against the possibility of a father desiring his own son's wife for himself; more particularly perhaps because the cows for her marriage have come from him.

This taboo separating father and daughter-in-law is one of the reasons for the age-village system which we must next discuss. For in Nyakyusa society father and son live in different villages.

## Age-villages

The most characteristic relationships of the Nyakyusa people are those which centre in the age-village. Villages and age-groups are common enough in other societies, and are familiar to all of us, but it is rare to find them combined; it is very uncommon to find, as we do among the Nyakyusa, that local groups of contemporaries live together for most or all of their lives.

T

Age-villages are formed by groups of men, all roughly of the same age, their wives and young children. Women belong to the villages of their husbands, young children to those of their fathers. The number of households in an age-village varies, but thirty to forty is a fair average. Girls, as we have seen, live at home until they marry, which they normally do soon after puberty, and then each goes to the house and joins the village of her husband. But boys, who marry later in life, leave home at about the age of ten or eleven and set up villages of their own.

(a) *Herd-boys*. Between the ages of about six and eleven the boys sleep at their fathers' houses and herd their fathers' cattle. This is a fulltime if not a very arduous occupation; the cattle are driven out about an hour after sunrise and return to be milked about 1 p.m.; after an hour or two they are again driven out and do not come back until sunset. The cattle of five to ten neighbours are usually herded together by their young sons; and so these boys spend all the day together for several years of their lives. This group of boys is the germ of the future age-village; it is a community with a common activity in the herding of the cattle, with a leader, and with laws and customs of its own.

'When we herd cows as boys', a friend of mine told me, 'there is always one who is obeyed by his fellows whatever he says. No one chooses him, he gains his leadership and his prestige by bodily strength. For always, when we are all boys together among the cows, we vie with one another and dispute about going to turn back straying cattle, or about fetching fire to cook the food we have brought with us. And so we start fighting, and we go on fighting until one of us beats all his fellows completely, and so becomes the leader. And then it is he who sends the others to turn back straying cattle, to fetch fire and to collect firewood. And he is greatly respected. He settles quarrels too. What we quarrel about most as boys is a particular insult; one says to another: "You are only a child, you are, I am your senior." This is always happening, and then it is the part of the one who is leader to set those two on to fight. We all stand round and watch and the one who first cries is proved the child.'

The herd-boys of my own acquaintance, a group of eleven altogether, told me that besides insulting one another like this, boys often cause trouble in their little community by stealing cow-bells from one another's cattle and hiding them away for future use. And one day, when I visited the local herd, the leader of the herd-boys told me they had caught two boys drowning a sheep that morning so as to be able to pretend it had drowned itself by accident, and then they would have had some of the meat to eat. 'We beat them very much', he told me, and he called one of the culprits to come and exhibit his weals. The leader further explained to me that such cases would not ever be reported at home unless the culprits themselves complained to their parents that they had been unjustly beaten. 'Then', he said, 'I should explain what they had done, and they would get beaten again.'

The time that is not spent in herding cows, in arranging and watching duels, and in punishing wrongdoers, is spent in playing various games, occasionally in pitched battles with neighbouring herd-boys, and in cooking and eating small amounts of food brought from home.

Friendships formed between members of this group sometimes last a lifetime. An old man once said to me of a friend of his who had died: 'We herded cows together when we were boys.'

As the boys one by one reach the age of ten or eleven, two important changes usually take place in their lives. Firstly, they leave the herding of cows to their younger brothers and themselves begin the business of hoeing the fields which will occupy them until they die; and secondly, they no longer sleep in the houses of their fathers but join an age-village of boys. These two changes usually, but not always, take place at the same time, and normally at about the age of ten or eleven years, well before puberty. But there are cases where special circumstances put the age of one or both of these changes later; I know one boy who herds his father's cattle although he has reached puberty, because he has no younger brother old enough to take over, and there are only five or six boys in his herd-group altogether. And in general I am told it is not uncommon for some boys who have reached puberty to be found still herding cattle. Again, in one age-village the boys leave home a little later than usual because there are leopards about, and it is dangerous for small boys to walk from the village of their fathers to that of the boys after dark.

(b) *The boys' village.* When a fair number of the sons of a village of married men have reached the right age, their fathers give them a piece of land to one side of the parent village on which to build. There they build little huts of reeds for themselves, sufficiently well thatched to keep out the heavy rain, and there they sleep. The building of the huts on this land begins in a playful manner, before the boys move. While they are still herding the cows and sleeping at home they build miniature huts there in their spare time, but do not sleep in them. When they move they build slightly more substantial huts with a better thatch. Until he marries each boy hoes his father's fields in his father's village and eats food cooked by his own mother at his father's house. But he sleeps with his friends. Thus between the time when he leaves home and his marriage each is a member of two villages, economically he still belongs to that of his father, socially to that of his own contemporaries. Though bachelors eat at their parents' homes, it is very rarely that they do not eat in the company of their own friends. A bachelor does not simply go home to eat by himself, but a group of bachelors, friends of the same boys' village, go round together eating at the house of each one's mother in turn.

In an age-village of married men there are always several different herds of cattle; and it is not only those from the same group of herd-boys that set up a new village together, but all the sons of the age-village. When a boy leaves the herd-group he joins a larger community, including the friends of his own age who have herded cows with him, but many others as well. Any boys' village is found to consist primarily of the sons of the members of some older village who originally gave the land for its building, but, as we shall see later, sons of other villages live there too.

At the beginning, when a group of boys starts a new age-village, or when boys join one already formed, they do not all have a hut to themselves: two or three friends share a hut. But later, as they grow older, each builds for himself. The younger ones build their huts of reeds, but the older ones try to get a few bamboos from their fathers or senior relatives and build more solid houses. Married men build entirely of bamboo, but often in a boys' village you will find a compromise between bamboo and reed, both being used in the same house, and the houses of bachelors, even though they be all of bamboo, are smaller than those of married men. The technique of good building is not very difficult, and the older boys instruct and help their juniors, as they join the village, to improve the skill playfully acquired as herd-boys so as to build more substantial huts.

One of the chief foods of the Nyakyusa is the banana; men plant bananas immediately round their huts, though their fields are mostly at a distance. And bachelors, while they continue to eat their main meals at their parents' village, plant bananas round their own huts as well. Bananas begin to bear very quickly, sometimes within a year of planting, and so, soon after the establishment of a boys' village, its members have bananas of their own, which they cook for themselves

PLATE XIX

5. A girl dancing at a wedding

6. Marriage-cattle brought at the *okokwa* ceremony of a chief's daughter, standing before her mother's hut

NYAKYUSA

PLATE XX

7. Drums at a funeral

8. The chief Porokoto—a typical Nyakyusa face

NYAKYUSA

and eat with their friends at odd times during the day. But they have as yet no fields.

There is no formal initiation of boys at puberty; but, on the other hand, the custom of leaving home and joining a boys' village is directly connected by the Nyakyusa with their ideas of decency in sexual life. They think it is perfectly all right to discuss sex openly among friends of about the same age but altogether wrong to discuss it either in the presence of, or with, their parents or those of their parents' generation. If a boy learns about love-making, in any way, from his parents the Nyakyusa think that he will not respect them properly, and that he himself will be a fool. A boy must learn these things from his immediate seniors and friends. One man said to me: 'If a boy after about ten years old stays at home to sleep, he is laughed at by his friends and his own parents send him away. They say: "If he sleeps at home he will hear what his parents talk about at night, the night is always full of lewd talk; and he may even see them undressing. He will grow up a fool, with little wisdom." You see at the boys' village', he went on to say, 'the older boys tell all sorts of stories, especially about women, they discuss love-making and women, and tell tales of their own conquests. The younger ones listen to these things and that is all right in the boys' village, that is how we learn. But we compare in our minds and think that if a boy stays at home it is as if he listened to all this from his parents, and people always do talk lewdly at night; and that is very bad, that is foolishness. But, in the boys' village it is good for the young ones to listen, that is how children grow up.'

On another occasion when I told this same man that in Europe many people thought it a good thing for boys to get sexual instruction from their parents and teachers he was shocked: 'But I think it is impossible', he protested, 'for parents to go into detail with their children; there is too much shame on both sides. And if they did, it would damage the children's respect for them.'

There is thus a correlation in this society between the age-village system at its genesis and the belief that a boys' dawning interest in sex must be informed, not by his parents, but by friends only a little older than himself.

Few men marry before twenty-five years of age, but affairs with girls begin before puberty. Affairs are related in detail to friends in the age-village, and the younger ones learn by listening; and they also learn when the older boys send them as messengers to the girls of their fancy.

Besides the more serious love-affairs which are carried on in secret, groups of boys from the same age-village commonly flirt with any girls they meet on the way, and it is then that the incest taboos are learnt. If one of the boys is known to be related to one of the girls, either through a common grandfather or great-grandfather, his companions send him away. 'Don't you see your sister is here? You cannot come!'

Contrary to a general belief about 'primitive' societies, homosexual intercourse is common in the boys' villages, between close friends, but there is no evidence of lasting perversion; homosexuality is said to be always *faute de mieux*. The older men in discussion dismiss it with the tolerant word 'adolescence', it appears never to be continued after marriage, and all except the feeble-minded get married sooner or later.

But life in a boys' village also gives its members much information and wisdom unconnected with sex. There, as we have seen, boys perfect their skill in building, and there also they learn to argue and express themselves with adult fluency. It is characteristic of the Nyakyusa legal system that small cases between neighbours are always first discussed and often finally settled in a friendly fashion in the presence of some friend or friends who act as arbitrators, without recourse to the constituted authorities. Small disputes about the eating of crops by cows, the possession of a cloth or some coppers, the ownership of a banana stem, and so on, occur in the boys' village as elsewhere, and as elsewhere the people concerned often argue out to a finish before some friend or neighbour. And by listening to such disputes, or participating in them either as judge or principal, the boys acquire rhetorical skill and some knowledge of law. In some boys' villages there is a recognized leader appointed by the political authorities of the chiefdom to settle graver disputes, in others there is not. The position of such a leader, where there is one, will be discussed later.

Above all, the boys' village gives to its members the conversation and company of more of their own contemporaries than did the group of herd-boys, and company the Nyakyusa hold to be the greatest of educators. In the most explicit discourse I heard on the value of company my informant explained that cleanliness, together with rhetorical and conversational skill, were all learned in company. These are his exact words: 'We say that it is by conversing with our friends that we gain wisdom; it is bad to sit quite silent always in men's company. A man who does this seems to us a fool, he learns no wisdom, he has only his own thoughts. And a man who does not spend time with other people is always dirty, he does not compare himself with any friend. We say that we learn cleanliness of body in company, the dirty ones learn from their more cleanly friends. Again if a man is accused to the chief and is unable to defend himself easily and with eloquence we mock at him and say: "What is the matter with you? Do you live all by yourself? How is it that you are so foolish?" We think that wisdom and cleanliness are the two great things learnt in company. We think it is bad to live alone far from other people, such a man learns nothing; he never learns to express himself well, to converse pleasantly with friends, or to argue a case with eloquence. It is better to live with other people.'

At first the sons of the parent village continue to join the boys' village as they grow up; but after some years, when the senior members of the boys' village are about seventeen or eighteen years old, the younger ones begin to be refused admittance to the village: 'They are children.' The young ones then either begin a new age-village of their own or else join a village which has already been started by the sons of a nearby men's village a little junior to that of their own fathers. If you inquire who are the members of such-and-such a boys' village you are always told that they are the sons of a particular village of men, but detailed investigation reveals the presence of some sons of other men's villages as well. Brothers, half-brothers, and other relatives are sometimes members of the same village, but more often not; and if they do belong to the same village, that is because they are near each other in age, and were born in the same village, not because they are kinsmen.

The members of the boys' village, which is now closed and no longer increases in numbers, continue to grow older, and after a time they begin to get married. Getting married, as we have seen, is often a gradual process; but it is not until he has his wife permanently with him that a young man can have fields of his own and eat their produce at his own place. The cultivation of land requires the co-operation of man and woman, cooking on any elaborate scale is a woman's business.

As the members of a boys' village marry the village does not move but it expands. The houses are built ever bigger and farther apart and the adjacent land is brought under cultivation. The boys' village with which I am best acquainted is in this transitional stage; it has fifty-three members altogether, the majority of whom are single, but some few are married, cultivate their own fields with their wives, and eat food cooked by their wives in their own houses. Of those who are single some again are betrothed to girls who visit them from time to time, but each still cultivates his father's fields and eats at his father's home.

(c) *The men's village.* It is now necessary to understand the system of men's villages and the general political organization in which the boys' villages finally take their place.

The number of age-villages in one chiefdom, all the members of which are married, varies with different circumstances, but the most usual number is from eight to fourteen. The age system is only broken by moving or by death; when a man dies his heir usually comes and lives where the dead man was living in his age-village. There he inherits the wives, the huts, the cows, and the land of his predecessor; he inherits the dead man's position in the village and often takes his personal name as well. The heir may be many years younger than his new neighbours, but he is now treated as their contemporary; he sits with them at ceremonies, he shares their rights at any division of meat. The age system in the villages is also broken by moving, for a stranger may come and be granted land in a village even though he is considerably older or younger than the bulk of its members. But otherwise members of a village are roughly contemporaries.

In a village of married men each has one or more bamboo huts for himself and his wives, with bananas round them; his homestead is close to those of his neighbours, while the main garden-lands of the whole group are at a distance in several blocks or all together. Boundaries between age-villages are not always apparent to a stranger; a solid hundred acres or so of houses and bananas may turn out to consist of two or three villages, each with its own organization, and each having blocks of garden-lands separate from the others.

In each village of married men, and usually in the older boys' villages as well, there is an appointed leader or great commoner (*olifumu*) who is originally chosen for the position by the great commoners of the senior age-villages of that chiefdom. They try to select a man who is wealthy, who comes from a respected family, who has personal ability in judging cases, who is popular with his fellows, and in the old days they looked also for qualities of courage and the ability to lead men in war. The qualities which the selectors look for in choosing a new great commoner are the clue to his functions. He is usually extremely hospitable to his neighbours, he judges their cases, he is their leader at ceremonies, and in the old days he led them in war also. He represents their desires to the chief, and it is through him and in consultation with him that the chief gives orders. Finally, each great commoner is believed to protect his own villagers from aggressive witchcraft, to shield people and cattle from the spiritual forces of evil.

So important is this position of great commoner that legal precautions are taken 'to prevent the great commoner becoming a chief', as several informants have put it to me. It is illegal to choose a great commoner from among the kinsmen of a chief; it is illegal to elect the son of a great commoner to that office in any age-village of his own contemporaries, though he may perhaps inherit the position in his father's village when his father dies.

The relationships which arise from common membership of an age-village are continually apparent in the Nyakyusa culture. Ceremonies such as funerals are not only meeting-places for relatives but also for the age-villagers; the great commoner in consultation with members of his village grants land and grazing rights to strangers who ask for them, and he settles many legal disputes between his neighbours. The village is, both for men and women, the chief field of friendship, conversation, and mutual hospitality; and its members recognize greater obligations towards one another than they do towards those outside. Before the coming of the Europeans the age-village was also a military unit, led by its own great commoner, in the constant fights between chiefdoms.

In most villages there are several herds of cattle which feed separately. The herd-boys, as we have seen, thus form separate groups within the village; so also do their fathers. The boys are related in the common activity of herding; the men, owners of the herd, by their joint interest in it and their common fear of witchcraft.

In the relationships of villagers the belief in witchcraft is a constantly recurring factor. It is believed that certain people, both men and women, have the power of harming their neighbours and their neighbours' cattle without taking any overt action whatever, without reciting any spells or performing any magical ritual at all.

Their influence, which is exercised at night in dreams, is only fully visible to those who are themselves endowed with this power; and to it are constantly attributed both sickness in men and the failure of cows to give milk. In this belief the elements of actual ill will and quarrelling, of actual sickness and the failure of cows to give milk, of actual dream experiences, are combined in a significant whole. Witches are of two kinds, they say; those who use their power rightly (*ava maŋga*) and those who use it wrongly (*avalɔsi*). The first kind are said generally to spend their dreams in trying to prevent the others from harming those whom they hate. The good witches are the 'defenders of the village', and in each village the great commoner is believed to be the first among them. In each group of men whose cows are herded together there is, again, commonly one man who has the reputation of defender of the herd, who is believed to protect the cows from the witchcraft of disgruntled individuals whether members of that small group or not. But if, at any time, a single person earns a general unpopularity in the village, whether by his pride, his meanness, or by wrongdoing, then it is believed that the defenders themselves lead the spiritual attack against him, and he falls sick. Such a blast of unpopularity acting through the power of witchcraft is called the 'breath of men' (*embεpo sya vandu*), and the belief in its efficacy is one of the chief sanctions of the accepted social order of Nyakyusa life.[1]

## *The Chiefdom and Wider Groups*

(a) *The 'coming out'.* Space forbids a full description of the relationships of villagers in all their intricate detail, but a short description of the 'coming out' (*ovosɔka*), which is at the same time the most important legal act and the most exciting ceremonial of Nyakyusa life, will, I hope, make the nature of the age-village clear, and will also provide us with an easy transition to the discussion of the organization of the chiefdom (*ekisu*).

I have never seen a 'coming out' properly; on one occasion I travelled to see one and arrived just a day late when all the important action and ceremonial was over, but I have had it fully described to me at different times by several people. Every chief (*omalafyalε*) is normally succeeded in his chieftainship by two sons, who divide his country between them. There are sometimes exceptions to this: in very large chiefdoms three or even four sons succeed, each taking a portion of the country; and in minor chiefdoms, that is in small chiefdoms which have come under the dominion of a neighbouring and powerful chief, only one son of the minor chief succeeds to the whole of that country.[2] But the rule is that two sons divide the country of their father. This rule worked well in the old days, for till quite lately the Nyakyusa have been expanding people in a district too large for their needs; and the combined countries of the two sons nearly always, in the old days, covered a greater area of effective occupation than the country of their

---

[1] Cf. Godfrey Wilson, 'An African Morality'.

[2] These minor chiefdoms have nothing to do with the present system of subordinating some chiefs to others (see below, section *b*).

father which they had divided. Now saturation point is approaching, or has come, and the rule makes for ever smaller and smaller chiefdoms. Various forces are tending to the alteration of the rule, but it is still a vital part of the constitution (see below).

The 'coming out' (*ovosɔka*) is a series of legal acts by which the country of an old chief and his great commoners is, with certain reservations, divided and handed over into the possession and control of his two sons and their respective great commoners. These legal acts are accompanied by much pomp and ceremony. It is at once the initiation of all the youth of the old chiefdom into public life, the constitution of two new political units, and the proclamation of two new chiefs. The 'coming out' not only consists of a series of legal acts and public ceremonies but of religious ritual as well; action is taken to increase the personal qualities appropriate in a chief, his wives, and his great commoners, and to secure prosperity for their people, by magical means.

When the eldest sons of his contemporaries reach the age of about thirty-three to thirty-five years the old chief is approached by his great commoners, who say: 'The sons have grown up, let us make the "coming out" for them.' After a period of delay, for he is unwilling to relinquish his own honour and power, the old chief agrees and the 'coming out' takes place. His two heirs, together with all the boys and young men, whether married or single, who are sons of the chief's contemporaries, are summoned to attend, according to their age-villages, at the old chief's principal house. When they arrive they wait there for two days, while the old great commoners discuss with their chief where to give the young men land, and whom they will select as great commoners of the young villages. We have already noted the principles which guide their choice of leaders. In many of the young village groups there are already leaders who have been previously appointed by the old great commoners, but these leaders are only temporary, they are not necessarily reappointed at the 'coming out'; at the 'coming out' 'everything is made new', the boundaries of the young age-villages are redrawn, and new great commoners appointed in them; only the groups of young men themselves remain unchanged.

The legal action which now takes place comprises three events: firstly, the public selection of new great commoners; secondly, the public appearance and the public recognition of the two young chiefs; and thirdly, the giving of land to the young age-villages.

When the old men have made up their minds, one of them goes among the crowd of young men and catches hold of those they have chosen in order of their seniority: First the one who is to be leader of the senior village of the first son of the old chief, then the leader of the senior village of his second son, then the leader of the next senior village of the first son, and so on. There are usually eight age-villages of young men; of these four will belong to the chiefdom of the first son, four to that of the second. The eight new great commoners are now publicly known, four in each new chiefdom.

The next stage of the action is the one from which the whole institution takes its name: the 'coming out'. The two young chiefs are secluded for a few hours in the hut of the old chief's first wife; there they receive various forms of magical treatment, and when it is finished, 'then', to quote the words of a great commoner who told me about his own coming out, 'the director of ceremonies said: "Get up!" The chiefs got up, and came out of the house to us, and we, the crowd of young men, said: "Come on!" and welcomed them. Then we all ran shouting and calling the war-cry towards the next chiefdom. In the old days we would have invaded that country for cows and brought them back and eaten them at the new huts which we built next. But that is finished now.' In this way the new chiefs are shown to their people.

Finally the young men are told exactly where to go and build, and the boundaries between the new chiefdoms and the villages of each are fixed; the old boys' villages are abandoned and the houses gradually pulled down and put up in their new places. At first the men of the four age-villages of each young chief just put up rough shelters to sleep in, all together on the place where the senior age-village of each new chiefdom will later be built, but after a month or two they separate, each village to its own place, and there they build their houses.

The land is now their own, they are no longer members of boys' villages, living on land given them at the side of the parent villages by their fathers; they are owners of the soil, full citizens, with chief and great commoners to rule them.

(b) *Organization and life of a single chiefdom.* A few months after the 'coming out' each of the two chiefs marries two wives. He may be married already, but the two whom he now takes rank as his great wives (*avehe avakolomba*) and their sons are his two heirs in the chieftainship. Young girls, daughters of neighbouring chiefs, are carried off with a show of force from their fathers' homes by the young chief's men, who, themselves, later send cows to regularize the position. The two great wives are thus married, not with the cows of their husband, but with those of the men whose sons their sons will one day rule.

Girls are carried off who are just about to reach puberty, and they stay at the home of one of the men of the old chief until their periods begin. When both have reached puberty they are initiated, not at their fathers' homes, but in the country of their husband, both together. At their initiation the old men and women of the country (contemporaries of the old, retiring, chief) play the part normally played by a girl's parents and their neighbours, while the young chief and his men take the usual part of a husband and his friends. And then, after the ceremonies are over, the two girls are given to the young chief as his wives. Houses are built for them separately, in the senior age-village of the new chiefdom for the first wife, in the next senior village for the second wife; and in this separation of dwelling-place is already apparent the future division of the chiefdom between their sons.

Within the chiefdom, and among the wives and children of the chief, two 'sides' (*embafu*) are recognized. In the normal country there are, at its beginning, two age-villages and half the wives of the chief on either side; for the junior wives, as they are married, are attached in a recognized order of seniority to one or the other of the two great wives, and have their own houses near them. This distinction of two sides is important in succession. If one of the two great wives bears no son, then the great commoners of the chiefdom often publicly accept the son of the next senior wife on that side as the heir to that half of the country; and, even if they do not do so during the old chief's lifetime, such a man has always a strong claim to the succession. And the two heirs each rank as head of one side of their father's family when he and his full-brothers are all dead.

Between the time of the two chiefs' 'coming out' and their own father's death there is between him and them a delicate balance of prestige and power. Each of the three, traditionally, has political authority in his own age-villages, but appeals in cases of inheritance may be taken from either of the young chiefs and their great commoners to the old chief and his great commoners, while the religious duties of chieftainship are exercised entirely by the old chief. During this transition period the functions of chieftainship are divided between three men, each with his own great commoners to assist him.

It is necessary to understand that an old chief is believed usually to die soon after the 'coming out' of his sons. The 'breath' of the people is believed to kill him because men love his sons rather than himself. When I asked about one chief (Mwakalukwa) who did not die till about fifteen years after the 'coming out' of his sons, I was told that his was an exceptional case: 'The people loved him very much because he helped them with the Government.' None the less such exceptions are not unusual. But, in any case, it is commonly said that 'after his sons' "coming out" the old chief's power decreases, while that of his sons increases'. When he dies his wives and cows are inherited by his full-brother, and to this brother also passes the religious leadership of both the two new chiefdoms, but all general or political power now normally[1] passes to the two sons. The period of transition is over, and the control of the age-villages of old men now passes to the two young chiefs and their great commoners, half to each side. The great commoners of the old chief, relinquishing most of their secular functions to their successors, enter upon new religious duties as priests in the worship of the chief who has just died, and this priesthood, as we shall see, they hand on to their sons. To the dead chief's full-brother go his wives and cattle, so that property and power are usually inherited separately; in all the cases which I have investigated, however, this brother has himself given some of the cows to the young chiefs, but the reasons for his action are still obscure to me. In so far as the dead chief's brother is still the religious head of both chiefdoms, the functions of chieftainship may be said still to be divided; but all the secular functions are now normally exercised by the young chiefs. And the religious functions also fall to them when all their father's full-brothers are dead.

Political authority is the general authority of one or more persons within a community, whether local or nomadic, which goes beyond the bounds of a single family, a leadership confined to no type of behaviour, but ordering a variety of social activities. Such an authority is wielded by a Nyakyusa chief, together with his great commoners, in his own chiefdom. There a number of legal, economic, religious,[2] and ceremonial activities are controlled by them; and there, before the coming of the Europeans, they had military leadership also. But

[1] Certain recent events have altered the working of this rule in some chiefdoms (see below).

[2] I am now speaking of the position of a chief after his father and all his father's full-brothers are dead, and before his own sons have 'come out'.

before that event no man had any wide political authority beyond the single chiefdom. The chiefs of Lubaga[1] had a far-reaching religious pre-eminence, but no general or political influence at all beyond their own country.

The only extensions of political power beyond a single chiefdom before European times, as far as I know, arose from the rivalry of brother chiefs. The division of an old chief's country into two was not always accepted by the young men concerned; quarrels and fighting between them were common, and the position established at the 'coming out' was sometimes modified by war. If one of the two decisively defeated the other, he took all his brother's cows and reduced him to a subordinate position. The land of the Nyakyusa is full of such minor chiefdoms; by the clerks who collect tax they are described as 'villages', but they are radically different from villages in their constitution. For, while they often consist only of a few score families, they are themselves articulated into age-villages and have at their head, not an elected great commoner (*olifumu*) but a hereditary chief (*omalafyale*). A minor chief marries in the ordinary way, like a commoner, and only one of his sons inherits his chieftainship; while his chiefdom, owing to its small size, is often simply divided into two villages, one for the old, one for the young men. To-day his position carries with it neither wealth nor power; he has some authority over his own people, but less than the great commoners of his powerful kinsman. Though some of the reasons for his subordination are to be found in modern conditions, it is clear that many of the factors have always operated.

Wars did not only occur between brothers; but when one chief defeated another who was more distantly related to him, he did not, apparently ever, reduce him to a minor position. He either took his cows and then left him alone, or killed him and set up a brother of his own as an independent though allied chief, or else, more rarely, killed him or drove him away, taking over the country and incorporating it in his own. So that, apart from the subordination of a defeated brother and his heirs, political authority always stopped at the boundaries of each separate chiefdom.[2]

The traditionally independent chiefdoms to-day vary in numbers from 100 to about 3,000 adult men.

[1] See below, pp. 288-9.
[2] Among the Ngɔnde people of Nyasaland there was a paramount chief Kyungu, with a far-reaching political authority; but there was no such chief among the Nyakyusa.

The coming of the German Administration in 1893 introduced a paramount political authority among the Nyakyusa for the first time, in the persons of European officials; while in 1926, a generation later, the British Administration created new Native Authorities under the District Officer and superior to the chiefs. The traditionally independent chiefs were grouped together in eleven court districts; in each district a 'Native Court' was set up, consisting of the various chiefs and their great commoners, under the hereditary presidency of one of the chiefs, who thereby became senior to all the others in that district. Salaries for chiefs have been introduced, and the senior chiefs receive far higher salaries than the others; while the meetings of each court are always held in the territory of the senior chief (*omalafyalɛ oŋkolomba*); and to it has now been transferred a great deal of the legal business which, before 1926, was transacted by each chief sitting with his own great commoners in his own chiefdom. The chiefs themselves were consulted in the selection of the Court Presidents, and those chosen were normally the chiefs with the greatest number of men in each particular court district. But those who have been subordinated to them still resent their authority.

In this account the term senior chief (*omalafyalɛ oŋkolomba*) denotes the President of a Native Court, chief (*omalafyalɛ*) means one of the traditionally independent chiefs, while minor chief (*omalafyalɛ onnandi*) means one of the subordinate chiefs, often with only 40–60 men under him.

The introduction of courts and salaries has brought an entirely new element into the relationship between old and young chiefs (see above). Only one of them can receive the salary and they commonly dispute about it. Quarrels are particularly frequent over the position of senior chief, for the presidency of a court carries with it a relatively large salary. Old senior chiefs cling to the position after their sons have 'come out', and when they die their full-brothers still dispute the position with the sons because of the salary involved. Such a situation could not have arisen before 1926, for then there was no comparable issue between them.

And the introduction of salaries has also had a most profound effect upon the relative status of the two young chiefs who 'come out' together. When an ordinary chief, with a small salary, dies the Government recognizes the first son alone as chief and pays the whole salary to him. This reduces the second son to the position of a minor chief as effectively as a defeat in war might have done in the old days. But while the action of warfare only occasionally led to the subordination of one of the brothers, this action of the Government does so invariably, and always subordinates the younger brother. When a senior chief dies, on the other hand, the salary is usually divided; the bulk of it goes to the first son, together with the position of senior chief, while to the second son is given the salary of an ordinary chief.

As the prestige and authority of a father in his family, or of a man among his neighbours, is closely connected with his wealth on the one hand, and with his believed religious powers on the other, so also the status of a chief among his people. He has more cows, more wives, more food than other men; he is spiritually responsible for the fertility of the land, the women, and the cattle of his chiefdom. But he is no autocrat, and all his public functions require for their exercise the co-operation of his great commoners.

Polygyny is, above all, the mark of a chief. Few commoners have more than five or six wives, but a chief frequently marries fifteen, thirty, forty, or even more; his wives weed and plant the fields which their unmarried sons hoe, and there is plenty of food for guests. Chiefs themselves hoe when they have time, and often they employ a poor man to hoe for them as well, rewarding him after a year or two with a cow. It is not possible for one man to satisfy so many women sexually, and it is generally said that every chief's wife, save the five or six who are his favourites, has a lover. But intrigues must be carried on with care, for their discovery means a great public scandal.

The extent of a chief's polygyny is conditioned by his control of cattle, and his income in cattle is derived mainly from inheritance and the marriages of his kinswomen. When his father dies his father's wives and cows pass to his father's full-brother, but they come to him and his brothers eventually when this man dies; while if the young chiefs have 'come out', it is common for their father's brother to hand over some, or even the bulk of the cattle, to them before his own death.

Before 1893 fighting between chiefdoms was common and, except between brother chiefs, the usual aim of fighting was, not conquest, but cows; wars were generally just cattle raids. And a substantial proportion of the cows captured in a successful raid went to increase the herds of the chief. This lost source of income is now supplied by Government salaries, which vary from 5s. to £15 a month.[1] The

---

[1] Salaries above 30s. a month are only paid to senior chiefs. No minor chief gets a Government salary, nor do great commoners. The local value of money is shown (a) by the tax (8s. p.a.), (b) by the wages of unskilled labour (6s. to 8s. p.m.).

price of a cow is £2; but many shillings are spent on clothes, bicycles, and beer, as well as on cows.

A chief, like any other rich man, maintains his prestige by hospitality; he constantly entertains his more notable subjects with beer; at the ceremonies of his family all his people gather in their age-villages and he kills cattle for them to eat. Chiefs seldom nowadays kill cattle except on ceremonial occasions, but in the old days of warfare they used also, I am told, to entertain their subjects with meat from time to time, in order to keep up their spirits for fighting. History is full of stories of Nyakyusa chiefs who attracted many men to their countries, and so gained great military strength, by the generosity and abundance of their feasts.

Every time a man or woman dies, a message must be sent to the chief, and at the burial he is given the whole breast and ribs (*akakwa*) of one of the cows which are killed by the family of the dead person at that time. He has the right to take food or milk from any of his subjects if he has need of it; but he should not take any man's beast without later returning another to him.

Apart from the now abandoned pursuit of cattle raiding the only profitable enterprises in which the members of a whole chiefdom jointly participate are those of hunting and fishing; in some chiefdoms, but not all, hunting is organized like warfare and fishing is a joint endeavour, both ordered by the chief.

Every chief has a title of ownership (*obwene nakyɔ*) to the land of his chiefdom and can evict any man he pleases (giving him another plot), if he wishes to build there himself; but his people also have titles of ownership to it, both collectively, under the leadership of the great commoners, and individually, each man to his own ground. It is the great commoners who, in consultation with their neighbours, give to the sons of each village land on which to build; it is they who, together, finally fix the boundaries of the young men's villages at their 'coming out'; it is they who, again in consultation with their neighbours, grant land to strangers who ask for it, though they must notify the chief and get his approval before doing so.

As the single great commoners settle disputes within their own villages, so the chief and great commoners together hear and decide cases within the chiefdom. Many of these legal actions are now settled in the courts, but not all of them; and, even when cases are going to court, preliminary hearings commonly take place before the chief first. Cases are conducted and witnesses interrogated by chief and great commoners together, and the decision which the chief pronounces is an expression of their general opinion.

Among the great commoners there is an order of seniority. The leaders of the two senior age-villages of the chief's own men play a prominent part at his 'coming out'; they each have a pre-eminent authority in one side of his chiefdom, and the other great commoners rank as their juniors, some on one side, some on the other. In the old days the two senior great commoners each led a whole side of the chiefdom in war.

The two most effective checks on the power of a chief are migration and witchcraft. Military strength used to depend upon the number of a chief's adherents; today the scale of his salary is similarly dependent; men are quite free to move, and there is a flow of adherents from unpopular chiefs. But unpopularity is most feared in its spiritual form of witchcraft. We have seen already that an adverse current of opinion is believed to act invisibly, as the 'breath of men', against an unpopular member of a village and to make him sick. So also the adverse opinion of a single village or of a whole chiefdom is believed to have power against a chief, to bring sickness or even death upon him. As in the single village, so in the whole chiefdom, the great commoners are the prime sources of this spiritual power; they are believed severally to protect the members of their own villages and jointly to protect their chief from the wanton attacks of witches; but if ever there is a just ground of offence they are believed to join their own power of witchcraft in the general attack. I know one chief who dare not give a judgement in a dispute between two of his villages for fear of the indignant witchcraft of the losing side. And a general unpopularity is believed always to lead, sooner or later, to a chief's death.

Chiefs also, like other men, fear the use of sorcery (i.e. destructive magic) against them, and use a number of protective 'medicines' (i.e. materials of magic) to protect themselves from it. They also use powerful 'medicines' to give themselves personal impressiveness, prestige, and authority among their people.

While in the families of commoners an ancestral spirit is only believed to affect the lives of his own descendants, the ancestors of a chief, on the other hand, are supposed to influence, for good or ill, the fortunes of whole chiefdoms. Rain and good crops, the fertility of women and cattle are dependent upon their good will, which in its turn is believed to depend upon a recurrent sacrifice of cows. And for this sacrifice the chiefs, their living descendants, are responsible. But, owing to the continuous division of chiefdoms every generation, several chiefs are concerned in each sacrifice; every dead chief is a source of misfortune or of blessing in the countries of all his direct descendants. And so the discussion of this part of the Nyakyusa religion leads us to the investigation of the groups which extend beyond the boundaries of a single chiefdom.

(c) *Groups wider than the chiefdom.* When a chief dies he is buried near the house of his senior great wife and trees are planted on his grave. The trees grow and form a sacred grove (*elisyeto*) hedged by taboos. Each of these groves is at first the religious centre of two, later of a number of chiefdoms, and in them the sacrifices are made. Responsibility for finding the cow for sacrifice in a particular grove rests with one of the living chiefs concerned, but responsibility for initiating the ritual and performing it lies not only with the chiefs but also with the hereditary priests (*avanyagɔ*) in each chiefdom. These hereditary priests are descended, some from the great commoners of the dead chief who is buried in that particular grove, some from his half-brothers. The ritual is esoteric; there is no gathering of the people at the sacrifice, and only chiefs and those with hereditary priesthoods come to it. But, on the other hand, everyone knows when a sacrifice is taking place, and, in spite of the influence of missions, most people in the pagan community believe in its efficacy.

Sacrifices are prompted either by actual misfortune or by prophecies of it. The sacrifices which I have seen myself were all stimulated by an actual shortage of food, and the hereditary priests have often told me that 'nowadays the chiefs do not listen to us until hunger comes'. But, traditionally, sacrifices are said to have been usually prompted by prophecies of coming misfortune which was then averted by them. In each chiefdom the ruling great commoners, the hereditary priests, and some private persons as well are believed to have the power of dreaming of misfortune (*okokunguluka*) before it comes. And the chiefs are said always to have listened to these dreams formerly and to have acted upon them.

Among the groves there is an order of seniority; the older the grove the more chiefdoms are concerned in the sacrifices there. And in Selya is the most important grove of all—Lubaga. All the chiefdoms of Selya, many of the Nyakyusa proper, and even some of the neighbouring chiefdoms of the Lugulu are traditionally concerned in its sacrifices. Lubaga, the Nyakyusa say, is the grove of Lwembe, one of the original chiefs who came down the Livingstone Mountains from the east, eight or nine generations ago; and from him all the present Selya chiefs are descended. The ancestor of the chiefs of the Nyakyusa proper was a brother of Lwembe; and though the Kukwe and Lugulu chiefs are not related, yet those of the Lugulu who are nearest to Lubaga used to send cows there for sacrifice as well, because of the great reputation that this grove had.

Sacrifices are still made in the country of the chief of Lubaga (Mwakisisya) for all the surrounding chiefdoms, but the full ritual has not been carried out for forty years. Traditionally each chief of Lubaga was ritually installed into a position somewhat resembling that of Sir James Frazer's 'Divine Kings', a position hedged with taboos, in which not only the sacrifices he made to Lwembe but his own health and fertility also were believed to be intimately connected with the prosperity of his own and neighbouring chiefdoms. But the present chief has never been properly installed, nor was his father before him. The sacrifices at Lubaga are believed to benefit not only the Nyakyusa but also the next tribe to the east, the Kinga, who live on the heights of the Livingstone Mountains; for Lwembe, they say, was born a Kinga and moved down the mountains to Lubaga, taking the fertility of the soil with him. And every year two hereditary Kinga priests come a three days' journey from their own country to participate in the sacrifice of a black cow to the spirits of Lwembe and his descendants.

Down by Lake Nyasa, in the extreme south-east of the Nyakyusa district, there is another equally sacred spot where sacrifices are made to Kyala, a younger brother of Lwembe.

The Christians and the Moslems form other religious groups which transcend the boundaries of a single chiefdom, but an examination of the Nyakyusa Christian and Moslem communities is beyond the scope of this essay.

The political group which is constituted by a court district, though only ten years old, is of great importance in Nyakyusa society; but here again the detailed examination of its organization and the relationships of its members is beyond the scope of this essay.

## BIBLIOGRAPHY FOR THE NYAKYUSA—NGƆNDƐ PEOPLE

COTTERILL, H. B. 'On the Nyassa and a Journey from the North End to Zanzibar', *Proceedings of the Royal Geographical Society*, xxii (1878).
CROSS, D. KERR. 'Geographical Notes of the Country between Lakes Nyassa, Rukwa, and Tanganyika', *The Scottish Geographical Magazine*, vi (1890).
—— 'Crater Lakes north of Lake Nyassa', *The Geographical Journal*, v (1895).

DIXEY, F. 'The Distribution of Population in Nyasaland', *Geog. Review* (New York), xviii (1928).

ELTON, J. F. *Travels and Researches among the Lakes and Mountains of Eastern and Central Africa*, London: John Murray (1879).

FOTHERINGHAM, L. M. *Adventures in Nyassaland: a Two Years' Struggle with Slave Dealers in East Africa*, London: Sampson Low, Marston, Searle and Rivington (1891).

FÜLLEBORN, F. *Das Deutsche Njassa und Ruvuma-Gebiet*, Berlin (1906).

HALL, R. DE Z. 'Local Migration in Tanganyika', *African Studies*, iv (1945).

HAMILTON, J. T. *Twenty Years of Pioneer Missions in Nyasaland*, Bethlehem, U.S.A.: Bethlehem Printing Co. (1912).

JOHNSTON, H. H. *British Central Africa*, London: Methuen (1897).

LUGARD, F. D. *The Rise of our East African Empire*, vol. i, Edinburgh and London: Blackwood and Sons (1893).

MACKENZIE, D. R. *The Spirit-Ridden Konde*, London: Seeley, Service and Co. (1925).

MERENSKY, A. *Deutsche Arbeit am Njasa*, Berlin (1894).

MOIR, F. L. M. *After Livingstone*, London: Hodder & Stoughton (1923).

MOREAU, R. E. 'Joking Relationships in Tanganyika', *Africa*, xiv (1943-4).

SANDERSON, M. 'Relationship Systems of the Wangonde and Wahenga Tribes of Nyasaland', *J.R.A.I.* liii (1923).

STEWART, J. 'The Second Circumnavigation of Lake Nyassa', *Proceedings of the Royal Geographical Society* (1879).

SWANN, A. J. *Fighting the Slave Hunters in Central Africa*, London: Seeley Service and Co. (1910).

THOMSON, J. *To the Central African Lakes and Back*, London: Sampson Low, Marston, Searle and Rivington (1881).

THURNWALD, R. C. *Black and White in East Africa*, London: Routledge and Sons (1935).

THWAITES, —. 'Wanyakyusa Agriculture', *East African Agricultural Journal*, ix (1944).

WILSON, G. 'An Introduction to Nyakyusa Society', *Bantu Studies*, x (1936).

—— 'An African Morality', *Africa*, ix (1936).

—— 'Introduction to Nyakyusa Law', *Africa*, x (1937).

—— *The Land Rights of Individuals among the Nyakyusa*, Livingstone: Rhodes–Livingstone Institute, Paper No. 1 (1938).

—— *The Constitution of Ngonde*, Livingstone: Rhodes–Livingstone Institute, Paper No. 3 (1939).

—— 'Nyakyusa Conventions of Burial', *Bantu Studies*, x (1939).

WILSON, M. 'An African Christian Morality', *Africa*, x (1937).

—— 'Nyakyusa Kinship', in *African Systems of Kinship and Marriage*, edited by A. R. Radcliffe-Brown and C. D. Forde, London: Oxford University Press (1950).

YOUNG, E. D. 'On a Recent Sojourn at Lake Nyassa, Central Africa', *Proceedings of the Royal Geographical Society*, xxi (1877).

Reference may also be made to Census Reports for Nyasaland and Tanganyika Territory; to the annual Reports of the Agricultural, Education, and Medical Department in both Territories; to annual Provincial Reports, and to Government reports on specific topics such as the following:

Tanganyika Territory: *Native Administration Memoranda*, No. II, 'Native Courts' (1930); No. III, 'Native Treasuries' (1930).

C. WILCOCKS, *Tuberculosis in Tanganyika Territory* (1938).

A. J. W. HORNBY, *Denudation and Soil Erosion in Nyasaland*, Nyasaland Department of Agriculture, Bulletin No. II (1934).

Nyasaland Protectorate: *Report on Emigrant Labour* (1935).

# THE YAO
# OF SOUTHERN NYASALAND[1]

*By* J. C. MITCHELL

## I. HUMAN GEOGRAPHY

*Topography*

NYASALAND takes its name from Lake Nyasa, which is the most conspicuous natural feature in the area. The lake is about 50 miles broad and about 300 miles long, and it is part of the Great Rift Valley which continues southwards. The altitude of the lake is about 1,600 feet above mean sea-level. On the west banks the Vipya and Nyika highlands rise almost vertically from the coast-line, while on the east shore there are corresponding highlands in Portuguese East Africa. To the north and north-east are the Livingstone Mountains, while to the south are the Shire valley and the Shire highlands. The area with which this paper is concerned lies between the Shire highlands in the south and the lake in the north.

Lake Nyasa is fed by innumerable streams draining from the highlands to the west and east of the lake. These find outlet in the Shire river which empties into Lake Malombe, 7 miles south of Lake Nyasa, and this in turn empties into the Shire river again, flowing southwards down a large valley to the Zambezi. On the eastern side of the Shire river, about 15 miles from it and 25 miles south of Lake Malombe, the valley rises to a slight ridge called the Makongwa ridge. This ridge is about 2,400 feet above mean sea-level and forms a watershed between the Shire on the west and Lakes Chilwa and Chiuta-Amaramba in the east. Lake Chilwa lies almost due east of the administrative town of Zomba, which is in the northern Shire highlands, and it is about 30 miles south of the Makongwa ridge. There is no outlet from Lake Chilwa, and it is in consequence slightly brackish. Lake Chiuta is about 30 miles to the north-east of Makongwa ridge

[1] This essay is a preliminary study based on fieldwork from September 1946 to September 1947. I wish to record my gratitude to my colleagues of the Rhodes–Livingstone Institute, Dr. E. Colson and Mr. J. A. Barnes; to the staff of the Institute of Social Anthropology, Oxford, Prof. E. E. Evans-Pritchard, Dr. M. Fortes, and particularly Dr. Max Gluckman, who have helped with this paper and suggested some valuable improvements. I wish also to record my thanks to those officers of the Nyasaland Administration who have allowed me to make use of official records and who have helped me and my work in many ways.

and drains into Lake Amaramba in Portuguese Territory. It empties into the Lujenda river which flows into the Rovuma to the Indian Ocean. To the north of the Makongwa ridge and north-west of Lake Chiuta there are more highlands, amongst which Mount Mangoche at 5,400 feet is the most notable. The terrain between the foothills of Mount Mangoche and Mount Chikala in the south is almost flat with occasional hillocks of steep sides and conical shape. It is flat in the sense that there are no great hills and valleys, but there is of course the watershed along the Makongwa ridge. The country falls rapidly to the Shire valley in the west and more gently to Lakes Chilwa and Chiuta in the east. Many small streams flow in the summer but are dry in winter, and here and there are marshy patches (*dambos*).

To summarize, there is a col lying between the hilly Mangoche area in the north and the Shire highlands in the south, which falls rapidly 1,000 feet to the Shire valley in the west and gently about 500 feet to Lakes Chilwa and Chiuta in the east. It is in this area that most of the survey that is recorded in this paper was done. This area lies between the co-ordinates 15° 05′ S. 35° 25′ E., 15° 05′S. 35° 50′ E., 14° 30′ S. 35° 25′ E., and 14° 30′ S. 35° 45′ E., and includes most of what was known as the Upper Shire or Liwonde District east of the Shire river, comprising the areas under the jurisdiction of the Yao Native Authorities Kawinga, Liwonde, and Nyambi. All generalizations in this paper refer to this area alone.

### Rainfall, Soil, and Vegetation

As shown strikingly in Diagram 1, the rainfall is confined almost entirely to the months between November and April. The rest of the year is virtually dry. Both Whites and Blacks divide the year into 'dry' and 'wet' seasons. The Yao call the dry season *cau* and the wet season *cuku*. The rain in the first part of the rainy season falls in heavy showers. This causes a very heavy run-off, flooding of the rivers and lake shores, and, of course, much soil erosion. Most of the roads into the area are impassable and vehicular traffic stops for the middle part of the rainy season. Practically no social activities take place during the rainy season and the people are mainly concerned with their growing crops. When the rain ends at the end of April and the weather becomes dry again, social activity increases. The people start to make long-distance visits when the harvests have been reaped. In the middle of the dry season the boys' and girls' initiation ceremonies start and dances of various sorts are held nightly. At this time too danger from lions is less because the game tend to gather at well-watered places and the lions stay with the game. All initiation ceremonies are completed by the time that the first rains come in mid-November.

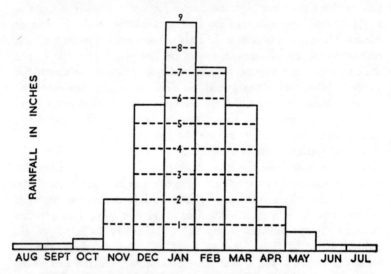

DIAGRAM 1. Average monthly rainfall: Liwonde Station, 1904–32.
Source: A. J. W. Hornby: 'The Climate of Central Nyasaland. Nyasaland Protectorate', *Dept. of Agriculture Bulletin*, No. 9, Dec. 1933.

Surface water-supplies affect markedly the distribution of the population. During the rainy season most villages can find a pool of rain-
water deep enough for their use only a few hundred yards away. As the
dry season approaches, however, these pools dry up and the people
are forced to go farther and farther afield to river-beds where, if there
is no running water, they have a shallow well which will yield sufficient
water for their purposes.[1]

The Administration has sunk wells in many waterless and therefore
uninhabited places, and it reports that soon after the construction of
a well, villages moved there and started gardens.[2] Ordinarily, however, women have seldom to go for water farther than about a mile.

The climate is warm with the maximum temperature immediately
before and during the early rains, i.e. September to December. During
May to August the temperature falls to quite a low level. Hornby

[1] See also F. Dixey, 'The Distribution of the Population of Nyasaland', pp. 274 ff.
where the relation of water-supply to the population distribution is fully discussed.
[2] Nyasaland Protectorate Report on Native Affairs, p. 47.

records that the mean maximum temperature for Liwonde is 82·3 and the mean minimum temperature is 59·3. These are for Liwonde Station, and they are probably a few degrees higher than the temperatures in the slightly higher part of the country where this study was made.[1]

The soils are said to be variable. The Agricultural Officer at Zomba in his report for 1944 said:

'In the valley of the Shire it may be described as rich sandy alluvium. Around the hills the soil is chiefly red with a high percentage of clay and small percentage of sand. Much of the soil in the ridge of Highland stretching from the Chikala hills in the south to the hills near Mount Mangoche in the north [i.e. the Makongwa ridge] is sandy and poor with pockets of good rich soil here and there. The soil improves as the land slopes down each side of the ridge to the west to the Shire valley and to the east to the shores of Lake Chilwa and Lake Chiuta in the north.'[2]

The natural vegetation has been largely cut out with the agricultural activity of the people. That which remains is mainly light forest of trees 20 and 30 feet high with thin undergrowth. In the marshlands there are no trees, but thick grass predominates. Along the streambeds the vegetation is of the rain-forest or tropical type with large trees, suspended lianas, and thick undergrowth. Along the lake shores of Chilwa and Chiuta are grasslands, but the area is marshy and liable to inundation and is little inhabited.

*Population*

Within the areas mentioned there is a fairly large population. The following table gives the population of the areas under the jurisdiction of the three Yao Native Authorities where I worked.

TABLE I

*Total Population in Kawinga, Liwonde, and Nyambi Areas*

| N.A. | Area | 1926 | | 1931 | | 1945 | |
|---|---|---|---|---|---|---|---|
| | | Pop. | Density | Pop. | Density | Pop. | Density |
| Kawinga . | 682 | 24,752 | 36·3 | 29,305 | 43·0 | 44,789 | 65·7 |
| Liwonde . | 396 | 8,174 | 20·6 | 8,821 | 22·3 | 12,716 | 32·1 |
| Nyambi . | 140 | 6,238 | 44·5 | 5,405 | 38·6 | 7,335 | 52·4 |
| Total . | 1,218 | 39,154 | 32·1 | 43,531 | 35·7 | 64,840 | 53·2 |

Sources: Areas from Nyasaland Government file 60/14/39 in Zomba. Population from the Nyasaland Census for these years, abstracted from the crude returns at the District Commissioner's office in Zomba.

[1] A. J. W. Hornby, 'The Climate of Central Nyasaland'.
[2] Agricultural Survey of Zomba District.

These figures are based on actual population counts and are therefore more reliable than the usual estimates of population given for African territories. They show that these areas are fairly heavily populated. As far as I know there have been no boundary changes since 1926, and, since the census was conducted in the same way, it seems reasonable to assume that the population has been increasing. The figures show an increase of 2·69 per cent. a year since 1926, though the increase has been greater in the last fourteen years than in the first five years. At this rate the population will double itself in twenty-six years. During the period following the turn of the century there was a large amount of immigration into British Nyasaland from Portuguese Nyasaland. The extent of this immigration can never be known. Most of it was a gradual movement into British territory in order, according to informants, to escape Portuguese ill treatment. Most of these immigrants were of the Nguru (Lomwe) tribes. To what extent this has continued to the present time it is hard to judge. There is almost certainly some movement to and fro across the Nyasaland–Portuguese East African border and there is no way of telling from extant quantitative sources the degree of immigration. A check on this is available from a calculation of the net reproduction rate of the people amongst whom I worked. This figure worked out to about 2.[1] The net reproduction rate is a measure which, given that the prevailing female mortality rates will persist in the future, indicates the degree to which mothers today are producing enough daughters to replace them in the reproductive process. With a net reproduction rate of 2 the population will double itself in a generation. This agrees roughly with the rate of increase calculated from the census figures and suggests that the immigration has ceased. This is supported by field observations that most larger villages have been in the area for twenty years or more.

The population is by no means homogeneous, tribally or linguistically, but culturally the tribes are all very similar. Table II shows the tribal make-up of the three areas. These proportions should not be taken to represent accurately the ethnic composition of the area. Certain people often call themselves Yao when questioned. This is particularly so among the Mpotola, who are an immigrant people who have completely lost their own language and have adopted Yao language

---

[1] The detailed argument and calculation of this figure is in my paper 'An Estimate of Fertility of Some Yao Hamlets in Liwonde District of Southern Nyasaland', *Africa*, xix. 4 (October 1949), pp. 293–308.

## TABLE II

### Tribal Composition of the Three Areas, 1945

| Area | Total Pop. | Tribes (percentages) | | | |
|---|---|---|---|---|---|
| | | Yao | Nguru | Nyanja | Ngoni |
| Kawinga . . | 44,789 | 48·6 | 35·7 | 14·5 | 1·2 |
| Liwonde . . | 12,716 | 75·1 | 19·6 | 5·2 | 0·1 |
| Nyambi . . | 7,335 | 73·2 | 26·8 | — | — |
| Total . . | 64,840 | 56·8 | 31·4 | 11·0 | 0·8 |

Source: Nyasaland Census 1945. Abstracted from the crude returns at the District Commissioner's office in Zomba.

and customs. The Nguru also prefer to call themselves Yao, and there is good reason for this, as will be seen below.

The table shows, and general observation confirms, that the largest group is the Yao. This paper deals primarily with the Yao, but a few words should be said about the other groups who live in close inter-action with the Yao. 'Nguru' is a term applied by the Yao to a large group of people who call themselves 'Alomwe'. These people come from that part of Portuguese East Africa immediately to the east. They speak a group of dialects mutually intelligible and widely dif-ferent from either Yao or Nyanja. Culturally and in social make-up, they are similar to the Yao and Nyanja, being matrilineal and matri-local and living in small kinship groups of matrilineal kin. Their mystic and ritual beliefs are similar. Some of the linguistic groups that form this congeries are the Shirima, Kokhola, Metho, Thokwani, Ratha, Makua, Nahara, Marenje, Nyamwelo, Mihavani, and Nikhukhu. These are the people who were immigrating in such large numbers into the British territories in the early days of its history. In fact, today they predominate in the Cholo and Chiradzulu Districts.

The Nyanja were the original inhabitants of the area but have been almost completely displaced by the Yao in all areas, except in Liwonde's along the Shire river, and in Kawinga's along Lake Shirwa in the section under Sub-Native Authority Mposa. Linguistically they are more akin to the Yao than to the Lomwe, but their language is yet unintelligible to the Yao. Culturally they appear to be similar to the Yao, and they have accepted certain Yao institutions such as the boys' initiation ceremonies (*lupanda*) and have been fitted into the Yao social and political structure.

The Ngoni, of whom there are very few here, are concentrated on the south side of the Chikala range in the areas of Chamba and Mposa, who are Sub-Native Authorities to Kawinga. They are the remnants of various Zulu raids that were made into Nyasaland during the last two or three decades of the nineteenth century. As far as I could ascertain they have adopted Nyanja language and ways.

*Agriculture*

The population supports itself almost entirely from its agricultural produce grown in the area. Traditionally, men are absent from Yao villages, formerly in trading and slave-raiding expeditions, nowadays as soldiers and labour migrants to Southern Rhodesia or to the Union of South Africa. The absentees contribute substantially to the economic welfare of the area, but the people support themselves mainly on both subsistence and cash crops.

*Subsistence crops.* No crop is entirely a subsistence crop. Any produce is likely to be sold for cash. The average Yao family needs cash in order to satisfy some of its wants. Salt has to be bought from the local Indian traders or African canteen holders. Cloth and other clothing are necessities and must be bought. Certain dues and fines, formerly paid in kind or slaves, are today paid in cash, as compensation for adultery, diviners' fees, initiation masters' fees, marriage gifts. When cash is needed at any particular moment it is almost always obtained by the expedient of selling home-grown produce or by catching a load of fish at the lake and hawking it for sale round the villages.

There are some crops, however, that are looked upon as food crops and others as cash crops. The food crops (in order of importance) are: first, maize (*cimanga*); second, cassava (*inangwa*); third, sorghum (*mapemba*); fourth, finger millet (*usanje*); fifth, sweet potatoes (*mbatata*); sixth, ground-nuts (*ntesa*); seventh, legumes of various sorts. The first three are staples. Maize and sorghum are eaten in about equal quantities, while cassava is eaten more often raw as a light midday meal than as porridge made from flour. Ground-nuts and the other legumes are used mainly as relishes, as are a wide range of greens such as cassava leaves, sweet potatoes, pumpkin leaves, and various wild leaves. The flour made from the maize is prepared as a stiff porridge for the adults who eat it together with one of the relishes. Usually this relish is vegetable, but sometimes it is dried fish and more rarely either chicken or some other meat.

Rice is grown near Lake Shirwa. Though it is mainly sold in markets run by the Agricultural Department, it is relished by the people who eat it at funeral feasts, which consist largely of foodstuffs that the dead person has left.

A certain amount of fruit, both wild and cultivated, is eaten. Mango trees abound in the area, and during the middle of the wet season there is an abundance of this fruit. Otherwise there are bananas and papaws in plentiful supply and much smaller quantities of oranges and lemons.

*Cash crops*. By far the most important cash crop in the area is tobacco. This is a dark smoke-cured variety used for pipe tobacco and cigars. The crop is encouraged by the Government and a large part of the Agricultural Department's duties is concerned with the production and distribution of seeds and supervising the growing and curing of tobacco. Individual Yao grow, cure, and grade their own tobacco, and when it is ready transport it to the local tobacco market. All tobacco grown by Africans is marketed by a Government sponsored organization, the Native Tobacco Board, which buys the entire crop from the growers at current prices according to the grade of the tobacco. Prices are sufficiently high to cover the overhead costs, and though the organization does not aim to make a profit, net profits have accrued and have been earmarked for African development schemes. The markets are placed in the areas where the tobacco is grown so that the growers can sell their crops near by at prices comparable with those in the tobacco centres in Limbe. It is difficult to arrive at the annual value of the tobacco sales for each individual Yao, but the Agricultural Officer at Zomba estimated this as follows:

### TABLE III
*Annual Cash Value of Tobacco Grown*

| Year | No. of growers | Amount in lb. | Cash value | Mean price | Mean lb. per grower | Mean cash | | |
|------|------|------|------|------|------|------|------|------|
| *Nyambi Market* | | | £ | d. | | £ | s. | d. |
| 1941–2 | 716 | 302,860 | 5,047 | 3·99 | 423 | 7 | 1 | 0 |
| 1942–3 | 1,601 | 361,904 | 5,253 | 3·48 | 226 | 3 | 5 | 7 |
| 1943–4 | 1,318 | 349,443 | 5,583 | 3·84 | 265 | 4 | 4 | 8 |
| *Mlomba Market* | | | | | | | | |
| 1941–2 | 339 | 91,104 | 1,648 | 4·34 | 268 | 4 | 17 | 2 |
| 1942–3 | 505 | 103,573 | 1,791 | 4·15 | 205 | 3 | 10 | 11 |
| 1943–4 | 474 | 115,486 | 2,442 | 5·15 | 244 | 5 | 3 | 0 |

Source: Agricultural Survey by the Agricultural Assistant, Zomba.

These earnings are means. The range is considerable. Some men are able to command the services of others and are able to sell their crops for £90 and more. Tobacco is undoubtedly the main cash crop in the area.

In addition to these sales a certain amount of tobacco is sold internally, i.e. by African to African. Usually this tobacco is made up of poor-grade leaves which have been rejected by the Native Tobacco Board. This tobacco is plaited into rolls and sold in chunks as chewing tobacco. It is difficult to gauge the extent of this internal trade, but my impression is that it is not great and that the growers would sooner sell on the market than privately. As far as I could ascertain little tobacco is smoked, and most is chewed.

The Government fixes the minimum price for ground-nuts which are sold at Government controlled markets to licensed buyers. These buyers are almost entirely Indian traders from the Shire Highlands. The controlled price for ground-nuts during the buying season June–July 1947 was 2d. a 1-lb. tin of shelled nuts. It is not possible to say at this stage what amount of cash this yields to the average seller, but it is fairly certain that it is not more than a few shillings during the year, though good growers get a good return per ground-nut garden, and many Africans prefer growing ground-nuts rather than tobacco. Ground-nuts are also used by the Africans as a food crop and they also express the oil. A few villages have primitive presses, copied, I am told, from a design used by the Arabs. The oil is used for cooking and also as a decorative embrocation.

Rice is bought at Agricultural Department markets at controlled prices by the Agricultural Department. These sales are, however, only made near the lake shores, especially Lake Chilwa, and do not affect the main region under study.

All other crops are sometimes sold along the road and at Government produce markets. The price of surplus maize sold in Government produce markets is controlled, though there is no control of the sale of maize between Africans, or of maize flour which is often sold by women who need money. An important way in which cash is obtained, especially by women, is through the sale of beer. Under Government encouragement club-houses have been erected in order that drunkenness may be controlled. Beer must be sold in these club-houses after a sixpenny licence has been purchased from the local authority. This beer is sold at about 3d. per quart and the average brewing will net about 10s.

*Agricultural Technique*

There are two types of garden in the area. There is the ordinary garden in which staples are grown (*mgunda*, pl. *migunda*) and there are gardens along the stream-beds which are especially valuable in the dry season (*litimbe*, pl. *matimbe*). Each household owns one or more of the former plots as well as a few smaller plots for tobacco and legumes. Not every household has a stream garden.

*Staple gardens.* The main gardens are cultivated on a variation of the slash-and-burn type of cultivation common in Central Africa. The area which is to be a new garden is prepared by cutting out the timber in it. The whole area cleared becomes the garden and not part as amongst the Bemba. Larger trees are pollarded and the branches piled round the trunks. Brushwood and smaller branches are piled in heaps throughout the clearing. When these are dry they are burnt, usually just before the rainy season, i.e. about September–October. The ash and soil is then hoed into elongated ridges along which the grain is planted. Hornby notes that 'cut timber has in the past been largely destroyed by fire and the toil of preparing the generally friable soil at the commencement of the rains is far from excessive'.[1] In second and subsequent years the stalks from the previous year together with all the weeds and other brush collected from the garden are piled into heaps and burned as before. Gardens are cultivated for many years, some certainly for more than five, but I have no accurate details on this point yet. If necessary, gardens are increased each year by cutting new timber. Villages seem to be fairly well fixed, some of them having been in their present sites for thirty years and more.

Some soils are recognized as being suitable for maize and some for sorghum. A man may have two gardens, in areas where the soils differ. There are signs of widespread impoverishment of the soil, and maize in many places is beginning to show yellow leaves, due, I believe, to lack of available nitrogen in the soil. This phenomenon is attributed by the Africans not to impoverishment of the soil but to the fact that the rains have come from the west. Rains from the west are bad and those from the east are good. Gardens are cleared in August and the rubbish heaped ready for burning. The vegetation is thus left to dry thoroughly. After burning the seeds are planted during late November. From this date onwards the people are very busy. The gardens have to be kept clean and free of weeds. Baboons and

[1] Hornby, 'The Climate of Central Nyasaland', p. 6.

X

bush-pigs root out the new seeds from the soil and an almost ceaseless watch must be kept on the gardens. Usually a man will spend most of his nights and days at the gardens. By February and March green maize is available to supplement the diet which has already become rather skimpy. By the end of April the crops are ready to be harvested. Usually this is done by man and wife, the man plucking the crop and the woman carrying it back to the village. Maize is stored in wicker-work containers called *ngokwe*, while sorghum is stored in the huts on a stand called *ligulu*. It is said that the smoke in the hut keeps the sorghum clear of weevils.

Cassava is planted in large mounds made by turning the turfs over so that the roots are on the outside of the mound and vegetable matter is in the inside. Cassava slips are then planted in this heap of rotting vegetable matter. They are planted at any time of the year and seem to be reaped at any time. Roots are usually dried on the roofs of huts and other suitable places.

Legumes are usually planted in smaller gardens or interplanted with the main crop. Ground-nuts are usually planted in a special small garden since they need special cultivation and hand-weeding. The ground-nut harvest is shelled and kept in small mud-plastered wicker containers which have only a small hole in the top. These are called *cikusi* and are designed to be rat-proof.

Tobacco is planted initially in nurseries in the stream gardens since it has to be hand-watered in the seedling stage. When they are large enough the plants are transplanted to larger gardens especially selected for their suitability. The seedlings are planted in the early rainy season (October–November) and transplanting begins late December. The leaves are ready to be plucked for curing in March–April and soon afterwards they are marketed.

Sweet-potatoes are planted in the late rainy season and are ready for eating about May. Sweet-potatoes are not easily stored and are usually kept in pits lined with ashes. They are for this reason not a very popular crop and are grown more for their leaves, which are boiled, than for the tubers.

*Stream gardens.* The value of the stream garden is that it yields out-of-season crops, usually maize, beans, and pumpkins. A little rice is sometimes grown in the stream garden and sugar-cane is an important crop socially, if not economically, since it is necessary in the initiation ceremonies. Stream gardens have a scarcity value since there is not enough stream bank available for every one. Boundaries are very carefully observed and land disputes centre on stream gardens more than on any other type of land.

*Livestock.* No cattle are found over the greater part of the area, which is supposed to have tsetse fly, though there are some cattle nearer Zomba. There are a few goats and sheep, but the number is so small that it is insignificant. The Agricultural Officer for Zomba gave figures for live-stock in 1939: 85 cattle, 218 sheep, and 127 goats. This is for a total population that he quoted to be 106,050. The ubiquitous chicken plays a far more important role in the lives of the people and is used on most important ceremonial occasions such as marriage feasts, funeral feasts, when approaching a chief, &c.

## The General Standard of Living

The Yao possess few skills with which their standard of living might be improved. All cultivation is done by hoe and axe, and apart from knives there is little other technological equipment. Men make mats from reeds and palm-leaf and also baskets, while the women make their own pottery from clay. A very few households are able to sport a tea-pot and cups. The furniture inside the huts is usually confined to a bed made from poles and laced with ropes plaited from grass, possibly a wooden stool, and sometimes a trunk which someone has brought from Southern Rhodesia. Most houses are substantially built from stout poles laced with bamboos and the interstices filled with mud. The inner and outer walls are plastered with a sand from the marshland which sets hard and forms a fine smooth surface. The roof is thatched with grass. Panelled doors and glassed windows are becoming more and more popular as are deck chairs and furniture made by local craftsmen from a local palm (*ciwali*). Most houses are built on a rectangular pattern, though a few of the old-fashioned circular huts can still be seen in parts.

The long robes characteristic of the Moslems (called *kanzu* locally; I believe a Swahili term) are worn by the men, though many of the younger men now wear European dress. Men of status often possess waistcoats and jackets of intricate design and of varied colours. Women usually wear a simple blouse and robe, though for ceremonial purposes clean, coloured robes are worn with a white cloth round the waist and a matching cloth round the head.

In the rural areas there are usually a few craftsmen who ply their trades. There are a few carpenters whose services are much in demand by those sections of the population who want panelled doors, glassed windows, coffins, sturdy furniture, &c. Blacksmiths no longer smelt their own metal but nevertheless are kept busy making arrow-heads and knives from scrap metal (particularly from discarded motor-car spring-leaves). In addition these blacksmiths are usually skilled tin-smiths and are able to construct cups and watering-cans for those who want them. Watering-cans are used by tobacco growers who need to water tobacco seedlings. In addition to these there are, of course, the leeches and diviners whose services are always needed. A few enter-prising men have also set up what they call 'canteens' at the roadsides and, under a trading licence purchased from the local Native Authority court-house, sell refreshments and items such as cigarettes, matches, sugar, salt, and trinkets to the passers-by.

On the whole, those who are competent to make comparative judgements maintain that the Yao live on a fairly high standard of living for Central Africans. They appear to be well fed and clean, the villages are usually neat and clean and sanitary with substantial and neat houses.

## II. HISTORICAL BACKGROUND

*Arab Influence*

To understand the Yao we must start with the Arab colonization of the east coast of Africa. We know that the Arabs had colonized it as early as A.D. 700. They were a mercantile people and their trading was so well advanced that by the end of the twelfth century they founded Kilwa as an *entrepôt*, about due east of the north end of Lake Nyasa.[1] When Vasco da Gama sailed up the east coast in 1498 he found that the Arabs had well-established posts all along the coast. The Portuguese and the Arabs became rivals for the trade of the African interior and this rivalry was to continue for many centuries. In 1698 the Imam of Oman drove the Portuguese out as far south as Cape Delgado, to where the Arabs had sole control of the east coast.[2]

The Yao say that their traditional home is between the Lujenda and Rovuma rivers east of Lake Nyasa. The interest of the Arabs was mainly in ivory and slaves, but also in tobacco and beeswax. There can be no doubt but that their trading expeditions had passed through the Yao territory, especially since the Rovuma valley serves as the most convenient route into Central Africa from Kilwa. We can be fairly

[1] Hichens, 'Islam in Africa', p. 114.
[2] Pim, *Economic History of Tropical Africa*, p. 19.

PLATE XXI

2. Young woman of Kawinga area showing typical decorative scarifications

YAO

1. Chieftain Chiwalo II of Kawinga area

PLATE XXII

3. New garden under preparation. Brushwood cut out and piled in heaps ready for burning in October in Kawinga area

4. Gardens being burnt at end of dry season in Kawinga area

YAO

certain that Yao contact with the Arabs had been going on for some time, at least 200 years, before the Europeans appeared on the scene.

Although it is fairly certain that the Jesuits from the Zambezi had explored the Shire valley and the Lake regions, little information has been left to us about the inhabitants of those areas.[1] One of the earliest references to the Yao is recorded by Dr. Francisco José de Laçerda in a letter dated 22 March 1798 addressed to the Minister of State of Portugal. In it he outlines his proposed visit to the Kazembe of the Wisa country. It is quite obvious that the Yao were serious competitors with the Portuguese for the land trade. Laçerda writes:

'The dry goods hitherto imported into this country [i.e. Wisa country] have been bought by the Mujao, indirectly or directly, from the Arabs of Zanzibar and its vicinity. Hence these people received all the ivory exported from the possession of the Casembe; whereas formerly it passed in great quantities through our port of Mozambique.'[2]

It is reasonable to assume that because of their geographical position the Yao had conducted a considerable trade between the interior and the coast, mainly of cloths and guns against slaves and ivory (the two are inseparable since slaves were the cheapest way of transporting ivory to the coast). Their trade in slaves led to their major conflict with the British.

When Livingstone made his expedition up the Rovuma in 1866 he found abundant evidence of the influence of the Arabs. Speaking of the Yao chief Mataka, he says: 'He gave me a square house to live in, and indeed most of the houses here are square for the Arabs are imitated in everything.'[3] Livingstone mentions in particular the slave trade that the Yao were carrying on in Kilwa. He records that:

'The Waiyau generally are still the most active agents the slave traders have. The caravan leaders from Kilwa arrive at a Waiyau village, show the goods they have brought, are treated liberally by the elders and told to wait and enjoy themselves, slaves enough to purchase all will be procured: then a foray is made against the Manganja who have few or no guns. The Waiyau who come against them are abundantly supplied with both by their coast guests. Several of the low coast Arabs, who differ in nothing from the Waiyau, usually accompany the foray, and do business on their own account.'[4]

---

[1] Burton mentions in a footnote to *Laçerda's Journey to the Casembe*, p. 37, that a missionary, João Santos, had resided in this area from 1586 to 1597.

[2] Burton, *Lands of the Casembe*, p. 37.

[3] Waller, *The Last Journals of David Livingstone*, p. 73.

[4] Ibid., p. 78.

*Yao Movements*

Even before Livingstone had made his expedition up the Rovuma valley, there had been a large-scale movement of the Yao out of their traditional home in all directions. The tradition is that the name Yao is taken from a hill, grass covered but treeless, which is situated somewhere between Mwembe (in Portuguese East Africa) and the Luchilingo range.[1] It is convenient to divide the history of the Yao into two major episodes, firstly the movement from the Hill Yao to other hills, and secondly the movement into and within the Nyasaland Protectorate.

*Episode I. The scattering of the tribes from the Hill Yao.* The exact cause of the scattering of the tribes from their traditional home is not clear. Abdallah suggests that it must have been some internal dissension.[2] Whatever the cause, the tribe broke up into a number of sections each of which settled at yet another hill and took their name from that hill. Yohannah B. Abdallah lists ten divisions,[3] but since only four have penetrated into British Nyasaland we need only consider these.

Those that finally came into Nyasaland were:

1. The *Achisi Yao*, who went to live at Mchisi Hill.
2. The *Amasaninga Yao*, who went to live near the Lisaninga Hill near the Lutwisi river in Portuguese East Africa.
3. The *Amangoche Yao*, who settled at Mount Mangoche near Fort Johnston, south of Lake Nyasa.
4. The *Amachinga Yao*, who settled near the Mandimba Hill, are called Amachinga because of the serrated edge of the range in which the Mandimba Hill is situated (*lichinga* = a fence).

*Episode II. The displacement of the divisions from their homes.*[4] In time, each of the four sections mentioned found its way into Nyasaland. Briefly the details:

1. The *Achisi Yao* are represented in Nyasaland by those Yao under N. A. Katuli in Fort Johnston District. The 1945 census showed that there were 12,187 Yao under this chief and this is 4·3 per cent. of the total Yao population of British Nyasaland. Of course, not all Yao under Katuli are Achisi Yao and there are no doubt Achisi Yao elsewhere in small numbers, but if we estimate the proportion as 5 per cent. we see that it is a small and relatively unimportant group.

[1] Abdallah, *Chiikala cha Wayao*, p. 7.  [2] Ibid., p. 8.
[3] Ibid., p. 9.
[4] For information on areas which I did not visit I have drawn heavily from the administrative file 'Historical Notes on Districts'.

2. The *Amasaninga Yao* are represented in British Nyasaland by those Yao under N. A. Makanjira, and they are roughly 5 per cent. of the total population of the Yao of the Territory. Makanjira himself is said to have been of Nyanja origin and to have moved to the Lisaninga Hills, where he acquired a mixed following of Amasaninga Yao and Nyanja, and moved in by conquest to the area round Fort Maguire, where he is now established. There are offshoots of this group in Dowa District across Lake Nyasa.

3. The *Amangoche Yao* are of much greater importance and at present constitute about half of the Yao population of the Territory. During the early part of the nineteenth century, while it was at Mangoche Mountain, this group was attacked by the Amachinga Yao under Nkata and Kawinga. The Amangoche Yao were displaced by this invasion and fled in all directions. Most migrated southwards and settled in the Shire highlands, where their representatives Mlumbe, Chikowe, Kapeni, Matipwiri, and others are found today.

4. The *Amachinga Yao*[1] were probably displaced from their traditional home at Mandimba on the Lujenda river in Portuguese East Africa by attacks by the Lomwe inhabitants in the east. They say that widespread famines followed the war and forced most of the migration to take place. Present-day representatives of this group are Nkata, Jalasi, Mponda, Msamala, Kawinga, and Liwonde in the Fort Johnston and Zomba (Liwonde) Districts.

It should not be thought that the Yao invasion into Nyasaland was a military incursion of the Ngoni type. Definite evidence on the exact form of the invasion is not available, but informants maintain that the first immigrants into the country came peacefully and in family groups (*mbumba*). Often the immigrants found succour with Nyanja groups there. Sometimes this hospitality was claimed because the Yao had the same clan names as the Nyanja. The Yao soon took the opportunity presented by internecine struggles among the Nyanja to consolidate their position in the country.

When Livingstone passed the lake in 1866 he found Mponda living in approximately the same place as his heir does today, and he mentions that Kawinga was living on the west of Lake Malombe.[2] He also mentions that the Machinga dominated the whole of this area, showing that by this time considerable movement had taken place into

[1] For a more detailed history of this group, especially of the Malemia group, see Stannus, 'The Wayao of Nyasaland', p. 233.
[2] Waller, *The Last Journals of David Livingstone*, p. 109.

the area. When the Church of Scotland Mission was established in Blantyre in 1876 Duff Macdonald recorded that the dispositions of the chiefs were as follows: Mlumbe to the north-west of Zomba; Kapeni near Blantyre at Sochi; Mpama at Chiradzulu; Kawinga at Chikala; Malemia on the south-west side of Mount Zomba; Matipwiri at Mount Mlanje.[1] Except for Kawinga, these are the positions where these groups are today. At this time therefore most of the movement into Nyasaland had ceased and the Yao invaders had already set themselves up as ruling classes over the indigenous Nyanja. At the same time the Ngoni were making frequent forays into the Shire highlands and the rest of southern Nyasaland, so that the position was far from being stable.

## White Settlement

The first White settlements in the area were missionary.[2] The Universities Mission to Central Africa made an unsuccessful settlement in the highlands in 1861. From 1862 until 1876 there were a few expeditions and visitors to the southern part of Nyasaland. It was not until 1876 that the next permanent settlement was made. This was the Church of Scotland Mission founded in Blantyre. After this the permanent White population in Nyasaland increased and more and more came to be known about it. In 1878 the African Lakes Company was founded with the object of taking the trading activities of the missions off their hands. In 1878 Capt. F. Elton, who was consul at Mozambique, obtained permission to conduct an expedition to Lake Nyasa to inquire into the slave trade. In the meantime antislavery sentiment in Britain, following the publication of Livingstone's reports of its horrors in Africa, led to a great interest in suppressing it. From 1885 until the close of the century, Britain followed a militant policy against all slave-traders and amongst them were the Yao. In 1889 the Portuguese appeared at the confluence of the Ruo and Shire rivers with a large military expedition which they maintained was scientific. As a direct result of this expedition, on 21 September 1889 the Acting Consul declared the territory north of the Ruo to be a British protectorate. The next year Mr. A. Sharpe made treaties with all the native chiefs in the area and these treaties were later ratified by the Anglo-Portuguese Convention of June 1891.

---

[1] Macdonald, *Africana*, vol. i, p. 31.

[2] For the general history of Nyasaland I have used mainly Murray, *A Handbook of Nyasaland*.

The pacification of Nyasaland was largely the suppression of the slave-trade. The Yao were the chief protagonists of the trade, so that Acting Commissioner Sharpe was able to write in his annual report in 1897: 'The Yaos . . . were the chief slave raiders for the Arabs, and in consequence nearly all our expeditions from 1891 to 1895 were undertaken against various sections of this tribe.'[1] A sum of £10,000 was spent a year, largely in providing a police force, and as early as 1891 a raid was made on Chikumbu, a Yao slave-trader, who had attacked a European's coffee plantations in the Mlanje area. After this there was a continual series of punitive expeditions against various native groups, usually after some slaving incident, which precipitated British action. Capt. Maguire was killed in 1891 by Makanjira's men and shortly afterwards the British forces suffered a reverse at the hands of Jalasi. Unsuccessful attacks had been made on Kawinga's stronghold at Chikala. It was clear that sterner measures were needed and in 1893 two contingents each of 100 Sikhs arrived. With this force more active measures were taken and the slave route to Quilimane through the Mlanje District was controlled. In 1893 the Protectorate was divided into administrative divisions and collectors were appointed in each. A hut tax of 3s. was introduced and White claims to land and mineral rights were settled with the chiefs, and it was laid down that all large estates had to have certificates of claim. A postal system and coinage were introduced. In 1894 the Yao chief Makanjira was attacked and thoroughly defeated. In 1895 there was a concerted effort on the part of the three Machinga chiefs Kawinga, Jalasi, and Matipwiri to oust the British from the highlands. This commenced with an attack by Kawinga on the friendly chief Malemia in the Zomba area. A force was sent to protect the missionaries at Domasi and this force stopped the main onslaught. After that the stronghold of Chikala was scaled and Kawinga completely dislodged. He retreated to the east and Matipwiri and his relative Mtirimanja were captured. After this the power of these chiefs was completely broken and no more risings were attempted in southern Nyasaland until 1915. In 1896 Katuli, an adherent of Jalasi, was captured, and in the same year Liwonde, who had so far eluded capture, was apprehended and sent as a political prisoner to Chiromo in the extreme south of the Protectorate.

In the meantime the Portuguese were making similar punitive expeditions into that territory due east of the Protectorate and many refugees came into Nyasaland from Portuguese East Africa. Notable

[1] Annual Report 1896, C. 8438, p. 12.

amongst these were the Mpotola groups under Chikweo and Ngokwe who are today settled near Lake Chiuta.

One of the early acts of the Administration was to disarm the Yao. The Yao felt the loss of their arms very keenly and even today express their displeasure, saying: 'We are now as children. The Whites have taken our guns away.' Collectors of Revenue were appointed in the districts into which the country was divided in 1893. Though these collectors had as their main function the collection of taxes, they did, however, undertake the administration of the whole district. To what extent they were effective in the early part of the Administration is not clear. An early administrator has recorded that 'The District Officers . . . had little influence beyond their near neighbourhood. The stations were mere footholds to be extended later under more peaceful conditions.'[1] The footholds were extended apace after the final subjugation of the Yao. The tax system had been introduced in 1893. By 1906 the system was accepted so well that inability to pay the tax was considered sufficient ground for divorce of a man by his wife.[2] The Africans had by 1903 begun to enter into the economic life of the country. As early as that date there was correspondence about the recruiting of labour in Nyasaland for employment on the mines in the Transvaal.[3] At the death of Kawinga III (Kawinga of the Anthill) in 1905, the Collector interfered in the succession and caused the appointment of the successor by secret ballot.[4] In 1911 the Witchcraft Ordinance was passed and this made illegal an institution which was fundamental to the social life of the Yao. In 1912 the District Administration (Natives) Ordinance was passed. This ordinance recognized the necessity for utilizing the indigenous political institutions for efficient administration. Accordingly village headmen were appointed officially and a principal village headman amongst these was considered to be in some authority over the others. The attitude of the Administration at this time was that the indigenous institution of chieftaincy should not be recognized as such. District Officers were warned that in selecting and recommending headmen to be a principal headman they were to consider the individual's merits. Principal head-

---

[1] Cardew, 'Nyasaland in 1894–5', p. 51.

[2] Duff, *Nyasaland under the Foreign Office*, p. 315. See p. 327, where this is discussed more fully.

[3] *Correspondence re Recruiting of Labour*, Col. 1531, &c.

[4] Recorded in the District Book for the Upper Shire 1908 now in the District Commissioner's Office in Zomba.

men were not to be appointed merely because they were chiefs in the indigenous structure. To what extent these admonitions were heeded it is impossible to say. The fact remains that all the principal headmen selected in the area with which this study is concerned were chiefs on their own account.

African troops played an active part in the 1914–18 War. Not only were large numbers of men used in carrying war supplies from the railhead at Blantyre to Fort Johnston on the lake for transmission to Karonga, a supply base for the German East African campaign, but African troops were also engaged in the fighting itself. Prominent in these active troops were the Yao. As early as 1895 the fighting qualities of the Yao had been noted by the Acting Commissioner Sharpe, who wrote:

'In 1895 fifty friendly Yao were enlisted as an experiment, and took part in the operations against Zarafi and Makanjira [Yao chiefs] and the Arabs at North Nyasa. In every fight they were well to the front and showed such sterling military qualities that it was decided to disband the Makua and replace them by Yao.'[1]

Therefore twenty years after the last Yao autonomous groups were dissolved they were willing to fight for the Administration. In 1924 the District Administration Ordinance was revised. In the meantime, even if the Administration was not officially recognizing the operation of tribal politics, they did, in fact, continue. When principal headman Liwonde died in 1921, his sister's son, who would be the traditional heir by Yao custom, became principal headman in his stead. In 1933 Indirect Rule was introduced by the Native Courts Ordinance of the same year. The details involving the introduction of this ordinance are discussed more fully below (p. 345). At this point it is sufficient to record that the first reaction to this ordinance seems to have been a series of squabbles over boundaries. The Provincial Commissioner reported in 1936:

'Yao doubts and jealousies about the boundaries of several authorities have been occupying the minds of the chiefs to the detriment of their Administration. The most important dispute came to a head in May when the action of a village headman in the disputed boundary presented an opportunity for firm and decisive action by the Provincial Commissioner. At a big baraza attended by both N. A. Kawinga and N. A. Liwonde, the chiefs concerned, the matter was finally settled and it is pleasing to record that the old feud has

[1] Annual Report 1896, C. 8438.

now ended amicably by the protagonists calling upon one another with all due pomp and ceremony.'[1]

In 1934 a training course for chiefs was introduced as part of the function of the Jeanes' Training Centre. Chiefs who are young enough are sent to this course for a period of four months, during which time they are trained in various aspects of European administration, e.g. agriculture, legal procedure, hygiene, writing, &c. In 1939, when the Second World War broke out, the Nyasaland Government started recruiting. Kawinga was approached to assist in the recruiting campaign. He co-operated with the Government as did the other Native Authorities, so that a high recruiting rate was shown for this area. In 1946 a Southern Province African Council was established. In this council Native Authorities and other responsible Africans can take a part in the government of the Southern Province by expressing their opinions at the conferences.

*The Present General Economic and Political Situation in Nyasaland*

The 1945 Census of Nyasaland showed that the total population of the Territory was 2,049,914, of whom 1,948 or 0·1 per cent. were White, 2,804 were Asiatic (almost entirely Indian), and the rest or 99·8 per cent. were African.[2] The White population may be classified into four main groups: the mission staffs accounting for 25 per cent. of the gainfully employed population (1,074); the Government staffs accounting for about 22 per cent.; the planters accounting for about 24 per cent.; and the commercial and professional who comprise about 29 per cent. Among the Indian population by far the greatest proportion of the gainfully employed (1,233) were employed in private businesses, mostly in the form of trading stores of various types. About 80 per cent. were employed like this. The rest were engaged in various occupations requiring some measure of skill, such as railway employees, clerks, tailors, transport contractors, &c. The Indian and White populations are concentrated in the Shire highlands (70 per cent. of both Indian and White populations) and the Dedza highlands (none of the Indian population and 14 per cent. of the White population). The distribution of the African population in various occupations was not available from the census, but we may say that a small proportion of literate Africans are employed in clerical positions by the White and Indian undertakings, but by far the majority who work in the Terri-

[1] Provincial Commissioner's Report, 1936, p. 20.
[2] There are a few hundred Euro-Africans whom I have ignored.

tory do so as unskilled labourers, labourers, and personal servants. In addition to this the major part of the population relies on subsistence or semi-subsistence cultivation for its livelihood.

## III. VILLAGE ORGANIZATION

*Introduction*

The Yao are settled in discrete clusters of huts which are scattered fairly evenly over most of the territory and which are called *misi* (sing. *musi*). This term is usually translated as 'village'. If we retain the term to connote simple clusters of huts, we are justified in this translation. But the term village is used by the Administration for a rather different grouping of huts altogether. It refers to a number of such discrete clusters of huts under the jurisdiction of a man who is called the 'village headman'.

I propose to use the terms hamlet, thorp, and village and administrative village to distinguish different combinations of hut-clusters. Briefly, I use the general term village for any discrete cluster of huts. I sub-divide villages into hamlets and thorps, according to their internal social composition. I use the term 'administrative village' for the group of villages under an administrative village headman. The implications of these definitions will appear as the analysis proceeds.

*Kinship, the Basis of Village Structure*

In the past all Yao had a clan name (sing. *lukosyo*, plur. *ngosyo*) which was inherited from the mother by both sons and daughters. The word *lukosyo*, which I have translated as clan name, actually has a meaning of *sort* or *kind*. The word *mtundu*, which is used more for non-human categories, may sometimes be used instead of it. When a person is asked what his *lukosyo* is he is as likely to answer Yao or Machinga as to give his clan name. On the whole though, the word is used much more for the clan name than otherwise. Nowadays the importance of the clan name has declined. Relatives of important people, notably of the so-called chiefs and the administrative village headmen, remember their clan names, but in many of the commoner families, while descent is still reckoned through the mother, the clan name is sometimes taken from the father. Informants say this is due to the influence of Islam which is the prevailing faith. Clan names such as *apiri, amilasi, ambeŵe, abanda, asimbiri, amwali*, &c., are found in the Marawi group,

Lake Tonga of Chinteche District, and among the Mpotola and Lomwe groups from Portuguese East Africa.[1] As far as I am aware, these clan names in Yao have no English equivalent and do not refer to animals, birds, or things as do the clan names of some other Central African tribes. The clans (i.e. the people having the same clan names) were exogamous, but nowadays it is quite common for a young couple not to know each other's clan name and for people of the same clan name to marry. This may be associated with the practice of domestic slavery, an institution which has affected village make-up and which is discussed in greater detail later. Briefly, a slave wife took her husband's clan name, and her children having their father's clan name could marry their seminal brothers and sisters by another slave wife with the same clan name. At this point it should be noted that it was customary for a person to call out his clan name after sneezing, and this was a means whereby many lost relatives were discovered and clan bonds re-established. When the Yao moved into Nyasaland they found succour with Nyanja groups with the same clan names. Today the men of status with the same clan name as the chief call him by kinship terms.

The Yao think of their line of descent as if it were a tree. They look upon the founding ancestor as the trunk (*lipata*, *likolo*) from which many branches (*nyambi*) have developed. A common theme at installation ceremonies of village headmen, when kinship matters are uppermost in the minds of the people, is the comparison of the family of the headman with a tree, some branches of which have borne fruit while others have not. Within the large, somewhat vague kinship grouping of the clan, more specific kinship groupings are recognized. These are called *mawele* (sing. *liwele* = a breast) or *milango* (sing. *mlango* = a doorway). They contain all those people who are supposed to be descended from a common ancestress. These groupings, corresponding to Fortes's maximal lineage,[2] are sometimes referred to as 'the people of someone'; e.g. *acina Masumba*, 'the people of Masumba', where Masumba was the founding ancestress, or the brother of the founding ancestress. Sometimes the clan name is mentioned when referring to these matrilineage groups so that we may find mentioned *ambrewe acina Masumba*, i.e. 'Masumba people amongst the *ambewe*'.

---

[1] Some Yao groups, notably that under Katuli, do not have this set of clan names at all.

[2] M. Fortes, *The Dynamics of Clanship among the Tallensi*, p. 30. I have been greatly stimulated by this book and acknowledge the debt I owe to its author.

Often the direct line of descent from the founding ancestress is not known beyond the most recent three or four generations. Larger sub-divisions within the maximal matrilineage group are sometimes distinguished by further differentiating the founding ancestress as *acina Lipwatika acina Masala*, i.e. 'the people of Lipwatika of the people of Masala'. Those people who can definitely trace their descent from a common ancestress say that they are of one breast (*liŵele limope*), and this concept is especially important when we have to analyse the larger villages. It is important to realize that the Yao do not think of the matrilineage group except in reference to some social situation. As the situation changes, so the matrilineage group may expand or contract to include or exclude certain people. The term *liŵele* when used as a kinship term serves to define a group in a specific situation. Within a village, for example, the situation in which lineage groups most commonly interact, there may be four matrilineage groups each of which is descended from a different ancestress. Here the matrilineage groups are undifferentiated in relation to each other, and are opposed to one another as components of the whole village.

Usually matrilineage groups within a maximal matrilineage are arranged in an hierarchical system based upon the putative sibling rank of the ancestresses. One matrilineage group may be referred to as 'the large breast' (*liŵele lyakulungwa*) in contradistinction to the 'smaller breasts'. The importance of this arrangement of rank lies in the inheritance of status and rank.

There are few social situations in which the maximal matrilineage group is mobilized. I shall show later on that matrilineage groups seldom persist in time for long and the maximal matrilineage group is invariably dispersed as a number of medial matrilineage groups. Commonly, matrilineage groups of four or five total generational span (i.e. from founding ancestress to new-born babies) form spatial groups, and it is upon matrilineage groups of this order that most attention is directed in the rest of this paper.

Matrilineage groups of this order usually live together as hamlets or as parts of thorps. Almost always each member of the matrilineage group can trace his descent back to the common ancestress (*likolo*). Occasionally the matrilineage groups are split into two sections where the actual descent from the founding ancestress to one of the groups is unknown. I have already said that in the village situation the matrilineage groups are undifferentiated and opposed to each other. Each matrilineage group, however, is differentiated internally, and here the most important corporate group is the group of siblings, corresponding to Fortes's effective minimal lineage.[1] In this group the emphasis is placed upon the relationship of a man to his uterine sister.[2] Because Yao marriage is usually matrilocal the women of the matrilineage group form the localized group whereas the men are dispersed. Therefore within any localized matrilineage group, groups of uterine sisters are differentiated from each other, but always in reference to a man who is usually their eldest brother. It is around the relationship of a man to his sisters that these groups are organized,[3] and to appreciate intra-lineage group relations the structure of the sibling groups must be understood. The Yao word *mbumba*,[4] which I translate as sorority-group, embodies in particular this conception. The word *mbumba* is never used to refer to a single woman, though in the plural as *acambumba* it is used to mean merely two or more women. When used possessively in connexion with a man, however, it means a group of women corporately organized around their relationships to him, this relationship almost always being that of brother to sister. Though the word 'sorority-group' may give the impression of meaning a group of women organized on a principle of sisterhood, I want to emphasize that, although the women in this case are corporately organized, they are organized around a principle of their common and like relationship to a single man. Of course, in actual fact there is little difference whether their unity is expressed as sisterhood or in relation to a common male leader. In point of fact, a woman cannot 'own a sorority-

[1] Fortes, *The Dynamics of Clanship, &c.*, p. 192.

[2] I use the word 'uterine' to mean born of one mother regardless of paternity. This I use in combination with sister, brother, or sibling. Uterine sisters are therefore girls who have one mother though they may have different fathers. I use the word seminal in the opposite sense to this, i.e. having the same father regardless of maternity. I use these terms instead of the terms maternal or paternal half-brother because I wish to indicate that the fact of paternity of uterine siblings, or of maternity of seminal siblings, is irrelevant. I suggest that the term 'maternal or paternal half-brother' should be retained where differential parentage is important as with paternal half-brothers in patrilineal societies. Full siblings are, of course, siblings who have the same parents.

[3] For a description of a similar relationship in a matrilineal-matrilocal people see Richards, A. I., *Land Labour and Diet in Northern Rhodesia*, p. 115.

[4] Both Sanderson and Hetherwick translate this word merely as 'woman', though Sanderson says that it literally means 'pot-maker'. I have been unable to confirm that it means 'pot-maker', but it actually has a larger connotation than merely 'woman'. See Sanderson, *A Yao Grammar*, p. 176, and Hetherwick, *A Handbook of the Yao Language*, p. 227.

group'.[1] She may belong to the sorority-group of her brother, but she herself will call the sorority-group to which she belongs her 'sisters'.

The man around whom the sorority-group is organized will refer to it as 'my sorority-group' (*mbumba jangu*). When he does so he will refer to a distinct set of women to whom he has specific duties. A man's sorority-group includes ideally his own uterine sisters and their female matrilineal descendants. The daughters of a man's sister, however, are also the sorority-group of his sister's son, so that theoretically any woman may at one moment belong to a number of sorority-groups, her brother's, her mother's brother's, her mother's mother's brother's, &c. But the effective one is usually that of her brother if he is an adult. As the boys in the family grow up they gradually assume the responsibility for their sisters and their mother's brothers relax their control. Small domestic disputes are referred first to the brothers and only later to the mother's brothers. The mother's brothers as they grow older take less and less active part in regulating the affairs of their sisters' descendants. Their position becomes more that of referees and consultants than active participants in day-to-day domestic affairs. The situation of the mother's brother in the structure is well summed up by his Yao designation *mkogowogona*, which literally translated is 'the recumbent log'. An old person who is too old to walk about and pursue actively his structural duties is compared with a log which lies at the doorway. As the duties of the warden of a sorority-group are taken over by the younger men in the matrilineage group, each in respect of his own sorority-group, so the older man is merely kept informed by each warden of the affairs that have taken place and only actively arbitrates in a case which is too difficult for his sister's son or sister's daughter's son to handle. The relationship of junior and senior wardens in the matrilineage group is most clearly shown in the marriage ceremony, where ideally the mother's brother and the elder brother of both bride and bridegroom appear as marriage sureties.

By the simple process of emphasizing the unity of the sibling groups, therefore, the matrilineage group is differentiated both into older and younger generations, so that each sorority-group in the charge of a sister's son is seen against the sorority-group of his mother's brother, and also into sibling groups of the same generation. The tensions that exist in this situation are expressed as tensions between the mother's

---

[1] This point was made to me by Mr. M. G. Marwick, who has studied a people with a similar organization, the Cewa of eastern Northern Rhodesia.

Y

brothers and sister's sons and also between collateral brothers. In any tense situation the lineage groups tends to crystallize into sibling groups. The following case illustrates this.

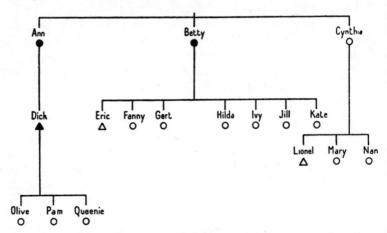

CASE I[1]

Ann and her two younger sisters, Betty and Cynthia, moved into Nyasaland about 1920 and Ann's son Dick had charge of the hamlet. Later Ann died and then Dick went to work in Salisbury leaving the hamlet in the charge of Ann's sister, Betty. In 1936, while Dick was in Salisbury, he was killed. Eric was selected to take his name and to take charge of the hamlet. Lionel, the son of Cynthia and the mother's younger sister's son of Eric, resented this and voiced his opinion. Eventually after a quarrel Lionel decided to move away and live elsewhere. With him went Mary and Nan, also Olive, Pam, and Queenie. Not one of Fanny, Gert, Hilda, Ivy, Jill, or Kate went with him.

This case illustrates how the sibling groups tend to keep together. In times of stress leading to a break-up of a village, siblings tend to stand together and form groups of their own so that each woman in the matrilineage becomes a point of potential cleavage.

A man who stands in the position of being responsible for the sorority-group is referred to as *asyene mbumba*. The word *asyene* is usually translated as 'owner'.[2] This is a mistranslation if we use the word 'owner' to imply the possession of property rights over an object. A closer translation of the word *asyene* would in this case be the person

---

[1] In this village case-history and in subsequent ones I use fictitious names.

[2] See Hetherwick, *A Handbook of the Yao Language*, p. 103, where he says *asyene chilambo* = owner of the country, *asyene musi* = the headman of the village. Also Sanderson; *A Yao Grammar*, p. 164, where he translates *asyene* as the 'owner'.

with whom an object is identified. The word is also used to indicate an emphatic form of the personal pronoun, so that *asyene* in this sense would be translated as 'he himself'.[1] This use of the personal pronoun seems to be consistent with the more accurate translation I have suggested, viz. in this sense it would mean a man identified with himself and no one else.[2] Therefore I propose to translate the term *asyene mbumba* as 'warden of the sorority-group'.

While ideally the warden of the sorority-group is the eldest son of the children of a woman, in practice this is not always so. If the eldest son is incapable of performing these duties, his younger brother will take them over. Any man is responsible for his sisters. Brothers are collectively referred to as the wardens (*acinsyene*) of the sisters. But among themselves sibling rank takes precedence and the eldest amongst them is expected to take action on behalf of his sisters. In the absence of the elder brother, any brother who is available, providing he has been initiated,[3] may take over the duties. In those families where no uterine brother or collateral brother is immediately available, which happens frequently because of labour migration, a seminal brother or some other relative acting on behalf of the uterine brother may assume the duties.

The duties of the warden to his sorority-group emerge mainly when the smooth relations of everyday life are disturbed. He is responsible for the behaviour of the women in his charge and any complaint about their behaviour is reported to him. Should one appear in court he will have to be present in the court-house. Should one of his 'sisters' be fined he will be responsible for the payment of the fine. In the marriage negotiations he plays an important part and these will be more clearly defined later in connexion with marriage. If his sister or her child fall ill it is his duty to see that a diviner is consulted and suitable treatment prescribed and secured. In domestic discord the

[1] Sanderson, *A Yao Grammar*, p. 57. *Asyene* has also the meaning of 'the owner', 'the master'.

[2] Wagner finds a similar difference in the Logoli word *ovwene*. He says: 'This term refers both to "ownership" of objects and of persons. It differs, of course, from our concept of the ownership in several respects. Thus the *omwene* (owner) of a person is the one who has not only the foremost rights over him but also the foremost obligations towards him.' This is exactly parallel to the Yao word *asyene*. See Wagner, 'The Political Organization of the Bantu of Kavirondo', in M. Fortes and E. E. Evans-Pritchard (eds.), *African Political Systems*, p. 216.

[3] Yao boys are initiated at between 8 and 12 years of age, but seldom take over the duties of warden until they are adult.

woman's husband will immediately report the matter to the warden
of the sorority-group. The warden has important duties in mourning
ritual, for he has to be chief mourner at his sisters' or his sisters'
children's deaths, and must provide the medicine necessary for the
ceremonial purification which ends the mourning period. Formerly
these obligations of a man to his sorority-group were counterbalanced
in rights that he had in them as a group, in that he could sell some of
them into slavery for his own personal reasons. This aspect of the
relationship has now fallen away, of course, but nevertheless the important point remains that nowadays, even as in the past, a man
achieves status and independence through his sorority-group. A
man's status in a Yao community depends on the number of persons
that he controls, and should he one day wish to set out and form a
hamlet of his own, independent of other village headmen, he can do
so only through the co-operation of his sorority-group.

The sorority-group is reflected in the system of kinship nomenclature. A man calls his sister *alumbwangu*, i.e. 'my sister', and she can
refer to him by the same term. This indicates the special reciprocal
relationship that exists between a man and his sisters. However,
usually a woman will call any brother, older or younger than she,
*acimweni*, which, though generally translated as 'elder brother', is
probably a term used more for people in some respected position,
since the chief of an area is also called *mcimweni* which appears to be
the same word. A woman thus calls *any* brother *acimweni* because any
brother may stand in the relation of warden of her sorority-group to
her. A man only calls his elder, and not his younger, brother, *acimweni*,
since it is only the former who stands in a similar position to him. A
man calls his younger brother by another term *mpwanga* since a
younger brother can in ordinary circumstances never stand in this
relationship to his elder brother. Sisters usually call each other *cemwali*,
and call their younger sisters *mpwanga*. Within the sibling-group
itself there are also tensions which lead to fracture. The warden of the
sorority-group's duties to his younger brothers are similar to his duties
to his sisters. It is important to notice that the warden refers to his
sorority-group as 'my sorority-group' (*mbumba jangu*), but his
younger brothers must refer to it as 'our sorority-group' (*mbumba jetu*).
The warden's younger uterine brothers and those by his mother's
younger sisters are all called by a special term *acapwanga* (sing.
*mpwanga*), which can be translated as 'my younger siblings of the
same sex'. They in turn call him *acimweni* or *akuluwangu*, which may

PLATE XXIII

5. A typical hamlet and setting in Nyambi area

6. Women pounding maize—a typical village scene in Kawinga area

YAO

PLATE XXIV

7. Installation of a village headman in Kawinga area. The headman has come out of the hut and is seated on a chair at slight left centre of the picture

8. Chieftain offering flour at the grass-sheds just before an initiation ceremony for boys in Kawinga area

YAO

be translated as 'my elder brother.' The term *acimweni* is often used
as an honorific title, but *akuluwanga* is never used thus. The relationship between brothers is a complex one. It is ambivalent and elements
of love and hate intermingle in it. A man is largely responsible for his
younger brother's doings. Where a man's younger brother was away
working in Salisbury when his wife committed adultery, the elder
brother summoned the guilty adulterer and had him pay compensation against his younger brother's wishes. When a man appears in
court the responsible elder brother must appear with him. Whenever
a man wanted in a case cannot be found, the court and the plaintiff
look for his elder brother. In a case where an African was assaulted by
a White another African standing by joined in to protect the one who
was assaulted. He afterwards explained his action: 'I would rather
he hit me than hit my elder brother.' With this feeling of responsibility
there is, however, also repressed hostility which emerges in certain
situations. The reef that wrecks the relations between brothers is the
control of the sorority-group. The following case-history illustrates
this.

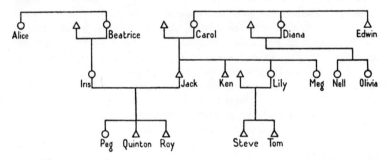

CASE II

Until 1945 there were about forty huts in the village called Jack, after
the headman. The village, however, today is much reduced in size and the
reason for this is the inefficiency of the headman Jack. He did not take action
when the people in his village fell ill. One day his younger brother Ken, who
was married at another village, was sent for and told by his mother that his
sister and her children were ill. He wanted to know what the cause of the illness was, and when he was told that they did not know he wished to know why.
He was told that the headman Jack was seldom to be seen at their huts. Ken
promised that he would see Jack the next day. He sent for his sister's sons,
Steve and Tom, and told them that they would have to go and see Jack, and,
if necessary, consult a diviner.

The following morning Ken approached Jack with his two sister's sons, Steve and Tom, and asked him why he had not attended to the sick people. Jack said that he had no time since he left early in the morning to keep the baboons from his millet garden and only came back late at night. Ken then said that he wanted to consult a diviner. The headman agreed and sent for his two sons, Quinton and Roy, to accompany Ken. The diviner foretold that the woman would die but that the children would recover. In order to check the divination, Ken, Steve, and Tom took a chicken and submitted it to the poison ordeal. The chicken died, indicating the guilt of Jack, and they cut off its head and took it to a man Edwin who stood in the relationship of mother's brother to Jack. Edwin was married at another village. Edwin could not believe what he was told and gave Ken another chicken and told him to repeat the test. Again the chicken died and Ken brought back its head to Edwin.

Edwin now approached Jack and accused him of sorcery. Jack denied the charge, saying that the diviner was lying. Edwin cited the chickens and Jack could make no answer. Edwin thereupon upbraided him for wickedness, telling him that he should not kill people merely for the sake of a garden, that his name was a famous one, and that a village headman could not live without people. Edwin also told him that he must be brought before a court.

Soon after this the sick woman died. After the funeral, Edwin assembled the people and told them that at the conclusion of the funeral feast the case would be considered. Edwin called a man Frank, who was unrelated to the group, so that he could arbitrate in the case. The accusations of sorcery were made against Jack and the chicken test was cited. Jack could make no defence. Ken announced at this point, that he could have nothing more to do with Jack and that he would take the remainder of the children elsewhere and leave Jack to hoe the garden as much as he liked. Frank tried to induce Ken to stay, but to no avail. Ken took twenty-two huts with him to a place some twenty miles away.

Those that stayed behind with Jack were Gwen and Hazel, classificatory sisters of Jack, and Peg, Iris, Alice, and their descendants making up the remaining eighteen huts.

Those that went with Ken were Carol, Diana, Lily, Meg, and their children, who made up the rest of the twenty-two huts.

I have quoted this case fully because it illustrates a number of important points. It shows very clearly the way in which the brothers compete for the right to care for their sisters. Younger brothers are jealous of the efficiency of their elder brothers in this matter. Behind this jealousy is a most important value. This is the value which is very common in Central Africa, and very prominent in the minds of the Yao: that status is associated with the number of dependants a man has. Ken could only achieve status in the eyes of his fellow men by acquiring dependants and the way in which he could do this was to take control of the sorority-group. It is significant that the arbitrator Frank tried to prevent Ken from taking the sorority-group away. Villages are conceived of as units and a certain sentiment is attached to their continuance. The break-up of a village is regarded as a distressing affair. But, on the other hand, part of the value placed on having dependants is, of course, the dislike of having them taken away, and Frank acting under the appreciation of this feeling, and on behalf of Jack in this matter, tried to prevent it. This motif in Yao culture appears again and again in different forms. It appeared in the pre-White days as the institution of domestic slavery. It appears also in the relationship of the chief to his subjects, where the subjects, appreciative of the value with which they are regarded by the chief as followers, are in turn able to use this to bring pressure to bear on the chief in order to achieve their own wishes. This they often do, merely by threatening to go to another chieftaincy. This will be more fully discussed in a later section.

Another interesting point is that the tensions between the brothers Jack and Ken in case II are expressed in an idiom of sorcery. A few notes on Yao beliefs in sorcery will make this clearer. The Yao believe that most illnesses, and certainly sudden illnesses, are due to the evil machinations of some close relative. They believe that this is done partly so that the sorcerer (he uses medicine to perpetrate the crime) can partake of a necrophagous feast with fellow sorcerers when the victim has died. Sorcerers can be discovered by consulting a diviner. The method of divining is similar in principle to that of the Azande in consulting an oracle,[1] i.e. the consultant submits to the diviner for the consideration of his divining instrument (usually a rattle or gourd in the case of the Yao) the names of the people whom he suspects and, for that reason, the people to whom he feels hostile. The finding of the diviner can be checked by the administration of the poison (*mwai*) to a chicken, and should the person whom the chicken represents be a sorcerer, the chicken will die.[2] A high proportion of accusations of sorcery are made between brothers, and it is certain that beliefs in sorcery provide an excellent medium for the expression of hostility between brothers.

The result of the opposition of brothers and of cross-cousins (see p. 335) is that sorority-groups tend to hive off and found hamlets of their own. Therefore the simplest type of spatial grouping among the

[1] See Evans-Pritchard, *Witchcraft, Oracles and Magic among the Azande*, pp. 99 ff.
[2] Yao sorcery beliefs will be more fully discussed in a paper at some later date.

Yao is the hamlet. In a typical hamlet of five huts, for example, there were a woman, her son, her two daughters, her daughter's daughter, and their spouses and unmarried children. The hamlet, however, does not remain a simple kin-group of this nature. The structural changes that take place in it are discussed under the social composition of the thorp.

## Matrilocal Marriage

Thus far we have considered the fundamental grouping in Yao social life: the sorority-group which is organized around the relation of a man to his uterine sisters. In its simplest form it is found in the hamlet. Before the larger clusters of huts can be analysed the institution of matrilocal marriage must be considered. Most marriages contracted in rural Yao areas can be classified as intra-village or inter-village, using the term village in this sense to mean any discrete cluster of huts. The spouses in intra-village marriages both live in the village before marriage, and usually they are related by kinship ties entailing preferential marriage rights. Inter-village marriages are contracted by people who are members of different villages or hamlets, and though they may be, they are not often, kinship marriages. Inter-village marriages may either be patrilocal or matrilocal, and in Yao rural areas most marriages existing at any one moment are matrilocal.

Usually a young man seeks to marry at about the age of eighteen or nineteen. When he notices a likely girl, say at a feast, he makes discreet inquiries to find out her village, or he may ask the woman herself. Whether he approaches the woman with a direct proposal or whether he finds out from some other person the village from which she comes, he must next approach her 'brother'. This is, of course, the warden of the sorority-group. It is proper that he should not reveal that he has already discussed the question of marriage with his bride-to-be. The warden tells the suitor to return at some other time so that he can consult the woman. When the man returns the warden is in a position to answer the proposal. Should she refuse, the warden has no power to force the woman to marry. If she agrees, the man starts to sleep with her in her hut, or if she has no hut, in some vacant hut or the kitchen of some hut. In the meantime he makes arrangements to build a hut of his own. After he has lived with the woman for some time the warden of the woman's sorority-group approaches him and asks him where his home is and the name of a person who can be approached about the marriage negotiations. The young husband then usually gives the name of his 'elder brother' or the warden of his sorority-group. Accordingly the woman's warden goes to that village to seek him out. There is a formalized approach in this matter. Usually the woman's warden will approach the man's warden and ask him whether anything has been lost from the village. The warden of the man either guessing what the visit is about, or possibly having been forewarned of the visit, mentions that a chicken cock has been lost. The woman's warden then replies that the cock is in her village and that he is looking for a hen. Thereupon arrangements are made for the solemnization of the marriage. The marriage is solemnized by a simple ceremony usually translated as the 'witness ceremony' (*cingoswe*). It is conducted in the hut of the woman. Two members of the kin of each side are present in a representative capacity. Collectively they are called the marriage sureties (*acinamangoswe*). The senior of these officials is the *mkogowogona*, whom I shall call the first marriage-surety. He is usually the mother's brother of the man or woman. The junior marriage-surety is called *mkupamame* (the sweeper away of dew) and is usually a warden of the sorority-group of the man or woman[1] or sometimes merely a brother. He is called 'the sweeper away of dew' because it is he who comes to the hut of the married couple early in the morning before the dew has evaporated, should there be any domestic discord. At the marriage-witness ceremony, flour which has been especially pounded for the occasion is cooked into porridge by female relatives of both sides, one pot being prepared by each side. The man's group in addition brings a cockerel which is slaughtered and prepared as a relish and the bride's group kills and prepares a hen. When the food is ready it is formally exchanged, the bride's people eating the cockerel and the suitor's people eating the hen. This exchange of food symbolizes the exchange of the members of each group and this is often vocalized in a short speech made after the ceremony in which each first marriage-surety representing his kin-group proclaims that they have each gained a member. At the same time the couple is warned that all differences in their married life are to be referred to the two marriage-sureties. After this ceremony the parties disperse to their villages and the couple start their life together.

The marriage-sureties are intimately concerned in the life of the young couple, and appear in it constantly. The bride's warden usually lives in the same village as she does (not necessarily so) and so is always present should any difficulty arise. Difficulties frequently do arise and

[1] He is of the same generation as the couple, i.e. the effective warden. See p. 319.

the injured party immediately turns to the marriage-surety. Usually the aggrieved woman or her husband goes to the bride's warden. Domestic quarrels may arise over many small things in domestic life —poor cooking on the part of the wife or a husband's lack of money to give his wife clothing are two common causes. The most common cause by far is adultery. If he is cuckolded the aggrieved man usually reports the matter to the woman's brother, i.e. to the bride's warden, without delay. He then delivers a summons to the guilty man. These cases are tried in court and it is important that the marriage-sureties should be there; in fact, the case cannot proceed if they are not. If no marriage-witness ceremony has been performed, the union is not looked upon as a legal marriage and no claim can be made by the husband against an adulterer. One informant summarizing the Yao attitude to this said: 'Marriage without marriage-sureties is only friendship.' An adulterer is looked upon as a thief, and it is interesting to note that if a woman were to be found carrying food to a man who is not her kinsman, it is sufficient ground for her husband to assume that she has been committing adultery. At the court, in adultery cases, the woman is usually asked to choose whether she wants to remain married to her husband or whether she wants to divorce him and to marry the adulterer. The assessment of the compensation to be paid by the adulterer to the husband of the woman depends on her decision. It is usually somewhat higher if she leaves her husband for the adulterer, and should she decide to marry the adulterer, he is obliged to take her as his wife. It is unusual for the bride's warden to interfere with her decision. He, however, is called upon to pay a fine of about 10s. on behalf of his sister if she refuses to keep her husband. Occasionally the warden does refuse to have the adulterer as husband to his sister, in which case the woman may either go and live in the man's village or the man may live in concubinage with the woman without the protection of the marriage-sureties.

A man, if unsuitable, can be sent away from the village by the woman's group. If he can show that he gave no grounds for divorce, he can claim compensation from the woman's sorority-group. Hence the members of the sorority-group are careful about the way in which they chase a man from the village. They try to make his position as awkward as they can so that he leaves the village of his own accord. On divorce, a man will claim from his wife the clothes and other gifts that he gave to her. He also claims the furniture he has bought and the door and window-frames he built into the hut. There is no marriage-payment among the Yao, though a few small gifts are usually made to a man's mother-in-law and these are not reclaimed.

In Nyasaland a tax used to be levied on all huts in a village, and on males over the apparent age of sixteen if they did not have huts. Widows were exempt from this tax, but the wives of labour migrants were not. Under Ordinance,No. 14 of 1939 the hut and plural taxation were abolished and a poll-tax was imposed on all African male residents over the apparent age of eighteen. However, the tax is still looked upon as a hut tax, and unless the husband pays the tax, the woman is expected to find it. This is immediately the responsibility of the woman's warden and he therefore brings pressure to bear on the husband to pay the hut tax. Thus the payment of the tax becomes a point over which there is much conflict between the husbands in the village and the wardens of their wives. When he sues for compensation in an adultery case a man will stoutly maintain that he has paid the hut tax regularly; and conversely, if the wife's warden can prove the husband has not paid the tax, he can claim that the husband was not carrying out his marital duties and that therefore the marriage should be annulled. This attitude to the hut tax became apparent quite early in the history of taxation (p. 310). It is quite usual for a labour migrant, when returning to Nyasaland, first of all to visit a tax office and pay off his tax arrears. Then he proceeds to his mother's village where he gets a report on his wife's fidelity. Should he learn that she has been unfaithful, then he has a clear way to legal action.

Marriage-sureties also play an important part in the activities that follow on the sickness of any member of the new family. Should man, wife, or child fall ill, it is usual for the marriage-sureties to arrange amongst themselves to consult a diviner and thus discover the cause of the illness. Should a marriage-surety refuse to do this, it is tantamount to admitting sorcery.

It is clear from what has been said that the function of the marriage-surety is not merely that of a witness. The word *acinamangoswe* has been translated as 'marriage witness',[1] but for the reason stated, I prefer to use the word 'surety' used by Macdonald,[2] which much more closely describes his functions. It should be noted that a surety need not personally witness a marriage to be surety to it. The obligations of a surety to a marriage can be delegated to some other person or a complete stranger may play the part in the actual marriage-witness

---

[1] Stannus, 'The Wayao of Nyasaland', p. 234, uses 'sponsor'.
[2] Macdonald, *Africana*, vol. i, p. 118.

ceremony, in place of the brother or mother's brother, who will be surety to that marriage afterwards.

### The Position of the Husbands in the Village

Yao villagers call the men who have married into villages *akamwini*, which I have translated as 'husbands'. The unenviable position of husbands in matrilineal-matrilocal societies has been well described by Richards in her studies of the Bemba people of Northern Rhodesia.[1] The husband is in a similar position among the Yao. He lives in a village with his mother-in-law, frequently in the very next hut to hers. He is by custom obliged in the early stages of marriage to avoid her, and to treat his father-in-law with great respect. The relationship with his father-in-law may become easier in time: that with his mother-in-law always remain tense. Furthermore, the son-in-law is expected to do all sorts of odd jobs for his mother-in-law, such as repairing a leaky roof, perhaps rebuilding her hut, building her a drying-stand for her sorghum, &c. He is, however, not expected to work in her garden as in some other matrilineal tribes. He is expected to work in his wife's garden, and if he does not do so he is subjected to a battery of caustic remarks from his mother-in-law and even deprived of food.

The husband's relations with the male members of the matrilineal descent group in the village are no easier. Husbands are seen to be strangers and their alien sympathies in certain situations are recognized by the Yao and are often formally expressed. Thus, one notability addressed a new village headman on the occasion of his installation: 'Beware how you treat the men who have married into the village. They have it in their power to break the village.' Only a small proportion of a husband's time is spent in the village into which he has married. While doing censuses, for example, I found that it was always difficult to get information about the husbands in the village, because they were frequently not there and usually very little was known about them beyond the village from which they came. The villagers excused their ignorance on this score saying: 'They are only husbands here—how should we know?' I found that husbands were often away on a visit to their matrilineal relatives' village.

Of particular importance for an analysis of the structure of the Yao village is the relationship of husbands to their brothers-in-law. The

[1] A. I. Richards, 'Mother-right among the Central Bantu', p. 267, and *Bemba Marriage and Present Economic Conditions*, pp. 33 ff.

relationships between a man who has married into a sorority-group and its warden, and to a lesser extent with the other male members of the descent group, contain elements of conflict and of co-operation, rooted in their respective relationships with their common object of interest—the wife and sister. The general term used between a man who has married into the village and the members of the descent-group in the same generation as his wife is simply *alamu* [brother- (or sister-) in-law]. However, the husband calls the senior members of his wife's matrilineage out of respect by terms used for senior siblings: he calls his wife's elder brother *acimweni*, while he calls the younger brothers *alamu*; he calls the oldest sister *cemwali*, while the younger are still *alamu* to him. This nomenclature is out of respect and does not alter the fundamental relationship of the husbands in the village to the male members of the descent-group. Furthermore, the two categories are further differentiated in that while all husbands in the village are called *alamu* by the male members of the descent-group, the husbands among themselves call each other by the kinship terms which we have translated as older and younger brother (*acimweni* and *mpwanga*), depending on whether they have married older or younger sisters, while they call the wives of the members of the descent-group 'sisters'.

The relationship between brothers-in-law or sisters-in-law is one of mutual respect, and marriage between people who call each other by these terms is prohibited. Since the structure of the Yao village is further illuminated by the relationship between the husbands and the brothers, a more detailed analysis of this relationship is relevant. Though we may term the formalized relationship between a man and his wife's brother 'respectful', behind this screen lies an attitude of hostility. A man is supposed to offer a chair to his wife's brother while he sits on the ground. On other occasions the tensions that exist in their relationships may flare into open conflict. A husband in the village and his wife's brother—particularly the warden of the sorority-group—co-operate in certain situations, especially those relating to the children born to the husband and his wife. They must both consult a diviner if the child falls ill, though the husband is not so concerned when his wife falls ill. It is to the wife's brother that a man looks for recompense if his wife's behaviour is not all that it should be. At the same time, however, it is to her brother that his wife appeals if she is dissatisfied with her husband's behaviour, and the brother is often able to wield considerable power over the husband in this respect.

A man living in Salisbury was able to write to his mother and tell her to send away the man who was living with his sister as he was bringing home with him a friend who was much more suitable. A second element of conflict appears in their competition for the affection of the woman and her children. This aspect has been dealt with in other societies and need not be enlarged upon here. A third source of conflict may lie in the repressed sexual attitudes of a man to his sisters, and thus to the men who have sexual access to them. It is notable that during the initiation instruction of boys, the sexual inaccessibility of a man's sister and his mother is particularly emphasized. Sexual relations are prohibited between a man and his sister-in-law, his mother-in-law, his sister, and his mother and those people who, by extension, are called by these terms. This prohibition is particularly strong in the case of the sister and mother. After a boy has been initiated he may not enter the house of his mother, or his sister, though these prohibitions may be ceremonially relaxed. Also, the Yao believe that one of the methods of acquiring the power to practise sorcery is to sleep with one's sister or mother. This act is placed in a category of execrable acts, with killing by sorcery a child of the sorority-group or sleeping on the mother's grave. Thus the man who has sexual access to another's sister is able to perform acts which are taboo to the latter, and this may be a further element in the tension that exists between a man and his wife's brother.

The following case illustrates the ease with which the relationship between a woman's husband and her brother may be disturbed.

Case III. John had married into a village shortly after his discharge from the Army. He had some tobacco in his hut, and one day his wife's brother, Peter, went into the hut and took it. When John came back he asked his wife who had taken the tobacco and she told him that her brother had. When John expressed his disapproval, his wife went to her brother Peter and told him that John had cursed at him. Peter therefore brought the tobacco back to John. John wanted to know why Peter was bringing the tobacco to him and Peter replied that he had heard that John had cursed him over the tobacco, and now he was repaying. John later mentioned this to his wife and wanted to know if she had been to complain to her brother. She said that she had and that he could do what he liked about it. Some days later there was a quarrel between John and his wife, so John went and reported the matter to Peter, who said that if John were not satisfied with the woman he could go back to his village. Peter said that he was not going to pursue the matter. John accordingly went to his village. After a month at home John found that his

wife had not come to his village to seek a reconciliation, so he summoned his
wife to court.

This case shows how easily the relationship between a man and his
wife's brother is disturbed by a trifle and exaggerated into a conflict.
It also shows that the bonds between brother and sister are much
stronger than those between husband and wife. The woman in this
case sided with her brother, though she must have known that this
might lead to divorce.

Thus far I have described the fundamental structure of Yao society.
Briefly, there is a distinct sense of lineage unity. The Yao tend to see
themselves as members of matrilineages set against each other by their
descent from different ancestresses. To outsiders each matrilineage
group appears to be an undifferentiated unit, but from within the
lineage group is differentiated into segments of descendants from
different women. The feeling of sibling unity is strong, and I have
described on page 316 how the Yao conceive the sorority-group to be
essentially the group of sisters under the wardenship of their brother.
The tendency for each sorority-group fully to express its autonomy by
forming an independent hamlet is counteracted by the feeling of
lineage unity whereby the effective wardens of sorority-groups are subjected to the authority of some genealogically superior kinsman (p. 317).
The Yao inherit kinship terms with status and names (see p. 341).
Today almost any village headman can indicate another whom he calls
'mother's brother' and who exercises some authority over him. The
direct genealogical connexion between these headmen and their
mother's brothers are usually forgotten, but the relationship of
authority and subordination is inherited by each succeeding headman,
so that their position in regard to each other remains fixed. Case II
cited on page 321 provides an instance where a village headman who
stood in the relationship of mother's brother to a lineage group was
summoned to hear a dispute in a village. The relationships of lineage
groups and the villages that develop about them are ordered in a
lineage framework in which authority rests with genealogical superiority. Because of the propensity of sorority-groups to establish independent villages, the lineage structure is not closely organized on a territorial
basis. The man who stands in the relationship of mother's brother to a particular village may live many miles away, while the nearest neighbours may
be foreigners. The relationship between sections which have broken away
from a village are maintained and perpetuated in a lineage framework in
spite of the physical distance between the sections.

*The Social Composition of the Thorp*

At the beginning of this chapter on village organization I distinguished between what I called hamlets and thorps. Each adult (spouses excepted) in a hamlet can trace his or her relationship directly by matrilineal descent to a common ancestress. The thorp is a different type of settlement. The spouses of the members of a descent-group do not form a group in the accepted sense of the word, i.e. they do not co-operate in corporate action. They may co-operate individually with members of the descent-group, but do not do so corporately. The effective group in a hamlet is the descent-group, and if we define the adults in the effective group as effective members, we may define the hamlet as a discrete settlement in which all the effective members are of the same descent-group. In the more complex settlements, which I call thorps, there may be more than one corporate group. The following table lists the effective members in a thorp of some thirty-nine huts and a total population of 132.

TABLE IV

*Effective Members of Groups in a Thorp*

| Group | Total survivors | | | Total in thorp | | |
|---|---|---|---|---|---|---|
| | ♂ | ♀ | T | ♂ | ♀ | T |
| Headman's lineage . . . . | 10 | 26 | 36 | 2 | 25 | 27 |
| Founder's son's lineage . . . | .. | 4 | 4 | .. | 3 | 3 |
| Founder's daughter's son's lineage . | 2 | 2 | 4 | 2 | 2 | 4 |
| Total . . . . . | 12 | 32 | 44 | 4 | 30 | 34 |

The two men in the founder's daughter's son's matrilineage living in the thorp are doing so because they have married relatives within the thorps. Of the headman's lineage we notice that only 2 of the 10 men are living in the thorp: the rest are married matrilocally elsewhere. Of the women, 2 of the headman's matrilineage have contracted intra-village marriage, so that we may say 28 of 30 have married matrilocally (93 per cent.). This suggests that though most men tend to live in their wives' villages, not all men do. At this point it is necessary to consider patrilocal marriage in this context.

Almost all marriages are at first matrilocal, but they may have become converted to a patrilocal marriage after some years have elapsed. Other marriages are patrilocal from the start. To marry a woman patrilocally is known by the term *kulowosya* in distinction to the ordinary matrilocal marrying which is called *kulombela*. The major factor which determines whether a man will live in his wife's village or whether he will take her to live in his own village is his relative status. In other words, the wife of the village headman must live patrilocally, and if she marries him after he has succeeded to a title, she does so from the start. More frequently, however, it is some time before he succeeds, when he moves from his wife's village to his own and brings his wife and children with him. Not only village headmen bring their wives to live in the village but wardens of sorority-groups tend to do so also. On divorce or death of her husband, the wife may return to her own sorority-group, and the determining factor seems to be whether her children have grown up in the village or not. If her daughters, in particular, have grown up in a village, they tend to marry and set up a group of households around their mother in the village of their father. In this way, within any enlarging village, there tends to develop a second sorority-group, and hence a matrilineage related to the headman's matrilineage by a patrilateral link or by a series of mixed patrilateral and matrilateral links. For example, the lineage group that has developed around the headman's wife, in time, has a warden to live patrilocally, and about his wife, in turn, there develops yet another group. As each village headman dies and is succeeded by his heir, so other foreign women are brought into the village, and so more and more cognatically linked matrilineages are introduced into the village. Schematically this may be represented by the following diagram.

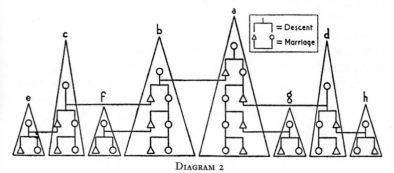

DIAGRAM 2

*The relationship of matrilineages in a thorp*

In this diagram each triangle represents the matrilineages descended from the wives of successive heirs or male descendants of the

village founder *a* (♀). Expressing all relationships to *a* the members in
each triangle are:

| Triangle | Members |
|---|---|
| a | S; D; DS; DD; DDS; DDD; DDDS; DDDD; &c.[1] |
| b | SS; SD; SDS; SDD; SDDS; SDDD; &c. |
| c | SSS; SSD; SSDS; SSDD; &c. |
| d | DSS; DSD; DSDS; DSDD; &c. |
| e | SSSS; SSSD; &c. |
| f | SDSS; SDSD; &c. |
| g | DDSS; DDSD; &c. |
| h | DSSS; DSSD; &c. |

The triangles *b*, *d*, and *g* are matrilineal descendants of the wives of
various village headmen. Succession is usually to a man's eldest
sister's first-born son. Hence these groups are connected to the headman's matrilineage by one patrilateral link. The triangles *h*, *c*, and *f*
are the matrilineages which have developed around the wives of
wardens of sorority-groups, who have married patrilocally, and are
thus connected to the headman's matrilineage by two patrilateral
links. Triangle *e* is represented by the matrilineage which has developed
around the warden of the sorority-group who was the son of a previous village headman. This group is thus connected to the headman's
matrilineage by three patrilateral links.

From this point of view we can define the thorp among the Yao as a
discrete settlement in which the effective members are articulated
into two or more related groups. All Yao villages can be placed somewhere on a continuum, which ranges from the hamlet as a simple
settlement to the multiple lineage-group thorp as a complex settlement. Were this process of multiplication of groups within the village
to continue, the number of groups in a thorp would, under monogamy, double itself with each generation. Under polygyny the groups
in the village may proliferate at a much higher rate than suggested. In
one thorp the founder's son had thirteen slave wives, and of these
seven had set up matrilineages, whose members are still found in the
thorp today. It is more common for the present-day headman only to
have one wife living patrilocally with him, but in the past when slavery
was still part of the normal social structure this was not so. Nowadays
there are a few who have a second wife in the village with them.

But the process of proliferation does not continue unchecked. It is
noteworthy that few Yao villages have a time depth of more than about
five generations. In other words, all the villagers are able to trace their

[1] D = daughter; S = son.

descent from a common ancestor who is removed only two or three generations from the average middle-aged person. In many villages a line of previous bearers of the name of the headman can be traced for five or six generations, but their collaterals have been forgotten and only those from whom villagers are descended are remembered. These are, as I said, two or three generations back in village history. This suggests that as the villages become too large and too complex they tend to break up into smaller autonomous groups which set up as independent villages. When independent villages are established in this way they usually move some distance away from the parent village. Though the general relationship between the villages may be remembered (see p. 337) the actual genealogical ties are forgotten. One of the outstanding features of Yao social organization is the instability of their villages. New villages are for ever being founded by sections that have hived off from parent villages.

## Intra-village Marriage and Cross-cousin Relationships

However, marriages between cross-cousins to some extent counter these processes of fission. I have dealt with inter-village marriages which may be patrilocal or matrilocal and come now to intra-village marriages. These are mainly between cross-cousins but may be between other relatives, who, however, are usually called 'cross-cousin' by the Yao.[1] An examination of the internal structure of a Yao village shows that the relationship of cross-cousins is important. The headman's wife who lives patrilocally belongs to a foreign sorority-group. She is a stranger and is often made to feel it, and there is frequently tension between a man's sisters and his wife or wives. This is fully realized by the Yao, and it is made clear to a village headman by old and experienced men when he is ceremonially installed. One adjured a village headman: 'As you have wives, do not listen to what they say. They may be lying. Sometimes they will quarrel with your sisters and say that your sisters have been insulting you. This is false. When you hear these reports you may be unfair to your sisters and the people will say that you have broken your village through listening to nonsense.' The headman's wife is called *alamu* by her husband's sisters, and as explained above (p. 331), this term suggests a certain amount of diffidence and respect covering tension.

The children of a headman and the children of his sisters call each other *asiwani*, which we translate as cross-cousin. The cross-cousin

---

[1] Children by slave wives of the same father, for example, may marry.

relationship is characterized by a joking relationship and this should be seen in relation to the village situation. The group of cross-cousins of the village headman's children form an opposed group and act together against the headman's children in certain situations. Yet there is also a strong tradition of cross-cousin marriage amongst the Yao. These marriages, informants say, are unstable, and they attribute this to the continuance into married life of the joking relationship that existed before. My general impression of the divorce rate confirms this, but unfortunately I am unable to confirm this quantitatively. A complicating factor is that many first marriages are made between cross-cousins, hence there are likely to be more divorces amongst them.

The kinship terminology also reflects the importance of cross-cousin marriage. A mother's brother's wife is called by the term *akwegwe* by a man or woman. This is also a self-reciprocal term between a person and his or her parent-in-law. Similarly the children of a cross-cousin are called 'my children' (*mwanangu*). If a man marries one's female cross-cousin he is called not 'brother-in-law' but 'my younger brother'. Informants say this is because, if a man does not marry his cross-cousin, then his younger brother should do so. A father's sister's children are also called cross-cousin, but the father's sister's husband is called 'father' (*atati*), not 'father-in-law' (*akwegwe*). This becomes significant if we consider the situation in which kinship relations are most effective, i.e. in the village. The children of a headman look upon all of their father's sisters as belonging to his matrilineal group and call them 'female fathers' (*atati ŵakongwe*). The children of this group of women they call 'cross-cousin'. All the men in the village they look upon as 'fathers'.

From the point of view of the village headman's sister's children, all the women of the matrilineage of the headman and of his generation are called 'mother', but are differentiated by whether they are senior or junior according to whether they are older or younger than the speaker's own mother. All the men married to these women are called 'father' and are thus undifferentiated. The only man who stands in the special relationship of authority is the headman, who is called by a special term *akwelume* which we have translated as 'mother's brother'.[1]

---

[1] It is interesting to note that the roots of this word seem to be that of *akwegwe* (parent-in-law) and *mlume* (male) and not, as Radcliffe-Brown has pointed out for other African tribes, composed of the roots for mother and male. See Radcliffe-Brown, 'The Mother's Brother in South Africa'.

It follows from what has been said that if cross-cousin marriage takes place between two members of a village, the internal constitution of the group is simplified, particularly if it is the warden of the patrilaterally linked sorority-groups who has married thus. Instead of his bringing in a foreign woman about whom will develop a related lineage, he will have married one of his father's matrilineage members so that the unity of the village is further solidified.

Not all intra-village marriages are, in fact, marriages between cross-cousins. Grandchildren of the same grandfather by different grandmothers may marry, but it is clear that in any case where such marriages avoid the introduction of foreign women into the group, the solidarity of the village is increased.

### Village Histories

A Yao village does not persist unchanged in time. Though the villagers in any particular village consider their village to be a persisting unit, the weaknesses immanent in its kinship structure eventually cause its disintegration and reconstitution in the same form, but with different personnel. Histories of different villages show the same general characteristics. Villages are composed of kinsfolk who can trace their descent from a common ancestress, either matrilineally directly or through some patrilateral link or links. Before this founding ancestress, only three or four generations back in the village history, other ancestresses are known to have existed, but the collaterals have been forgotten and today villagers only know that village A is related to village B, and that the relationship of the two headmen is that of father to son or mother's brother to sister's son. In some of the older villages, groups are known to have hived off and set up independent existences elsewhere. The gradual break-up of large villages and the growth of smaller new villages is continually going on. This, of course, is the exterior aspect of the internal structure of the village which has been so far described. Villages usually fragment in particular patterns and it is as well to illustrate the ways in which this occurs. Earlier (case I, p. 318) I described the break-up of a village and the segmentation of the parts is clearly seen. The segmentation was here preceded by tension between a man and his mother's younger sister's son. Later (case II, p. 321) I cited a division in a village which occurred where once again the tension was expressed in the competition of brothers, but in this case the other main type of fission is exemplified in that the matrilineage group involved moved out with their new leader-elect, while the original headman was left with his children and other relatives, but not his matrilineal relatives.

In other cases complete fragmentation of villages takes place. In addition to the way in which related lineage-groups move out of a village, the headman's lineage-group itself may segment into sorority-groups which move away to establish independent hamlets. A large village may disintegrate and give rise to five or six related but independent hamlets. As these groups settle down in areas they are become now hamlets or, at the most, very simple and small thorps. But inherently in their structure operate the same structural weaknesses which brought about the establishment of those new villages, and which in due course will cause their extinction or at least modification.

## IV. THE VILLAGE IN POLITICAL STRUCTURE

### The Village as a Basic Unit

I have already outlined the internal structure of villages. Hamlets and thorps are internally differentiated, but to the outsider these villages appear to be undifferentiated wholes. This section deals with the relationships of villages to each other in the larger framework of political structure.

Villages are scattered fairly evenly, though there are areas where there is no population because there is no surface water. Villages also seem to be placed more closely along the streams for the same reason. On the whole there are no great differentiating economic and ecological factors. They all live in the same terrain and live at the same economic level. I exclude from this analysis the villages along the lake shores, which I have not yet visited and which may show other features.

Villages are known by the name of the founder, and this name is inherited by the village headmen who are his heirs. It is difficult to over-emphasize the importance of the concept of 'village' in the life of the Yao. They think, for example, of places in terms of the location of villages in those areas. A man will fix an occurrence as taking place at 'such-and-such village'. The road to Zomba is conceived of as a number of stages between villages. The Yao indicate geographical location by reference to the nearby social groupings. The exception to this general rule is the chief's village. Usually the court village is known by some other name than that of the chief. Kawinga's court village is called 'Nanyumbu' and Nyambi's 'Malundani', these being hills in the near vicinity of these villages. This distinction is probably to avoid confusion with the larger area, the sub-district under the jurisdiction of Kawinga or Nyambi, which is also known by the chief's name as 'At Kawinga's'.

In the same way, people are fixed as having come from or as belonging to certain villages. A man may thus be distinguished as John of Tom's village. The unity of villages against similar groups is also clearly shown in the initiation ceremonies. For example, in the boys' initiation ceremonies (*lupanda*) the initiates are housed in grass-sheds before they are taken to the circumcision spot. These long grass-sheds (*masakasa*) are divided into smaller compartments each of which houses the boys from one particular village. As a rule boys from different villages are not mixed together in these compartments. The undifferentiated nature of the village to outsiders is also shown by the *awilo* relationship that existed between certain villages in the past. As far as I could gather these relationships no longer persist. Briefly the *awilo* (burial men) were the men who prepared a corpse for burial and who carried the corpse to the grave and interred it. Since relatives were by custom not allowed to handle the corpse of a dead kinsman, it was essential that the burial men be unrelated. The burial men also had certain duties to perform in the mourning ceremonies and during these they stood in an asymmetrical joking relationship with all members of the village in which the death had taken place. They could in fact go so far as to take a child in slavery if the child was found unattended. After the mourning ceremonies were over the joking relationship persisted in a less intense form, not only between the particular burial men and the villages, but between the village of the burial man as a whole and the village where the death took place. Any unrelated man who happened to be in or near a village when a death took place could perform these duties, so that burial-men relationships between villages arose in a haphazard way.

## The Village Headman

I have from time to time mentioned the village headman. Now his position in the social structure can be more easily appreciated. I use the term village headman to denote the person who is the recognized leader of the village. In a hamlet it may be the warden of a sorority-group, and in a thorp it may be a senior matrilineal descendant of the village founder. In general, a village and its headman are identified by a name which is matrilineally inherited. The usual rule is succession by a man's sister's first-born son, though it is not followed if this man is considered to be unsuitable for the position. Village headmen can usually trace their descent back through three or four village headmen to the first whom they consider the founder of the village.

When a headman is installed he is said to 'enter the name' (*ajinjila lina*). For the more important village headmen the actual installation ceremony is an occasion of great rejoicing. The successor is selected by the village members, the children of the predecessor having a great deal of weight in this decision. At the appointed time, in company with one or two other notabilities, some important village headman (not the chief) calls the nominated heir to some isolated place. When he is safely alone the officiating headman strikes the heir on the forehead with his fist, knocking him to the ground. The others immediately seize the heir and shout that 'So-and-so is here!' calling the name of the dead headman, which is the name that the heir is to assume. In the past a special hut of cloth was built, and the heir placed in it. Nowadays he is taken to a hut in the village. The woman have been told to brew beer for the important day of 'coming out of the hut' (*kukopoka nyumba*). In the meantime the heir is kept in his hut. On the day previous to his coming out, he is dressed completely in clothes as a corpse is and carried to the hut of the wife of his predecessor. This move is marked by great jollification and the villagers shout out that the dead headman has returned from the grave. The heir now spends the whole night in the hut in company with some important old headmen who instruct him in the mode of behaviour he will have to adopt now that he has become a village headman. During this time he is given a ritual meal which is designed to test whether he is a sorcerer or not. He is given three dishes of meat with a plate of stiff porridge. He is told to eat the one that he likes best. Unknown to him (so I am told), one of the dishes contains human flesh. If he is a sorcerer he will choose the human flesh after tasting it, and leave the other two. If he is no sorcerer, he will vomit after eating the human flesh.[1] If he is no sorcerer the villagers are told and they rejoice. If he is a sorcerer he must be treated to cure him of his evil propensities. Thereafter proceedings continue.

The next morning the heir is ceremonially brought out in front of his predecessor's hut, placed in a chair, and dressed in his finest clothing, with his wife and his predecessor's wife on either side of the chair. This is the actual ceremony which is known as 'coming out of the hut'. It is the climax to the installation. The heir is considered to have

[1] This test is based on the belief that sorcerers assemble to disinter corpses and eat their flesh. I have briefly described this on page 323.

succeeded at this point. The people now assemble about him while he and his wives assume a posture correct for initiates, i.e. silent and with heads bowed. Local notabilities make speeches, usually to the headman and his sisters, strongly tinged with a moral flavour, emphasizing in particular the evils of conflict and strife and the possibility of a break-up of a village should the village headman fail in his duties. The headman is told to eschew sorcery and not to listen to the tales of his wives about his sisters because of the results that this has—the dissolution of the village as a unit. The sisters in turn are urged to respect the man, not to refer to him by his name, but to use the descriptive title *mwenye* (chief). Gifts are made to the headman in the form of coppers which are showered at his feet. At the conclusion the headman and his wives are taken inside the hut and the mass of people who have collected go about the business of merry-making and beer-drinking.

From now on the successor is considered to be identical with his predecessor. The Yao deny that the soul of the dead man returns to the new headman as the Bemba believe.[1] Nevertheless the successor seems to take over the social position and duties, in fact the whole social personality, of his predecessor. We have seen that the successor assumes the name of the predecessor and after the 'coming out of the hut' he is no longer referred to by his previous name. Furthermore, he inherits the wives of his predecessor since he has to undertake the duties of husband towards them though no new marriage ceremony is performed. He need not necessarily sleep with them and he can release them from their sexual obligations towards him and allow them to marry other men. It is interesting to note that if the successor has previously married his predecessor's daughter (i.e. his cross-cousin), then his duty of providing for the mother of his cross-cousin ceases.

A striking fact about a man's succession to the position of headman is that with the name of his predecessor he also assumes his terms of address to kinsmen. The successor now calls the children of his predecessor 'my children'. Men previously called 'mother's brother' he may now call 'younger brother'. As far as I could discover, the terms for his father and mother remain unchanged. Patterns of behaviour to non-kin also change. For example, the friends of the predecessor, i.e. those who were entitled to share a mat with him, are now the friends of the

---

[1] The Bemba believe that each man has a *mupashi* or guardian spirit which must be inherited by the successor who takes his name, bow, social status, and obligations as well as the spirit and the right to approach this spirit in prayer. See Richards, 'Mother-right among the Central Bantu', pp. 267 ff.

successor. The more valuable property also passes to the successor. Here the Administration's decisions about the loan of rifles is particularly puzzling to the Yao. Rifles are loaned to responsible headmen to destroy dangerous and destructive game. When a headman dies the Administration recalls the rifle. Should the successor wish to borrow the rifle he is placed on a long waiting list. The Administration maintains that the loan was made to an individual who is now dead. This separation is impossible to the Yao. For them the successor is virtually the same man as the predecessor.

The term *asyene musi* is used to denote the 'village headman',[1] but the more important village headmen are called 'chief' (*mwenye*). It is impolite to call a village headman by his name. He should always be addressed as 'chief' or by some kinship term. The village headman is distinguished from the commoners in several ways. The most obvious of these are the duties he has to the villagers. A village headman may be, of course, a warden of a sorority-group as well as a village headman. But there are many wardens of sorority-groups who are not village headmen. A thorp may have many sorority-groups living in it each of which has its own warden. It has only one village headman. When a sorority-group moves away from its parent village and establishes a hamlet of its own, the warden of the sorority-group assumes a new role in the political sphere and he becomes a village headman. Previously he was a warden of his sorority-group, but the relationship of his sorority-group with others was expressed through the headman of the parent village. Now he represents his sorority-group as an autonomous unit. In general the village headman is responsible for the members of his village to the chief and other political functionaries. In the past he was required to propitiate the village ancestors at various times, and to conduct the simple first-fruits ceremonies. Nowadays much of what he has to do stems from his position as an administrative village headman or from the administrative machinery in other ways. For example, a village headman has to see that the village is kept clean and that a refuse-pit is dug. The paths between villages must be kept clean and the village headman is approached by the District Commissioners when labour is needed for public works. When the District Commissioner appears on his tour it is customary for the villagers to give him gifts of flour and chickens. These gifts are usually provided by the village headmen and each is expected to provide a gift. The chief

[1] The general remarks about the meaning of the word *asyene*, made on page 318 and page 319 (footnote 2), should be recalled.

also looks upon the village headman as a representative of the village. The more important village headmen must report to the chief the arrival of any new hamlets which have come to live in their vicinity.

The village headman is also distinguished from common villagers in that he is subject to certain mystical dangers that commoners are not. He is, for example, particularly and always susceptible to the contagion of death. He may not prepare the corpse of a commoner for burial. Should he eat the chicken which is brought to him to announce the death of a villager he will contract a disease (*ndaka*) involving swelling of the legs. At the same time he is entitled to certain dues from the villagers, the most notable of which is a cup of beer which has to be given to him from each brewing in his village.

### The Status of Village Headmen

From time to time I have mentioned 'important village headmen'. Village headmen are ranked in status and their rank is shown by a number of insignia. The most important factor in reckoning the rank of a village headman is the size of a village under his command. The part that having dependants plays in the internal organization of the village has already been noted (p. 322). A village headman's status is often connected with the number of his dependants, as in a statement 'he is a big man—he has many huts'. But of almost equal importance are the historical associations of a man. Descendants of the first invaders of the land are reckoned superior to the later immigrants. Though a village headman may have had many dependants in the past, the inherent instability of Yao villages may reduce his dependants. His rank nevertheless tends to persist.

A man's achievement of status, mainly by having the power that goes with acquiring dependants, is recognized by the chief in the area in various ways. One of the most important of these is by allowing village headmen to hold initiation ceremonies. A successful initiation depends upon the goodwill of the ancestors of the chief. The sanction of the ancestors for an initiation ceremony is obtained by the chief's sacrificing at the ancestral shrine, which is usually a tree in the neighbourhood of his hut. The offering consists of pouring a cone of flour, which has been especially pounded for the occasion, at the base of the trunk of the tree. Should the cone collapse during the night following the sacrifice, this is taken to mean that the ancestors are not willing to sanction the initiation ceremony. The sacrifice will then be repeated in a few days' time. The chief may, if he sees fit, delegate the right to hold such initiation ceremonies to various headmen. This right includes the right to approach the ancestors of the area through the village headman's own ancestors, and is therefore called 'having a sacrifice basket' (*kukola ciselo*). The duties of the chief or village headman in the initiation are primarily: obtaining the sanction of the ancestors for the initiation; blessing the grass-sheds in which the initiates are kept before they are circumcised and proceed to the bush-school (*ndagala*), and to which they return before the end of the initiation period; and blessing each initiate and his or her mother before the ceremony. He himself takes no part in the actual ceremony and, in fact, is not allowed to go to the grass-sheds or bush-school. The actual ceremonies, the operation and the instruction, are carried out by specialists (*m'mchira* = tailmen) who have magical zebra tails which play an important part in the ceremony. The tailmen may or may not be village headmen, except that if they have the right to conduct initiation ceremonies they may not also be tailmen. For the ritual part that the village headman plays in this activity he is paid small sums by the relatives of the initiates. Financial as well as status benefit is therefore derived from having the right to conduct initiation ceremonies. In general it is considered more important to have a boys' initiation ceremony (*lupanda*) than to have a girls' (*ciputu*). Some headmen are entitled to hold both.

Only a few headmen in the area are allowed to wear a plain scarlet piece of cloth (*mlangali*) around the forehead. This is a mark of great status. The right to wear this band is granted by the chief. I know no person who has the right to wear a red band who is not a village headman. Successors are entitled to wear the band if they renew the permission and those who migrate into a new area are also entitled to wear a band if they wore one before and obtain the permission of the chief in the new area. All village headmen of importance are also given a special type of greeting. This is the Arabic type of greeting (*subaḥe*) accompanied by a slight bow of the upper half of the body while the left hand is placed on the chest. In addition to these distinctions, more important headmen are buried in the village instead of in common graveyards. The grave of a headman in a village is called *nsati*, and special permission to bury a headman in the village must be obtained from the chief before it can be done. The corpse of the village headman must be prepared for burial by other village headmen of like standing. During trials at the chief's courts the village headmen of standing take up their position under the veranda of the chief's hut while the commoners sit in the open court-yard. Important village headmen take up their position near the chief. In the initiation ceremonies the leader of the group of initiates will be either a son or a sister's son of the chief or village headman of standing. Rank therefore is clearly recognized among village headmen.

The status of village headmen also operates in other ways. The most important of these is that of arbitrating in disputes. Disputes are settled in one of two ways. They may be settled either in the local Native Authority court-house constituted in terms of the Native Courts Ordinance (1933), or they may be settled by the arbitration of the chief or an important village headman. Generally speaking the cases settled in the court-house are those which do not offend the White ideas of justice and morality. Examples are cases concerning adultery, petty theft, assaults, &c. Of the cases tried outside the court-house we may distinguish two types. Firstly, there are the minor disputes of everyday life. A quarrel between two women is an example of the type of case that may be settled by the arbitration of the village headmen. Secondly, more serious charges, especially those involving accusations of sorcery, of homicide due to a breach of taboos, and the like are also settled outside the court-house. In these cases either the chief or the most important village headman in the area may be called in to arbitrate. It should not be construed from this that village headmen do not take part in the proceedings inside the court-house. Village headmen attend the court and express opinions and question the witnesses. However, the decision in this situation is made by the paid court assessor and the punishment is awarded by the chief or Native Authority.

Another way in which the status of the village headman is reflected is in the placing of mosques. In the area I visited, nearly all Yao professed to be Moslems. A certain proportion of those who claimed to be Moslems could not be held to be so, even by their own standards. This became apparent during the month of Ramadan when these people did not observe the fast. A considerable proportion of the population are practising Moslems. Mosques are built in most Moslem villages and in addition to these there are larger mosques built at the villages of chiefs and important headmen. The village mosques are used during Ramadan for morning and sunset prayers (the midday and other daily prayers are not observed). The larger mosques are used for the prayers held at midday on every Friday. For these prayers the Moslems from the neighbourhood assemble and hold a joint prayer

under the leadership of a local 'teacher' (*mwalimu*). In the neighbourhood of a chief's village the mosque is usually placed in the chief's
village, but in the outer areas the large mosques are situated in the
villages of the important Moslem headmen.

A third way in which the status of the village headmen is reflected
is by means of administrative villages. Under the District Administration (Natives) Ordinance 1912, village headmen were recognized by
the Administration. They were given certain duties to perform and
received a small yearly remuneration. At the same time the Administration ruled that before a village headman could be recognized as an
administrative village headman there must be twenty huts under his
care. Where villages were too small to fulfil this requirement they were
considered by the Administration merely to be part of a larger administrative village under an administrative village headman. Administrative villages therefore are not necessarily social units in that they do
not necessarily act corporately. Under one village headman there
may be three or four hamlets and thorps completely unrelated to the
administrative headman and sometimes even relatively unknown to
him, having only recently moved into the area under his jurisdiction.
It is not clear from the records how the administrative village headmen were chosen. Probably they were chosen by the District Residents
in consultation with the chief. Nowadays it is obvious that all those
who have indigenous marks of rank—i.e. wear red bands, have initiation ceremonies, were associated with the first invaders into the
country, &c.—are administrative village headmen. New administrative village headmen are continually arising. In itself, to be an administrative village headman, 'to have a book' as it is phrased in the
vernacular, is a mark of status. There is consequently a certain amount
of competition amongst village headmen to acquire enough followers
so that they might present a good enough case to be appointed. To be
made an administrative village headman, apart from the financial
benefits that accrue from it, is a tangible and objective expression of
success in the Yao scheme of values, since it implies that one has sufficient dependants or followers to be considered a relatively independent leader. To be appointed, a village headman must make his application to the District Commissioner through the Native Authority.
Therefore he must first of all convince the chief of his right to this
consideration. In doing this he is in competition with his fellow village
headmen who are trying to achieve the same purpose. After he has
convinced the chief of the strength of his claim, the chief transmits his

claim to the District Commissioner who considers the application now, not in terms of the relationships of the chief and village headman, but rather from the broader administrative point of view.

## The Chief and the Village Headman

I have, from time to time, mentioned the chief. In this section I wish to describe the relationship between the chief and the village headmen. At the outset it is important to realize that I have used the word 'chief' and the phrase 'Native Authority' for the same individual, but not for the same social personality. The interaction of the chief and his subjects can be conceived as taking place in two fields. In the first field the chief may interact as a social personality in the structure in terms of an indigenous system of values. The personality who sacrifices to his ancestors in a rain prayer, or who deliberates on the granting of the right to conduct an initiation ceremony to a village headman, I call 'chief', since the interaction takes place in reference to a system of values which was part of the culture before the coming of the Whites. In the second field, the personality who punishes a man because he has infringed the Native Authority regulations, the personality who acts as an agent in the Administration, I call 'Native Authority'.[1] In an actual situation the two aspects of a man's personality cannot be isolated. For sociological analysis, however, it is useful to consider the position of the chief and the Native Authority in two interlocking structures.

The historical evidence available suggests that there has never been a strong centralized Yao state. History as represented by both the Yao themselves and by reports of early pioneers suggests that the Yao political groups were small, dominated by military and commercial leaders, who held their fellows so long as they retained their military and commercial leadership. The Yao talk of the early chiefs as warriors and rich men with many slaves, able to send caravans of ivory to the coast. Duff Macdonald records 'the chief may otherwise have less influence than a powerful headman, and we have known cases where he simply contented himself with grumbling when his headmen acted contrary to his desire'.[2] He tells of a village headman who demanded from a chief the murderer of one of his villagers. He records: 'Chelomoni, a Blantyre headman, was attacked when on a journey, by another

[1] I realize that a Native Authority in terms of section 2 of the Native Authority Ordinance (1933) might be 'a native council or group of natives declared to be or established as a Native Authority'. In these areas, however, the Native Authorities were all chiefs and not councils.     [2] Macdonald, *Africana*, vol. i, p. 157.

headman and had his wife taken from him. He was himself wounded by an arrow, and came to the Station bleeding very profusely. The outrage called for some remonstration, and Chelomoni's villagers at once prepared to march upon the offender.[1] Later he says: 'Nkanda of Cherasulo was at first a headman of Kumpama's but rebelled and lives on the southern side of that mountain.'[2] The evidence seems to point to a number of largely autonomous village headmen under the partial domination of the chief. Histories of various Yao groups abound with examples of important village headmen who launched out and became independent leaders. In those days the chief himself was a village headman with his own village and he is still so today. Some of the village headmen in a chief's area carry the same insignia of rank that the chief himself does. In terms of the indigenous system of values therefore the chief is in competition with his village headmen and on much the same footing. He has only certain ritual sanctions over his headmen because of the power of his ancestors. The ancestors of the present chiefs are recognized to have been immensely powerful people. Periodically the chief sacrifices flour to them at the tree-shrines either in rain ceremonies or in some impending or actual calamity, threatening the whole tribe.

With the introduction of British rule far-reaching changes took place. One of the most important of these is that village headmen, who in the old days might have been able to move out of one chief's area, and by conquest set up a new chieftaincy of his own, must today for ever remain a village headman. The Administration has imposed a limiting structure upon them. The chiefs have been recognized as Native Authorities and the Administration will not willingly recognize new and additional ones. Competition between village headmen and the chief nevertheless continues. Village headmen compete with each other to become administrative village headmen and to receive recognition by being allowed to hold initiation ceremonies, to be allowed to wear red bands, &c. The chief, on the other hand, tries to resist these claims realizing that in allowing too many headmen to have the same insignia of rank he reduces the value of these insignia in the eyes of his subjects. In one chiefdom there are many who are entitled to wear the red band. In another only one or two have the distinction. In the first chiefdom the people realize that to wear the red band is no great distinction. For the same reason the chief opposes the too common holding of initiation rights. He therefore opposes the demands of

[1] Macdonald, *Africana*, vol. i, p. 128.          [2] Ibid., p. 32.

the village headmen, arguing in one case that the village headman's village was too close to the chief's. The village headmen have a certain amount of power in that they are able to threaten to move away from the chieftaincy thereby reducing its strength. On one such occasion when a village headman had been refused the right to hold a boys' initiation ceremony and had threatened to move his village to another area, the chief immediately offered the headman a girls' initiation basket. To some extent there is also some economic competition between the village headmen and the chief, but this is the setting of the general economic life of the area. The chiefs are able as a rule to grow more tobacco than the village headmen and commoners, and for this reason and for some others (e.g. they are paid a relatively high salary) they are able to keep up a higher standard of living. Nevertheless some villagers who have been to the Mines in South Africa and Southern Rhodesia may have more goods and finer clothes than either chiefs or village headmen.

## The Chiefs and the British Administration

The position of those chiefs who have been appointed Native Authorities has been strengthened. A Native Authority has behind him the backing of the Administration and in certain situations he may emphasize this. For example, in a speech at the installation of a headman that he had championed against the wishes of the villagers, a chief said: 'This man has been chosen by me as being the best candidate, and the Governor agrees with me.'

Before the British Administration commenced the chiefs had a number of court officials. These were the *Nduna* or counsellors, who were a number of important village headmen who advised the chief in state matters, such as where famine was expected, where wars might profitably be prosecuted, and who settled the disputes of the chief and his wives or the chief and his family. These counsellors were usually called 'friend' (*anganga*) by the chief, and their position of honour was inherited by their heirs. In addition to the counsellors there were also court assessors (*mapungu*). Court assessors were chosen for their eloquence and wisdom. Unlike the counsellors they were not necessarily village headmen, in fact some have been slaves. Also their position was not inherited but they were replaced by others chosen by the chief and his counsellors. The court assessors used to live at the chief's court and subjects could only approach the chief through the court assessors. An assessor's more important duties, however, were to sift evidence and cross-examine witnesses at cases. After this he would convey a summary of the case to the chief, who would in turn award compensation. Under the British Administration the importance of the counsellors has waned. Provision is made by the Administration for the remuneration of a certain number of court assessors at the courts of Native Authorities. Counsellors who have no function in the court have not been recognized. The result is that the tendency has been to appoint the counsellors to the position of court assessors, thereby causing some confusion of function of the original officials. At the same time the Native Authority has a small bureaucracy stationed at his court and in various small ways this bureaucracy is beginning to take over the functions that were formerly carried out by the court assessors and counsellors. The court sergeant, for example, now shows visitors to the chief. The court clerk advises the chief on certain matters.

Finally, all Yao who have gone from Nyasaland to work in Southern Rhodesia and South Africa, have been lumped together and classified with Nyanja, Nguru, Cewa, and all other tribes in Nyasaland as 'Nyasa boys'. The two senior battalions of the King's African Rifles, the first and second, have always been recruited from Nyasaland and are looked upon as being Nyasa regiments, as against the battalions from other Territories. In the towns a semi-political organization has developed amongst the clerks and teachers and other literates. In these ways affiliations are developing between Yao groups which were formerly hostile, and between tribal groups which were formerly at war. The local affiliations to village and chief, though still of major importance, are gradually giving place to affiliations of a broader kind in which the Africans see themselves as a part of a larger world order.

## BIBLIOGRAPHY FOR THE YAO AND KINDRED PEOPLES

ABDALLAH, YOHANNAH B. *Chiikala cha Wayao*, edited and translated by M. Sanderson as *The History of the Yaos*, Zomba: Government Printer (1919).

ABRAHAM, J. C. *Census Report for Nyasaland, 1931*, Zomba: Government Printer (1931).

BRUWER, J. 'Kinship Terminology among the Cewa of the Eastern Province of Northern Rhodesia', *African Studies*, vii. 4 (December 1948).

—— 'The Composition of a Cewa Village', *African Studies*, viii. 4 (December 1949).

—— 'Kinship among the Cewa of Northern Rhodesia and Nyasaland', *African Studies*, ix. 1 (March 1950).

BUCHANAN, J. *The Shire Highlands*, London: Blackwoods (1885).

BURTON, SIR R. F. *The Lands of Cazembe: Laçerda's Journey to Cazembe in 1798* (translated and annotated), London: J. Murray (1873).

CARDEW, C. A. 'Nyasaland in 1894–5', *The Nyasaland Journal*, i. 1 (January 1948).

CASSON, J. C. 'Agricultural Labour Conditions in Nyasaland', *Assoc. Sci. Agron. Col.*, Elampes (1910).

*Census Report for Nyasaland, 1945*, Zomba: Government Printer.

CODRINGTON, R. 'The Central Angoniland District of the Protectorate', *Geographical Journal*, xi. 15 (May 1898), pp. 509–22.

DIXEY, F. 'The Distribution of the Population of Nyasaland', *The Geographical Review*, xviii (April 1928).

DUFF, H. L. *Nyasaland under the Foreign Office*, London: George Bell (1903).

DULY, A. W. R. 'The Lower Shire District: Notes on Land Tenure and Individual Rights', *Nyasaland Journal*, i. 2 (July 1948), pp. 11–44.

ELMSLIE, W. A. *Among the Wild Angoni*, Edinburgh: Oliphant and Ferrier (1899).

FULLERBORN, F. *Das Deutsche Njassa-und-Ruvuma Gebiet*, Berlin (1906).

GOVERNMENT REPORTS. Foreign Office: *Correspondence re Operation against Slave Traders in British Central Africa*, London: H.M.S.O., Command 7925 (1896) and Command 8013 (1896).

—— *Colonial Report, Annual, No. 472, British Central African Protectorate, Report for 1904–5*.

—— *Agricultural Survey of Zomba District by the Assistant Agriculturalist*, Zomba (1945), Government File.

—— *Annual Report of the Provincial Commissioner, Southern Province for the Year ending Dec. 1936*, Zomba: Government Printer (1937).

—— *Correspondence re Recruiting of Labour in the British Central African Protectorate for Employment in the Transvaal, 1903–1908*, London: H.M.S.O., Col. Off. Ref. Col. 1531, 1950, and 3993.

—— *Historical Notes on Districts in the Southern Province extracted from The District Annual Reports for 1936*, File 58/37 Provincial Commissioner's Office, Blantyre.

—— *Report of the Consul and Acting Commissioner Sharpe on the Trade and General Condition of the British Central African Protectorate for April 1896 to March 31st 1897*, London: H.M.S.O., Accounts and Papers (Africa), No. 5 (1897), C. 8438.

—— *Report on Native Affairs, Nyasaland Protectorate*, Zomba: Government Printer (1931).

—— *Report of Commission of Enquiry into Occupation of Land*, Zomba: Government Printer (1920).

GARBUTT, H. E. 'Witchcraft in Nyasa (Manganga, Yao, Achawa), communicated to writers', *J.R.A.I.* li (1911).

—— 'Native Customs in Nyasa and the Yao', *Man*, xii (1912), p. 20.

*Handbook of the Nyassa Company* (Portuguese Nyasaland), London (1898).

HARRIES, LYNDON. *The Initiation Rites of the Makonde Tribe*, Livingstone: Rhodes–Livingstone Institute, Communication No. 3 (1944).

—— 'Some Riddles of the Makua People', *African Studies*, i. 4 (December 1944).

HECKEL, B. *The Yao Tribe, Their Culture and Education*, University of London Institute of Education, Studies and Reports, iv (1935).

HETHERWICK, A. *A Handbook of the Yao Language*, London: S.P.C.K. (1902).

HETHERWICK, A. Note on Yao in *Nyasa News*, November 1893, p. 64.

—— 'Some Animistic Beliefs among the Yaos', *J.R.A.I.* xxxii (1902).

—— 'Islam and Christianity in Nyasaland', *Moslem World*, xvii. 2 (April 1927).

HICHENS, W. 'Islam in Africa' in Arberry, A. J. and Landau, R., *Islam Today*, London (1943).

HONAKER, S. W. *Portuguese East Africa, Its Resources, Industries and Trade*, Dept. of Commerce, Bureau of Foreign and Domestic Commerce, Special Consular Reports, No. 85, Washington: Government Printing Office (1923).

HORNBY, A. J. W. 'The Climate of Central Nyasaland', *Department of Agriculture Bulletin*, No. 9 (December 1933), Zomba: Government Printer.

HYNDE, R. S. 'Marriage and Relationship among the Yaos', *Nyasa News*, vii (1895), pp. 217–18.

JOHNSON, W. P. 'Discovery of the Source of the Lujenda', *Proc. Royal Geographical Society*, viii (August 1882), pp. 480–4.

—— 'Seven Years Travel in the Region East of Lake Nyasa', *Proc. R.G.S.* viii (August 1884), pp. 313–36.

—— 'The Yao, A Defence and a Suggestion', *Occasional Papers from Nyasa News* (November 1893).

—— 'More about the Yaos', *Occasional Papers from Nyasa*, Likoma (1894).

—— *Nyasa the Great Water*, London: Oxford University Press (1922).

JOHNSTON, H. H. *British Central Africa*, London: Methuen (1897).

JUNOD, H. P. 'Notes on the Ethnographical Situation in Portuguese East Africa', *Bantu Studies*, x. 3 (September 1936).

LACEY, A. T. *Report of the Commission Appointed to Enquire into Emigrant Labour*, Zomba: Government Printer (1935).

LAWS, R. *Reminiscences of Livingstonia*, Edinburgh: Oliver and Boyd (1934).

LAWSON, A. 'An Outline of the Relationship System of the Nyanja and Yao Tribes in South Nyasaland', *African Studies*, viii. 4 (December 1949).

LIVINGSTONE, D. and C. *Narrative of an Expedition to the Zambesi and its Tributaries, and of the Discovery of Lakes Shirwa and Nyassa, 1858–64*, London: John Murray (1865).

MACDONALD, DUFF. *Africana, or the Heart of Heathen Africa* (two volumes), London: Simpkin Marshall and Co. (1882).

MAPLES, C. 'Mtonya', *Nyasa News*, No. 1 (August 1893).

—— 'Unangu', *Nyasa News*, No. 2 (November 1893).

—— 'Makualand between the Rivers Rovuma and Luli', *Proc. R.G.S.* (February 1882), p. 86.

MARWICK, M. G. 'Another Modern Anti-witchcraft Movement in East Central Africa', *Africa* xx. 2 (April 1950).

MAUGHAN, R. C. F. *Africa as I have known it*, London: John Murray (1929).

MITCHELL, J. C. (with M. Gluckman and J. A. Barnes), 'The Village Headman in British Central Africa', *Africa*, xix. 2 (April 1949).

—— 'The Political Organization of the Yao of Southern Nyasaland', *African Studies*, viii. 3 (September 1949).

—— 'An Estimate of Fertility in Some Yao Hamlets in Liwonde District of Southern Nyasaland', *Africa*, xix. 4 (October 1949).

MOGGRIDGE, L. T. 'The Nyasaland Tribes, their Customs, and their Poison Ordeal', *J.R.A.I.* xxxii (1902).

MOIR, F. L. M. *After Livingstone: An African Trade Romance*, London: Hodder and Stoughton (no date).

MOREAU, R. E. 'The Joking Relationship (*Utani*) in Tanganyika', *Tanganyika Notes and Records*, xii (December 1941).

M.T.K. 'The Yaos in the Shire Highlands', *Nyasa News*, No. 4 (1894), pp. 121–3.

MURRAY, S. S. (compiler). *A Handbook of Nyasaland*, Zomba: Government Printer (1932).

—— 'Native Customs in Nyasaland', *Nada*, xvi (1939).

O'NEILL, H. E. 'Journey from Mozambique to Lakes Shirwa and Amaramba', *Proc. R.G.S.* (1883–4).

—— *The Mozambique and Nyasa Slave Trade* (1885).

PIM, SIR A. *The Economic History of Tropical Africa*, London: Oxford University Press (1940).

PRETORIUS, J. L. 'The Terms of Relationship of the Cewa', *Nyasaland Journal*, ii. 1 (January 1949), pp. 44–52.

RANGELEY, W. H. J. 'Notes on Cewa Tribal Law', *Nyasaland Journal*, i. 3 (December 1948), pp. 1–68.

—— ' "Nyau" in Kotakota District', ibid., ii. 2 (July 1949), pp. 35–49.

ROOME, W. J. W. *A Great Emancipation: A Missionary Survey of Nyasaland*, London World Dominion Press (1937).

ROWLEY, H. *The Story of the Universities Mission to Central Africa, from its Commencement under Bishop Mackenzie, to its Withdrawal from the Zambesi*, London: Saunders, Otley and Co. (1866).

—— *Twenty Years in Central Africa*, London: Wells Gardner, Darton, and Co. (3rd edition, 1889).

SANDERSON, M. *A Yao Grammar*, London: S.P.C.K. (1922).

—— 'Ceremonial Purification of the Yao', *Man*, xxii (1922), p. 55.

—— 'Relationship Systems among the Yao', *J.R.A.I.* 1 (1920).

SCLATER, B. L. 'Routes and Districts in Southern Nyasaland', *Geographical Journal*, ii (November 1893), pp. 403–23.

STANNUS, H. S. 'The Wa Yao of Nyasaland', *Harvard African Studies* (1923), Varia Africana, iii, pp. 229–372.

—— 'Notes on Some Tribes of British Central Africa', *J.R.A.I.* xl (1910).

—— and DAVEY, J. B. 'Initiation Ceremony for Boys among the Yao of Nyasaland' *J.R.A.I.* xliii (1913).

THEAL, G. M. *Records of South East Africa*, Printed for the Government of the Cap Colony (1899).

THOMPSON, J. 'Notes on the Basin of the River Rovuma, East Africa', *Proc. R.G.S* ii (February 1882), pp. 65–79.

WALLER, H. *The Last Journals of David Livingstone in Central Africa from 1865 to his Death*, London: John Murray (1874).

WERNER, A. *Native Tribes of British Central Africa*, London: Constable (1905).

WEULE, K. *Negerleben in Ost Afrika* (1908), translated by A. Werner as *Native Life in East Africa*, London: Pitman (1909).

—— *Wissenschaftliche Ergebnissen einer ethnographischen Forschungsreise* (1908).

YOUNG, CULLEN. 'Note on Maravi Origin and Migration', *African Studies*, xi. 1 (March 1950).

YOUNG, E. D. *Nyassa, A Journal of Adventure* (1877).

# SOME 'SHONA' TRIBES OF
# SOUTHERN RHODESIA

*By* J. F. HOLLEMAN

## I. INTRODUCTION

*Identification*

THIS contribution deals with a number of tribal groupings in central Mashonaland, Southern Rhodesia. The area in which these people live is roughly triangular and covers approximately 2,700 square miles. It comprises the central and southern portions of the Sabi Native Reserve (Buhera District), the whole of the Wedza Native Reserve (Marandellas District), and the Narira Native Reserve (Charter District).

The people described are: a Hera tribe under the Nyashanu chieftainship (Sabi Reserve); two autonomous fractions of the once dominating, now widely scattered, Rozwi tribe, the one under the Musarurwa chieftainship (Narira Reserve), the other under the Rozani chieftainship (Wedza Reserve); and a Mbire tribe under the Swoswe chieftainship (Wedza Reserve). All these are commonly regarded as belonging to the Zezuru cluster of the 'Shona' tribes, but it is doubtful if such classification can be justified on ethnological grounds as no detailed comparative study has yet been attempted.[1] From a native point of view this affiliation is meaningless, as it is not supported by any special ties of a political or other nature. Few, if any, have an intelligent conception of a 'Zezuru cluster' as distinct from, say, a Karanga or Manyika cluster (which seems to be justified on linguistic grounds), and questioning on the subject of such affiliation produces only vague and often confused views. Mbire and Rozwi informants may admit that they speak 'Cizezuru'; the Hera usually maintain that they speak Cikaranga or, specifically, Cihera. It seems advisable to reserve an ethnological classification of Shona tribes until a wider comparative study has been made.

---

[1] Major works such as C. Bullock's *Mashona Laws and Customs* and his *The Mashona*, and the writings of F. W. T. Posselt (e.g. the collection *Fact and Fiction*), though containing much valuable information, are too generalized to serve as a basis for classification. The rest of the Shona literature is mainly topical.

From the outset it is useful to know that the tribal communities mentioned above are fragments of what were probably once greater centralized units occupying certain portions of Southern Rhodesia.

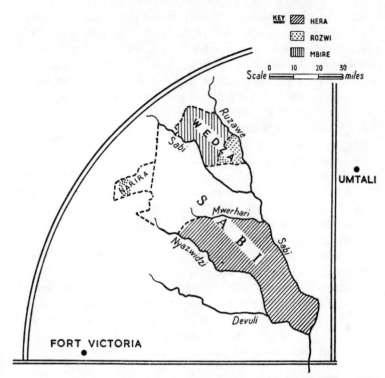

*The Wedza, Narira, and part of the Sabi Reserves, Mashonaland.*

Of these the Rozwi once dominated the country, but their power was broken up by Swazi, Ndebele, and Europeans. Having lost this centralized authority, numerous fractions of the Rozwi clan are now dotted all over the country, living side by side and on a more or less equal footing with various other tribal communities which, likewise broken loose from their original anchorage, have established themselves (often after a considerable period of wandering and unrest) as independent offshoots of their old parent bodies.

The result is not only that the tribes commonly referred to as 'Mashona' lack the centralized political authority of a paramount chief, but also that there can hardly be any question of a specific and distinctive tribal pattern pertaining to, say, Rozwi, or Mbire, or Hera. Especially during the generally peaceful conditions of the past half-century inter-tribal contact has been free and frequent. Whatever distinctive or exclusive clan features there may have been in the past have become common property of tribal communities living in close contact in the same locality. So that it would be safer now to ascribe minor variations and specific tendencies to a certain *locality* where they are found, instead of labelling them with the particular clan name of one of the communities living in such locality. It will be found, for instance, that the Rozwi grouping in the Wedza Reserve present a pattern of law and custom practically identical with that of their immediate neighbours in the same reserve, the Mbire (Swoswe's people), but differ in certain aspects from their fellow clansmen living as an autonomous community in the Narira Reserve. And that the Mtekedza section of the Hera, which some generations ago broke away from the main Hera body, more closely resemble their Njanja neighbours (Charter District) than their brother section (Nyashanu's people) who are living in the central and southern part of the Sabi Reserve, some 40–80 miles to the south.

In describing the general pattern common to all the communities living in central Mashonaland, the usefully inclusive but foreign (Ndebele?) term 'Shona' will be used, because there seems to exist no indigenous term which could be used conveniently as a common denominator. When variations of this general pattern occur, the locality should be noted, in spite of the fact that reference will inevitably be made to particular tribal groupings.

## Habitat

The people described in this paper live under roughly similar geographical and climatic conditions. The country is mostly slightly undulating highland with altitudes varying from 4,500 feet in the Narira Reserve to around 3,600 feet in the Wedza Reserve, falling to 2,000 feet in the south-east corner of the Sabi Reserve. The flat surface is every now and then broken by peculiar granite formations from sixty to several hundred feet high, giving, on a gigantic scale, the impression that numerous truck-loads of boulders had been carelessly dumped all over a golf-links. In the Narira and northern Sabi Reserves these formations are less numerous than in the southern parts of the Sabi and Wedza Reserves, where they may form chains and clusters stretching for many miles over the broken plains.

In the southern Wedza and Sabi Reserves there is still a considerable amount of woodland (in the latter area even a fair amount of small and big game); the Narira Reserve and northern Wedza Reserve are practically denuded and the Government has made a modest start with afforestation.

The quality of arable land is fair and in normal years the rainfall is sufficient (20–30 inches; less in the sparsely populated southern Sabi Reserve) for agriculture, the principal mode of subsistence. Although Land Officials are never optimistic when contemplating the dangers of soil erosion through overstocking, careless (i.e. traditional) cultivation, deforestation, &c., the country is comparatively little eroded. The Administration is taking widespread and energetic measures (centralization of villages, separation of ploughing and grazing areas, contour ridging, destocking, &c.) to forestall the fate of, say, some parts of the Transkei or Zululand.

Surface water remains a problem, as rivers and streams crossing the country lose most (sometimes all) of their water towards the end of the dry season (May–October). There are relatively few springs and pans, and in spite of energetic efforts on the part of Government officials to sink wells and build dams, people have found it difficult in some parts (especially Sabi Reserve) to find water for livestock or even domestic use.

## Subsistence

The population mainly subsists on agriculture, maize and millet being the staple crops, though a fair amount of sorghum, monkeynuts, beans, and rice is also raised. In the areas not yet touched by the Administration's policy of centralization (southern Sabi Reserve), where traditional methods of agriculture (inadequate, wasteful breaking up and 'scratching' of the soil, and broadcasting seed over an extensive acreage, without the use of fertilizers or rotation of crops, &c.) prevail, the people have been satisfied with a crop of $1\frac{1}{2}$ to 4 bags per acre. The new policy is, however, slowly being enforced throughout the country, entailing a severe limitation and stricter control of arable land, and a more intensive cultivation of fields. Those individuals who are sensitive to improved methods of cultivation seem to be able to raise 20 to 25 bags per acre without difficulty. But in spite of widespread use of trained African demonstrators and demonstration plots, the Administration is fighting an uphill struggle against what some officials regard as 'inexplicable lethargy', 'stupid and short-sighted conservatism', or 'almost criminal lack of responsibility', regarding improved use of the land.

Although agriculture is by far the most important means of sub-sistence, a sizeable number of cattle and smaller livestock (goats, sheep, some pigs) is found, mostly of a poor to mediocre quality, though officially sponsored schemes for improvement of stock have been in operation for some time. In spite of their numbers (which the Administration is anxious to cut down to less than one-half), live-stock are still maintained mainly for marriage (*rovoro*) and ritual pur-poses. Milk and meat do not form a regular part of the traditional daily diet, the first mostly being consumed by herd-boys and other small children, the second mostly becoming available at ritual functions (*kupirirana*; *bira*). Native butchers are, however, establishing business to a rapidly increasing extent, and regular sales of stock (as part of the Administration's destocking scheme) are bound to introduce and develop a more 'economic' element in cattle husbandry.

## II. LOCAL GROUPINGS

Tribal organization is based on three different local groupings, the biggest of which is the 'tribe' (*nyika*) controlled by an independent, hereditary chieftain (*ishe*). The tribe is divided into several tribal wards (*dunhu*, pl. *matunhu*) each under the control of a hereditary ward head (*sadunhu*). And the *dunhu* comprises a number of separate villages (*musha*, pl. *misha*) each under a headman (*samusha*).

I shall deal with these units separately.

### The Village—Musha

The picture presented by village groupings in central Mashonaland is not uniform. In most of the central and southern Sabi Reserve (Hera under Nyashanu chieftainship) the people live in tiny villages, each under control of a hereditary headman, and widely scattered over the country. These villages lack the neat, fixed pattern of the Zulu or Xhosa villages and consist of a small cluster of thatched pole-and-mud huts built around or facing an open space (*civara, dare*) on which one or two shady trees may have been left standing. No efforts are made to fence in the village, but occasionally a line of berry-carrying shrubs may be found on one or more sides, serving as cover for an open-air cooking-place or small vegetable garden, or separating two adjoining villages.

Granaries (*dura*; *tsapi*) are often found on a nearby lowly protruding solid rock (*ruwari*) whose flat surface also serves as a threshing-floor.[1] Goat and chicken pens are usually placed on the *civara*, while cattle kraals (*danga*) are built a little distance away, outside the cluster of living huts.

The population of these villages varies considerably, from a single family of half a dozen souls to more composite groups of relatives numbering a few score.

Distance between the villages varies from a few dozen yards to a few miles, and though it is commonly stated that 'relatives like to live near each other', greater or smaller physical distance between villages is not always a safe gauge to measure the intimacy, or even existence, of kinship relationships between neighbours.

In cases where the village is divided, two or more sections of the same village may be found as separate hamlets at some distance from each other. Though no outward signs of a closer unity between them may be apparent, the term *musha* then applies to such a collection as a whole, while each of the component hamlets (including the principal one) is regarded as its *mana* (pl. *mamama*).

Fields cultivated by members of the villages are found in the immediate vicinity, often forming a solid block upon which the boundaries of the individual gardens are hardly observable. Owing to the particular character of traditional cultivation, in which the village population starts to cultivate a given tract of virgin land, using the same gardens for two to three years, and extending (*kuwandurira*) their reclamation for another few years until the most suitable land is exhausted, the villages are shifted every six to eight years or so, depending upon the available amount of arable land in the immediate vicinity. This process presented little difficulty in the past as land used to be ample and dwellings are easily built.

In theory a distinction is made between grazing area (*ufuro*) and ploughing area (*urime*), in that cattle have to be grazed at a safe distance from fields actually under cultivation. But as there is little or no control over the movements of villages in search of suitable ploughing areas, cattle are grazed wherever there happens to be food for them, as long as they are kept out of the fields under actual cultivation. Except in those cases where the landed interests of two different villages touch each other, there are no formal boundaries marking the extent of a

---

[1] All storage huts are built, wherever possible, on a bare rock foundation as protection against white ants. Sleeping quarters, however, are never built on rock.

village's land rights. One of the principal features of Shona land tenure in this area is the establishment of a 'sphere of interest' with due regard to existing rights of neighbouring others, and the gradual expansion of such sphere into those directions where no other conflicting interests can reasonably be expected.

In the other areas, the Wedza and Narira Reserves, where the Government's policy of centralization has been operating for some years, the picture is different. The villages (again *misha*, under control of hereditary headmen) are, on the whole, considerably bigger than in the above described parts of the Sabi Reserve, and the composition of the village population often more varied and consequently more complicated. The main element binding villagers together remains, however, that of kinship.

Due to the order to build on a surveyed 'line', which separates large ploughing areas from grazing areas, the villages have assumed the appearance of single streets (the original *dare* or *civara*) flanked on both sides by a single straight row of huts,[1] the length of the street depending on the size of the village community. Villages numbering 40–60 people are common, and those having 100–150 inhabitants are not exceptional.

The bigger villages are usually, but not necessarily, split into two to five *mamana* (sections), in which case the continuity of the 'line' may be interrupted by empty gaps of twenty to a few hundred yards between the built-up sections, by low hedges, or even by two or three strategically placed stones on the open *civara*. Nowhere, however, is the idea of 'exclusiveness' carried out so far that a section or village has found it necessary to build or grow a fence hedge *around* their place of residence. Typical of the principle of free intercourse between villages, the newfangled hedges (in which there is always an opening left) and the solitary stone beacons are referred to as the 'gate' (Eng.) and not as the *mugano* (boundary) of a village.

As in the traditional villages, small livestock and chickens are usually kept on the *civara* while cattle kraals are built at some distance behind their owners' huts.

With the centralization programme in progress, and the issue of arable land under stricter control, not only individual gardens belonging to members of the same village, but also fields belonging to people of different villages built along the same 'line', are situated more

---

[1] Each round living hut (*imba*) usually faces a square type store hut (*bozi*) belonging to the same family unit, across the street.

closely together and, after reclaiming the comparatively small margin allowed for natural expansion and new issue, the ploughing area tends to become continuous blocks of fields extending over several square miles. And woodland has disappeared almost completely.

## Village Organization

The *musha* (village) is controlled by an hereditary headman, the *samusha*, who is the head of the principal family unit which originally founded the village. Membership of the village is based on kinship and/or residence within the common homestead. But a member who has been absent for a considerable time will not lose his membership unless there is clear evidence that he will not return. Nowadays the inclusion of a person's name on the tax register of a certain village headman has become generally accepted as proof of his membership of such village—a point of evidence which is often raised in connexion with garden disputes or the position of a person who has been away from home for a long time.

In the southern Sabi Reserve the small village communities mainly consist of single agnatic units, a father with his wife or wives and unmarried children, often with one or more married sons and their families. But not seldom other relatives may live in his village, such as children of his sister or father's sister, maternal kin, or a few in-laws. These people may come singly or with their families, submitting to the authority of the village headman, as do his own children. In the bigger villages, elsewhere, the number of these non-agnatic kinsmen is proportionately greater than in the villages of the southern Sabi. It was found that in the latter area the members of the headman's family (excluding their wives) composed about two-thirds of the average village population. In the centralized areas not more than about one-third of the number of villagers belonged to their headman's own family, while the rest of the population consisted of family units which were cognates or in-laws of the headman, or sometimes not related at all. The bigger amongst these other family units may attain some measure of independence as separate village sections (*mana*) under the control of their own family heads (*samana*) who remain, however, responsible to the headman.

The *first* establishment of a new village as an independent community requires the sanction of the headman of the tribal ward (ward-head), and in case of a foreigner coming from outside the tribal boundaries, also of the chief. After permission to establish an independent village has been received, the ward-head (*sadunhu*) or his representative will show the new headman where he can build his village and cultivate his gardens. The ward-head formally confirms the allocation by driving a peg (*kudzikira bango*) into the ground on the spot where the hut of the headman's principal wife (*vahosi*) is to be built. A preferential right to a cultivation area is vested by making some distinctive marks in the middle of the selected area, usually by cutting some branches from one or more trees and piling them up around the trunks (*kubatira gombo*).

The new homestead is built collectively by all villagers, usually with the assistance of neighbours against the compensation of ample quantities of beer provided for the occasion by the new headman. Before its occupation the village is ritually fortified by sexual intercourse between the headman and his first wife.

Garden sites are allotted by the headman to all eligible members of his village after he has selected sites for himself and his immediate dependants. If the village has several subsections the headman will indicate to the heads of these sections (*samana*) the approximate extent of their areas, after which they, in turn, will provide for the people under their control. A husband receives his allocation on behalf of his individual family and is expected to allot separate portions to each of his wives. Young men about to marry are usually given their own fields to enable them to build up a stock of grain; grown-up, unmarried daughters may be given a corner of their mother's field in which to cultivate some crops which they are allowed to sell or barter in order to buy themselves clothes, small livestock, or anything they may require with a view to marriage. All allocations, whether made to individuals or to family units, allow for reasonable future expansion.

Although every individual cultivator has a full and indisputable right to the crops he (or she) raises and is entitled to the full use of his field without interference from others, the land itself is never regarded as individual property.[1] The nearest approach to Western 'ownership' is the right of 'Bantu-ownership' held by the village *as a collective unit* in respect of the collectivity of fields (under actual cultivation or lying fallow with a view of recultivation). This right is controlled by the headman in his capacity as representative of the village community. But the individual members and sub-units of this

[1] Neither does it fall within the meaning of any of the common terms for 'property' or 'possession'. It is, in the words of one informant, 'something you use and abandon again, it is never yours in the sense a beast or a plough or even a wife can be yours'.

community are entitled to exercise a *right of use* to their individual shares in the collective property, as long as they retain their membership of the village and the village itself remains in a position to exercise its Bantu-ownership.[1]

When the original allotment, made to the village by the ward-head, proves insufficient even after making use of the available surrounding land, the headman is entitled to search for a new cultivation area and village site within the boundaries of the ward. When land is generally ample and a conflict with the landed interests of other villages unlikely, he can select new land without prior permission from the ward-head. But in areas where arable land is not so plentiful, or when he intends to make use of a site abandoned by another village, the headman is expected to approach the ward-head for confirmation of his choice. In neither case is there a repetition of the formal 'planting of the peg' necessary for a first establishment. But usually, because a village is normally moved a few months before the start of the new planting season, the headman himself will mark one or more trees on the site of his intended cultivation as a visible sign that he has vested a preferential right over the area pending actual reclamation by his villagers.

The functions of a headman are essentially those of the head of a family group. His first duty is to see that the individual family units under his control are in a position to sustain themselves, and he is therefore primarily responsible to provide sufficient acreage for their needs in the manner described above.

The headman has jurisdiction to adjudicate in any dispute between members of his village. These are essentially minor cases, such as petty jealousy and scolding (*kutuka*) between women, strife between husband and wife, disobedience of grown-up children towards their parents, and garden disputes, &c. In these matters his function is rather that of an arbitrator trying to settle a dispute (*kuenzanisa nyaya*) in an informal manner than of a judge formally deciding a case (*kutonga mhoswa*). A fine (*muripo*) will seldom be levied against a guilty village member, and if this happens it is by way of exacting a concrete token of goodwill and reconciliation. There are no court fees payable

[1] A village loses its right of Bantu-ownership: (*a*) when it moves beyond the boundaries of the tribal ward (*kutama*), that is, when it ceases to be a member community of the old ward; (*b*) when its new site and cultivation area, though within the same ward territory, are so far removed from the old sites that it would be impracticable to continue to use them. But when a village moves only a relatively short distance (*kusuduruka*) so that the old sites are still within reach, it retains a preferential right to them.

to the headman, and the whole procedure has the character of a family circle, presided over by the family head, jointly ironing out any differences between two or more of its members.

Whenever the matter is so serious that the headman does not feel able to reach a satisfactory solution, he will make a preliminary investigation into the nature of the conflict and present the case to the ward-head for his decision or advice. When one of the villagers under his control becomes involved in a legal conflict with someone belonging to another village and the matter cannot be settled between the parties, it is the responsibility of the headman to see that his villager obeys the summons of the ward-head and to represent his man in court. And although the headman will not be held personally responsible for any eventual compensation unless the wrongdoer belongs to his own family, he is expected to use all his authority to see that such compensation is duly paid by the party under his control. Similarly, if any villager has an action against a member of another village his headman usually acts as formal complainant on his behalf.[1]

As the head of a family group the headman officiates in matters of family ritual, dedicating or sacrificing cattle to the family ancestral spirits, and calling upon them for assistance in case of illness or other misfortunes. When seed for the next planting season has to be magically treated it is his duty to engage a magician (*nganga*) for the purpose.

European administration has imposed a few new duties upon the headman. One of these is the collection of various taxes from taxable members in his village. This responsibility has had a curious effect upon his position as tribal official. It has not only resulted in the substitution for the traditional term *samusha* of the new title *sabuku* ('keeper of the book'), which is now most commonly used, but the custody of a village tax-register has, in fact, become a primary badge of the headman's office. Where, in the past, *kudzikira bango* ('planting the peg') marked the formal recognition of a community as an independent *musha*, the granting of a separate tax-register to a person would nowadays be regarded as concrete proof of his being a headman (*samusha*), and to entrust the head of a village section (*samana*) with

---

[1] I have seen many cases at the chief's or ward-head's court postponed because the court refused to deal with the matter owing to the absence of the headman of one of the parties. Asked why his presence was considered essential even if he could not be held responsible for the payment of the compensation, the answer was usually that 'he ought to be there to listen so that he would know what was going on in connexion with his village members', or 'he is like a father to anyone living in his village, and a father ought to know what his child is doing'.

his own tax-book would have the effect of creating a new village community under his control, independent of the original village unity.

The headman is assisted in his duties by the elders of the village, section heads (if any), or the heads of the family units comprising the village. Together they form an informal village council, meeting at irregular times whenever it is deemed advisable, to discuss matters of village or family interest. The head of a big village usually has one or two deputies, highly trusted kinsmen, who receive notifications or listen to complaints before these are transmitted to him, and who act as his spokesmen or personal messengers. There is no recognized term[1] for these village officials, but they are often either a younger brother (*mununguna*), son-in-law, or sister's husband (*mukuwasha*) or a sister's son (*muzukuru*) of the headman. These men are never formally appointed to their duties, nor do they receive any fixed or regular compensation, though they may, occasionally, receive small presents from the headman.

As the head of a family group the headman may require the members of his family to help him occasionally with the cultivation of his fields (*zunde*) without compensating them (though he will, if he feels like it, provide some food for them). Such obligation may be extended to cognates (e.g. sister's children) living under his control, while a daughter's or sister's husband will often do so voluntarily. But the headman cannot exact such services beyond this narrow circle of relatives without exceeding his traditional authority.

Nowadays he often acts as official witness to the registration of marriages contracted in his village, for which duties he is entitled to a small fixed fee.[2]

Within the village every individual family unit, consisting of a husband, his wife or wives, and their unmarried children, provides for its own subsistence. When a man has only one wife they will usually jointly cultivate one field on which the main crops, maize and millet, are raised, and their bigger children are required to help them as far as possible.[3] Usually a woman also has a small plot on which she grows native vegetables, beans, monkey-nuts, in so far as these are not interplanted amongst the main crops.

---

[1] The term *mupoterwi*, meaning 'a person to whom one turns first', is sometimes used in this connexion.     [2] G.N. No. 36/1918.

[3] A frequent complaint by parents of school-going children is that they are 'unable to cultivate their gardens properly owing to the absence of their children'.

There is, in connexion with agricultural work, no fixed division of labour based on sex, and people of both sexes and all ages are often busy in the same field doing the same work. Ploughing with oxen is normally done by men, but especially during their absence women frequently handle the animals.

A man with more than one wife has a separate field (*zunde*) which he cultivates with the help of his wives and children, all working together when necessary (e.g. with weeding), or taking turns as directed by the husband.

Each co-wife has her own field (*munda*), and is left free in her choice of cultivation as long as she keeps her children well fed. Each co-wife must provide a plate of food for her husband at every mealtime, and he will take care to eat from every plate.[1]

A diligent housewife often produces more than she needs for her domestic use, and sells or barters the surplus for extra clothes, small livestock, or simple luxuries. A husband will seldom interfere in these transactions.

Although the daily work in the village and on the lands is performed by the members of the families amongst themselves, there are frequent instances in which members of different families or belonging to different neighbouring villages combine their efforts and work collectively and in rotation on each other's fields. The more limited of these activities is called (*ma*)*jangano*, in which two to six householders arrange a schedule for reciprocal aid in connexion with specific tasks (for instance, cutting bush for fresh fields, ploughing, weeding, reaping). On such occasions there is no compensation for the work, but the host for the day may provide some relish (*muriwo*), or a few handfuls of fried monkey-nuts at noon.

A more extensive form of collective activity is provided by the *nhimbe*, a body of neighbouring villagers of both sexes working in rotation on the field of whichever member has prepared a large quantity of beer (*doro*) for the occasion, without which no *nhimbe* party would work. *Nhimbe* groups are non-political in the sense that membership is based on a proximity of residence which is not bound to any political boundaries. The geographical situation of a village determines its membership of a particular *nhimbe* group. As a loosely organized body the importance of the *nhimbe* can hardly be over-estimated. In conservative areas people state without hesitation

---

[1] One of the clearest signs that a wife has lost her husband's favour is his refusal to taste the food she has prepared for him.

that 'no one is able to do all his cultivation alone' [i.e. only with his family]. Every field-holder, man or woman, has at least a few *nhimbe* parties during every season, depending on the size of the field and the prospects of the season.[1] Participation in the *nhimbe* system, both as host and as working guest, is a matter of social urgency, because any-one who, for some reason or other, keeps himself and his family apart from these activities cuts himself off from social life. The economic value of the *nhimbe* may be debatable, as a very considerable portion of the day-time is spent on leisurely gossip and drinking, and the people usually end the day's work with dancing and singing into the late hours of the night. But socially it is, perhaps, the brightest aspect of native life, and some idea of its significance may be gauged from the fact that one *nhimbe* group, consisting of the members of nine small villages in the central Sabi Reserve, had gathered about 180 times for collective work on the fields of its members during one reasonably good season.

### Tribal Ward—Dunhu

The next bigger local unit found in central Mashonaland is the *dunhu* (pl. *matunhu*), the tribal 'ward'. In contrast to the traditional hamlet or village (*musha*) which, as a unit, had no fixed territorial limits, the *dunhu* is well defined. Its boundaries are determined usually by rivers, streams, hill-tops, and like natural geographic features. As a local unit it greatly varies in size and numbers of population.

In the southern Sabi Reserve, where the population is widely scattered and political authority much more differentiated than in the Wedza and Narira Reserves, the wards are, like the villages there, on the whole much smaller. Accurate topographic surveys of these indig-enous units are not available, but I would estimate the average tribal ward in the first-mentioned area to be between 25 and 35 square miles, though some are considerably bigger or smaller. Com-pared with this, the Rozwi territory (Rozani chieftainship) in the southern Wedza Reserve, which three generations ago was an autono-mous ward owing allegiance to the Mbire chieftain, Swoswe, covers approximately 125 square miles. It has since become an independent chieftainship, subdivided into three recognized tribal wards measuring about 35, 40, and 50 square miles respectively. The remaining greater

---

[1] In a good season the average field-holder may have one or two parties for clearing and ploughing a fresh field; two or three parties for weeding; one or two parties for reaping; and one or two (very generous) parties for threshing.

portion of the Wedza Reserve, approximately 315 square miles, is occupied by only four tribal wards under the Mbire chieftainship.

When we compare some population figures relating to the southern Sabi and Wedza Reserves, the contrast is even greater. A village census was taken (October 1946) in two tribal wards in the Sabi Reserve which, I think, fairly represent the average ward in that area. One tribal ward numbered just over 170 people (children included) spread over fifteen separate hamlets (*misha*); the other, which belonged to a vassal unit, had about 180 inhabitants living in fourteen different hamlets. When a similar census was taken (1947) in the smallest tribal ward of the Rozwi section in the Wedza Reserve (centralized area) the total of its fourteen component villages reached just over 1,100.

In the following table a few more tribal wards with their respective populations are given.[1] Under group I are four tribal wards belonging to the Mbire people under Swoswe's chieftainship; group II, three wards under Rozwi (Rozani) authority; group III, two wards mentioned above, forming part of the Hera (Nyashanu) tribe in the Sabi Reserve.

| | Tribal ward | No. of villages | No. of taxpayers | Total population |
|---|---|---|---|---|
| Group I . . | Makwarimba . . | 96 | 1,517 | 7,479 |
| | Cadoka . . . | 50 | 795 | 3,829 |
| | Cigodora . . | 45 | 710 | 3,442 |
| | Musanu . . . | 8 | 114 | 564 |
| Group II . . | Rozani . . . | 14 | 203 | 1,104 |
| | Gonesu . . . | 20 | 319 | 1,560 |
| | Ushe . . . | 20 | 309 | 1,607 |
| Group III . . | Mafuruse . . | 13 | ? | 171 |
| | Nemadziva . . | 14 | ? | 182 |

*Distribution of villages and population in tribal wards*

In spite of this divergence the basic internal structure of the ward and its function are the same in all three reserves. It is a political unit occupying a distinctly demarcated territory under control of a *sadunhu*.

[1] In September 1947 Mr. R. Howman, Assistant Native Commissioner at Wedza, made an unofficial count of the people in his reserve, based on information obtained from headmen at tax-paying time. He has kindly permitted me to use his figures (groups I and II). About the same time I undertook a more detailed census covering only the Rozani ward (also included in Mr. Howman's figures).

PLATE XXV

1. Village at Gonoreshumba, Southern Sabi Reserve, showing living and storage huts. Wall decorations are unusual

2. Wherever possible store-huts are built on solid rocks. The huts, empty at the end of the dry season, are dilapidated

SHONA

PLATE XXVI

3. Typical lay-out of a village in the centralized area of Southern Wedza Reserve. Directly behind the living quarters is an open calves pen and covered goat pen. In the background a portion of another section belonging to the same village

4. A preferential right to a piece of virgin land has been vested by cutting branches from a number of trees and piling them up around the trunks, in Southern Sabi Reserve

SHONA

It comprises a varying number (see table) of separate and mutually independent villages (*misha*) which, collectively, are under the political control of the ward-head. As a rule the ward has a nuclear body of agnatic kinsmen who are spread over more than one village, and whose family head is the hereditary head of the ward. If he belongs to the lineage which controls the tribal territory (*nyika*) of which his ward is a part, he is called *jinda* (pl. *macinda*).[1] To the agnatic nucleus other villages may be attached, some of them related by marriage or by cognatic ties, to the ward-head. Some villages, however, are not related at all to him, but have submitted to his authority because they chose to live in the area controlled by him.

The unity of the ward as an autonomous community is, therefore, based partly on genealogical and partly on territorial grounds. In fact, a study of Shona land tenure reveals that its function as an exclusive land unit is probably its most characteristic feature. It is the autonomous ward community which, as a well-defined, component part of the tribe (*nyika*), holds the *communal right* over all the territory within its boundaries. It is as an accepted and eligible member of this community that a person may make use of the land for building and cultivating purposes.[2] When this happens the communal right of the ward appears to be largely suspended from the areas actually held and used by member villages, while it remains fully extended over the rest of the ward territory in which no such individualized rights are vested. These latter portions thus remain available for the reasonable requirements of all ward members and may be used collectively for grazing purposes, while the natural resources (firewood, wild fruits, honey, water, game, pot clay, &c.) may be tapped by them.

Even from the individualized (village) areas the communal right is never completely lifted. It may be temporarily pushed back in favour of the right of Bantu-ownership, and this suspension may last as long as the latter right remains effective. But its latent grip is resumed, partially or fully, as a matter of course as soon as Bantu-ownership

---

[1] The term *jinda*, in a general sense, includes all male members of the chief's own lineage living under his political control, and as such it stands in opposition to *mutorwa*, 'foreigner', that is, anyone not belonging to the chief's lineage. As a political term it is usually reserved for those agnates of the chief occupying positions of considerable authority, such as ward-head. Occasionally, and incorrectly, ward-heads *not* belonging to the chief's lineage are also referred to as *macinda*.

[2] Such land is, as we have seen, held by the collective *village community* in Bantu-ownership, while individual portions of the village allotment may be cultivated under a right of use of the holders.

either weakens or ceases. Such a resurgence of the communal right can be observed when a village leaves for another ward or moves to new sites. The village may sometimes retain a preferential right to the previous site and abandoned gardens, but if not, its former possessions will return automatically and fully under the control of the communal right of the ward; it may be seen seasonally when, as soon as the fields have been reaped, cattle are allowed to graze on the stover regardless of field ownership.

Evidence that Bantu-ownership is never quite free from limitations due to the communal right can be found in the duty of villages to allow non-members access to surface water within their area, or passage through their villages or fields (provided, of course, that no damage is done to property), to pick wild fruit and berries from trees or shrubs standing on or near their allotments.

In short, once a person is accepted as a member of the ward community he can avail himself of a village and garden site and of the natural resources of the common ward territory, but always with due regard to the established rights of his fellow members and subject to the limitations due to the communal right.

As the representative of the ward community the ward-head is primarily responsible for upholding the communal right. We have seen evidence of this in his actions relating to the establishment of new villages, when he or his representative formally sanctions the transaction by driving a peg into the ground. He is further expected to take action in order to protect the interests of his community against unlawful use of the common territory by ward members or strangers. He is the obvious arbitrator in land disputes between villages.

But his functions extend beyond these limits, as he has authority to try and settle any legal conflict arising within his area, which would fall within the scope of his jurisdiction. This means that his tribunal is also a court of appeal to which village headmen will bring cases which they failed to settle. According to Shona law the *sadunhu* is entitled to similar court fees to the chief of the tribe, though on a much lesser scale.[1] Unlike the village tribunals, the court of the ward-head has a more or less formal procedure.[2]

---

[1] If his court is a recognized 'native court' within the meaning of *section five* of the Native Law and Courts Act, 1937, he is entitled to receive a hearing fee of five shillings for every case (G.N. No. 108/1938). There is, in this respect, no difference between chiefs and ward-heads.

[2] Complaints are formally lodged; parties are summoned on behalf of the ward-

In principle, serious cases like those arising from witchcraft, homicide, stock theft, &c., are excluded from the jurisdiction of a ward-head, but in practice his authority is generally limited by the realization that an appeal lies from his court to the court of the chief. The result is (and probably has been in the past) that the ward-head will rarely give judgement unless he has reason to believe that the parties will abide by his decision. This means that *any* conflict in which either party remains adamant is usually referred to the chief's court without reaching a solution in the ward-head's court.

The ward-head also has other than juridical duties. At the end of the agricultural season, when crops have been reaped, he initiates a kind of thanksgiving celebration (Hera, *mushosho*; Rozwi, *muswa*; Mbire, *rukoto*). For this purpose all family heads in the ward have to bring a basket of grain (*swanda*) to his village, and large quantities of beer are prepared there. The whole ward population comes together to drink, sing, and dance, after the beer has been dedicated by the ward-head to his ancestral spirits and the unknown spirits of the original 'owners of the country' (*vasanyika*).[1] The celebration stresses the unity of the ward community and is still held after a good harvest in many wards. But it is rapidly falling into disuse in the centralized areas.

In times of drought, and formerly at the beginning of every new season, a similar ritual (*mukwerera*) was held to ask for plentiful rains, but these occasions, too, are getting rare, and are being replaced by small-scale efforts on the part of the heads of individual villages or families.

A ward-head used to be entitled to occasional free labour from the members of his ward, who were called up a few times every year to work in his garden (*zunde*). The idea behind these communal efforts is the same as in the case of a family head who may require the services of members of his family for the production of food because he is responsible for providing for them in times of need. The ward-head, too, is regarded as a 'father' of his people, and expected to provide hospitality and food when needed. The people therefore gave such

head by a court messenger (*muyai, sinene, mudzimbahwe*), who often also acts as intermediary (*mupoterwi*) between the parties and the court; after the court fees and the remuneration of the messenger have been paid the case is heard in open court by two or more assessors in the presence of the ward-head, who finally summarizes the case, interprets the law in question, and gives judgement.

[1] Some pots of beer made from millet (*rukweza*) are placed at the graves of known ancestors, and under big trees in the forest for the spirits of the unknown *vasanyika*.

services as a matter of course, realizing that it was in their own interest to keep his granaries well filled. The ward-head was not obliged to compensate his people for these services, but he would often prepare food for them when they worked in his fields 'so that they would work happily'. Because the same communal aid was due to the chief of the tribe the ward-head would take care that his people would respond generously to the chief's call for work. Nowadays this useful institution, so often misinterpreted as 'forced' or 'tribute' labour, has practically ceased to exist, having been replaced by the reciprocal activities of the ordinary *nhimbe* parties.

## The Tribe—Nyika

The *nyika* is the widest tribal grouping functioning as a political and territorial unit. It comprises the area and people controlled by an independent and hereditary chieftain (*ishe*, pl. *madzishe*).

The population of the *nyika* can be roughly classified into two main categories. The first and most important (though not the most numerous) are the members of the nuclear patrilineage or, rather, portion of patrilineage, upon and around which the political and territorial unity is built. The chief belongs to this agnatic body. Probably the bulk of the population is, however, made up of small and large communities belonging to a greater number of other lineages, and which owe allegiance to the chief. Members of the first-mentioned category are called *va(ma)cinda* (sing. *jinda*).[1] In contrast to the *macinda* the members of all other lineages, regardless of their rank or position in the tribe, are referred to as *vatorwa*, 'foreigners'. This classification does not imply a position of political or social subordination or inferiority of *vatorwa* generally to *macinda* generally. It mainly serves to distinguish between members belonging to the same lineage as the chief's and people of different origin. No *mucinda* (*jinda*), unless he actually occupies a position of authority in the tribal organization, ranks socially higher than a *mutorwa*.

The *nyika* is usually made up of (or divided into) several wards (*matunhu*) which are often (but not always) controlled by hereditary heads of minor 'houses' of the lineage section which forms the genealogical framework of the tribe. Sometimes, however, one or more wards are built upon the genealogy of an important 'foreigner' who had originally submitted to the authority of the chief, but had been

[1] See page 379, note 1.

given a defined portion of the tribal territory and the power to control his own growing body of kinsmen and those of other kin who chose to live in his ward.

By way of comparison it may be stated that the Rozwi tribe (Rozani chieftainship) in the Wedza Reserve consists of three tribal wards, each under control of a *jinda*, the head of a minor house of the Rozwi lineage; the Mbire tribe in the same reserve has three wards controlled by houses of the Mbire lineage, and one under control of a *mutorwa* (a Mwenyi group); the Rozwi tribe (Musarurwa chieftainship) in the Narira Reserve has five wards belonging to houses of the Rozwi lineage and one belonging to a 'foreigner' (a Hera). In the great Hera (Nyashanu) tribe in the Sabi Reserve a very much greater differentiation has taken place. I was unable to get accurate information on the number of autonomous tribal wards which owe allegiance to the Nyashanu chief, partly because some of the units referred to as *dunhu* were so small, both in territory and in numbers of population, that they hardly deserved to be regarded as such;[1] and partly because a number of influential village headmen had assumed greater authority than (according to their rivals) they were entitled to. The comparatively long vacancy in the chieftainship (since 1943) has added to the confusion. I would, however, estimate the total number of wards to be around forty to forty-five. Of these about twenty-five are represented by houses of the Hera lineage, while in the others the ruling elements are 'foreigners'.

These 'foreign' elements have become politically incorporated in the tribal body. They have asked for, and received, from the head of the nuclear group, the chief, permission to settle within the boundaries of the territory controlled by him. In the act of asking permission, and in the allocation by the chief's representative of a place to settle (and both these actions are often accompanied by concrete tokens of tribute and submission to the chief's authority), political subordination to his authority is implicit.

The origin of these foreigners may be as varied as the number of groups in which they present themselves. In cases where they have been granted some degree of autonomy as component tribal wards, they may have come as a large family group with their associated kindred,

---

[1] Commenting on their size, informants said these were *katunhu* (diminutive of *dunhu*), but they rejected the suggestion that these units were merely composite villages (*misha*) on the grounds that their territory was demarcated, and that their headmen had been given certain privileges pertaining to a *sadunhu* (ward-head).

broken away from their parent body in search of suitable land or political safety. Often their original tribal unity had been shattered by invading Ndebele or for some other reason, in which case broken remnants rallied around their family head, seeking political affiliation with another chief, from whom they expected protection. Very often, however, they have come (and are still coming) as individual families, eager to settle with or in the vicinity of their maternal or uterine relatives, or with in-laws. This is the reason why the bulk of the foreign population (*vatorwa*) is not organized into its own territorial units (*matunhu*), but is found elsewhere as minority elements in villages headed by members of the ruling clan, or in its own villages as foreign units forming part of the political and social structure of an existing tribal ward.

Also the agnatic nucleus, as it is made up of sections or houses (*imba*, pl. *dzimba*) of the ruling clan, and living within the common tribal area, shows a considerable measure of dispersal. Probably the majority of these kinsmen will be found in wards controlled by a house of their own clan, and may form part of the genealogical hierarchy of such house. Often, however, small fragments of the ruling lineage live in wards controlled by 'foreign' groups. In this manner they may, in such wards, occupy a similar position to that outlined above in connexion with foreign elements. That is, although they belong to the ruling clan (section) and are living within the tribal boundaries, they are nevertheless under control of a *mutorwa*, and are component parts of the 'foreign' unity (village or ward) as represented by him.

Of greater political consequence is the division of the ruling clan-section into those 'houses' which are still eligible to produce a successor to the chieftainship and those which are not.

According to the broad principles of collateral succession in these areas, all male agnatic descendants of a common forefather are eligible to succeed to his hereditary name and position as head of the house which he founded. The same principles apply, in theory at least, to the chieftainship. Nevertheless, there may be a number of houses of the ruling lineage section which are excluded from the chieftainship. Two main reasons for such exclusion may be advanced. The first is that the chieftainship may be based upon a genealogical hierarchy which is represented by a comparatively young section of an older, broken-up lineage unity, and that various other sections of the old lineage have become politically affiliated with such young section. In these cases (the two Rozwi tribes in the Wedza and Narira Reserves are examples) the chief's political authority extends over the other sections, but the chieftainship itself is confined to the particular section of which he is the genealogical head.[1]

The other reason for the exclusion of certain agnatic sections from the chieftainship is that in the past conflict between rival houses putting up candidates for the chieftainship resulted in the exclusion of defeated houses (and their descendants) from the chieftainship. To prevent a complete splitting up of political unity such defeated houses were often granted a certain measure of political and territorial autonomy within the tribal framework as controlled by the victorious house. In this manner various component houses of a common lineage group obtained hereditary control over defined portions (*matunhu*) of the tribal territory, acknowledging the political superiority of a chieftainship in which they could no longer participate. This position is illustrated amongst the Mbire in the Wedza Reserve and (to a far greater extent and degree of variation) amongst the Hera of the southern Sabi Reserve. In the latter area only about one-quarter of the number of minor houses (Hera lineage) in control of tribal wards are considered to belong to the *gadzingo*, that is, the section from which candidates for the Nyashanu chieftainship can be drawn.

It follows that the framework of tribal organization is provided by a segment or segments of the patrilineage to which the chief belongs. But political unity is only partly based on the genealogy of the house which bears the traditional and hereditary name of the chieftainship (*ushe*) and which may extend over only a comparatively small section of the agnatic body (Hera, *gadzingo*). It is further based on the formal recognition of the political superiority of the chief's house by agnatic units falling outside the dominant house, and by subordinate units of foreign origin.

But such political unity is only effective within the limits of a common, and in principle inalienable, tribal territory. This territory is held by the tribal community under the communal right in which all eligible members share according to their reasonable requirements. It is protected as an entity against unlawful intrusion from without, and its internal use may be controlled, when necessary, for the common good. Such control is exercised in the first instance by the chief as representative of the tribe, but for administrative purposes the land may be divided into demarcated portions which become the common

---

[1] More about this situation caused by the breaking up of old lineage structures will be said below, when the *imba* is discussed as a genealogical grouping.

territory of ward communities, but only as component parts of the inclusive tribal unity.

The unity of tribe and land is a natural conception. It is based economically on the fact that the tribe depends exclusively on its own territory for its subsistence; it is legally supported by the occupation of successive generations of tribesmen; and religiously and magically this conception is strengthened by the belief that the founding tribal ancestors established the communal right on the land for the benefit of future generations of their own kin (and of those incorporated into the tribal unity), and that their spirits are still closely interested in and connected with the land.[1]

The functions of the chief are essentially the same as those mentioned in connexion with the ward-head, but, obviously, his authority is much greater. Under tribal law the chief's court had full jurisdiction over members under the control of the chief. It acted as a court of the first instance in matters considered so serious that their impact was considered to affect the whole tribal community, such as homicide, witchcraft, and offences against the chief's person. It acted as a final court of appeal in connexion with all disputes and offences which failed to reach a satisfactory solution in the courts of the ward-heads. Nowadays the jurisdiction of the chief, in so far as his court has been constituted under the provisions of the Native Law and Courts Act, is severely curtailed. He still has very considerable jurisdiction in civil cases to which Shona law is applicable, but no criminal jurisdiction.[2] But subject to a few innovations (such as formal appointment and recognition of court assessors, register of court cases, fixed court fees, and supervision by the native commissioner) the Act wisely allows these courts to function largely according to traditional principles of procedure and evidence.[3]

The formalities of court procedure are stricter at the chief's court than at the courts of ward-heads, but the essential characteristics are the same. On the one hand one finds expressions of deference for the superiority of the tribunal[4] and the position of the chief (or ward-head), such as frequent clapping of hands and the initial humility of

[1] Evidence of this connexion can be found, for instance, in the *mushosho* celebrations mentioned before. When these are held by foreign ward-heads a representative of the ruling clan must be present to establish contact with the 'spirit owners' of the land.      [2] § 6(3), Act 33, 1937.      [3] § 7, Act 33, 1937.

[4] The term for bringing an action is *kukwira pa dare*, lit. 'to climb the court', and the relative token by which a hearing is obtained is called *gwiro*.

parties and witnesses. On the other hand there is the realization that this is a common tribal forum in which every aggrieved party can, within limits, give vent to his pent-up feelings, and in which all present may, after formally expressing their respect to the chief, freely give their opinion on the merits of the case. The presiding chief or ward-head, in fact, does little more than listen to the arguments of the parties, witnesses, councillors, and members of the public, until the case, having reached a stage of finality in their hands, is formally presented to him for decision. By this time the relevant legal principles have been elaborately discussed in public and the chief has had ample opportunity to sense the opinion of the majority. Usually he gives his decision accordingly after summarizing the main points of the conflict.

The chief's ritual functions are mostly confined to the propitiation of the ancestral spirits of his own clan. For this purpose he may dedicate a bull to the spirit of the founder of his house, or sacrifice such an animal when the spirit requires it. Great tribal rituals are, however, singularly few in number. The above-mentioned 'thanks-giving cele-brations' (*mushosho, rukoto, muswa*) at the end of a good season do not appear ever to have been held by the chief on behalf of the whole tribe. Neither were the yearly rain ceremonies (*mukwerera*) held on a tribal scale, although in times of severe drought (even nowadays) the chief might send a deputation with gifts to a famous rain-maker.

The importance of rituals (*bira*) is usually measured by the remoteness of the ancestor whose spirit has to be propitiated, which in practice means the sacrificial killing of a bull which had been previously dedicated to the spirit by having the ancestral name bestowed upon it. But even when an important animal is being sacrificed the ritual is usually attended by only a few high-ranking clan members and a small number of other close relatives of the chief, giving an intimate and exclusive character to the occasion.

At least on two occasions, the death of a chief and, especially, the installation of a new chief, when the people gather to meet and honour their head, the whole tribe, including foreign incorporated elements, seems to be involved in the ritual proceedings.

The Shona Chief derived his income from various sources. One of these was court fees, which formerly consisted of one or two goats, payable by both parties. When he gave a successful decision involving many head of cattle the grateful complainant would often give his chief a beast by way of *kutenda* (thank you). But in cases such as homicide or incest, in which the whole community was thought to have been exposed to magical danger, the beast or other animal which the accused had to pay to the court was killed and eaten by the public and not retained by the chief.

The chief has the right to receive tribute of various parts of some game, such as elephant tusks, lion skins, and some portions of other big game killed on his territory. Especially mentioned as exclusively royal game is the scaly ant-eater (Hera, *harakabvuka*), a delicacy which may be eaten only by an independent and lawful chief.[1] But hunters bringing these tributes could expect to be compensated by the chief.

At his installation a new chief receives gifts of tribute and recognition (*civuciro*) from his ward-heads, village headmen, and important members of his family under his control, and even neighbouring chieftains who wish to avoid the impression of being hostile to him will send gifts in kind or money. These gifts, which vary from a half-crown to a head of cattle, have a dual purpose of being expressions of rejoicing (*kupemberera*) and of recognition of his political superiority (*kuvucira*) by his subjects. In the latter sense they are in practice obligatory, as failure to give them immediately raises the presumption of insubordination.[2]

The chief also had the right to communal aid from his subjects, who could be called up a few times a year to work in his fields (*zunde*). Although it is usually stated that the chief was under no obligation to compensate for these services because they were regarded as being for the common good,[3] he would often prepare food and kill a beast to entertain his people.[4] As stated before, this institution has largely fallen into disuse, and a chief who needs a large body of people to help him

[1] During a long vacancy in the Nyashanu (Hera) chieftainship a man caught one of these animals and presented it to the person whom he believed to be the rightful candidate. This caused a sharp reaction from the supporters of a rival candidate.

[2] When Cangu was installed as Rozani Chief (Rozwi tribe, Wedza Reserve) two of his village headmen failed to give *civuciro*. They were later summoned by him to explain why 'they had been angry with the chief'. After they had found some excuse and had given a gift of five shillings, they offered an additional two shillings 'to break the arrow' (*civuna museve*), that is, to remove the threat which was implied in their initial behaviour.

[3] A Hera informant maintained that when a hungry man took food from the chief's *zunde* this could hardly be regarded as 'theft', because a needy subject had the right to be fed by the chief, and the chief's gardens were cultivated by his people to meet such emergencies.

[4] Evidence of this was given by a Rozwi spokesman, who stated that the late Rozani Chief insisted on being given prior notification when ward-heads intended to bring their people to his fields so that he would have time to prepare food for them.

with the cultivation of his lands will nowadays prepare beer for the ordinary *nhimbe* (collective beer- and work-party).

Informants deny that in the past a chief would receive some tribute or recognition fee from foreigners who had obtained his permission to settle in his country. These people would, however, after having completed their village, brew beer 'to show the village to the chief' (*kuratidza ishe musha*). In this gesture, which appears to be obligatory only in the case of people settling as independent village communities, and not when they become members of an existing village, the element of gratitude and of submission to the chief's authority is implicit. Nowadays a *civuciro* gift of about five shillings is usually paid to the chief by *any* foreigner upon his application for settlement, and this new custom tends to dispense with the necessity of holding a beer-party in honour of the chief.

A new source of income for the chief is provided by the establishment of African businesses in the reserves, as it has become accepted practice that people setting up a store, butchery, tailoring business, &c., pay the chief about twenty or thirty shillings (apart from the amount they have to pay into revenue for their trading licences).

The chief is assisted in his duties by tribal officials, who can be divided into two classes. The first class comprises the hereditary heads of wards and villages whose normal duty it is to control the domestic affairs of their respective local units, but who, on irregular occasions, may be called to the *muzinda* (chief's village) in an advisory capacity. As councillors of the chief they are called *gota* (pl. *makota*). The second class consists of a number of people who, mainly on account of their close relationship with the ruling chief, have been selected by him to be his personal advisers and henchmen. They may include his younger brother or an elder son, a sister's or father's sister's son, or a sister's husband, that is, people regarding whom kinship law provides a particularly suitable pattern of subordination, loyalty, or intimacy. They usually stay in or near the chief's village so that their services are constantly available. They serve as intermediary between tribal subjects and the chief, arraigning parties for trial at the chief's court, and acting as his messengers and spokesmen, as his companions on journeys, or as court assessors. They are generally called *makota* or *makurugota*,[1] but descriptive terms may be used in connexion with their particular duties.

---

[1] Except when they belong to the chief's own clan, in which case they are called *macinda*.

Being chosen as close relatives of the chief their positions are not hereditary, since every new chief will select his personal advisers from amongst his own circle of near relatives. But through their close and regular association with the chief and the influence they exercise at the chief's court their position in tribal affairs is in a sense more important than that of ward-heads, who are *ex officio* councillors of the chief.

Specific mention must be made of the sister's or father's sister's son of the chief who, as his *muzukuru*, is more than anyone else in the lawful position to criticize the chief and check his actions when necessary. This relative is, in fact, the only person who has jurisdiction in actions to which the chief himself is a party, and who acts as arbitrator in disputes within the chief's own family.[1]

## Succession to the Chieftainship

Succession to the chieftainship is governed by the common principles of collateral succession prevailing in central Mashonaland.[2] According to these principles the oldest son, regardless of the position or rank of his mother, succeeds to the personal name and the position of his father. When he dies his next younger brother or half-brother succeeds to the father's name, until the generation of sons of the father is exhausted and the oldest grandson succeeds to the name and position of his grandfather, the determining factor again being the order of birth amongst collateral grandsons. Minor variations occur from place to place,[3] but one important implication is found everywhere: only males actually descended through the agnatic line from a common forefather can ever succeed to his name and the genealogical (or political) position which such name represents. A man cannot, for instance, succeed to his brother's own name and position, but he

[1] His position is the same as that of any sister's son (*muzukuru*) regarding his mother's brother's (*sekuru*) family, about which details have been given in my *Pattern of Hera Kinship*, Rhodes–Livingstone Paper No. 17. But the occupation of this privileged position in connexion with the person who happens to be the chief of the tribe obviously carries considerable political implications, and it is safe to say that during the reign of his mother's brother this *muzukuru* is one of the most influential persons in tribal affairs.

[2] These rules differ from the rule of primogeniture from the chief wife which is common amongst South African tribes.

[3] For instance, in the Narira Reserve it appears to be the rule that after a son of one house has succeeded to his father's name his full-brother should, for the time being at least, step aside in favour of a half-brother, even if the latter happens to be his junior in age. The reason given for this rule is that one house should not, on account of its many sons, be in a position to dominate other houses for an unduly long time.

may, after his brother, succeed to the name of their common father or forefather.[1]

Especially in the case of an old and established chieftainship, its succession may involve the candidatures of numerous clansmen between whom agnatic relations may be very remote. As it is the relative age on a certain generation-level which is, in principle, the determining factor, it is often difficult to know who is the oldest and therefore most eligible of the candidates. It is the task of tribal elders, mostly belonging to the ruling clan, and of other important kinsmen to determine which candidate has the best rights to become chief. In the event of serious rivalry recourse may be had to a *swikiro* (spiritual medium) of an important ancestor to ascertain the views and wishes of the ancestral spirits.

There is no doubt that other than legal considerations may sometimes influence the succession. A common excuse for by-passing a rightful heir is some serious physical disability, especially blindness. Other heirs have been by-passed on account of their temporary absence from the tribal territory. Of at least one[2] it is reported that he refused to accept the chieftainship because he considered himself too poor to fulfil his duties properly. And previous insubordination by a minor house has led in more than one case to the permanent exclusion of that house and its descendants from the chieftainship.

Most Shona chiefs in the past owed allegiance to the then dominating Rozwi clan, and their succession was subject to the approval of the Rozwi Paramount Chief. Some of this old superiority is still preserved today as a mere formality, and the important Nyashanu Chief (Hera) is, for instance, 'crowned' (*kugadzira*) by a representative of the Rozwi clan.

In some respects there is evidence of a genealogical lineage coherence beyond the limits of political unity. On the death or installation

---

[1] This point may cause friction in tribes which represent an affiliation of remnants of an old lineage section, the political unity of which has broken down. When the chieftainship is re-established on the basis of one of these houses, the other houses, of which some may be incorporated into the new political unity, cannot participate in the succession to the new chieftainship. The fact that there may still be question of a succession to the name and now purely genealogical position of the founder of the old unity in which these other houses do share, has sometimes resulted in a conflict between genealogical seniority and political superiority. Examples of such conflicts are fairly common, for instance amongst the Hera of the southern Sabi and the Rozwi of the Wedza Reserve.

[2] A Murozwi in connexion with the Musarurwa chieftainship.

2C

of an independent chieftain representatives of other sections of the lineage may gather from all over the country as an expression of a clan unity which has lost all political significance in everyday life.

## III. GENEALOGICAL GROUPINGS

It has become clear that in each of the political units mentioned above (*musha*, village; *dunhu*, tribal ward; *nyika*, 'tribe') the composition and structure of the community is, to a varying extent, determined by kinship ties. It is therefore necessary to examine briefly the principal genealogical groupings, and to see how far they fit into, or form the background of, the political and social structure of Shona society.

*Patrilineage—Rudzi*

The patrilineage (*rudzi*) is a wide and nowadays widely scattered body of people sharing the same totemic clan name (*mutupo*) and the same sub-clan name (*cidawo*).[1]

Nowhere, as far as I am able to judge, does the *rudzi* as a whole function as a political entity. Its main significance lies in the fact that on the strength of a common *mutupo* and *cidawo* people claim a common origin through the agnatic line, even when actual kinship cannot be traced, and that the lineage being exogamous, intermarriage between members is, in principle, forbidden. But even this rule is breaking down in cases where actual relationship between the parties can no longer be traced, and different political affiliation seems to neutralize the effects of such remote kinship. Especially amongst members of the Rozwi lineage, whose numerous fragments are spread all over the country as so many independent political bodies, intermarriage between members belonging to different fragments is, in fact, fairly common.

Clan names (pl. *mitupo*) are, as a rule, of totemic origin, sub-clan names (pl. *zwidawo*) not. For the tribal units under discussion these names are:

Rozwi: *mutupo*, Moyo (heart); *cidawo*, Mondizo.
Hera: *mutupo*, Shava (eland); *cidawo*, Museyamwa (a prop).
Mbire: *mutupo*, Soko (monkey); *cidawo*, Mondizo.[2]

---

[1] A common *mutupo* alone does not establish kinship, and the suggestion that some kind of functional grouping might exist, based solely on *mutupo*, is inconceivable to the native mind.

[2] The original Mbire *cidawo* was Vudzijena ('grey hair'). One of the Mbire progenitors (Nyahuye?) was a *muzukuru* (sister's son) of a Rozwi king and became so

People are expected to refrain from eating their totem animal (or part of animal), but I have found no trace of any special ritual in connexion with the totem animal.

Due to the fact that several sub-clan names are connected with one and the same clan name, it is the *cidawo* rather than the *mutupo* which serves as the distinctive feature of the *rudzi* (lineage). To call a man by his *cidawo* is to honour and respect him as an individual member of a lineage of which he is proud, and it is therefore the customary and correct thing to do whenever individual relations are not close enough to use personal names, or when the occasion demands a more formal attitude (e.g. a son who is being publicly reprimanded by his father will address his father by his sub-clan name; a person addressing anyone in authority on formal occasions, such as a court case, will use the latter's *cidawo*).

A child gets the *mutupo* and *cidawo* of his legal father. A premarital child will be given the *mutupo* and *cidawo* of his natural father, if he is known (which is usually the case), and if there is any likelihood of his father marrying his mother, or that he will pay the customary compensation (*maputiro*) to the mother's family. In the very rare cases[1] where the natural father of a premarital child is not known, it is given the *mutupo* and *cidawo* of its mother.

As said before, I have found no example of a lineage (*rudzi*) functioning as a corporate whole, nor as a recognized political unit, nor as an occasional all-inclusive gathering for particular ritual purposes.

But lineage *sections* of varying width and depth usually form the genealogical framework of such major political groupings as *nyika* (tribe) and *dunhu* (tribal ward). And between these units, which are politically and mutually independent, a vague and wider association may sometimes obtain, and be expressed on such occasions as the death of the head of an important section or the installation of his successor. Representatives of neighbouring sections of kinsmen are then invited to be present.

closely associated with the Rozwi that he adopted their *cidawo*, Mondizo. Another Mbire section then took Kumene (meaning unknown) as *cidawo*; yet another, probably older, split occurred when an heir to the Mbire chieftainship was by-passed, and thereupon established his own branch with the distinctive *cidawo* Shungwasha, or Mrewa (from *kurewa*, to by-pass). While the two first-mentioned clan segments are still both known under the appellation Mbire, the Mrewa segment became the Washawasha tribe.

[1] Rare, because it would mean that the mother is unable to name the father of her child. Normally her testimony is regarded as conclusive evidence in Shona law.

The collateral system of succession to ancestral names rather favours a momentary revival of such wider unity. For instance when, in the words of Shona informants, 'the name of Mambo [one of the oldest and greatest ancestral names of the Rozwi clan] came to our place', the small and relatively insignificant Musarurwa branch of the Rozwi lineage in the Narira Reserve, which had produced the successor, became the focal point of nation-wide Rozwi interest. ('Many great chiefs from very far came to attend the installation of the new Mambo.') But now, only a few score years later, old informants who had actually witnessed the occasion failed to enumerate more than a few names of those great ones who had been present. Lacking any closer or more regular ties, the incident had come rather as a surprise, and had left little more than a vague and fleeting sense of affiliation, the very width of which could be appreciated by a few, but confused the majority of clansmen.

## Family Group—Cizwarwa

Of much greater practical importance than the *rudzi* is the *cizwarwa*, a group of agnates which can be said to comprise the first- and second-generation descendants in the agnatic line of one man, that is, his sons, daughters, and sons' children. A few informants were inclined to limit the *cizwarwa* to the first- and second-generation descendants of one man *and* one wife, but it seems that such a limited conception is only advanced when there is strife between the various 'houses' of the common grandfather and a conflict in connexion with the family estate. It finds no support in law.

When asked to describe the *cizwarwa* informants may state that the unit comprises 'people belonging to one *rudzi* (patrilineage) who live together and come together for ritual purposes (*kupirirana*)'. The first requisite is not always borne out in practice, but the second reveals an essential feature of the *cizwarwa*. It is the family group functioning in close ritual unity, calling upon the spirit of its common *tateguru* (father's father)[1] for support. In dealings with the hierarchy of ancestral spirits, many of whose names have already been forgotten by the living, the spirit of the *tateguru* is the closest intermediary between the

---

[1] The term *tateguru* is especially used for the *spirits* of the father's father and older agnatic ascendants. The Njanja and Rozwi of the Narira Reserve also use this term when *speaking of* a living father's father. But when the old man is *addressed* in person all, except the Hera of the southern Sabi Reserve, will use the term *sekuru* (grandfather). The Hera will address their father's father as *baba mukuru*, which really means 'elder father', the common term for a father's elder brother.

PLATE XXVII

5. Complainant is sitting with his back to the camera, and is questioned by two assessors to the right and left of him

6. Same court session as above. Wives of parties listening to the proceedings. Girl with white head-cloth is co-defendant in adultery case

SHONA

PLATE XXVIII

7. The first drink before the work at a Southern Sabi *nhimbe* party is started. Although all work together, men and women have separate pots of beer

8. These Southern Sabi children join in the collective activities of a *nhimbe* party. These youngsters have started to thresh millet while their parents are still gathered around the beer pots

SHONA

living and the dead. The common form of address at these occasions includes the request: '. . . and you, our *tateguru*, will tell the others, whose names we have forgotten. . . .'

To be effective, *all* the members of the *cizwarwa* should be present at a *bira* (ritual gathering). Informants explain: 'Even when there is trouble between the houses of one *cizwarwa*, all should be there. Our *tateguru* would be very angry if he saw that some of his children had been left out.'

Kinsmen outside the *cizwarwa* grouping may (and, if within reach, will) be invited to a *bira*, as are close relatives by marriage and nearby cognates, but their presence, though desirable, is not essential.

A person sneezing (*kuhocira*) or kicking his toe against a stone will exclaim, '*Tateguru wangu*, So-and-so [naming his father's father]', with such strict regularity that this has proved to be a simple and most reliable check upon kinship affiliation.

The statement that members of one *cizwarwa* 'live together' in one locality need not be correct in practice. One reason is that the *cizwarwa* includes females, and marriage being in principle patrilocal, married women usually live away from their own families. Another reason is that the male members of a family do not always stick together as a local unit over a time-span of two generations; and although it is reasonable to suppose that in the past local unity prevailed for a longer time than it does nowadays, a check upon family histories clearly shows that also in the past brothers (especially of different houses) tended to drift apart after the death of their father, and that this tendency became more marked in the second descending generation. What one finds is that a portion of the *cizwarwa* has preserved some unity as a local body (though it may be spread over more than one independent village), while the remainder is scattered, having taken up residence elsewhere in independent villages or with other relatives (mother's family, in-laws, &c.) or with friends. Their whereabouts are, however, known, and on such occasions as serious illness or death within the *cizwarwa*, or the succession to the name of the common ancestor, or the distribution of a member's estate (*kurovaguva*), they will be called together as a genealogical unit.

From an estate point of view the *cizwarwa* in the past probably presented a closer unity in that its members, when in need of assistance (especially in connexion with marriage cattle), could appeal to the recognized family head (i.e. the one bearing the name of the *tateguru*) who could then avail himself of the assets of any of the component family units and direct these towards the relief of the needy member. This conception of the estates of individual families being pooled into a wider common estate in which each and all members share as of right, and which is controlled by the head of the *cizwarwa*, has lost much of its communal character. In the Narira and Wedza Reserves (more exposed to Western influence) more than in the remote parts of the central and southern Sabi Reserves, the element of 'house preference' (in principle already existing even under the old conditions) has become more accentuated. The *cizwarwa* now presents a picture in which the various sub-units are inclined to regard their individual estates as their exclusive own, and they resent the idea of a wider communal control on a *cizwarwa* basis. Members are still sensitive to the appeal of needy relatives, but help is extended on a reciprocal rather than communal basis. That is, in the past cattle needed for, say, house A, could be obtained from house B as part of the common estate, and house B, when itself later in need, might be helped with cattle found in house C of the same family group, because all three houses participated in one common unity of *cizwarwa*-and-estate; but nowadays such transactions are likely to result in specific debtor and creditor relationships between houses A and B, or between B and C, because each house is apt to emphasize its own proprietary rights.

In the Narira Reserve, where the process of individualization of sub-units is farthest developed, such reciprocity is practised between full-brothers after the death of their father; while in remote parts of the Sabi Reserve a common family estate may still be a reality amongst children of two half-brothers, that is, still on a *cizwarwa* basis.

Speaking generally, it would appear that the *cizwarwa* has preserved its unity only in connexion with its own ritual functions.

### 'House'—Imba

Any subdivision of the lineage (*rudzi*), from the largest to the smallest, could be (and often is) correctly referred to as *imba* of So-and-so (name of its founder). The term is therefore mainly used in practice to distinguish such unit from other like units forming part of a wider common agnatic grouping. An example is given in the accompanying diagram. People would refer to Bunhu (a headman of the Rozwi lineage in the Narira Reserve) as belonging to the *imba* of his father Banwa, as distinct from his father's brother's son Cinyimo who, being a child of Zhakata (brother of Banwa), would belong to the house of Zhakata.

Both Banwa and Zhakata belong (with their children) to the house of Bunhu's father Madziwire who, together with his brothers Mukundwa, Mupfururirwa, &c. (and their descendants), would be included in the

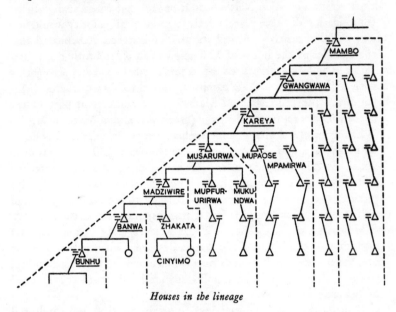

*Houses in the lineage*

house of Bunhu's father's father's father, Musarurwa, which is now the name of the chieftainship of an independent *nyika*. The last-mentioned house would, with similar houses (Mupaose, Mpamirwa, &c.), belong to the next greater house of Kareya, which in turn would be part of the house of Gwangwawa, which, again, would fall under the house of Mambo, which is one of the most famous segments of the Rozwi lineage.

At some generation-levels the term *imba* could be identified with a distinct *political* unity. In the above genealogy, for instance, the house of Musarurwa represents an independent *ushe* (chieftainship) and *nyika*, the political unity and territory under a chieftainship bearing the distinctive name 'Musarurwa'. The name Madziwire represents a tribal ward (*dunhu*) in the Musarurwa *nyika*, while the still younger name of Bunhu would represent an independent village grouping (*musha*) within the *dunhu* of Madziwire.

This does not mean that in practice 'house' groupings on different generation-levels would necessarily have their sequel as political groupings of a similarly inclusive character. On the contrary, a study of various genealogies would establish the fact that in relatively few cases have genealogical house groupings become consolidated as distinct political entities. Neither can it be said that where such political consolidation did take place, relative genealogical seniority would find its parallel in relative political status. For instance, it appeared that the founder of the house of Mupaose was an elder brother of Musarurwa. The former, however, represents a tribal ward and is, together with a 'brother house' (Mpamirwa) and three 'sons' houses' (Mukundwa, Mupfururirwa, and Madziwire), a component part of the *nyika* which is represented by the (brother) house of Musarurwa.

Examples of a similar divergence between genealogical and political rank can be found almost everywhere (see below). The situation in which genealogically equal and even senior groupings are attached and politically subordinate to a junior house of the same lineage (which, at some time in the past, managed to establish a wider and politically superior unity) is found amongst the Hera in the southern Sabi Reserve, the Rozwi of the Wedza Reserve, and (in minor aspects) also amongst the Mbire of the Wedza Reserve. This situation is of the greatest importance in connexion with succession to the chieftainship, from which members of such politically affiliated 'brother' or 'father' houses are excluded.

If many *dzimba* (houses) failed to attain political and territorial autonomy, the disintegration of large houses which once did exist as such was equally common. The process of parent houses splitting up into component smaller houses is a natural feature of genealogical descent. It is also the obvious structural mechanism through which the authority of a senior unit can be expanded politically as well as territorially. But when such centralized authority fails to maintain itself against pressure from without or within, disintegration will take place, and roughly according to the same natural principles of division. The seams which formerly held the major component parts together in the old unity now become the outlines of younger, separate, and mutually independent political units, each controlled by its own centralized authority. In this process of disintegration the units which subsequently consolidated themselves (within the limits of the old common territory or elsewhere) after a period of wandering, may have a similar structure to the old unit, in that their nuclei are provided by houses of the old lineage group, which have become rallying-points for other lineage members and the structural framework for a new political unity. But there are differences. In the old unity, as far as can be gathered from vague and often confused evidence, the relative political status of sub-units roughly corresponded with the genealogical rank of the houses by which their unity was represented. But in the new setting, as has been indicated, such correspondence often fails. The reason probably is that neither the splitting up of the original unit nor the consolidation of new units, in spite of their following a genealogical pattern, occurred at one particular generation-level of the old genealogy. If this had happened the picture today would have been that of several independent units, each based on the solidarity of 'sons'' houses of the original 'parent' house and unity. These independent 'sons'' houses would incorporate sub-units represented by a number of 'sons' sons'' houses, thus preserving, for each new unit, one single genealogical and political hierarchy. In this hierarchy, on the basis of the prevailing principles of collateral succession, each of the component 'sons' sons'' houses (or their subsections) could, in due course, provide a successor to the position of head of the new political unit, because all would have been members of such a house.

But this picture applies nowadays only to that section of the tribal grouping which represents the dominant nucleus, that is, the house of the founder of the new political unity; it does not include sections of the old lineage grouping which, although politically attached to the new tribal grouping, have their origin outside the dominant house. Some of these sections may represent houses which are genealogically senior, or at least equal, to the ruling house. I have mentioned the Rozwi tribe in the Narira Reserve, in which lineage groupings have become politically and territorially consolidated in tribal wards (*matunhu*), three of which belong to 'sons' houses' of the house of Musarurwa, and two to houses which are genealogically 'brothers' to Musarurwa.[1] Although these two 'brother houses' are component parts of the political unity of the tribe, they fall outside the genealogical hierarchy of the house of Musarurwa, and cannot therefore produce a successor to the Musarurwa chieftainship.

In the small Rozwi tribe in the Wedza Reserve political cohesion is based upon the affiliation of three Rozwi houses: Rozani, Musinganete (Gonesu), and Ushe. The first two are 'brothers' out of the house of Mbava whose political unity was broken some generations ago. The

---

[1] One of the tribal wards under this chieftainship is controlled by the house of a 'foreigner' (*mutorwa*) of the Hera lineage, and does not, therefore, fall under this discussion.

third Rozwi house, that of Ushe, is genealogically much more remote. After a period of wandering along different routes these young houses settled in the southern portion of the Mbire (Swoswe) area, where the house of Rozani established a chieftainship of that name (with the assistance of the Administration) to which the house of Musinganete became affiliated. Because the house of Rozani founded the new chieftainship, members of the houses of Musinganete and Ushe, while owing political allegiance to Rozani, do not form part of the genealogical hierarchy of the latter, and are therefore excluded from the chieftainship.

The Hera tribe in the southern Sabi Reserve offers examples of a slightly different character. Here, too, the original lineage unity under the house of Mbire broke up long ago, resulting in various splits between major houses. One or two houses broke away completely and established their own territorial and political independence (e.g. the Masarirambi branch or house under the Mtekedza chieftainship in the Charter district); but other splits, which occurred from time to time, did not always result in complete independence or territorial separation. After the Masarirambi branch had moved away its remaining brother house of Makumire faced a major internal split between its two sons' houses, Mushumba (the elder) and Dukuta. After some bitter fighting the defeated Mushumba people entrenched themselves behind the Marabada range of hills and became, so to say, a political island within a wider territory controlled by Dukuta. In course of time one of the junior houses of the Dukuta section (probably grandson Matema) re-established the chieftainship under a new name, 'Nyashanu', now based on the hierarchy of the house of Matema, to which numerous other houses of the original Hera lineage unity (as founded principally by the old house of Makumire) owed allegiance, but without being able to participate in the succession to the Nyashanu chieftainship. Some of these affiliated houses are definitely genealogically senior to Nyashanu (e.g. Mushumba); others are at least of an equal generation-level, such as the houses of Mudahose (Cirozwa) and Mundandi (Muradzikwa); while numerous other houses represent the remnants of some obscure older branches (e.g. Mutepfe and Murambinda).

The house of Matema had to pay for the exclusiveness of its chieftainship. The price was the recognition of a considerable number of the other houses as politically and territorially autonomous units, under the formal political superiority of the Nyashanu Chief. The whole tribal structure became a confederation of a few big, and many tiny, house units of the same lineage, each boasting a considerable autonomy politically and territorially (*matunhu*), but presenting a more or less united front against the outside world.

Internally, however, the confederation itches with discomfort and strife. The bigger houses, like those of Mushumba and Mundandi, though accepting the formal superiority of Nyashanu, do not recognize the court of the chief as a court of appeal. The heads of some other smaller houses claim to possess virtually the same prerogatives (e.g. in connexion with hunting tribute) as the Nyashanu Chief. At present, due to a long-standing vacancy in the chieftainship, various houses outside the Matema branch have again advanced the old claim that the Hera chieftainship is a heritage older than Matema, and that its succession should, therefore, be based upon a wider genealogical hierarchy in which they, too, could participate. The result of all this is that the centralized authority of the Nyashanu Chief is practically limited to those areas under control of houses of the Matema branch (and especially the house of Makuwa—'Mawire'), and exists in name only beyond these limits.

So far we have dealt only with *imba* as an agnatic unit founded upon a common *male* ancestor; and from a wider genealogical and political point of view this is the most common conception. But dealing with smaller agnatic groupings, such as are found within the limits of a *cizwarwa* (family group), and then especially in connexion with the family estate, *imba* is more commonly used for units based on a common *mother* or *father's mother*. A man who marries more than one wife thereby establishes the nuclei of so many houses (*dzimba*) within which the sense of cohesion is based upon a common *genetrix* (*dumbu rimwe* = one womb). While the structural and political aspects of lineage groupings are expressed in terms of 'patri-groupings' based on a common *male* ascendant, the *estate* is closely connected with the 'matri-group',[1] that is, the *imba* seen as a unit originated from one mother or father's mother. These two groupings are, of course, integral parts of the same *agnatic* body, and their functions are naturally complementary. For instance, succession to the *position* and *name* of the founder of the *imba* as a patri-group takes place on the basis of seniority in *age* and *generation* in the male hierarchy. This means that as a rule the succession is not influenced by the rank or position of the house of a

---

[1] The terms 'matri-group' and 'patri-group' are being used here for convenience sake. It should be clear that 'matri-group' has nothing to do here with 'matrilineal'.

candidate's mother: an elder son born of a second wife will thus precede a younger son born of a first wife, the criterion being that 'it is the blood of the father that counts'.[1]

But when we turn to succession to, and distribution of, a deceased man's *estate*,[2] it is apparently the 'blood of the mother' that counts most heavily: *imba* is now interpreted as a matri-group within the patrilineal setting. We find a preferential right of a full-brother to cattle due for or received from the marriage of his full-sister, often to the exclusion of an elder half-brother who would rank first in the succession to the father's name and position. Similarly, a successful preferential claim may often be advanced by a man to the widow of his full-brother against the half-brother who would rank higher in genealogical hierarchy.

Without enlarging upon this subject we may state that as soon as the estate factor comes into play (and this seldom happens outside the limits of the *cizwarwa*) the matri-groups are accentuated; but when the structural and political aspects are concerned this differentiation loses its significance and *imba* is thought of in terms of patri-groupings.

## Other Kinship Groupings

In no community, small or great, are the kinship relationships of a purely agnatic character. Exogamy and patrilocal[3] marriages being the rule, women belonging to various other clans form a more or less permanent part of any local agnatic grouping. With every marriage special and intimate ties of relationship (*ukuma okurovorana*) are established between in-laws, and it is not seldom that some in-laws live together in the same village (*musha*) or section of a village (*mana*).

[1] So strong, indeed, is this principle that I have found numerous examples in which it was extended to a man's sons begotten and born out of wedlock.

[2] *'Estate'*, as a native conception, is 'organic' rather than 'economic', in the sense that it represents, primarily and ultimately (even today), the capacity to reproduce as an agnatic unit. For this reason a widow with child-bearing capacity is a primary 'asset' in a deceased man's estate (*nhaka*); while cattle and unmarried daughters, being directly or indirectly convertible into 'wives', rank a close second in importance. This interpretation of estate is not an academic abstraction. It is the natural and logical outcome of the Shona kinship system, about which more will be said in a forthcoming book on *Shona Customary Law*, to be published by the Rhodes-Livingstone Institute. It is particularly and essentially a native conception, so obvious and common that failure to recognize and accept it as such may lead (and has led) to grievous misunderstanding whenever disputes about cattle, wives, and widows are brought to a European court.

[3] 'Patrilocal' in the sense that a wife will follow her husband to his residence, and not vice versa.

Very often, too, a person prefers to stay with his *vasekuru* (mother's family), with whom he is on very intimate terms, rather than with his own paternal kin. An analysis of the composition of Shona villages shows that, after the nuclear agnatic body of kinsmen, the uterine elements (*vazukuru* of the village headman) are usually numerically strongest in the village. This situation is also influenced by the fact that divorced or separated women, or wives whose husbands are engaged in long-term employment outside the native reserves, like to go back to their parental homes, taking their small children with them. Apart from these relatives, almost any combination of relationship may be found in the same village or neighbourhood.

## Kindred—Mhuri

A group of kindred, both agnatic and cognatic, living together with their wives and children in the same village or neighbourhood so that they maintain regular contact and have a sense of unity, is known as a *mhuri*. It is difficult to define this term precisely, as almost any combination of relatives living in the same locality may regard themselves as a *mhuri*.

When a person refers to his *mhuri*, he first thinks of his wives and children and other agnatic dependants (brothers' families, sisters) living under his control. But he also includes in his *mhuri* such blood-relatives (maternal and uterine), living in his village or village section or in nearby villages, over whom he can exercise some measure of informal authority. Regarding these latter relatives his authority is based on personal rather than legal grounds. A certain non-political unity obtains amongst such groupings of kindred, based on near kinship and proximity of residence. These factors make intimate participation in the joys and trials of each of the members possible, resulting in an *ad hoc* unity expressed on such occasions as birth, marriage, domestic troubles, illness, and death, when the *mhuri* gathers to celebrate, mourn, or discuss matters of family interest.

The term *samhuri* ('family head') sometimes applies to a man merely in his capacity as head of his own family unit, the small agnatic grouping which could also be labelled as *imba*; but it also implies his having authority over non-agnatic blood-relatives living under his jurisdiction, in which case the term *samhuri* becomes synonymous with *samusha* (village headman). In fact, in many small villages the composition of the population is such that it would constitute a single *mhuri*.

Yet there are obvious differences between a *mhuri* and a *musha* or an *imba*. The *musha* is predominantly, but not exclusively, a kinship unit; the *mhuri* is exclusively based on kinship. Membership of a *musha* community is founded upon common residence in the same village settlement; the members of a *mhuri* do not necessarily live in one village. The *musha* is a tightly organized unit with a distinctly political and autonomous character; the *mhuri* is neither political nor autonomous, and as a social body has no organization which it can regard as its specific own.

The difference between *mhuri* and *imba* is also clear. Though both are exclusively genealogical groupings, the *imba* is a purely agnatic unit comprising members of the same patrilineage having a common genitor or genetrix, and it is a conception which could be expanded almost indefinitely in space and time; the *mhuri* includes agnatic, maternal, and uterine blood-relatives and affines married to these, but in spite of its wider genealogical basis it is almost invariably limited to near relatives who happen to live in the same neighbourhood. In the *imba* the genealogical aspect is framed within the structure of a unilineal hierarchy with a fixed pattern of seniority and rank, and with principles of succession based on these; the *mhuri* is multilineal in its composition and its indefinite structure makes no provision for hereditary succession to the position of *samhuri*.

## BIBLIOGRAPHY FOR THE 'SHONA'

Since an annotated bibliography on the 'Shona' has been published in I. Schapera (ed.), *Select Bibliography of South African Native Life and Affairs*, London: Oxford University Press (1941), covering books and articles up to the end of 1938, a short list of standard works is given, followed by titles published since 1938.

### Standard Works

BULLOCK, C. *Mashona Laws and Customs*, Salisbury: Argus Co. (1913).

—— *The Mashona*, Cape Town: Juta (1928); expanded as *The Mashona and the Matabele*, Cape Town and Johannesburg: Juta and Co. Ltd. (1950).

POSSELT, F. W. T. *A Survey of the Native Tribes of Southern Rhodesia*, Salisbury: Government of Southern Rhodesia (1927).

——*Ethnographical Sketch of the Natives of Southern Rhodesia*. Official Year Book of Southern Rhodesia, No. 2, pp. 750–61. Salisbury: Government Printer (1930).

—— *Fact and Fiction. A Short Account of the Natives of Southern Rhodesia*, Bulawayo: Rhodesian Printing and Publishing Co. (1935).

### Articles and Books since 1938

BERNARDI, B. *The Social Structure of the Kraal among the Zezuru in Musami, Southern Rhodesia*, Cape Town: Communications from the School of African Studies, University of Cape Town, New Series No. 23 (1950).

CHILD, H. F. 'Etiquette and Relationship Terms', *Nada*, xxv (1948).

CHINYANDURA. 'The Tribes of Mambo', ibid. xxiv (1947).

FRANKLIN, H. 'The Native Ironworkers of Enkeldoorn District and their Art', ibid. xxii (1945).

GROSE, R. 'The Crowning of the Cherara Chief', *Rhodesia Scientific Association*, xxxvi (1938).

HOLLEMAN, J. F. *The Pattern of Hera Kinship*, Cape Town: Oxford University Press for the Rhodes–Livingstone Institute (1949).

MACIWENYIKA, J. *Ngano* (folklore), London: Sheldon Press (1943).

POSSELT, F. W. T. 'Trees in the Religious Ritual of the Bantu of Southern Rhodesia', *Man*, xxxix (1939), p. 110.

RICHARDS, J. B. 'The Mlimo—Beliefs and Practices of the Kalanga', *Nada*, xix (1942).

ROBERTS, J. G. 'A Southern Rhodesian Totem', ibid. xxiv (1947).

—— 'Totemism, Zimbabwe and the Barozwi', ibid.

SICARD, H. v. 'The Origin of Some of the Tribes in the Belingwe Reserve', ibid. xxv (1948).

SOUTHERN RHODESIA GOVERNMENT: Reports of the Secretary for Native Affairs and Chief Native Commissioner for the years 1941–5. Salisbury: Government Stationery Office (1947).

—— *Report of the Native Trade and Production Commission, 1944*, Salisbury: Government Stationery Office, C.S.R. 1945.

STEAD, W. H. 'The Clan Organization and Kinship System of Some Shona Tribes', *African Studies*, v. 1 (March 1946).

—— 'Some Notes on the Manyika', *Nada*, xxv (1948).

TAPSON, R. R. 'Notes on Mrozwi Occupation of Sebungwe', ibid. xxi (1944).

# GENERAL BIBLIOGRAPHY

The following books are referred to in various essays, but do not fall under the specialized bibliographies. We do not cite here books or articles by one of the writers referred to by another, since details of these are given in the relevant special bibliography. (e.g. Richards quoted by Mitchell.)

DOKE, C. M. *Bantu: Modern Grammatical, Phonetical, and Lexicographical Studies since 1860*, London: Percy, Lund, Humphries and Co. (1945).

EVANS-PRITCHARD, E. E. *Witchcraft, Oracles and Magic among the Azande*, Oxford: Clarendon Press (1937).

FORTES, M. *The Dynamics of Clanship among the Tallensi*, London: Oxford University Press (1945).

—— and EVANS-PRITCHARD, E. E. *African Political Systems*, London: Oxford University Press (1940).

GLUCKMAN, M. 'The Kingdom of the Zulu of South Africa', in *African Political Systems*.

GUTHRIE, M. *The Classification of the Bantu Languages*, London: Oxford University Press (1948).

KUPER, H. *An African Aristocracy: Rank among the Swazi of the Protectorate*, London: Oxford University Press (1947).

—— *The Uniform of Colour: A Study of White–Black Relationships in Swaziland*, Johannesburg: University of the Witwatersrand Press (1947).

NADEL, S. F. *The Nuba*, London: Oxford University Press (1947).

RADCLIFFE-BROWN, A. R. 'The Mother's Brother in South Africa', *South African Journal of Science*, xxi (1923).

—— 'Patrilineal and Matrilineal Succession', *Iowa Law Review*, xx. 2 (1935).

WAGNER, G. 'The Political Organization of the Bantu of Kavirondo', in *African Political Systems*.

# INDEX

Abdallah, Yohannah B., 306.
Achewa villages, 204 n.
African consciousness of identity, 18–19.
— Lakes Company, 308.
— Representative Council, 56, 239, 240.
— *Studies*, viii.
Agricultural Officer, 299, 303.
Alomwe, 297.
Aluyi or Aluyana, 1.
— the, of the plain, 19.
Anglo-Portuguese Convention, 1891, 308.
Angola, immigrants from, 6.
Angoni villages, 204 n.
Arabs, 5, 253, 305, 309, 311.
Arab colonization, 304.
Arab slave trade, 305.
Arab slavers, 100.
Arab traders, 165, 166, 167, 170, 189.

Baganda, the, 130.
Balovale, 1, 6, 17, 24, 25, 59.
bananas, 272–3.
Bangweolu, Lake, 164, 166, 178, 190.
Bantu, the Southern, 165, 171, 188, 189.
— the Central, 165, 190.
'Bantu-ownership' of land, 362, 363, 369–70.
*Bantu Studies*, vii.
Bantu Zone, Central linguistic, 94.
Barnes, J. A., vii, viii, 94 n.
Barotse, 1.
— immigrants into, 6.
— kingdom, 94, 100.
— — Tribes of the, 87–9.
— loyalty to the British Crown, 18.
— nation, composition of, 6.
— Province, population of, 88.
— — size of, 6.
Barotseland, 165.
— National Council, 17.
— — — subjects discussed at, 17–18.
— Tribal distribution in, 16.
Basuto, 1.
Batonga (Tonga people), 96 n.
Bechuana, 1.
Bechuanaland Protectorate, 171.
Beit Railway Trust, vii.
Bemba, the, 13, 301, 328, 341.

Bemba (*cont.*)
Bemba of Northern Rhodesia, vii, 164.
ancestor worship, 184.
ancestral spirit, 169, 174, 176, 182.
area, 165.
bad spirits, 186.
betrothal present, 180, 182.
bilateral kinship group, 176, 179.
bilateral nature of kinship, 175.
burial groves of chiefs, 184–5.
captain of the troops, 169.
centralized government, 168.
charms, 187.
chief worship, 184–5, 189, 191.
chief's authority, 169–70.
— duties, 170.
— followers, 169–70.
— funeral rites, 184–5, 189, 191.
— judicial powers, 170.
— mother (Candamukulu), 168.
— supernatural sanctions, 169.
— wealth, 170.
chiefs' relic shrines, 169, 185.
chieftainship, 168–71.
children's upbringing, 175.
clan names, 178.
clans, 178.
clans in ceremonial life, 179.
classificatory granddaughters, 181.
complementary clans, 179, 191.
councillors, 169.
country, 194.
Crocodile clan, 169, 179.
— totem, 168.
cross-cousins, 178, 181.
deserted sites of villages, 172.
destructive magic, 188.
economic life, 166.
father's sister, 175.
fire ritual, 186, 189, 191.
first chief's wives, 185.
geographical situation, 164, 166.
girls' initiation ceremony, 180, 182, 183, 191.
guardian spirits, 169, 185, 186.
handicrafts, 167.
hereditary headmen, appointment and functions of, 171–2.
hereditary priests, 169, 178, 184, 185.
human sacrifice, 185, 189.

PRINTED IN
GREAT BRITAIN
AT THE
UNIVERSITY PRESS
OXFORD
BY
CHARLES BATEY
PRINTER
TO THE
UNIVERSITY

REPRINTED IN GREAT BRITAIN BY PHOTO OFFSET
BY
BUTLER & TANNER LTD.
FROME AND LONDON